Encyclopedia of Social Work

19th
Edition

2003 Supplement

Encyclopedia of Social Work

19th
Edition

2003 Supplement

Encyclopedia Supplement Committee

Richard A. English, *Editor-in-Chief*

Diana DiNitto
Edith M. Freeman
Gary Holden

Martha N. Ozawa
Lynn Videka-Sherman

NASW PRESS

National Association of Social Workers
Washington, DC

Terry Mizrahi, PhD, MSW, *President*
Elizabeth J. Clark, PhD, ACSW, MPH, *Executive Director*

Encyclopedia of Social Work, 19th Edition, 2003 Supplement

Publisher	Cheryl Y. Bradley
Executive Editor	Paula L. Delo
Staff Editors	Andre Barnett
	Susan Fisher
	William Schroeder
Editorial Assistant	Christina Bromley
Copy Editor	Louise Goines
Proofreader	Gail Martin, Editorial Associates
Indexer	Leonard Rosenbaum

ISSN: 0071-0237

First impression, June 2003
Second impression, June 2004

Printed in the United States of America

Encyclopedia Supplement Committee

Contents

Preface and Acknowledgments   ix

How to Use the Encyclopedia   xi

Introduction by *Nazneen S. Mayadas*   xv

Appendixes

Preface and Acknowledgments

The *2003 Supplement* to the 19th edition of the *Encyclopedia of Social Work* is released during a time of great national and global uncertainty. The United States was still contending with the aftermath of September 11, 2001, as the war with Iraq was declared on March 20, 2003. At such a juncture, social workers everywhere need the benefit of new research on topics relevant to these unsettling times. The *Supplement* addresses many of these topics, such as social welfare, employment, and multiculturalism. As editors, our concerns about these issues from both national and global perspectives have been heightened since the terrorist attacks on the World Trade Center and the war in Iraq.

The five distinguished members of the *Encyclopedia of Social Work* Supplement Committee diligently collaborated in selecting topics ranging from employment to strengths-based practice. For their diligence, commitment, and thoughtfulness, I thank Diana DiNitto of the University of Texas at Austin for her personal attention to many details of this project; Edith M. Freeman of the University of Kansas; Gary Holden of New York University; Martha N. Ozawa of Washington University; and Lynn Videka-Sherman of the University at Albany, State University of New York.

In selecting the topics in this *Supplement*, the committee members carefully reviewed the three-volume 19th edition of the *Encyclopedia of Social Work* and the 1997 *Supplement*. They needed to ensure that the topics not only reflected significant concerns of the new century, but also considered the ever-changing political, economic, and social landscape.

The committee identified potential authors, drafted the criteria by which manuscripts were judged, and reviewed each submission. Their commitment and dedication made the *2003 Encyclopedia Supplement* possible.

I also extend my sincerest appreciation to the 17 authors whose work is compiled here. Their consummate professionalism proved invaluable as they balanced writing and rewriting their pieces with the daily rigors of demanding careers. The result is a superb body of work.

To the staff of the NASW Press, many thanks for providing excellent editorial support.

And to the social work practitioners, researchers, educators, and students, it is with great pride that we present to you the *Encyclopedia of Social Work, 2003 Supplement*.

Richard A. English, PhD, MSW, *Editor-in-Chief*
Dean
School of Social Work
Howard University
Washington, DC

April 2003

How to Use the Encyclopedia

For the 19th edition of the *Encyclopedia of Social* Work, the editorial board attempted to collect the most current scholarly analyses of practice and research. Reflecting the breadth of the diverse social work profession, the three-volume set, published in March 1995, contains 290 entries, representing the work of nearly 350 authors. The 1997 *Supplement* added 30 new entries, and the 2003 *Supplement* adds 17 new entries. It also includes the same search tools for readers featured in the *Encyclopedia*.

CONTENT

For the 2003 *Supplement,* the Encyclopedia Supplement Committee commissioned 17 new entries to address emerging topics and to reflect changes in the profession and in society. New entries expand coverage of such areas as

> Education
> Employment
> Medicare and Medicaid
> Mental Illness
> Social Welfare.

The *Supplement* also includes the 1999 *NASW Code of Ethics.*

ORGANIZATION OF THE ENCYCLOPEDIA

The 19th edition, which consists of 290 entries and 142 biographies, is published in three volumes:

> Volume 1: A–E
> Volume 2: F–O
> Volume 3: P–Y and biographies

Each volume contains a full table of contents and an index to make it easier for readers to locate entries. The *Supplement* contains many of the same search features as the 19th edition.

Entries have been placed in alphabetic order, word by word; colons within a title precipitate a secondary sort. The following example illustrates the pattern:

> Asian Americans Overview
> Asian Americans: Chinese
> Asian Americans: Japanese
> Asian Americans: Southeast Asians
> Asian Indians

SEARCH TOOLS

Readers may open a volume and turn to the appropriate place in the alphabet to find the information they seek. Several tools have also been incorporated to help readers find a specific topic or a set of related topics.

Detailed Table of Contents

Each volume contains a complete table of contents for the full *Encyclopedia*. Entry titles, stated as simply and descriptively as possible, are listed in alphabetic order, and the names of authors and the opening page number are given.

Subject Cross-References

Although we have attempted to place entries where readers are most likely to look, many terms might be used interchangeably. Therefore, numerous subject cross-references have been inserted into the 2003 *Supplement* to help readers find entries in the *Encyclopedia* and its supplements. For example, in the 2003 *Supplement*, you will find the following cross-references:

> **Income**
> *See* Employment and Earnings, *2003*
> **PIE**
> *See* Person-in-Environment, *Volume* 3

An italic year or volume number following the entry title indicates where that entry can be found. "Employment and Earnings" is a topic in the 2003 *Supplement*, while "Person-in-Environment" can be found in Volume 3 of the *Encyclopedia*.

Comprehensive Index

The highly detailed, easy-to-follow index is your best source for organizations, federal legislation, and places. Browsing through the index will lead you to a wide range of key topics. The index also includes cross-references (such as OAA. *See* Old Age Assistance—Title I) and "see also" references (such as Prisons. *See also* Community-Based Corrections; Family-Based Corrections).

Reader's Guides

Reader's Guides will help you locate entries on related topics. Reader's Guides are interspersed throughout the 19th edition, with entries in alphabetic order. A comprehensive list of all of the Reader's Guides, including entries from the

1997 *Supplement*, can be found in Appendix 2, at the back of this edition. Entries that appeared in the previous *Supplement* will be followed by the year *1997*. Titles of new entries (those included in this *Supplement)* will be followed by the year *2003*. The remaining titles may be found in the *Encyclopedia*. For example, the HIV/AIDS Reader's Guide box (below) can be found in Volume 2 of the *Encyclopedia*, on page 1256.

READER'S GUIDE

HIV/AIDS

The following entries contain information on this general topic:

HIV/AIDS Overview
HIV/AIDS: Direct Practice
HIV/AIDS: Men
HIV/AIDS: Pediatric
HIV/AIDS: Women

We have attempted to provide as many ways to find a subject as possible. For example, you will find entries related to people of color in several Reader's Guides:

Cultural Competence
National Origin Groups
People of Color
Racial and Ethnic Groups
Special Populations

A list of Reader's Guides appears at the end of this section as well as on page xxii in the 19th edition of the *Encyclopedia*.

For Further Information

Another way to find related entries is to review the additional titles at the end of each entry. For example, at the end of the "Medicare and Medicaid: Health Policy" entry, you will find the following list:

For further information see

Aging: Public Policy Issues and Trends; Federal Social Legislation from 1961 to 1994; Health Care: Financing; Health Care: Policy Development, *1997;* Health Care: Reform Initiatives; Health Services Systems Policy; Long-Term Care; Managed Care; Social Security

The year *1997* after "Health Care: Policy Development" means that this entry can be found in the 1997 *Supplement.* Entries not followed by a year in italics can be found in one of the three volumes of the *Encyclopedia*, in alphabetic order.

Key Words

Authors have supplied up to five key words or key word phrases that most succinctly describe the content of the entry. You may use these to search for other entries in the index.

Authors

Authors are listed with the title of the entry in the table of contents, and there is a byline immediately following the entry title in the text. At the end of each entry, you will find the author's position and address as they were at the time the *2003 Supplement* was published.

Bibliographic Information

Authors' sources are cited using the author–date citation style. References are listed immediately following each entry.

Many entries also include a "Further Reading" list. The materials in these listings, although not specifically mentioned in the text of the entry, provide additional helpful information on the topic.

CONCLUSION

Many people—the editorial board, the supplement committee, authors, and staff—have collaborated to create an up-to-date reference work that presents the richness, the vitality, and the depth of social work knowledge. We hope that it will be useful to scholars, practitioners, and students as they continue to expand the knowledge base.

LISTING OF READER'S GUIDES
(For full Reader's Guides see Appendix 2.)

Abuse and Neglect
Adolescents
Adults
African Americans
Aging
AIDS/HIV
Asian Americans
Assessment
Budgeting
Child Abuse
Children and Youths
Clinical Social Work
Community
Computer Use
Courts and Corrections
Crisis Intervention
Cultural Competence
Death and Dying
Direct Practice
Disabilities
Education
Employment
Ethics
Families
Feminist Practice
Fields of Practice
Finances

Foster Care
Fundraising
Gay Men
Gerontology
Group Work
Health
Hispanics/Latinos
History
HIV/AIDS
Homelessness
Homosexuality
Immigrants
Income Security
Information Systems
International Issues
Justice
Legal Issues
Legal Regulation
Legislation
Lesbians
Management
Medical Care
Men
Mental Health
National Origin Groups
Needs Assessment
Parenting
People of Color

Planning
Poverty
Professional Associations
Public Assistance
Public Policy
Public Social Services
Racial and Ethnic Groups
Regulation of Social Work
Religion and Spirituality
Research
Residential Care
Sexual Abuse
Sexuality
Social Services Delivery
Social Supports
Social Welfare
Social Work Education
Social Work Profession
Special Populations
Staff Development
Substance Abuse
Third-Party Payments
Treatment Approaches
Vendorship
Violence
Welfare
Women

Introduction

Nazneen S. Mayadas

The *Encyclopedia of Social Work* Supplement Committee and its chair are to be congratulated on their hard work and dedication in putting together a renowned panel of authors to give their perspectives on the developments that have taken place in social work since the publication of the *1997 Encyclopedia Supplement*. The authors selected by the Supplement Committee are widely recognized experts in their respective fields who bring state-of-the-art knowledge and expertise to this *Supplement*. Thanks are also due to the National Association of Social Workers (NASW) editorial and publication staff whose management and support behind the scenes are, as always, invaluable and professional. This is especially so for a complex project such as this that is also important to the profession.

Social work is socially constructed; it is a profession that parallels societal conditions, and because social conditions are constantly in the throes of change, this mutability is also reflected in the profession. The *Encyclopedia of Social Work* is designed to mirror changes and to maintain a record of these transitions. This task is discharged with excellence and deliberation in the present volume, which succeeds the *1997 Encyclopedia Supplement*. To update an already well-researched and comprehensive encyclopedia is not only a formidable and challenging task, but it also demands considerable care and deliberate attention to detail to avoid duplicating and reiterating materials published in previous volumes. The *Encyclopedia of Social Work* is a major source of professional consultation for educators, for students and practitioners of social work, and for members of other related disciplines and professions. It also serves as an archive of the development of social work theory and knowledge. Hence, information provided in its pages must satisfy multiple requirements and demands. The *2003 Supplement* to the *Encyclopedia of Social Work* has met these challenges remarkably well and has identified trends that are currently evident in the knowledge base of the profession and in service delivery and practice. The entries in this volume reflect some of the key changes seen in American social work in the last decade of the 20th century and at the turn of the millennium. At the same time, they reflect current and future developments in the profession. This volume selects aspects of three major themes: professional practice and education, social work research and social policy, and economic influences. Not only will readers find key developments of the past decade superbly and succinctly written, but they will also find excellent pointers for further study.

The section on social work research includes a fine historical entry that traces the early origins of social work research and discusses the tension between a scientific and a practice-based approach. The development of the Institute for the Advancement of Social Work Research represents a major research initiative for the profession and marks an important new phase in the development of social work research. It is a national initiative coordinating collaboration between various social work education constituency organizations and benefits from federal funds through the research centers established by the National Institute of Mental Health. The focus on outcomes from the 1990s onward, which was driven by managed care and other funding bodies to demonstrate effectiveness of social work intervention, led to the adoption from the medical profession of an evidence-based approach to practice. This historical perspective and the related entry on guidelines for evidence-based practice pose an interesting question for the future direction of the profession. Is the development of an evidence-based approach consistent with the postmodern constructivist era in which we live? The section on participatory and stakeholder-based research reflects this latter perspective and enables readers to address this question of compatibility and future direction for the profession. The Supplement Committee must be credited for highlighting a key philosophical issue in a practical way by including topics the authors address so effectively while giving a comprehensive, yet succinct, overview of the main issues.

In the policy-related sections, one entry summarizes issues and challenges in the Medicaid and Medicare programs as a result of legislative, economic, and demographic changes. Other entries address the welfare reform initiative and its consequences. "Temporary Assistance for Needy Families" concisely summarizes the effect of welfare reform and makes a telling recommendation that future initiatives might do better to focus on reducing poverty rather than reducing the poverty rolls. An illustration of the social construction of social work is given in "Conservatism and Social Welfare." The dominance of the conservatives should not, it is argued, allow social welfare to atrophy; rather, social welfare should be accommodated by linkages with market-based strategies such as asset and credit-building programs and microenterprise initiatives. Traditional welfare services might be reborn, suggests the author, and Community Financial Services would be the focus of intervention.

"Empowerment Zone, Microenterprise, and Asset Building" explores in further detail how these market-based strategies for poverty reduction have been implemented. Further entries that address the economics of poverty support this approach: one explores the implications of the contingent labor market, including issues relating to health benefits, health and safety, gender, and stigma. A chastening point here is that even social work and social work education are not free from contingent labor issues. Two sections address other economic issues; one addresses employment earnings and labor market supply issues, the other addresses retirement and pensions. This strong focus on economics and poverty is a great strength of this *Encyclopedia Supplement.* Indeed, it may usher in a new approach to poverty studies.

One might even venture to say this could herald a watershed or new direction for social work in the 21st century as the knowledge base adapts to new economic and political conditions. In this way, the committee has demonstrated excellent vision. They have fulfilled their task in producing the signpost. It is up to the rest of us to explore new directions, to be well informed about these new approaches, and to be open to extending our knowledge in unfamiliar areas that may challenge us and require new skills. If the profession is to continue to be relevant and offer the best service to clients, we can do well to use these writings as guidelines for further investigation, research, and practice in the service of our clients. The emphasis on economic empowerment resembles the strengths perspective in clinical practice. The application of concepts across practice levels, which do not emphasize the spurious dichotomy between micro and macro levels of

practice, may well require a new curriculum design in social work education, and these ideas may spawn new models of social work practice.

This potential for substantial change is further explored in the entries that deal with social work practice. In fact "Empirically Based Interventions" boldly asserts that this approach has the "potential to revolutionize the practice of social work, to the betterment of clients' lives and of the citizenry as a whole." Certainly, the international Campbell collaboration, founded in 1996 and modeled after the Cochrane collaboration in health care, marks a new approach to international and to interdisciplinary collaboration in practice and parallels developments in the field of medicine in evidence-based practice. These collaborative initiatives of global networks collect and disseminate systematic reviews of research on the effectiveness of interventions. The Cochrane collaboration focuses on health care and the Campbell collaboration focuses on the behavioral sciences. As society becomes more outcome focused, research in social work gains prominence and supports accountability in practice. If social work interventions are indeed responsible for exchange in the target system, then it is imperative that theories are rigorously tested for further application. A good example of this is evidence-based practice that builds its interventions on tested knowledge. Research and practice are two sides of a single coin, each contributing to the development of knowledge for practice. "Evidence-Based Practice Guidelines" is an important companion to this entry. It describes the recent trends and proposals for a new approach to social work practice that would move away from the theory-based approach to the adoption of a practice guidelines approach, similar to the medical profession. This entry discusses the advantages and disadvantages associated with such a transition and raises questions such as, "Is the knowledge base of the profession sufficiently developed to support such an approach?" This is a practice trend dependent on research knowledge and is still in its infancy, but it is to the credit of the committee that they have selected these key new approaches for inclusion in this *Supplement.*

"Hate Crimes" recounts crimes of all kinds, including church arson, genocide and ethnic cleansing, domestic terrorism, and appalling violence to individuals such as those that resulted in the deaths of James Byrd and Matthew Shepard. The role of social work and public policy is thoroughly explored. Intergroup tensions are a common factor in this entry and the one on multiculturalism, which raises interesting issues concerning the power of words on actions and concerning dualist philosophy that reinforces the rather limiting and paternalistic traditional dichotomy of "us and them." The author contends that "true multiculturalism is a movement for a just and equal world, and that we must work to transform the individual self and institutional structures to create this world as well as our group identities." A multicultural perspective centralizes the role of culture, with cultural diversity as the organizing concept. Currently the terms "diversity" and "minority cultures" are used interchangeably. This reinforces the inequitable proclivity to stratify society on ethnic lines. Diversity and multiculturalism must be accepted as a normal human condition. Only then will a truly equitable society be achieved. An entry on strengths perspective summarizes this now well-established approach, and one on people with severe and persistent mental illness documents an area of central interest in social work practice because social workers provide a considerable proportion of the available services to people with mental illness.

Two entries provide important overviews: one addresses the future of social work education, while the other addresses social work practice. "Social Work Education and the Future" is a comprehensive review of many factors influencing social work education, such as globalization, race, racism, devolution, downsizing, social and economic health, aging, and growth in the number of schools of social work. Technology and economic globalization, it is argued, have shrunk the world to a global village, which facilitates interdependence and communication. Within this context, the authors speak to the post–September 11 necessity of internationalizing the Council on Social Work Education (CSWE) curriculum

standards for accreditation. The authors discuss the combined effort of the two national arms of the profession, NASW and CSWE, to build a new paradigm of social work education that would recognize multiculturalism and internationalism. More operational measures of internationalism would include faculty and student intercountry exchanges, with specific learning goals and opportunities for language acquisition.

"The Future of Social Work Practice" provides an excellent structural analysis of the profession and demonstrates that social work is an expanding profession, with promising employment opportunities anticipated over the next two decades. In addition, an NASW task force notes that social workers are equipped with the skills for international development work. New areas of practice, such as corporate, forensic or judicial practice, and Internet-based counseling, among others, are considered.

Readers beware! Exciting and potentially radical changes are highlighted in this *Supplement* from the perspectives of both practice and policy: do not be taken in by the reserved and objective academic approach of these entries. The contents of this volume will revolutionize the profession of social work in the search for a more just and equitable society and more effective services to individuals. This volume has admirably fulfilled its functions of both documenting and reflecting current practice, presenting and evaluating new trends, and highlighting possible future directions. Explore, critique, and analyze these ideas, and as you read, the authors will take you on a journey into the 21st century. How these new approaches are received, tested, and applied will influence the future shape of social work practice.

Nazneen S. Mayadas, DSW, ACSW, is chair, NASW Publications Committee, and professor of social work, School of Social Work, University of Texas at Arlington, Box 19129, Arlington, TX 76019–0129.

C

Confidentiality

See Legal Issues: Confidentiality and Privileged Communication, *Volume 2;* Legal Issues: Recent Developments in Confidentiality and Privilege, *1997*

Conservatism and Social Welfare
David Stoesz

Conservatism is often negatively associated with social welfare, yet its influence has been profound; as the 21st century unfolds, it will continue to shape social policy. That conservatism should play a prominent role in American social welfare is virtually assured by structural features in the contemporary mixed welfare economy. Ginsberg (2000) has observed that the political, economic, and philosophical precepts of conservatism have been embedded in American society. The political economy of the West is democratic–capitalist, designating a primary role for market economics. In the United States, the independent sector, including nonprofit organizations and private philanthropy, has made important contributions to the well-being of disadvantaged populations. Conservative preferences for markets to deliver services, expansion of private property, and consumer choice also have been compatible with social workers in private practice.

Social work's apprehension about conservatism is primarily due to the profession's affirmation of the liberal formulation of the welfare state. According to classic liberalism, government should provide benefits to underserved populations unconditionally as an entitlement. The liberal welfare state was instituted with the Social Security Act of 1935 and expanded significantly with the War on Poverty of the mid-1960s. Wilensky and Lebeaux (1965) identified two conceptions of social welfare: the *residual* (conservative) orientation relied on social welfare only when the "safety net"—the market, families, friends, and government—failed; the *institutional* (liberal) orientation viewed welfare as a social structure, like public education, essential for the functioning of a modern society. Significantly, Wilensky and Lebeaux hypothesized that the residual conception would be surpassed by the institutional as social welfare became more necessary for industrial society. By the 1980s, however, the liberal welfare state was in retreat, raising fundamental doubts about the prospect of replicating the northern European welfare state ideal in the United States.

The two-term presidency of Ronald Reagan during the 1980s found liberalism being replaced by a conservatism that has defined domestic policy, shaping not only the framework of policy options, but also the details of existing programs. Conservatives had long been critical of the liberal welfare state, denouncing it for high taxation, inferior service, a turgid bureaucracy, and a disaffected public (Yergin & Stanislaw, 1998). This critique was radicalized during the 1980s by an insurgency of "traditionalist" conservatives who advocated for the infusion of Christian values into social policy and pressed a cultural agenda consisting of restricting abortion, reinserting religion in public schools, and denying the civil rights of women, racial minorities, and homosexuals (Stoesz, 1996). Although the traditionalist agenda was contrary to the principles advocated by "libertarian" conservatives, it galvanized many Americans who were not affiliated with the dominant political parties and who were concerned about the deterioration of traditional values; these independent voters swung to the "Right," accounting for the electoral success of the Republican Party.

The triumph of Republican conservatives did not go unnoticed. Indeed, the conservative shift in public philosophy became so compelling that many Democrats, members of the party most supportive of the welfare state, adopted more centrist positions. The conservative assault on social programs reached its zenith during the 1990s when Republicans attained control of Congress and President Bill Clinton capitulated to their power by signing a welfare reform act that many liberals bitterly opposed. Thus, the retreat of welfare state liberalism and the rise of the traditionalist Right have had a profound effect on social policy, an influence that has been contrary to the mission of social work.

Recent events suggest a reconciliation of the liberal versus conservative polemic. Beginning with the creation of the Democratic Leadership Council during the 1980s, young political leaders such as Bill Clinton and Al Gore pulled the Democratic Party to the center, calling for a "third way" in governance—distinct from the progovernment liberalism and promarket conservatism that had defined American ideology during most of the 20th century. The third way movement soon spread to Europe, providing a platform for a new generation of politicians (Giddens, 1999). In the United States, Republicans fashioned "compassionate" conservatism as a way to soften the "traditionalist" conservatism that had begun to repel many liberal and independent voters. As the conservative momentum in domestic affairs continues, in all likelihood, the future will witness an emergent ideology that meets the requirements of postindustrial society, one that is as postliberal as it is postconservative.

History of Conservatism

Since its inception, strong conservative currents have shaped the American social welfare system. Abolitionists introduced the first federal social program during the Civil War. The Freedman's Bureau, established to help emancipated slaves become self-sufficient, was terminated by southern congressmen six years after its creation (Franklin, 1980). Yet, federal pensions paid to Union veterans swelled, eventually consuming 40 percent of the federal budget (Skocpol, 1992). Ironically, these first federal social programs were the creation of the Republican Party.

Modern social welfare is understood as a product of industrialization and its attendant social problems: urbanization and immigration. Indeed, the first modern impulses in American social welfare were proposed by "progressive" Republicans who worked within a conservative ideological framework (Morris, 2001). Progressive reformers established mothers' pensions in the states, and these served as precursors to family welfare, which was established under Title IV of the 1935 Social Security Act. Gordon (1994) has observed that progressive "maternalists" deferred to conservatives in the creation of family welfare in two ways: states were allowed to establish eligibility criteria as well as benefit levels, and the rightful place of

mothers was presumed to be in the home. Cash benefits for wageworkers, overwhelmingly men, were federalized through unemployment compensation and social security—programs that mimicked private insurance schemes. Since its inception, then, the American welfare state has been consistent with conservative values of work and family life.

The War on Poverty introduced programs that augmented the welfare state and also reflected conservative influences. Medicare and Medicaid, established in 1965, reimbursed private medical providers, catalyzing a burgeoning market in health care. Despite the significant expansion of public assistance benefits to people who were poor during the War on Poverty, benefits were consistently set according to the conservative principle of "less eligibility," requiring that they be less than the lowest prevailing wage so as not to subvert the work ethic. During the 1970s, two important and rather different programs were inaugurated, and these, too, reflected conservative principles: the Health Maintenance Organization Act of 1973 provided incentives for private managed care companies to subscribe members, and in 1975 the Earned Income Tax Credit (EITC) authorized a refundable benefit for low-wage workers. Subsequent to the War on Poverty, the welfare state continued to expand through programs that complemented conservatism.

The Conservative Revolution

Although conservative influences were evident in the programs and benefits of the welfare state, conservatives voiced increasing misgivings about the expansion of federal social programs. The conservative indictment of social programs was twofold. Aware that virtually all social programs were open-ended entitlements, conservatives were concerned about that part of the federal budget that was not subject to containment. Increasingly, social programs were consuming larger portions of federal expenditures, a problem that would inevitably worsen when baby boomers became eligible for social security and Medicare. To the extent that social program expenditures were on autopilot, they crowded out discretionary allocations, annual appropriations that included everything from defense to student loans to health research. A subordinate issue related specifically to public assistance programs: unconditional welfare benefits were associated with multiple social problems—generational welfare dependency, teenage pregnancy and out-of-wedlock births, dropping out of high school, among others—all considered problems of the "underclass." Rather than alleviating poverty, conservatives alleged that liberal social programs actually exacerbated the underclass (Novak, 1987; Stoesz, 2000).

The conservative case against the welfare state would have proved to be little more than right-wing rhetoric had it not been for the concerted efforts of conservative think tanks. Bridling at the liberal imprint on social policy, wealthy individuals and foundations began channeling significant funds to conservative policy institutes during the 1970s. In Washington, DC, the American Enterprise Institute and the Heritage Foundation acquired dozens of policy analysts to critique liberal social programs and propose alternatives, a venture that was complemented by the Manhattan Institute in New York City and the Hoover Institution in Stanford, California. Using sophisticated and aggressive methods for disseminating ideas, the conservative think tanks quickly eclipsed the more staid liberal think tanks, such as the Brookings Institution and the Urban Institute, and began to dominate the social policy debate (Stoesz, 1988, 1999). With the election of Ronald Reagan to the presidency in 1980, dozens of analysts from conservative think tanks assumed appointed positions within the federal government from which they would begin to alter the liberal vector in social policy.

During the 1980s, conservative policy institutes proved particularly adept at fielding young scholars and promoting their work to the public. Among them, two would rise to prominence, essentially defining the welfare reform debate through to the end of the century: Charles Murray and Lawrence Mead. A previously unknown scholar, Murray had written a monograph for the American Enterprise Institute contending that welfare benefits aggravated poverty. Subsequently, a patron of the Manhattan Institute subsidized a book on the idea, and, not long thereafter, Murray (1984) presented *Losing Ground* to a standing-room-only audience at the Heritage Foundation. Murray attained notoriety by proposing a bold "thought experiment," "scrapping the entire federal welfare and income support structure for working-aged persons" (p. 227). Whereas Murray's draconian notion captured the conservative imagination, Mead's proposal was more pragmatic. Noting that receipt of public assistance benefits was unconditional, in *Beyond Entitlement,* Mead (1986) proposed making benefits dependent on specific behaviors, such as employment and school attendance. By

holding welfare recipients to the same standards of conduct expected of the nonpoor, Mead argued that welfare policy could be a mechanism for reversing the proliferation of underclass behaviors. Both of these ideas would become features of conservative welfare reform by mandating that welfare recipients obtain employment and imposing time limits on their receipt of benefits.

A growing group of disenchanted liberals watched with alarm as conservatives dominated social policy during the 1980s and vowed to avenge the Democratic presidential campaign losses of 1980, 1984, and 1988. In order to pull the Democratic Party to the Right, the Democratic Leadership Council was created, and a centrist think tank, the Progressive Policy Institute, was appended to it. Noting public ambivalence about social welfare (Cook & Barrett, 1992), "neoliberal" Democrats moved on several tracks. Because of the solid support on most fronts for social security and Medicare, neoliberals continued to endorse these programs. However, eroding public sentiment for public assistance, commonly called "welfare," led to a reversal of traditional liberal positions, so that work and time limits were endorsed. A third initiative advocated by neoliberals focused on "civic society," a reinforcement of nonprofit, community-based organizations to restore mainstream norms in troubled neighborhoods. As had been the case for conservatives during the 1970s, neoliberalism would have been so much rhetoric had not two of its champions, Bill Clinton and Al Gore, been elected in 1992. With their reelection in 1996, the neoliberal imprint on social policy would be indelible.

POLICY LEGACY

The conservative influence on social policy has been profound. Indeed, the impact was similar to the hegemony enjoyed by liberals earlier in the 20th century: The popularity of liberal social programs was such that Richard Nixon, a conservative Republican, signed major expansions of federal social programs during his presidency. By the 1990s the ideological dominance had been reversed with Bill Clinton, a Democrat, acceding to congressional conservatives by signing the 1996 welfare reform act, known as the Personal Responsibility and Work Opportunity Reconciliation Act (PRWORA). As the following list shows, conservative changes in social policy have been extensive:

- The 1981 Omnibus Budget and Reconciliation Act (OBRA) cut the Title XX block grant by 20 percent, penalized public assistance recipients who persisted in working, and encouraged states to seek waivers for innovations in the provision of cash assistance to poor families.

- The Family Support Act of 1988 mandated that beneficiaries of family assistance enroll in a training or education program or enter the labor market, in which event they would be provided with transitional benefits for child care, health care, and transportation.
- In 1989 catastrophic health insurance was repealed the year after it was instituted, the first retraction of a social insurance program in the history of the American welfare state.
- In 1993 the Health Security Act, which was an initiative to extend health care to all Americans in a way that complemented the expanding managed care industry, was soundly defeated.
- The 1993 Budget Act reinforced traditional income supplement programs by increasing the minimum wage as well as the earned income tax credit, despite outcries that benefits were going to many people who were not needy.
- The 1994 Riegle Community Development Act introduced the Community Development Financial Institutions Loan Fund, an application of community capitalism as a neighborhood development strategy.
- In 1996, PRWORA radically reformed welfare by converting an open-ended entitlement to a discretionary block grant that was devolved to the states, imposing targets on the number of beneficiaries who must be working, and instituting a five-year time limit on receipt of federal benefits. In addition, the PRWORA allowed private entities to subcontract in the provision of welfare, notably for-profit firms and faith-based nonprofits.

At the beginning of the 21st century, there is little evidence that the conservative dominance in social policy has diminished. The liberal wing of the Democratic Party continues to be marginal, recently evident in the failed presidential candidacy of Al Gore who ran a campaign based largely on liberal politics. Within the Republican Party, the influence of liberalism is extremely remote, though the emergence of compassionate conservatism may signal movement from the far Right toward the ideological center. In formulating compassionate conservatism, Republican candidate George W. Bush drew heavily on Marvin Olasky's thinking. Appearing on the eve of the Bush campaign in

2000, Olasky's *Compassionate Conservatism* outlined the breadth, as well as the controversy, of the concept:

> It is a full-fledged program with a carefully considered philosophy. It will face in the twenty-first century not easy acceptance but dug-in opposition. It will have to cross a river of suspicion concerning the role of religion in American society. It will have to get past numerous ideological machine-gun nests. Only political courage will enable compassionate conservatism to carry the day and transform America. (p. 68)

In his Philadelphia acceptance speech, Bush placed compassionate conservatism at the center of his campaign in order "to put conservative values and conservative ideas into the thick of the fight for justice and opportunity" (Didion, 2000, p. 68). Reiterating the theme at a University of Notre Dame commencement address, Bush identified compassionate conservatism as "the third stage of combating poverty in America" following President Johnson's War on Poverty and President Clinton's welfare reform (Allen, 2001). Accordingly, Bush established the White House Office of Faith-Based and Community Initiatives during his first year in office; then, in his 2002 State of the Union Address, he encouraged Americans to provide 2,000 hours of community service through the Freedom Corps (Stoesz, 2002). Thus, Bush asserted a revisionist centrism, portraying conservatism as a catalyst for social justice, a moral high ground long held by liberals. Subsequently, George W. Bush choreographed responses to the attacks of September 11 so masterfully that conservatism was once again the nation's unrivaled public philosophy (Dionne, 2002). Moreover, corporate influences in campaign financing, in funding policy institutes, and in providing human services will continue to shape social welfare in a conservative manner. As the past decades have so clearly demonstrated, conservatism is, indeed, a force with which social work must reckon.

SOCIAL POLICY INITIATIVES CONSISTENT WITH CONSERVATISM

Although liberals often claim that conservatives are inimical to social welfare, this is not the case; it would be more accurate to say that conservatives simply have a different understanding of who should help the needy. Consistent with residual welfare, conservatives prefer that the disadvantaged rely on the labor market, family and friends, and civic associations for assistance, not federal social programs. The conservative emphasis on individual initiative, private agencies, and financial capital *can* inspire new thinking about how to advance social welfare. In this respect, social work in private practice, including employee assistance programs, is consistent with using conservatism as a basis for enhancing life opportunities. Another example is replacing public social services with vouchers; this would not only allow welfare poor people to exercise choice in their selection of services providers, an option that most middle-class Americans take for granted, but also dismantle much of a welfare bureaucracy that has segregated poor people from the social mainstream (Stoesz, 1992). An illustration of how conservatism can be used to advance social welfare is "bootstrap capitalism," consisting of wage supplements, asset building, and community capitalism (Stoesz, 2000; earlier work by Stoesz & Saunders, 1999, referred to "welfare capitalism").

Wage Supplements
Wage subsidies reinforce the work ethic by augmenting earned income. Since its inception in 1975, the federal EITC has paid refunds to low-wage earners, primarily those with children. The EITC was intended to reduce the tax burden on working poor people, effectively supplementing their wages and making work more attractive than welfare. By the late 1990s, the EITC was budgeted at $30 billion annually, eclipsing Temporary Assistance for Needy Families and vying with Supplemental Security Income as the largest cash benefit welfare program. About a dozen states have established their own earned income credit (EIC) programs to complement the federal EITC. Not all state EIC programs are refundable, however, and they vary in benefits, paying from 25 percent to 43 percent of the federal EITC. Tax credits have also been available to employers who hire workers at low wages. The Work Opportunity Tax Credit took effect in 1996, reimbursing employers up to $2,400 per employee, effectively allowing them to supplement low wages.

Phelps (1997) has proposed a more direct wage subsidy, a graduated scale through which the supplement declines as wages rise. At the low end, someone earning a wage of $4.00 hourly would receive a subsidy of $3.00, totaling $7.00; at the high end, someone earning a wage of $12.00 would be augmented only $0.06, totaling $12.06. Phelps has estimated a fully implemented wage subsidy would cost about $125

billion, an amount that he claimed would be generated by collapsing the EITC, employer tax credits, and welfare. Also, Phelps has contended that this wage subsidy would also prevent future costs related to social control, especially incarceration and institutionalization of the underemployed and unemployed.

Asset Building
Accruing assets accelerates the upward mobility of poor people. Among the most perverse features of traditional welfare were its stringent limits on allowable assets, established at no more than $1,500 per family. As a result, welfare poor people were denied the ability to build assets, which could be used to buffer them against adversity. By contrast, more affluent Americans have been allowed a range of asset-building opportunities through tax expenditures granted for home mortgage interest, as well as employer contributions for retirement and health care packages—benefits that far exceed direct welfare benefits to poor people. Since OBRA of 1981, more than 40 states obtained waivers to modify welfare programs, and many elected to increase the limit on allowable assets (Strawn, Dacey, & McCart, 1994).

A more direct asset strategy is individual development accounts (IDAs), dedicated savings accounts in which the account holder's contribution is matched from an external source, such as the government or philanthropy, according to the account holder's income. As proposed by Sherraden (1991), IDAs have been incorporated into the PRWORA as well as the Assets for Independence Act of 1999 in order to encourage welfare poor people to finish college or vocational school, buy a home for the first time, or establish a business. Under the "Down Payment on the American Dream" initiative, the Corporation for Enterprise Development in conjunction with the Center for Social Development has received $15 million from private foundations to demonstrate IDAs in 13 sites across the nation. Subsequently, IDA participants were found to average savings of $33 per month, which accumulated to $845 over nine months when matching funds in varying amounts were included (Sherraden, 2000). Even specific behavioral changes due to IDAs have been documented because the program specifically encourages account holders to finish school, own a home, or start a business.

Another asset-building strategy is microcredit, imported from the Third World, where microloans have shown a surprising capacity to pull peasant women out of poverty by providing small dollar credits for business start-ups. Microenterprises have evolved slowly in the United States. Several states have established microcredit loan programs to encourage poor people to purchase homes or start businesses (Counts, 1996).

Community Capitalism

Neighborhood-based capitalism is evident in the 2,000 community development corporations (CDCs) that have evolved in response to the dramatic drop in government aid to cities since the early 1980s. Specialized CDCs, such as community development banks and credit unions, have been organized—Chicago's Shorebank, Ithaca's (New York) Alternative Credit Union, Durham's (North Carolina) Self-Help Credit Union, and the Marshall Heights Community Development Organization (Washington, DC)—in order to provide more extensive financial services to low-income families. Indeed, a subset of CDCs has been organized chiefly by women to meet the particular circumstances of female-headed households: housing, child care, and elder care (Gittell, Ortega-Bustamante, & Steffy, 1999).

Porter (1995) has claimed that urban neighborhoods represent a "major growth market of the future" (p. 59) and has prophesied the renaissance of inner-city markets. Despite the impoverished conditions of many urban neighborhoods, "depressed areas are great sources of funds (social security checks, welfare payments, earnings, private pensions, and so on)," noted Porter, "but these have been flowing to megabanks that use them elsewhere" (Minsky, 1993, p. 15). The deployment of community-based financial institutions to tap into this flow of funds for the benefit of neighborhoods was facilitated by the 1994 Riegle Community Development Act, which authorized $382 million for a community development rotating loan fund.

These illustrations of bootstrap capitalism could be integrated into an alternative to liberal poverty policy. If traditional welfare departments were converted to Community Financial Services (CFSs), a variety of conventional and innovative services could be provided. Conventional financial services could include savings, checking, and financial planning, and these could be complemented by innovations, such as economic literacy education, IDAs, and microcredit. Account holders could have a choice in which CFSs deposit their benefits, so that CFSs could be encouraged to compete for consumers. Electronic benefit transfers of cash benefits and food stamps could become power-

ful weapons to combat poverty if coupled with a savings strategy, such as IDAs. Account managers who have been trained in the microeconomics of low-income families could assist account holders.

A CFS strategy could also retain capital in poor neighborhoods. To capture capital, CFSs would recruit electronic benefit transfer accounts, help workers and employers maximize EITC and work opportunity tax credit benefits, encourage nonprofits to establish accounts as a way to make investments in their communities, solicit deposits from commercial banks as a way to meet their Community Reinvestment Act obligations, and ask government officials to deposit community development funds. Thus, the CFS strategy employs essentially conservative means to facilitate the integration of welfare and working poor people into the social mainstream.

FUTURE OF CONSERVATISM

Conservatism will continue to shape American social welfare, primarily through the devolution of federal functions to the states and the privatization of governmental functions.

Devolution

In *Laboratories of Democracy*, Osborne (1988) recounted his travels among a handful of governors who were struggling with fiscal compression—reduced federal revenues to the states while need for social welfare escalated—caused by Reagan administration policies. To his surprise, Osborne found that the governors he tracked were, of necessity, being imaginative and innovative in continuing to address the problems of state governance. Since the Nixon administration, various presidents have advocated devolving decision making to subordinate jurisdictions through various "federalism" initiatives. This has provoked a strong reaction on the part of social workers, because states had historically used states' rights as a basis for opposing efforts to advance social welfare, ranging from social reformer Dorothea Dix's failed attempt to use the federal government as an instrument of welfare reform to southern officials' objection to the Civil Rights Movement during continuing Jim Crow practices. A more tactical issue was the allocation of resources for advocacy subsequent to the establishment of the welfare state. Having invested heavily in organizational infrastructure in Washington, DC, to further lobby for elaboration of federal social programs, liberal interest groups, including social workers, were unprepared to reorient their work at the state capitals.

Rather than recognize the import of state and local prerogatives in social welfare and reallocate resources to state capitals and metropolitan areas, the social welfare lobbies have consistently opposed devolution, arguing that it was inimical to the American welfare state. For their part, conservatives were quick to point out that the objection was actually based on the social welfare lobby preserving its influence; the issue, conservatives alleged, was not the nation's welfare but that of the liberal advocacy organizations (Berger & Berger, 1983).

Devolution will remain a central issue in American social welfare. Historically, important social program activity has been a state responsibility, including child welfare, mental health, public health, and juvenile justice. The devolution of family welfare through the PRWORA further complements this tradition. On the other hand, the devolution of the Title XX Social Services block grant has gone virtually unnoticed, even though the reassignment of this function to the states was associated with protracted underfunding of children's services (Costin, Karger, & Stoesz, 1996). (Social workers could be more vigilant about social programming by the states by subscribing to Influencing State Policy [http://www.statepolicy.org/], an initiative to enhance the impact of social work at the state level.)

Privatization
Although the private sector has been a fixture of the mixed welfare economy, as evidenced in private philanthropy and private practice, privatization has become a volatile issue. The conservative suggestion that the private sector should completely *replace* government initiatives is, however, a signal departure from the historical role of the private sector in supplementing governmental welfare. For social workers who are keenly aware of the scope of human needs, the suggestion of a diminishing role of government is untenable. In this respect, Osborne (1992) emerged prophetic once again, having proposed in *Reinventing Government* that government establish the objectives of public policy but assign their execution to the private sector. During the last decades of the 20th century, conservatives advanced privatization on several fronts, eventually converting substantial segments of Kansas and New Jersey child welfare to private auspices. Indeed, the entire public welfare system of Texas would have been privatized had it not been for White House intercession.

Yet, privatization need not be antithetical to advancing social welfare. A new generation of

social entrepreneurs has emerged as experiments with markets reveal untapped opportunities, both locally and nationally. Shore (1999) has explored even more remote reaches of capitalism, founding Share Our Strength (SOS) and Community Wealth Ventures (CWV), hybrid organizations that profit from their roles in niche markets. By the late 1990s SOS and CWV had a payroll of $2.7 million and contributed $8.5 million to nutrition organizations serving poor people (Thompson, 1999). Although ventures such as SOS, CWV, and Second Harvest have not yet attained a scale comparable to that of more prominent organizations, their true value may be gauged more accurately by their pioneering work on the postindustrial frontier.

Although devolution and privatization have been part of the conservative assault on the welfare state, there is no reason these strategies cannot be used to advance social justice. A case can be made that the *future* of social welfare rests less with the salvaging of the monumental programs that articulated the American welfare state, essential though these have been for addressing problems attendant with industrialization, and more with the evolution of a new generation of ventures that exploit the features of the postindustrial environment. Because these have emerged outside of government, they have been suspect; having been started by social entrepreneurs, they have been ignored. Regardless, their irrepressible multiplication has resulted in a grudging recognition that a new way of doing business is evolving. These innovations share several features—their structure is flat, their process is interactive, their technology is transformative, their ownership is collaborative—that have become the tableau of future organizations. The policy infrastructure for this new era is now being forged at the same time, and in all likelihood the result will be a robust, dynamic social policy that is at once committed to sustaining the disadvantaged and, as importantly, also accelerating their upward mobility and reviving their communities. Such an achievement will be as disorienting for traditional liberals who have been inculcated with the necessity of federal entitlements as it is for traditional conservatives who have disdained civic responsibility. Whether under the guise of neoliberalism or compassionate conservatism, the policy environment is protean, not unlike that of the Progressive Era when groups of altruistic professionals seized the opportunities before them and laid the foundation for a century of social progress.

REFERENCES

Allen, M. (2001, May 21). President urges war on poverty. *Washington Post*, p. A1.

Berger, B., & Berger, P. (1983). *The war over the family*. Garden City, NY: Doubleday.

Cook, F., & Barrett, E. (1992). *Support for the American welfare state*. New York: Columbia University Press.

Costin, L., Karger, H., & Stoesz, D. (1996). *The politics of child abuse in America*. New York: Oxford University Press.

Counts, A. (1996). *Give us credit*. New Delhi, India: Research Press.

Didion, J. (2000, November 2). God's country. *New York Review of Books, 47*(2).

Dionne, E. J., Jr. (2002, January 27). Conservatism recast. *Washington Post*, p. B1.

Franklin, J. (1980). *From slavery to freedom*. New York: Knopf.

Giddens, A. (1999). *The third way*. Malden, MA: Blackwell.

Ginsberg, L. (2000). Conservative approaches to social policy. In J. Midgley, M. Tracy, & M. Livermore (Eds.), *The handbook of social policy*. Thousand Oaks, CA: Sage Publications.

Gittell, M., Ortega-Bustamante, I., & Steffy, T. (1999). *Women creating social capital and social change*. New York: City University of New York.

Gordon, L. (1994). *Pitied but not forgotten*. New York: Free Press.

Mead, L. (1986). *Beyond entitlement*. New York: Free Press.

Minsky, H. (1993). *Community development banking*. Annandale-on-Hudson, NY: Jerome Levy Economics Institute.

Morris, E. (2001). *Theodore rex*. New York: Random House.

Murray, C. (1984). *Losing ground*. New York: Basic Books.

Novak, M. (1987). *The new consensus on family and welfare*. Washington, DC: American Enterprise Institute.

Olasky, M. (2000). *Compassionate conservatism*. New York: Free Press.

Osborne, D. (1988). *Laboratories of democracy*. Boston: Harvard Business School Press.

Osborne, D. (1992). *Reinventing government*. Reading, MA: Addison-Wesley Press.

Phelps, E. (1997). *Rewarding work*. Cambridge, MA: Harvard University Press.

Porter, M. (1995). Competitive advantage in the inner city. *Harvard Business Review, 73*, 55–71.

Sherraden, M. (1991). *Assets and the poor*. Armonk, NY: M. E. Sharpe.

Sherraden, M. (2000). *Saving patterns in IDA programs*. St. Louis: Washington University, Center for Social Development.

Shore, W. (1999). *The cathedral within*. New York: Random House.

Skocpol, T. (1992). *Protecting soldiers and mothers*. Cambridge, MA: Harvard University Press.

Social Security Act of 1935, Ch. 531, 49 Stat. 620.

Stoesz, D. (1988). Packaging the conservative revolution. *Social Epistemology, 2*(2), 145–153.

Stoesz, D. (1992). *Social service vouchers*. Washington, DC: Progressive Policy Institute.

Stoesz, D. (1996). *Small change*. White Plains, NY: Longman.

Stoesz, D. (1999). Unraveling welfare reform. *Society, 36*(4), 53–61.

Stoesz, D. (2000). *A poverty of imagination*. Madison: University of Wisconsin Press.

Stoesz, D. (2002). The American welfare state at twilight. *Journal of Social Policy, 31*, 487–503.

Stoesz, D., & Saunders, D. (1999). Welfare capitalism. *Social Service Review, 73*, 380–400.

Strawn, J., Dacey, S., & McCart, L. (1994). *Final report: The National Governors' Association survey of state welfare reforms*. Washington, DC: National Governors' Association.

Thompson, T. (1999, December 19). Profit with honor. *Washington Post Magazine*, p. W6.

Wilensky, H., & Lebeaux, C. (1965). *Industrial society and social welfare*. New York: Free Press.

Yergin, D., & Stanislaw, J. (1998). *The commanding heights*. New York: Simon & Schuster.

David Stoesz, DSW, is professor of social work, Virginia Commonwealth University, 1001 W. Franklin Street, P.O. Box 842027, Richmond, VA 23284-2027 and an associate of policyAmerica, 8110 Carlyle Place, Alexandria, VA 22308.

For further information see

Aid to Families with Dependent Children; Criminal Justice: Social Work Roles; Federal Social Legislation from 1961 to 1994; Federal Social Legislation from 1994 to 1997, *1997;* Health Care: Policy Development, *1997;* Health Care: Reform Initiatives; Health Planning; Income Security Overview; JOBS Program; Progressive Social Work; Public Social Services; Public Social Welfare Expenditures; Sentencing of Criminal Offenders; Social Welfare Expenditures: Private, *1997;* Social Welfare History; Social Welfare Policy; Social Workers in Politics; Substance Abuse: Legal Issues; Temporary Assistance for Needy Families, *2003;* Temporary Assistance to Needy Families, *1997;* Voluntarism; World Social Situation, *1997*

Key Words

poverty	social programs
social justice	social welfare

Contingent Work in the United States
Kathleen Barker

Contingent work is one of the most controversial labor-related developments at the beginning of the 21st century. During the 1990s, an era in which corporations downsized the U.S. labor force and flushed workers onto unemployment rolls, creating an atmosphere in which workers were increasingly viewed as disposable, contingent work permeated the consciousness of American citizens. Fortune 500 firms—deteriorating symbols of employment in the United States—were eclipsed by Manpower, a temporary agency, which became the largest "employer" in the United States (Barker & Christensen, 1998). American workers suspected that long-term permanent jobs were being replaced with less certain or temporary positions with indefinite or short-term expectations and no access to internal labor markets, or "career ladders."

Although researchers have disagreed about a number of issues related to contingent work, most agree that contingent work represents a substantial change, or transition, in the employment relations model that dominated the United States from the latter part of the 19th century throughout the 20th century. This transition refers to the change from stable, permanent, and organizationally rooted jobs in advanced industrial societies to short-term, temporary, and less than full-time employment (Barker & Christensen, 1998; Pfeffer & Baron, 1988). In referring to aspects of this transition, Pfeffer and Baron coined the phrase "taking the workers back out." Organizations, in removing permanent workers from their ranks and replacing them with nonpermanent workers, were changing as well, from hierarchically controlled bureaucracies with strong administrative controls (for example, long-term employment relationships, internal career ladders) to firms that were smaller and "flexible" and did not emphasize firm-specific knowledge. Most importantly, workers in the same firm did not necessarily share a uniform relationship with their employer. Permanent full-time employees labor alongside people hired from temporary agencies, day workers, and independent contractors.

Is contingent work necessarily a new feature of American work life? No. Secondary or "peripheral" work has long been a feature of employment in the United States. According to Morse (1969), the Industrial Revolution entailed using millions of workers, immigrants, Native Americans, African Americans, and women in temporary, intermittent, and part-time arrangements. Working on the periphery was associated with a "second" class status within the workplace. However, contemporary contingent work deviates from the past in important ways. Although it still retains historical linkages to

many "bad" jobs in the secondary labor force, it has emerged in "good" jobs, that is, those jobs that are highly skilled, technical, executive, or professional.

In social work, the literature on contingent work is sparse. Using contingent work as a search term, a literature search in *Social Work Abstracts* in March 2002 resulted in only one article, Carr's (1996) analysis of self-employment. Similarly, no citations were uncovered for the term "nonstandard work," an umbrella term for work that is less than permanent and full time. This is surprising because welfare reform, erosion of health insurance, and worker health and safety are implicated in the emergence of contingent work. There is a growing list of differences in workplace experiences among American workers with which social work professionals must grapple. Comparable positions (engineer, accountant, graphic artist) do not specify equivalent work life conditions, such as pay, benefits, perks, and permanency. For instance, "high end" or professional contractors experience tensions between the benefits of a professional occupation and the job insecurity that professionals in permanent positions do not experience (Kunda, Barley, & Evans, 1999). One of the reasons for the paucity of literature on this topic may be due to competing definitions of contingent work that have dominated the social science literature in the 1990s.

Definitions of Contingent Work
Labor economist Audrey Freedman first introduced the term "contingent work" in 1985, defining it as a set of "conditional and transitory employment arrangements . . . initiated by a need for labor—usually because a company has an increased demand for a particular service or a product or technology, at a particular place, at a specific time" (p. 85). Plewes (1988)

saw parallels between the emergence of just-in-time inventory systems and a just-in-time workforce, an analogy tested in a comparison of just-in-time arrangements in the automotive parts industry and the temporary help services industry (U.S. Department of Labor, 1999). Other early definitions of contingent work saw it as comprised of temporary, self-employed, and contract workers and involuntary part-time workers (Belous, 1989; Christensen & Murphree, 1988). Others (for example, duRivage, 1992) emphasized the wage and benefit inadequacy of contingent work (for example, duRivage, Carré, & Tilly, 1998) or the limited scope of opportunities that accompanied contingent arrangements (Barker, 1993). Yet the term became muddled, notably in the media, by its application to a variety of workplace attachments. In 1996 Polivka of the U.S. Bureau of Labor Statistics (BLS) invoked a previously published textual definition of contingent work (see Polivka & Nardone, 1989): "Contingent work is any job in which an individual does not have an explicit or implicit contract for long-term employment" (1996, p. 4).

Thus, contingent work is an umbrella term that covers those arrangements in which workers have no implicit or explicit understanding that employment will continue (Cohany, Hipple, Nardone, Polivka, & Stewart, 1998; Polivka, 1996). Workers may be on call, temporary, self-employed, or independent contractors, and these categories also overlap with the designation of part-time and full-time schedules. The distinctive element of contingent work is that it is work identified solely as having limited duration, and the employer may be in either a direct or intermediary relationship with the worker (for example, a firm may hire a temporary worker directly or through a temporary help agency).

Although these conceptual definitions, including the Polivka (1996) definition, were useful in clarifying the core nature of contingent work, they did not resolve social scientists' arguments about the operational definition, or measurement, of contingent work. BLS statisticians created three possible definitions of contingent employment, ranging from the most restrictive to the most permissive, which resulted in three different estimates of contingent workers (see Cohany et al., 1998; Polivka, 1996, for detailed discussions). Based on the results of the first contingent work supplement (CWS) to the February 1995 *Current Population Survey,* the BLS calculated that there were between 2.7 million (most conservative estimate) and 6.0 million (most permissive estimate) contingent workers in the United States. They used three definitions to create three different estimates of the number of workers. The first estimate, 2.2 percent of the total workforce, defined the contingent sector as those wage and salary workers who expected their jobs would last for a year or less and who worked at their jobs for one year or less (Estimate 1—the narrowest estimate because it excluded all self-employed workers and independent contractors). The second estimate of 2.8 percent resulted when self-employed workers were included and workers expected their employment to last for an additional year or less and who had worked at their job or been self-employed for one year or less as self-employed or with a client firm (not temporary agency) to which they were assigned if they were temporary workers (Estimate 2). Finally, 4.9 percent of the workforce was contingent when the assumptions about job tenure were relaxed—this included all wage and salary employees and all self-employed and independent contractors but with different restrictions (Estimate 3—the broadest estimate). Even in Estimate 3, however, self-employed and independent contractors were included only if individuals expected their employment to last for a year or less and also if they had been working for that employer for one year or less. Wage and salary workers were included if they had their current job for more than a year and expected it to last for more than a year. Under the most inclusive definition (Estimate 3), BLS estimated that there were 6 million contingent workers in 1995.

The BLS definitions provided important starting points for many researchers but were not without controversy, mainly because researchers thought that BLS underestimated the number of workers in contingent jobs (Kalleberg et al., 1997; Spalter-Roth et al., 1997). "We see no reason to restrict the definition of workers in insecure jobs to only those people who have worked for their current employer for one year or less; the length of time one has already spent in a job has little relevancy to whether that job will continue in the future" (Kalleberg et al., 1997, p. 36). Kalleberg and colleagues defined contingent status as occurring when individuals reported job insecurity. They conceptualized a contingent job as part of a larger trend toward the creation of a nonstandard work arrangement (NSWA), an umbrella term that refers to a variety of employment attachments that are not "traditional." NSWAs refer to full-time and part-time, on-call, day labor, self-employment, independent contracting, and temporary work. Kalleberg and colleagues (1997, 2000) classified jobs as nonstandard work according to any one of the following criteria: there is the absence of an employer (for example, as in independent contracting); there is a distinction between the organization that employs the worker and the organization for whom the person works (for example, temporary work); or there is temporal instability associated with the job (temporary work, day labor, working for a contract company, and so forth). NSWAs include individuals who report their jobs are insecure (contingent workers) and those who do not.

Using the same database, but different operational definitions of contingent work, researchers have concluded that contingent work is much greater than the estimates provided by BLS. In the first reanalysis of the 1995 CWS using Kalleberg and colleagues' (1997) revised definition, Hudson (1999) found that 10.6 million workers were contingent. This was substantially higher than the 6 million figure resulting from the most permissive definition of contingent work used by BLS. The BLS classified 4.5 and 5.3 percent, respectively, of all working men and women as contingent in 1995. Using the revised definition, Kalleberg and colleagues (1997, 2000) found that 8.5 percent of all men and 9.8 percent of all women had jobs of uncertain or limited duration when all jobs were considered (that is, including full-time regular employment). In addition, when examining what proportion of nonstandard jobs were contingent, 17.9 percent of the women and 18.2 percent of the men reported their jobs were insecure. Subsequent reanalysis of the 1997 CWS revealed substantially similar trends, with 17.1 percent of women and 16.5 percent of men claiming their jobs were of limited or uncertain duration (Hudson, 1999). Slightly less than three out of 10 Americans (28.7 percent) held jobs that were nonstandard. Women were more likely to be employed in a nonstandard job (33.7 percent) than men (24.3 percent). Nonstandard jobs are more likely to pay low wages and offer no benefits compared with regular full-time jobs.

The lack of accord on the definition of contingent work has resulted in varying estimates of the number of contingent workers. As contingent jobs vary considerably, however, gross estimates as these do not provide adequate information about each type of contingent arrangement.

SCOPE AND CHARACTERISTICS OF CONTINGENT WORK

Because contingent work is not a single category, characteristics of three notable types of contingent work are next explored. In this section, the subcategories of contingent work are defined and enumerated. Occupational characteristics and trends regarding each of these subcategories of contingent work are also presented. Except where noted, the statistics are based on Hudson's (1999) reanalysis of the 1997 CWS.

Temporary Work

Temporary workers are all workers employed in the help-supply-services industry. "Temps" are hired through an intermediary, a temporary employment agency that pays the worker. Temps are also hired directly by employers for limited duration employment. Temps are distinguished from on-call workers, who are in a pool of workers and are called in as needed for variable time periods (for example, substitute teachers, musicians hired at a union hall, and so forth), and day laborers, who are self-employed and obtain employment by congregating at designated or known sites for selection by employers (for example, landscapers, agricultural workers, and so forth).

The expansion of the temporary help services industry is the most evident and rapid among all contingent relationships. According to Segal and Sullivan (1997), the industry has expanded at an annual rate of more than 11 percent. "Help supply services employment grew from 0.6 percent of the total private economy in 1982 to 2.7 percent in 1998—a rate of growth surpassing even computer and data processing employment" (U.S. Department of Labor, 1999, p. 18). In 1997 there were slightly more than 1.2 million individuals who claimed they were paid by a temporary help agency. Client firms pay a temporary agency for the wages of a worker plus some premium for providing workers on short notice for variable length assignments. Temporary workers work for agency clients in a variety of clerical and industrial settings. The most typical positions for female temporary help agency personnel are secretarial and nursing aides; assembly jobs and truck driving are common for men.

According to the 1997 CWS, the temporary help force tend to be young (about 25 percent under age 25), female (about 56 percent), and white (53 percent). African Americans (20.2 percent) and Hispanics (13 percent) are disproportionately represented in temporary work when compared with their participation in full-time regular work—11.6 percent and 10.3 percent, respectively. When women work in temporary jobs, they tend to earn less than men ($9.85 and $11.84, respectively). Compared with similar full-time workers with comparable education, region, age, marital status, citizenship, and ethnicity, temporary workers average from 15 percent to 18 percent less per hour. Nearly 7 percent of full-time temps receive health insurance coverage through their employers whereas only 1.8 percent of the part-time temps receive such coverage. Compared with full-time workers who receive health insurance coverage through their own employer (69 percent), temporary workers are severely disadvantaged. However, substantial numbers of temporary workers achieve health insurance coverage through other venues, with 43.1 percent of full-time temps and 60 percent of part-time temps reporting some coverage. Only 23.7 percent of the women and 10.7 percent of the men report flexibility or family reasons for working in their temporary help agency jobs.

On average, temporary jobs possess the worst job qualities (poor wages, insecurity, and ineligibility for fringe benefits and pensions) that are generally characteristic of "bad" jobs (Kalleberg, Reskin, & Hudson, 2000). An analysis of the 1997 CWS data shows that 68.6 percent of the women and 66.2 percent of the men in temporary jobs expressed uncertainty about the duration of their positions. This oxymoronic observation means that slightly more than 30 percent of temporary workers feel their jobs are not uncertain, and there are a number of reasons why this may be so.

Temporary work has become a permanent solution for employer staffing in the contemporary workplace (Cohany, 1996), but it has also engendered serious dilemmas for benefits and collective bargaining (Carré, duRivage, & Tilly, 1995; duRivage, 1992), workers' legal rights (Carnevale, Jennings, & Eisenmann, 1998), and safety concerns (McAllister, 1998; Rebitzer, 1998). The downsizing associated with the late 1980s and early 1990s resulted in large layoffs and an increase in temporary workers (not employees; see Gonos, 1998) who worked alongside full-time regular employees but received none of the benefits (for example, stock options, pension, training, and so forth) that regular employees received. An unknown number of firms came to rely on temporary workers but did not convert them to permanent status. The continual employment of these temps led

to the phenomena of "permatemps" (West, McClintock, & Engelbach, 2001). Some observers believe that permatemps exist to avoid paying for the fees associated with hiring an employee from a temporary firm and to avoid paying for the array of benefits extended to regular employees.

Universities also have their own corps of permatemps who comprise an unknown percentage of all faculty in the United States and have few if any benefits or participation in collective bargaining (Barker, 1995). In recent years, university adjuncts and corporate permatemps began to protest their conditions. The permatemps at Microsoft brought a class-action suit seeking retroactive rights to stock benefits. The permatemps argued that they were not employees but "common-law" employees because they were supervised on the job. An appeals court determined that independent contractors could also join the suit (Bernstein, 1999). Microsoft lost the case as well as an appeal to the U.S. Supreme Court. Similar other cases are being brought around the country as workers seek to restore more equality, and courts are responding by curtailing some of the more obvious violations of Internal Revenue Service codes regarding employee status.

On-Call and Day Labor Workers

Little has been known about on-call workers until the CWS survey in 1995 (Cohany, 1996). On-call workers report to work on an as-needed basis or when called and are considered wage and salary workers. Day laborers are self-employed and report to a site where employers can pick up laborers for work of a day or more. Typical on-call positions are associated with hospitals for women, construction for men, and elementary and secondary school positions for both men and women. According to Hudson (1999), there were almost 1.8 million on-call and day labor workers in 1997. Slightly more women than men (50.1 percent) are on-call or day laborer workers, but they tend to work different schedules, with men working full time (69 percent of all men) and women working part time (69.5 percent). Earlier studies of women working on call showed that they were similar to traditional workers in that nearly half were mothers with at least one child under six years of age (Cohany, 1996).

According to the 1997 CWS, part-time workers tend to be overwhelmingly white (73.8 percent) with African Americans (8.1 percent) and Hispanics (14.7 percent) comprising small sectors of on-call and day labor workers.

Compared with their participation in all employment (9.7 percent of all workers), Hispanics are overrepresented for on-call, day labor work. Women working on call average $11.04 per hour, whereas men average $12.67 per hour. Akin to part-time and temporary workers, on-call workers earn less ($12.64 per hour) than their full-time peers ($15.86 per hour). Compared with similar full-time workers with comparable education, age, marital status, citizenship, and ethnicity, on-call workers average from 9 percent to 21 percent less per hour. Slightly more than 42 percent of full-time on-call workers receive health insurance coverage from their employers. However, gender differences for on-call workers are significant with only 23.3 percent of women working on-call full-time jobs receiving benefits, although 51.3 percent of comparable men receive employer health benefits.

Hudson's (1999) analysis of preference for on-call work found that both women (52.5 percent) and men (56.3 percent) expressed a preference for traditional full-time jobs. In terms of insecurity about employment, 100 percent of women and 100 percent of men agreed that their jobs were of limited or uncertain duration.

Independent Contractors

In considering independent contractors, the CWS distinguishes independent contractors such as independent consultants and freelance workers from those who operate businesses such as restaurants or shops. Independent contractors are self-employed workers or wage and salary workers, and researchers found distinct characteristics for each type of independent contractor group. When independent contractors are in wage and salary jobs, they may earn a base pay plus some commission or incentive. Typical occupations are, for example, private household positions, real estate occupations, and street and door-to-door salespersons. Independent contractors who are self-employed are, for example, managers and administrators, small business owners, and carpenters. In 1997 there were almost 7 million self-employed independent contractors and 884,706 wage and salary independent contractors. Men predominate as self-employed independent contractors (75 percent) and less so as wage and salary independent contractors (65.1 percent).

In the 1997 CWS, independent contractors who are self-employed are overwhelmingly white (87.9 percent). African Americans (4.8 percent) and Hispanics (7.3 percent) comprise a disproportionately small portion within this group. Wage and salary independent contractors yield similar rates for whites (78.5 percent) but higher rates for African Americans (9.3 percent) and Hispanics (9.9 percent). Compared with their participation in all employment (10.6 percent of all workers), African Americans are underrepresented in self-employed independent contracting, and this results in a wage inequity because independent contracting pays the highest wages among all employment categories, both standard and nonstandard. Women working as independent contractors average $16.45 per hour, whereas men average $19.18 per hour. Compared with similar full-time workers with comparable education, region, age, marital status, citizenship, and ethnicity, independent contractors average from 1 percent to 7 percent less per hour. However, when Hudson (1999) controlled for job characteristics (industry, occupation, union membership, receipt of health insurance or pension, and so forth), independent contractors who are female earn 13 percent more than comparable full-time women, and men earn 20 percent more than comparable full-time men. Health benefit coverage for wage and salary independent contractors is minimal with only 9.6 percent of part-time independent contractors and 28.9 percent of full-time independent contractors receiving coverage through their employers. Full-time female independent contractors who are wage and salary workers are less likely (20.5 percent) to receive coverage than comparable men (34.1 percent). Although self-employed independent contractors receive no health insurance coverage from their client firms, fully 75.6 percent of full-time and 70.6 percent of part-time independent contractors obtain coverage elsewhere.

Hudson's (1999) analysis of preference found that independent contractors, especially women, largely prefer their working arrangements. In terms of insecurity about employment, 19.7 percent of women and 14.5 percent of men who are wage and salary independent contractors report their jobs are of limited or uncertain duration compared with 10.1 percent of the women and 5.9 percent of the men in self-employed independent contracting arrangements.

In summary, nonstandard work represents a substantial deviation from workplace arrangements that dominated most of the 20th century. Among nonstandard workers, contingent workers—on-call workers, day laborers, and temporary workers—report the highest levels of insecurity. Although not presented above, part-time workers, especially women, express substantial security. In Hudson's (1999) analysis of the 1997 CWS supplement, only 10.5 percent of women and 15.2 percent of men thought their regular part-time jobs were of uncertain duration or contingent. Temporaries are disproportionately African American and Hispanic and whites are overrepresented among the highest paying group, independent contractors. Analyses show that women and minority men are the most disadvantaged in part-time and temporary work (Rasell & Appelbaum, 1997). Minorities, however, are more likely to work in regular full-time work than in nonstandard work. Numerous commentators have observed that counting contingent workers is a relatively recent and controversial event. Trends are difficult to establish except in the case of temporary and part-time work.

Contingent Work in Social Work

When social workers work contingently, they are called "consultants," although many are also called "adjuncts." The status difference associated with either title merits reflection. These disparate opportunities for social work professionals signal an important and cautionary tale regarding the bifurcation of work roles and rights even within one profession (CWS data on the number of contingent social workers cannot be reliably cited due to small sampling of social work professionals and associated large standard errors). In fact, empirical representative data on social workers as workers are sparse. In their analysis, Barth and Pho (2001), citing the data inadequacies as well as contested definitions of who is a "social worker," have called for better data collection by the federal government and institutions on social workers' labor market experiences.

Strengths and Limitations of Contingent Work

Advocates of contingent staffing argue that it offers multiple benefits for firms through staffing flexibility, cutting direct labor costs, as well as reducing or eliminating benefit costs. In this view, contingent work is not necessarily underemployment. Contingent work can enhance workers' leverage in the marketplace, particularly for those workers whose skills are in demand (Abraham & Taylor, 1996). Professionals and managers are portable between firms and the opportunities those firms present. In terms of women with families, flexibility is often invoked as a benefit of contingent work. Critics, on the other hand, maintain that many contin-

gent workers are not portable but disposable. They argue that contingent work can result in a workplace of "haves and have-nots" in terms of benefits, especially health insurance (Farber & Levy, 2000); that it can exclude some workers systematically from many of the social, organizational, and skill opportunities associated with full-time employment (McAllister, 1998; Parker, 1994); and that certain contingent arrangements can obscure power arrangements, resulting in contradictory feelings of loyalty and excessive fear (Smith, 1998).

Flexibility. When flexibility of nonstandard arrangements is invoked by observers, it traditionally has been understood to refer to child care issues. Martella (1992) found that temporary work is inherently inflexible because most temporary work requires availability of the worker for assignments from 9 A.M. to 5 P.M., five days a week. Refusal to work means the possibility of being dropped by a temporary help agency. In addition, the organization 9to5 (2000) found that temporary agencies erect barriers to workers receiving unemployment insurance. In their investigation, 9to5 uncovered one firm that made applicants sign an employment contract that specified the worker would be classified as a voluntary quit if the worker did not accept any assignment. Parker's (1994) research supported the notion that temporary work is primarily about flexibility for the employer. Workers must stay "on-call without interruption" (p. 93), contributing to a bleeding between the borders of work and nonwork time, a trend observed for jobs in general (Bond, Galinsky, & Swanberg, 1998).

Portability. Not all contingent jobs are "bad" jobs. Researchers have found that contingent and nonstandard work varies considerably. Kalleberg and Schmidt (1995) have argued that organizations are most likely to use workers with the lowest and highest skills. In a study of organizational staffing practices, they found that higher prestige occupations are more likely to be temporaries because professionals and managers have portable skills they can transfer from one firm to another (see Parker, 1994). Rather than maintaining an expensive and intermittently needed group of specialized workers, firms are most likely to subcontract unique skills (Christensen, 1998). The two questions that emerge from this line of thinking are as follows: Do advantaged workers, such as professional and managerial women and men, benefit from contingent work as they juggle the competing demands of work and family? Do firms provide such workers with employer-sponsored family benefits?

Gender roles. Research has been conducted that compares the experiences of managers and professionals in nonstandard arrangements with those of peers in regular full-time jobs (Spalter-Roth et al., 1997). Using the 1995 CWS (U.S. Bureau of Labor Statistics, 1995), analysts found that mothers in dual-earner families in managerial and professional nonstandard arrangements work fewer hours per week than female peers in full-time regular employment. It was also found that men who are independent contractors or self-employed work more hours than their male peers in regular full-time employment. Thus, even at the managerial and professional levels, nonstandard work may reinforce traditional roles of women and men that are generally observed for all workers.

Health benefits. Research examining how firms with contingent workers apply their work–family policies is rare in the literature on contingent work and organizations. Christensen (1998) surveyed 21 firms and found that 20 used contingent workers on an increasing basis. All permanent employees were offered a range of work–family programs and policies (for example, flextime, flexplace, job sharing, relocation assistance, counseling, child care information assistance, part-time positions, maternity leave, parent groups, and so forth). Except for direct hire temporary employees, contingent workers are eligible for few benefits and then only at a handful of firms. Christensen pointed out that temporary agency workers (the predominant source of temporary help in those firms surveyed) and independent contractors are not employees of the firm. Therefore, firms are not legally obligated to provide such benefits (see Gonos, 1998). In addition, as contingent workers are not employees of a firm and are not covered by discrimination laws or the Occupational Safety and Health Act of 1970, providing family benefits to contingent workers would make it theoretically possible for workers to sue the employer *as if* they were employees (Christensen, 1998).

Health and safety issues. A variety of emerging employment relationships, such as joint employment between a contracting employer and a providing employment agency or company, are not adequately addressed by current labor law and policy. For example, to avoid liability for accidents, employers will avoid appearing as if they supervise or control contract workers. The appearance of such control extends to worker training (Rebitzer, 1998) with serious implications for worker health and safety (McAllister, 1998; Parker, 1994). In the petrochemical industry, contract workers were preferred because they were not provided with health benefits (Wells, Kochan, & Smith, 1991). They also were given more dangerous work even though they were not as experienced as direct hires or core employees. There was a lapse of supervision of contract workers that resulted in more accidents for contract workers than core workers. Attorneys had advised many of the companies to avoid a joint relationship, such as training or supervision, with the contract employees (Kochan, Wells, & Smith, 1992) because the National Labor Relations Board typically has failed to recognize joint employer liability (Carré et al., 1995). In fact, in the petrochemical industry one-third to one-half of such workers are not included in plant worker safety programs (Kochan et al., 1992). More recently, the Office of Occupational Safety and Health proposed a $2 million fine for a Wisconsin hospital and two temporary agencies that resulted from the hospital deploying untrained, unvaccinated housekeepers supplied by a temporary agency to emergency room and trauma units (Foley, 1998).

All industrial workers face hazards, but contingent industrial work hazards are amplified by unfamiliar coworkers and supervisors, as well as unfamiliarity with the physical layout and equipment of an employer's workplace (Parker, 1994). In a series of interviews with temporary workers, McAllister (1998) noted: "For the temp, everyone is a supervisor" (p. 229). She also found, however, that there is a lack of supervision or concern as well. Temporary workers reported a fear that filing for workers' compensation would result in retaliation—that is, unemployment.

Stigma. Exclusion from the wider community of workers is also many times premised on the use or creation of stigmatizing characteristics (Opotow, 1990). Observers have commented on how contingent workers are forced to announce their tenuous ties to a firm through wearing different clothing or uniforms (Wells et al., 1991), wearing different colored badges (Holmes, 2000; Smith, 1998), and using different entrances (Wells et al., 1991). Differential treatment is associated with part-time, temporary, and contractor status in many studies. "Difference" may also subsequently create a deficit model when employers use such jobs as a way to evade worker protections, such as unemployment compensation and occupational safety and health protections. Deficits are theorized to accumulate to the individual from structural conditions of work that are unavailable or denied, such as promotion opportunities, autonomy, challenge, opportunity to learn new skills, and other conditions (Barker, 1995). Barker found that temporary instructors, a misnomer in the higher education literature as "part time" when instructors are often temporary, reported difficulty in obtaining instructional duties beyond introductory courses. In a series of interviews, it appeared that "time" in a job or job-related experience did not qualify instructors for increasingly complex or specialized course content. McAllister (1998) and Parker (1994) reported comparable findings. To the degree that workers are negatively valued or stigmatized due to their contingent status, a deficit model of work experience is created. One implication is that employers will not evaluate contingent work experience fairly or positively when a worker competes for subsequent employment. In the case of higher education, subsequent follow-up with department chairs found that the more adjunct experience a fictional job candidate possessed, the lower the chance the candidate had of being recommended for hiring (Barker, 1998).

Ferber and Waldfogel (1998) provided mixed evidence regarding the accumulation of economic deficits. In an analysis of the National Longitudinal Survey of Youth, they found that participation in some nonstandard employment relationships resulted in economic deficits. Involuntary part-time experience provided negative effects on current wages for women, whereas both voluntary and involuntary part-time work negatively affected men's wages. Both men and women who reported current or past nontraditional employment were far less likely to have benefit coverage than the substantially smaller group who were always traditionally employed.

Selective inclusion or class disorganization. A strong sociological tradition in the study of work has entailed identifying forces that empower capital and depower workers' class interests. Using a perspective that focuses on the contradictions of worker identity, employer-driven flexibility, and commitment as a work ethic, Smith (1998) focused on the changes to the employment contract as a source of control and the organization of work. She has found that some firms used participative "teams" to maximize commitment of temporary workers and reduce the cost of labor while making no long-term commitment themselves to the workers. The ability of work teams to supplant management resulted in a conflation of identity for workers in an assembly line. Much like professional and highly educated workers whose identities were mediated by their desire to "act" like full-time faculty while denying their status differences (Barker, 1998), Smith reported that temporary assembly workers were "valued" by an employer as evidenced in their role in training both temporary and permanent workers. The value bestowed on temporary workers was vigorously pursued by them, especially to distinguish themselves as "good" as opposed to "bad" temporary workers.

LABOR LAW AND EMPLOYMENT LAW

Observers point out that contingent workers are not subject to the same labor and employment protections afforded other workers. This is due to the legal quagmire of employment relations in which contingent workers find themselves due to increasingly archaic labor and employment laws (Carnevale et al., 1998; Carré et al., 1995; duRivage, 1986). Federal legislation could be called inconsistent on most protective matters. Labor law and employment law have become increasingly out of date in both scope and ability to serve the needs of contemporary contingent workers. Most labor law is premised on full-time employment relationships (duRivage, 1992). Many contingent workers are not employees, are not covered by many labor and employment law conventions (for example, Fair Labor Standards Act, Equal Pay Act, Title VII of the Civil Rights Act of 1964), and are suffering from a range of problems from benefits and wages to retaliation for bringing an action against an employer (duRivage et al., 1998). Under Title VII and the Age Discrimination in Employment Act of 1967, existence of what is called an "employment relationship" is difficult to ascertain and mired in prior court rulings, which do not reflect changing employment relationships (Carnevale et al., 1998). Workplace rights and remedies are frozen in a past that idealized the full-time and permanent position. Future policies and laws need to address protecting workers, and a number of researchers have called for treating contingent and nonstandard workers as if they are full-time employees (Rasell & Appelbaum, 1997). In

LOMA LINDA UNIVERSITY

Julie Schaepper, M.P.H.
Community-Academic Partners in Service
(CAPS) Director

Office: (909) 651-5011
Pager: (909) 558-1717, 1786
Fax: (909) 558-0116
jschaepper@llu.edu

Cottage 80
24951 N. Circle Drive
Loma Linda, California 92350

making recommendations for labor law changes, duRivage (1992) noted that contingent work could be broadly defined in terms of the hardships workers face. It is interesting that this basis for defining contingent work is gaining currency as witnessed in recent statistical and theoretical work on "bad" jobs (Kalleberg et al., 2000) and the findings regarding accumulation of deficit. The National Labor Relations Act restricts access of part-time and contingent workers to union representation and participation in collective bargaining (duRivage et al., 1998). One idea is that an amendment to the labor relations act could include prehire agreements that would mandate that organizations hire only union workers (duRivage et al., 1998). Thus, even in high-turnover settings, unions would be motivated to organize part-time and contingent workers who would also retain their union membership and protections as they move from one work setting to another.

In addition to labor law reform, legislation is needed that would assure wage and benefit parity for part-time and contingent workers with full-time workers. There is no legal assurance of equality between workers of comparable skills and abilities with different work schedules. In addition, "whether workers choose nonstandard employment or have it imposed on them, key benefits should be socially guaranteed" (duRivage et al., 1998, p. 278), for example, health insurance and pensions that are portable. Finally, legislation is needed that prevents employers from employing temps for years on end to avoid paying employee benefits, such as pension and health care.

FUTURE CHALLENGES

As researchers debate the parsimony of contingent work as an analytic unit, most agree that the term does capture the sense that employment relations are changing and that there is an increase in poor-quality jobs. In the absence of private sector interest in correcting some of the worst abuses, some of the most important future research on contingent work will determine how labor laws and employment laws will protect these workers from such practices.

It is hoped that future research will relate the accumulation of economic deficits (wages, benefits, pensions) with the social deficits (training, ostracism, insecurity) of contingent employment. Research on the short- and long-term consequences of contingent work on careers and on the individual is needed in the areas of pension, social security, health benefits, work satisfaction, and productivity. What is the impact of contingent work on careers for different occupational groups? What are the dangers of contingent work to the individual during cyclic recessions? That is, are individuals and their families, due to a contingent work status, absorbing more of the risks, such as downsizing, than other workers during cyclic recessions? As more Americans are working without health benefits, are some contingent jobs a "cost" that corporations are passing along to the taxpayer? Under what conditions and for which educational and occupational groups does contingent work serve as a stepping-stone to more stable work?

Although some observers would claim that many individuals feel their full-time permanent jobs are "insecure," this misses the point that although impermanence may be an intermittent companion to permanent work arrangements, it is a constant companion for most contingent workers. Contingent workers are robbed to a large extent of the privileges still held by most full-time permanent employees, no matter how insecure permanent employees might be. In the wisdom that comes from hindsight, we may eventually recognize these contingent workers as the canaries in the mine shaft—they may reveal whether we can live with a model of employment relations that differs radically from the model that dominated most of the 20th century.

REFERENCES

Abraham, K., & Taylor, S. (1996). Firms' use of outside contractors: Theory and evidence. *Journal of Labor Economics, 14,* 394–424.

Age Discrimination in Employment Act of 1967. 29 U.S.C. § 651.

Barker, K. (1993). Changing assumptions and contingent solutions: The costs and benefits of women working full- and part-time. *Sex Roles, 28,* 47–71.

Barker, K. (1995). Contingent work: Research issues and the lens of moral exclusion. In L. Tetrick & J. Barling (Eds.), *Changing employment relations: Behavioral and social perspectives* (pp. 31–60). Washington, DC: American Psychological Association.

Barker, K. (1998). Toiling for piece-rates and accumulating deficits: Contingent work in higher education. In K. Barker & K. Christensen (Eds.), *Contingent work: American employment relations in transition* (pp. 195–220). Ithaca, NY: ILR Press.

Barker, K., & Christensen, K. (1998). Controversy and challenges raised by contingent work arrangements. In K. Barker & K. Christensen (Eds.), *Contingent work: American employment relations in transition* (pp. 1–18). Ithaca, NY: ILR Press.

Barth, M. C., & Pho, Y. (2001). *The labor market for social workers: A first look* (Tech. Rep.). New York: John A. Hartford Foundation.

Belous, R. (1989). *The contingent economy: The growth of the temporary, part-time and subcontracted workforce* (NPA Rep. No. 239). Washington, DC: National Planning Association.

Bernstein, A. (1999, May 31). Now, temp workers are a full-time headache. *Business Week*, p. 46.

Bond, J. T., Galinsky, E., & Swanberg, J. E. (1998). *The 1997 national study of the changing workforce*. New York: Families and Work Institute.

Carnevale, A. J., Jennings, L. A., & Eisenmann, J. M. (1998). Contingent workers and employment law. In K. Barker & K. Christensen (Eds.), *Contingent work: American employment relations in transition* (pp. 281–305). Ithaca, NY: ILR Press.

Carr, D. (1996). Two paths to self-employment? Women's and men's self-employment in the United States, 1980. *Work and Occupations, 23,* 26–53.

Carré, F. J., duRivage, V. L., & Tilly, C. (1995). Piecing together the fragmented workplace: Unions and public policy on flexible employment. In L. G. Flood (Ed.), *Unions and public policy* (pp. 13–34). Westport, CT: Greenwood Press.

Christensen, K. (1998). Countervailing human resource trends in family-sensitive firms. In K. Barker & K. Christensen (Eds.), *Contingent work: American employment relations in transition* (pp. 103–125). Ithaca, NY: ILR Press.

Christensen, K., & Murphree, M. (1988). Introduction to conference proceedings. In K. Christensen & M. Murphree (Eds.), *Flexible workstyles: A look at contingent labor* (Conf. Summary, pp. 1–4). Washington, DC: U.S. Department of Labor, Women's Bureau.

Civil Rights Act of 1964. 42 U.S.C. § 2000e.

Cohany, S. R. (1996, October). Workers in alternative employment arrangements. *Monthly Labor Review, 119,* 31–45.

Cohany, S. R., Hipple, S. F., Nardone, T. J., Polivka, A. E., & Stewart, J. C. (1998). Counting the workers: Results of the first survey. In K. Barker & K. Christensen (Eds.), *Contingent work: American employment relations in transition* (pp. 41–68). Ithaca, NY: ILR Press.

duRivage, V. L. (1986). *Working at the margins: Part-time and temporary workers in the United States.* Cleveland: 9to5.

duRivage, V. L. (1992). New policies for the part-time and contingent workforce. In V. L. duRivage (Ed.), *New policies for the part-time and contingent workforce* (pp. 89–122). Armonk, NY: M. E. Sharpe.

duRivage, V. L., Carré, F. J., & Tilly, C. (1998). Making labor law work for part-time and contingent workers. In K. Barker & K. Christensen (Eds.), *Contin-gent work: American employment relations in transition* (pp. 263–280). Ithaca, NY: ILR Press.

Farber, H. S., & Levy, H. (2000). Recent trends in employer-sponsored health insurance coverage: Are bad jobs getting worse? *Journal of Health Economics, 19,* 93–119.

Ferber, M. A., & Waldfogel, J. (1998, May). The long-term consequences of nontraditional employment. *Monthly Labor Review, 121,* 3–12.

Foley, M. P. (1998). Flexible work, hazardous work: The impact of temporary work arrangements on occupational safety and health in Washington State, 1991–1996. In I. Farquhar & A. Sorkin (Eds.), *Research in human capital and development* (Vol. 12, pp. 123–147). Stamford, CT: JAI Press.

Freedman, A. (1985). *The new look in wage policy and employee relations* (Conf. Board Rep. No. 865). New York: Conference Board.

Gonos, G. (1998). The interaction between market incentives and government actions. In K. Barker & K. Christensen (Eds.), *Contingent work: American employment relations in transition* (pp. 170–191). Ithaca, NY: ILR Press.

Holmes, S. (2000, July 1). Microsoft policy may jolt temp industry. *Los Angeles Times*, p. C1.

Hudson, K. (1999). *No shortage of nonstandard jobs: Nearly 30% of workers employed in part-time, temping, and other alternative arrangement* (Briefing paper). Washington, DC: Economic Policy Institute. Available: http://www.epinet.org/briefingpapers/hudson/hudson.pdf

Kalleberg, A. L., Rasell, M. E., Cassirer, N., Reskin, B. F., Hudson, K., Webster, D., Appelbaum, E., & Spalter-Roth, R. (1997). *Nonstandard work, substandard jobs: Flexible work arrangements in the U.S.* Washington, DC: Economic Policy Institute.

Kalleberg, A. L., Reskin, B. F., & Hudson, K. (2000). Bad jobs in America: Standard and nonstandard employment relations and job quality in the United States. *American Sociological Review, 65,* 256–278.

Kalleberg, A. L., & Schmidt, K. (1995). Contingent employment in organizations. In A. L. Kalleberg, D. Knoke, P. V. Marsden, & J. L. Spaeth (Eds.), *Organizations in America: Analyzing their structures and human resource practices* (pp. 253–275). Thousand Oaks, CA: Sage Publications.

Kochan, T. A., Wells, J. C., & Smith, M. (1992, Summer). Consequences of a failed I.R. system: Contract workers in the petrochemical industry. *Sloan Management Review, 33,* 79–89.

Kunda, G., Barley, S. R., & Evans, J. (1999). *Why do contractors contract? The theory and reality of high end contingent labor* [Online]. Stanford, CA: Stanford University, Department of Industrial Engineering and Engineering Management, Center for Work Technology and Organization.

Available: http://www.si.umich.edu/ICOS/MOTREV.html

Martella, M. (1992). *The rhetoric and realities of contingent work: The case of women in clerical temporary work.* Unpublished doctoral dissertation, Temple University, Philadelphia.

McAllister, J. (1998). Sisyphus at work in the warehouse: Temporary employment in Greenville, South Carolina. In K. Barker & K. Christensen (Eds.), *Contingent work: American employment relations in transition* (pp. 221–242). Ithaca, NY: ILR Press.

Morse, D. (1969). *The peripheral worker.* New York: Columbia University Press.

9to5. (2000). *Report on discriminatory hiring practices in temporary employment agencies* [Online]. Available: http://www.9to5.org/temp.html

Occupational Safety and Health Act of 1970. 29 U.S.C. § 651.

Opotow, S. (1990). Moral exclusion and injustice: An introduction. *Journal of Social Issues, 46,* 1–20.

Parker, R. E. (1994). *Flesh peddlers and warm bodies: The temporary help industry and its workers.* New Brunswick, NJ: Rutgers University Press.

Pfeffer, J., & Baron, J. (1988). Taking the workers back out: Recent trends in the structuring of employment. In B. Staw & L. Cummings (Eds.), *Research in organizational behavior* (Vol. 10, pp. 257–303). Greenwich, CT: JAI Press.

Plewes, T. J. (1988). Understanding the data on part-time and temporary employment. In K. Christensen & M. Murphree (Eds.), *Flexible workstyles: A look at contingent labor* (pp. 9–13). Washington, DC: U.S. Department of Labor, Women's Bureau.

Polivka, A. E. (1996, October). Contingent and alternative work arrangements defined. *Monthly Labor Review, 119,* 3–9.

Polivka, A. E., & Nardone, T. (1989, December). On the definition of "contingent work." *Monthly Labor Review, 112,* 9–16.

Rasell, E., & Appelbaum, E. (1997). Nonstandard work arrangements: A challenge for workers and labor unions. *Social Policy, 28,* 31–36.

Rebitzer, J. B. (1998). Job safety and contract workers in the petrochemical industry. In K. Barker & K. Christensen (Eds.), *Contingent work: American employment relations in transition* (pp. 243–259). Ithaca, NY: ILR Press.

Segal, L. M., & Sullivan, D. G. (1997). The growth of temporary services work. *Journal of Economic Perspectives, 11,* 117–136.

Smith, V. (1998). The fractured world of the temporary worker: Power, participation, and fragmentation in the contemporary workplace. *Social Problems, 45,* 411–430.

Spalter-Roth, R. M., Kalleberg, A. L., Rasell, R., Cassirer, N., Reskin, B., Hudson, K., Webster, D., Appelbaum, E., & Dooley, B. L. (1997). *Managing work and family: Nonstandard work arrangements among managers and professionals.* Washington, DC: Economic Policy Institute.

U.S. Bureau of Labor Statistics. (1995). *Contingent and alternative employment arrangements.* Report No. 900.

U.S. Department of Labor. (1999). "Just-in-time" inventories and labor: A study of two industries, 1990–1998. In *Report on the American workforce* (pp. 5–36). Washington, DC: U.S. Government Printing Office. Available: http://www.bls.gov/opub/rtaw/pdf/rtaw1999.pdf

Wells, J. C., Kochan, T. A., & Smith, M. (1991). *Managing work place safety and health: The case of contract labor in the U.S. petrochemical industry.* Beaumont, TX: Lamar University, John Gray Institute.

West, D., McClintock, L., & Engelbach, D. (2001). *PEOs and payrolling: A history of problems and a future without benefits* [Online]. Seattle: Center for a Changing Workforce. Available: http://www.cfcw.org/PEO.pdf

Kathleen Barker, PhD, is professor of psychology, Medgar Evers College of the City University of New York, Department of Psychology, 1650 Bedford Avenue, Brooklyn, NY 11225.

For further information see
Purchasing Social Services; Supervision and Consultation; Working Poor, *1997*

Key Words

independent contracting	self-employed/self-employment
part-time work	temporary work
pension benefits	

Cultural Diversity

See Ethnic-Sensitive Practice, *Volume 1;* Issues of Multiculturalism: Multicultural Practice, Cultural Diversity, and Competency, *2003*

E

Education

See Baccalaureate Social Workers, *1997;* School Social Work Overview, *Volume 3;* Social Work Education and the Future, *2003*

Empirically Based Interventions

Bruce A. Thyer

As this entry is being prepared, social work stands poised to fulfill its original mandate of being philosophically based on the foundations of natural science, with the conventional tools of empirical research associated with natural science being adopted as the profession's most effective approach to developing knowledge. This knowledge will yield psychosocial interventions effective in preventing and alleviating personal dysfunction and, ultimately it is hoped, large-scale social problems. Two major related movements, within and outside the profession, have brought about this happy state of affairs, movements known as *empirical clinical practice* and *evidence-based practice*, and the history of each will be briefly reviewed, concluding with a summary of the current situation and likely future developments.

EMPIRICAL CLINICAL PRACTICE

Empirical clinical practice, although having many precursors in social work and related fields, was firmly established in 1979 with the publication of a book written by social workers Siri Jayaratne and Rona Levy entitled *Empirical Clinical Practice*. In it, these authors made two not unreasonable assertions:

- Social workers should become skilled in and apply with their clients psychosocial interventions that have some credible amount of research evidence as to their efficacy.
- Social workers should empirically evaluate the outcomes of their work with clients, with single-system research designs (SSRDs) presented as one approach to undertake such evaluations.

During the succeeding two decades additional voices were added to this position (see review by Reid, 1994). In 1982 the Council on Social Work Education mandated that social work students should be taught research methods useful in the evaluation of one's own practice. Further and perhaps more sophisticated books appeared presenting the use of SSRDs, to the point that by the late 1990s over a dozen social work texts had been published exclusively devoted to this approach (including Tripodi, 1994), and almost all generalist research texts and a good many practice texts included one or more chapters describing it as

well. Several hundred examples of using SSRDs to evaluate social work practice have been published both in the United States (Thyer & Thyer, 1992) and in Great Britain (Kazi, 1998), and this approach is now widely recognized (see Gabor, Unrau, & Grinnell, 1998; Shaw & Lishman, 1999) as one of several practical methods to evaluate the outcomes of clinical and community-based practice (Thyer, 1998).

Parallel to these methodological developments, striking efforts were undertaken in the last quarter of the 20th century to empirically evaluate various psychosocial interventions, in an effort to produce generalizable knowledge regarding the effectiveness of certain treatments when applied to clients with particular problems. The major research designs used for evaluation have been SSRDs and, perhaps more credibly with respect to producing generalizable knowledge, nomothetic or group designs. Group designs, as with SSRDs, come in a variety of forms suitable for different types of field situations and practice arenas. The most credible (in terms of internal validity) type of group design is the randomized controlled clinical trial (RCT), which involves using control groups and random assignment of clients to varying conditions or alternative treatments, or perhaps to delayed treatment, placebo interventions, or to no treatment at all. In many respects, RCTs are the "gold standard" with respect to yielding reliable and generalizable knowledge, and their applications are increasing within social work, spurred perhaps by evident successes in related fields (Cnaan, 2001), especially in medicine.

However, the use of group designs of lesser potential internal validity is also seen as a valuable research enterprise, depending upon the nature of the question for which answers are sought. If one wishes to answer the question "Did clients seen at my agency improve over the course of their treatment?" then a simple group design such as the pretest–posttest design (O–X–O) may be an adequate approach to use (with "O" referring to an assessment period and "X" the period of treatment). However, if answers to more complex questions are sought, such as "Did my clients get better *because* of social work treatment?" or "Did more clients improve more than they would have with the simple passage of time?" then the use of more complex and better controlled group designs is necessary, approximating or including the rigor associated with the RCT (see Royse, Thyer, Padgett, & Logan, 2001).

Thus, the current state of affairs is that both SSRDs and group designs are seen as extremely useful tools in developing empirically justifiable outcome claims about particular clients seen by individual social workers or treated in particular programs, as well as necessary in developing information about treatment effectiveness that is generalizable across practitioners, clients, and services settings. There is recognition (as there always has been) of the importance of replicating tightly controlled research findings on the effectiveness of psychosocial treatments within the context of the naturalistic provision of social services in everyday life, with real clients and typical practitioners.

This application of empirical research to the development and testing of social work practices and other forms of psychosocial services has proven to be extremely productive. In 1993 members of Division 12 (clinical psychology) of the American Psychological Association established the Task Force on Promotion and Dissemination of Psychological Procedures ("Task Force," 1995) with a twofold purpose:

- to develop justifiable standards of evidence by which one can judge whether a particular treatment might be said to have credible evidence that it is effective in helping clients with a particular problem
- to compile a list of such empirically supported therapies.

Both endeavors were accomplished, although not without some controversy. The research criteria developed by the task force as a precondition for an intervention to be labeled as having "established" its efficacy included the following:

1. at least two good between-group design experiments demonstrating efficacy in one or more of the following ways:
   a. superior to pill or psychological placebo or to another treatment
   b. equivalent to an already established treatment in experiments with adequate sample sizes
2. a large series of single case designs ($N > 9$) demonstrating efficacy, including:
   a. good experimental designs and
   b. comparison of intervention to another treatment, as in point 1a above.

These studies must have used replicable treatment manuals or protocols to guide services delivery and have clearly described the characteristics of the clients, and two different investigators or treatment teams must have obtained positive outcomes (see Chambless et al., 1998, for further details). Although not particularly stringent standards, these serve as an excellent starting place for beginning to determine whether or not a particular treatment should be labeled as empirically supported. By applying these admittedly liberal criteria to the existing clinical research literature, a very large number of interventions emerged as empirically supported. Periodically updated lists of these "established" and "likely established" psychosocial interventions have been published (for example, Chambless et al., 1996, 1998; Sanderson & Woody, 1995; Task Force, 1995; Woody & Sanderson, 1998).

Although certain segments of the helping professions have been busy preparing scientific criteria to judge the credibility of interventions, and preparing compilations of interventions deemed credible, others within psychiatry, psychology, social work, and related fields have been working on practice guidelines (PGs), which are articles or monograph-length publications describing the "best" methods of helping clients with particular problems. The best of the PGs rely exclusively upon the types of empirical research literature described immediately above; others are so-called consensus statements or the appraisals of so-called experts. Sometimes consensus-based PGs are genuinely grounded in science, but sometimes they are derived more from the opinions of individual authorities. And some PGs are prepared by entities that have a vested interest in cost containment (for example, managed care organizations requiring brief therapies) or a particular treatment (for example, the pharmaceutical industry sponsoring drug-oriented PGs).

Practice guidelines may be developed within a particular discipline or prepared by interdisciplinary teams or organizations, with the latter arrangement the more preferable one. Psychologists may complain that a PG developed by psychiatrists understates the role of psychotherapy in treating a particular disorder, whereas psychiatrists may complain that a PG developed by psychologists places undue stress upon the side effects and high relapse rates attendant upon the use of psychotropic medications. Thus, interdisciplinary collaborations aimed at developing PGs and based upon reviews of scientific evidence, drawing upon research studies irrespective of the authors' disciplines, are the preferred model for the construction of PGs. It would be a mistake to try and develop social work PGs drawing only upon studies authored by social workers, or psychology PGs drawing only upon research authored by psychologists, and so forth—the information base of such PGs would be far too limited (see Thyer, in press).

Fortunately, NASW is collaborating with other disciplines in development of practice guidelines, which may be a very good thing, depending upon the credibility and ability of the representatives chosen by NASW to represent the social work perspective. The Society for Social Work and Research has representatives in the Campbell Collaboration who will be participating in the development of systematic reviews of the effectiveness of psychosocial interventions in the fields of criminal justice, education, and social welfare (see Schuerman et al., 2002). Social workers Matthew Howard and Jeffrey Jenson were guest editors of the May 1999 issue of the journal *Research on Social Work Practice*, which was devoted to the topic of PGs, and a new book edited by Rosen and Proctor (in press) is the latest social work treatment of the topic.

Evidence-based PGs made their appearance after the initial principles of empirical clinical practice were first articulated within social work and psychology. Basing one's choice of interventions (at least in part) upon sound PGs

can be seen as a derivative component of empirically oriented practice. Once sound research has shown that particular interventions are effective and efficacious, the development of well-proceduralized, practice-friendly treatment protocols describing the conduct of these selected interventions became possible. It is important to remain cognizant that not all PGs are empirically supported, and that the scientific evidentiary foundations of certain areas of practice (especially macropractice) remain weak. This requires ongoing efforts on the part of social workers to apply critical analytic thinking skills in the appraisal of PGs and other research products, and to keep abreast of the latest scientific developments.

A related development has been the appearance of practice textbooks that take a "problem-focused" organization (usually arranged by mental disorder) and then describe the appropriate (that is, empirically supported) assessment methods and interventions. These have now been published in the general literatures of psychotherapy (Giles, 1993), psychology and psychiatry (Hibbs & Jensen, 1996; Nathan & Gorman, 1998), and social work (Mattaini & Thyer, 1996; Thyer & Wodarski, 1998; Wodarski & Thyer, 1998). Similarly, special issues of professional journals have been entirely devoted to evidence-based empirically supported treatments, such as the June 1998 issue of the *Journal of Clinical Child Psychology* and the February 1998 issue of the *Journal of Consulting and Clinical Psychology*. These are exceedingly valuable educational resources for social work practitioners and students alike.

It may be contended that the rise of empirically based interventions has rendered obsolete the previously common practice of devoting practice texts to the presentation of some "theoretical" approach to understanding, assessing, and treating clients (for example, behavioral, psychodynamic, and so forth); or to the presentation of more generalized relatively "atheoretical" models (for example, task-centered, strengths-based, solution-focused, ecosystems, family-centered, group work, and so forth). Rather, the empirical practice approach attempts to present all methods of psychosocial interventions that are scientifically judged as effective, regardless of what theory or conceptual model they are supposedly based on. After all, why does one write textbooks—to advocate for a theory or model, or to present the most useful ways to help clients? The answer seems obvious.

The recognition that all interventions do not share the same levels of evidentiary support has given rise to the development of some tentative ethical standards, such as those raised by Thyer (1995) and Myers and Thyer (1997), who claimed that clients now have a right to be provided with empirically based interventions as first-choice treatment where these have been established. Unfortunately, NASW's *Code of Ethics* (1996) is rather lukewarm on the issue:

> Social workers should base practice on recognized knowledge, including empirically based knowledge, relevant to social work and social work ethics. (p. 22)

This standard places empirically based (that is, scientifically derived) knowledge as but one equal consideration among many other sources of knowledge, as opposed to elevating it above, say, traditional knowledge, practice wisdom, appeals to authority, and intuition. This is problematic because many fields can legitimately lay claim to these latter forms of knowledge, making it difficult to distinguish truly professional services provided by scientifically informed social workers.

More stringent was a related position taken by NASW's National Committee on Lesbian and Gay Issues (NCOLGI), contending that it is unethical for social workers to provide so-called reparative therapies to gay and lesbian clients (treatments aimed at "converting" their sexual orientation from homosexual to heterosexual):

> Proponents of reparative therapies claim— without documentation—many successes. They assert that their processes are supported by conclusive scientific data that are in fact little more than anecdotal. NCOLGI protests these efforts to "convert" people through irresponsible therapies . . . sweeping generalizations are made in the name of science, but without any of the rigor that science requires. Empirical research does not demonstrate . . . that sexual orientation (heterosexual or homosexual) can be changed through these so-called reparative therapies. (NASW, 1992, p. 1)

To condemn any treatment as unethical, in part because it lacks scientifically credible evidence of effectiveness, is a remarkable ethical standard indeed and one that, if adopted widely within social work, would begin to move us closer to the direction of evidence-based practice.

EVIDENCE-BASED PRACTICE

Evidence-based practice (EBP) has been a parallel but not dissimilar movement to empirical clinical practice. EBP was belatedly but formally established in medicine in the 1990s and has been defined as "the conscientious, explicit, and judicious use of the current best evidence in making decisions about the care of individual patients" (Sackett, Richardson, Rosenberg, & Haynes, 1997, p. 2). The language of EBP is now being widely applied to numerous medical specialties as well as related professions such as nursing, dentistry, psychology, pharmacy, and midwifery. As EBP crept into the psychiatric literature, the potential applications to clinical and other forms of social work practice have become obvious. In 1998 a new multidisciplinary journal was established— *Evidence-Based Mental Health*. An editorial in this journal clarified the relative role of scientific evidence versus other considerations in the selection of possible treatments:

> Evidence-based practice is a sharing of information with parents, a dialogue with them about the risks and benefits of various alternatives. An evidence-based practitioner does not "prescribe" a treatment, instead the parents and child are listened to, their values and cultural background are taken into consideration, and the particular and unique predicament of each child is appreciated. Our role is to help parents make informed choices and sympathise with their dilemma when ambiguity abounds. The evidence is presented in a balanced, hopeful, and optimistic fashion: "this is the best evidence we have, the situation is not a perfect fit, but there is reason to believe that if we follow this treatment there may be a beneficial outcome. What do you think?" (Szatmari, 1999, p. 7)

Implicit in this perspective is that the clinician is professionally obligated to present the scientific evidence, not unsubstantiated opinions, views of noted authorities, fads, or other types of information, in lieu of credible research findings. Social worker Eileen Gambrill (1999b) made clear that similar views guide EBP within our discipline:

> In EBP social workers seek out practice-related research findings regarding important practice decisions and share the results of their search with clients. If they find that there is no evidence that a method they recommend will help a client, they so inform the client and describe

their theoretical rationale for their recommendations. Clients are involved as informed participants. (p. 346)

There is anecdotal evidence that EBP is rapidly gaining in credibility and significance.

The first social work book incorporating the term EBP recently appeared in print (Corcoran, 2000), and others are in the offing (for example, Thyer & Kazi, 2003; Thyer, Wodarski, Harrison, & Myers, in press). On December 13, 1999, the Surgeon General of the United States David Satcher was quoted on National Public Radio: "Evidence-based treatment is treatment based upon the best available evidence," and the recent *Mental Health: A Report of the Surgeon General* (U.S. Department of Health and Human Services [USDHHS], 1999) contains the following statements:

The statements and conclusions throughout this report are documented by reference to studies published in the scientific literature. For the most part, this report cites studies of empirical—rather than theoretical—research. (USDHHS, 1999, p. 9)

A challenge for the Nation in the near-term future is to speed the transfer of new evidence-based treatments and prevention interventions into diverse service delivery settings and systems. (USDHHS, 1999, p. 14)

A variety of treatments of well-documented efficacy exists for the array of clearly defined mental and behavioral disorders that occur across the life span. (USDHHS, 1999, p. 3)

Gaps also exist between optimally effective treatment and what many individuals receive in actual practice settings. (USDHHS, 1999, p. 15)

A range of efficacious psychosocial and pharmacological treatments exist for many mental disorders in children. (USDHHS, 1999, p. 18)

Other professional and consumer groups are moving in this direction. For example, the Association for Science in Autism Treatment (ASAT) was founded in 1999 in part as a reaction to the widespread proliferation of ineffective treatments provided to consumers with autism. The ASAT (1999) mission statement is simple:

To disseminate accurate, scientifically sound information about autism and treatments for autism. To improve access to effective, science-based treatments for all people with autism, regardless of age, severity of condition, income, or place of residence. (p. 2)

The ASAT values statement is equally clear and compelling:

ASAT is committed to science as the most objective, time-tested and reliable approach to discerning between safe, effective autism treatments, and those that are harmful or ineffective. ASAT supports all scientifically sound research on the prevention, treatment and cure of autism, as well as all treatments for autism that are shown to be effective through solid scientific research, regardless of discipline or domain. (p. 2)

These elegant mission and values statements can serve as a role model for all social work professionals interested in promoting EBP within the human services. We can expect other advocacy constituencies to develop similar organizations aimed at promoting the conduct and application of research findings for other psychosocial problems as well.

The voice of evidence-based social work practice is also receiving more attention in Great Britain. For example:

Our basic argument is that social work activities, particularly those that can be described as "interventions," should be justified, wherever possible, by proofs of effectiveness, including, where possible, RCTs. . . . The interests of people dependent . . . on public welfare services, will be better served if welfare purchasers invest in strategies on proven effectiveness and if researchers focus their efforts on producing information that enable such decisions to be taken. An evidence-based approach does not, as is often assumed, defend and consolidate the power of professionals and the welfare empires that employ them. On the contrary, such an approach is fundamentally anti-authoritarian in nature, in that it challenges accepted wisdom and the power of vested interests. (Newman & Roberts, 1997, pp. 294–295)

In the mid-1990s the British government funded the Centre for Evidence-Based Social Services, headed by social worker Brian Sheldon and based at the University of Exeter. Sheldon's group funds outcome studies on social work practice, convenes conferences on evidence-based practice, and publishes a regular newsletter reporting centre activities. Many other contemporary British publications may be found supporting the growth of evidence-based social services (for example, Gambrill, 1999a; Gomm & Davies, 2000; MacDonald, 1994; Sheldon & Chilvers, 2000).

In 1997 NASW joined with nine other national mental health associations to produce the patient booklet titled *Your Mental Health Rights* (Joint Initiative of Mental Health Professional Organizations, 1997). Contained within this remarkable document is the statement, "Individuals have the right to be informed about the options available for treatment interventions and the effectiveness of the recommended treatment" (Cantor, 1999, p. 923). This is certainly consistent with the propositions of evidence-based practice. Also in 1997, Donna Shalala, U.S. Secretary for Health and Human Services, gave a talk at the University of Michigan, claiming:

> You've probably heard the expression, "We did everything right, we just didn't get the results we wanted." Well, when it comes to children, that kind of thinking—that kind of self-satisfaction—just won't cut it. Today, everything we do to improve the lives and destinies of children, whether it's research, policy, management, or just good intentions, is secondary to making sure we get the right outcomes. . . . I've steered the department toward making sure that what we do works. That means customer service, accountability, and measurable change. (Shalala, 1999, p. 709)

EVIDENCE-BASED PRACTICE AND THE FUTURE OF SOCIAL WORK

Many demands will be made upon our profession due to EBP, and they may require that we change many venerated practices (see, for example, Parker, 1997; Weiss, Catron, Harris, & Phung, 1999). In order to produce social workers prepared to successfully compete in the private marketplace and to practice effectively in the public sector, academics will have to relinquish their cherished freedom to teach any currently popular or theoretically preferred approach to intervention in favor of disseminating information and skills centered around contemporary and best empirically supported psychosocial treatments. This is professional behavior. Indeed, some recent (1999–2000) advertisements for social work faculty have stated applicants must be prepared to teach practice from an evidence-based perspective. As this trend continues, doctoral programs must focus research training on methods appropriate for evaluating services outcomes and less on building theoretical knowledge via hypothesis-testing studies; and MSW programs will attend more to the evidence-based foundations of didactic and practice course content. In May 2000 the faculty at the George Warren Brown School of Social Work at Washington University voted to adopt evidence-based practice as the central organizing theme for the MSW program (see Howard, McMillen, & Pollio, 2003). More schools will follow this pioneering example.

Although evidence-based practice is most extensively developed in the realm of clinical intervention in the field of mental disorders (Thyer, 2002a, 2002b), the purview of social work is much broader than this. Thus, evidence-based practices will have to be developed for other psychosocial problems not amenable to the categories found in the *Diagnostic and Statistical Manual of Mental Disorders* (American Psychiatric Association, 2000), troubles brought by clients to the attention of social workers such as spousal battering, child abuse and neglect, sexual abuse, chronic unemployment, school violence, health promotion, grief, racism, discrimination, and other forms of social injustice. There is nothing intrinsically different about these larger scale issues that will render them less amenable to the design and conduct of sound intervention research or to the promulgation of evidence-based practice guidelines (see, for example, Biglan, Glasgow, & Singer, 1990; Thyer, 1996). Indeed, considerable work already exists and may be consulted by social workers (for example, Mattaini & Thyer, 1996; Thyer, 2001; Wodarski & Thyer, 1998). It would be both inaccurate and a serious mistake to contend that we lack sufficient knowledge of effective interventions in these arenas to take the first steps toward promoting evidence-based practice.

The evidence that professionally trained social workers can help clients more effectively than members of the other human services, or even provide better care than that delivered by nonprofessionals, is rather slim (for example, Epstein, 1995, 1997, 1999; Stuart, 1970; see also Christiansen & Jacobson, 1994; Dawes, 1994). Platitudinous assertions that social workers somehow "care more" than members of other professions are a slender reed indeed to rely upon in terms of the future well-being of the field. We have an immense task—to demonstrate that clients with various difficulties who receive professional social work services do indeed get better; and to demonstrate that they improve more than they would have simply through the passage of time or through the receipt of credible placebo or bogus interventions, or at the hands of nonprofessional people. Then we must evaluate psychosocial interventions of established efficacy against newly developed programs and practices, and do this in the manifold areas of social work practice, micro through macro.

The subject matter of our field—human behavior in all of its marvelous complexity—is more difficult to investigate than nuclear physics. Answering the above challenges will require keen intellects, much hard work, and abundant resources. In addition, we cannot reasonably expect a continued flow of funds from the public and private cornucopia to support the ongoing provision of social work and social welfare services unless we set ourselves to this task.

Absent credible evidence that services provided by social workers help solve client and societal problems, why should the public and private sectors support the expensive social welfare empires currently found in the fields of mental health, health care, child welfare, and so forth? The tenets of evidence-based practice have the potential to revolutionize the practice of social work to the betterment of clients' lives and the citizenry as a whole. The present author is confident that the profession is up to this challenge and will be the better for having undertaken it.

REFERENCES

American Psychiatric Association. (2000). *Diagnostic and statistical manual of mental disorders* (4th ed.). Washington, DC: Author.

Association for Science in Autism Treatment. (1999, Fall). ASAT mission statement and values statement. *Science in Autism Treatment, 1,* 2.

Biglan, A., Glasgow, R. E., & Singer, G. (1990). The need for a science of larger social units. *Behavior Therapy, 21,* 195–215.

Cantor, D. W. (1999). Ensuring the future of professional psychology. *American Psychologist, 54,* 922–930.

Chambless, D. L., Baker, M. J., Baucom, D. H., Beutler, L. E., Calhoun, K. S., Crits-Christoph, P., et al. (1998). Update on empirically validated therapies. II. *Clinical Psychologist, 51,* 3–16.

Chambless, D. L., Sanderson, W., Shoham, V., Bennet-Johnson, S., Pope, K., Crits-Christoph, P., et al. (1996). An update on empirically validated therapies. *Clinical Psychologist, 49,* 5–18.

Christiansen, A., & Jacobson, N. S. (1994). Who (or what) can do psychotherapy: The status and challenge of nonprofessional therapies. *Psychological Science, 5,* 8–14.

Cnaan, R. (2001). Randomized controlled trials. In B. A. Thyer (Ed.), *Handbook of social work research methods* (pp. 177–192). Thousand Oaks, CA: Sage Publications.

Corcoran, J. (2000). *Evidence-based social work practice with families.* New York: Springer.

Dawes, R. (1994). *House of cards: Psychology and psychotherapy built on myth.* New York: Free Press.

Epstein, W. M. (1995). *The illusion of psychotherapy.* New Brunswick, NJ: Transaction Books.

Epstein, W. M. (1997). *Welfare in America: How social science fails the poor.* Madison: University of Wisconsin Press.

Epstein, W. M. (1999). *Children who could have been: The legacy of child welfare in wealthy America.* Madison: University of Wisconsin Press.

Gabor, P. A., Unrau, Y. A., & Grinnell, R. M. (1998). *Evaluation for social workers* (2nd ed.). Boston: Allyn & Bacon.

Gambrill, E. (1999a). Evidence-based clinical practice, evidence-based medicine and the Cochrane collaboration. *Journal of Behavior Therapy and Experimental Psychiatry, 30,* 1–14, 153–154.

Gambrill, E. (1999b). Evidence-based practice: An alternative to authority-based practice. *Families in Society, 80,* 341–350.

Giles, T. R. (Ed.). (1993). *Handbook of effective psychotherapy.* New York: Plenum Press.

Gomm, R., & Davies, C. (Eds.). (2000). *Using evidence in health and social care.* London: Sage Publications.

Hibbs, E. D., & Jensen, P. S. (Eds.). (1996). *Psychosocial treatments for child and adolescent disorders: Empirically based strategies for clinical practice.* Washington, DC: American Psychological Press.

Howard, M. O., McMillen, C. J., & Pollio, D. E. (2003). Teaching evidence-based practice: Toward a new paradigm for social work education. *Research on Social Work Practice, 13,* 234–259.

Jayaratne, S., & Levy, R. L. (1979). *Empirical clinical practice.* New York: Columbia University Press.

Joint Initiative of Mental Health Professional Organizations. (1997). *Your mental health rights* [Brochure]. Washington, DC: Author.

Kazi, M.A.F. (1998). *Single-case evaluation by social workers.* Aldershot, UK: Ashgate.

MacDonald, G. (1994). Developing empirically-based practice in probation. *British Journal of Social Work, 24,* 405–427.

Mattaini, M. A., & Thyer, B. A. (Eds.). (1996). *Finding solutions for social problems: Behavioral strategies for change.* Washington, DC: American Psychological Press.

Myers, L. L., & Thyer, B. A. (1997). Should social work clients have the right to effective treatment? *Social Work, 42,* 288–298.

Nathan, P. E., & Gorman, J. (Eds.). (1998). *A guide to treatments that work.* New York: Oxford University Press.

National Association of Social Workers. (1996). *NASW code of ethics.* Washington, DC: NASW Press.

National Association of Social Workers, National Committee on Lesbian and Gay Issues. (1992). *Position statement: "Reparative" or "conversion" therapies for lesbians and gay men.* Washington, DC: Author.

Newman, T., & Roberts, H. (1997). Assessing social work effectiveness in child care practice: The contribution of randomized controlled trials. *Child: Care, Health and Development, 23,* 287–296.

Parker, G. (1997). Case management: An evidence-based review fails to makes its case. *Current Opinion in Psychiatry, 10,* 261–263.

Reid, W. J. (1994). The empirical practice movement. *Social Service Review, 68,* 165–184.

Rosen, A., & Proctor, E. (Eds.). (in press). *Developing practice guidelines for social work interventions: Issues, methods, and research agenda.* New York: Columbia University Press.

Royse, D., Thyer, B. A., Padgett, D., & Logan, T. K. (2001). *Program evaluation: An introduction* (3rd ed.). Pacific Grove, CA: Wadsworth.

Sackett, D. L., Richardson, W. S., Rosenberg, W., & Haynes, R. R. (1997). *Evidence-based medicine: How to practice and teach EBP.* New York: Churchill-Livingston.

Sanderson, W. C., & Woody, S. (1995). Manuals for empirically validated treatments: A project of the Task Force on Psychological Interventions. *Clinical Psychologist, 48,* 7–11.

Schuerman, J., Soydan, H., MacDonald, G., Forslund, M., deMoya, D., & Boruch, R. (2002). The Campbell Collaboration. *Research on Social Work Practice, 12,* 309–317.

Shalala, D. (1999). The 1997–1998 Fedele F. and Iris M. memorial lecture. *Research on Social Work Practice, 9,* 708–715.

Shaw, I., & Lishman, J. (Eds.). (1999). *Evaluation and social work practice.* London: Sage Publications.

Sheldon, B., & Chilvers, R. (2000). *Evidence-based social care: A study of prospects and problems.* London: Russell House.

Stuart, R. B. (1970). *Trick or treatment: How and when psychotherapy fails.* Champaign, IL: Research Press.

Szatmari, P. (1999). Evidence-based child psychiatry and the two solitudes [Editorial]. *Evidence-Based Mental Health, 2,* 6–7.

Task Force on Promotion and Dissemination of Psychological Procedures. (1995). Training in and dissemination of empirically-validated psychological treatments: Report and recommendations. *Clinical Psychologist, 48,* 3–23.

Thyer, B. A. (1995). Promoting an empiricist agenda within the human services: An ethical and humanistic imperative. *Journal of Behavior Therapy and Experimental Psychiatry, 26,* 93–98.

Thyer, B. A. (1996). Behavior analysis and social welfare policy. In M. A. Mattaini & B. A. Thyer (Eds.), *Finding solutions to social problems: Behavioral strategies for change* (pp. 41–60). Washington, DC: American Psychological Press.

Thyer, B. A. (1998). Promoting research on community practice: Using single-system designs. In R. MacNair (Ed.), *Research strategies in community practice* (pp. 47–61). Binghamton, NY: Haworth Press.

Thyer, B. A. (2001). Evidence-based approaches to community practice. In K. Corcoran & H. Briggs (Eds.), *Structuring change: Effective practice for common client problems* (pp. 54–65). Chicago: Lyceum.

Thyer, B. A. (2002a). Evidence-based practice and clinical social work. *Evidence-Based Mental Health, 6,* 6–7.

Thyer, B. A. (2002b). Principles of evidence-based practice and treatment development. In A. R. Roberts & G. Greene (Eds.), *Social workers' desk reference* (pp. 739–743). New York: Oxford University Press.

Thyer, B. A. (in press). Social work should help develop interdisciplinary evidence-based practice guidelines, not discipline-specific ones. In A. Rosen & E. Proctor (Eds.), *Developing practice guidelines for social work interventions: Issues, methods, and research agenda.* New York: Columbia University Press.

Thyer, B. A., & Kazi, M.A.F. (Eds.). (2003). *International perspectives on evidence-based practice in social work.* Birmingham, UK: Venture Press.

Thyer, B. A., & Thyer, K. B. (1992). Single system research designs in social work practice: A bibliography. *Research on Social Work Practice, 2,* 99–116.

Thyer, B. A., & Wodarski, J. S. (Eds.). (1998). *Handbook of empirical social work practice—Volume 1: Mental disorders.* New York: John Wiley & Sons.

Thyer, B. A., Wodarski, J. S., Harrison, D. F., & Myers, L. L. (in press). *Cultural diversity and social work practice: An evidence-based approach.* Springfield, IL: Charles C Thomas.

Tripodi, T. (1994). *A primer on single subject design for clinical social workers.* Washington, DC: NASW Press.

U.S. Department of Health and Human Services. (1999). *Mental health: A report of the Surgeon General.* Rockville, MD: U.S. Department of Health and Human Services, Substance Abuse and Mental Health Services Administration, Center for Mental Health Services, National Institutes of Health, National Institute of Mental Health.

Weiss, B., Catron, T., Harris, V., & Phung, T. (1999). The effectiveness of traditional child psychotherapy. *Journal of Consulting and Clinical Psychology, 67,* 82–94.

Wodarski, J. S., & Thyer, B. A. (Eds.). (1998). *Handbook of empirical social work practice—Volume 2: Psychosocial problems and practice issues.* New York: John Wiley & Sons.

Woody, S. R., & Sanderson, W. C. (1998). Manuals for empirically supported treatments: An update. *Clinical Psychologist, 51,* 17–21.

Further Reading

Cournoyer, B. R., & Powers, G. T. (2002). Evidence-based social work: The quiet revolution continues. In A. R. Roberts & G. Greene (Eds.), *Social workers' desk reference* (pp. 798–807). New York: Oxford University Press.

Franklin, C. S. (2001). Onward to evidence-based practices for schools. *Children & Schools, 23,* 131–134.

Jordan, C., & Franklin, C. S. (2002). Treatment planning with families: An evidence-based approach. In A. R. Roberts & G. Greene (Eds.), *Social workers' desk reference* (pp. 252–255). New York: Oxford University Press.

Lloyd, E. (1998). Introducing evidence-based social welfare practice in a national child care agency. In A. Buchanan & B. Hudson (Eds.), *Parenting, schooling and children's behaviour* (pp. 161–177). Aldershot, UK: Ashgate.

MacDonald, G. (1998). Promoting evidence-based practice in child protection. *Clinical Child Psychology & Psychiatry, 31,* 71–85.

Parry, G. (2000). Evidence-based psychotherapy: An overview. In N. Rowland & S. Goss (Eds.), *Evidence-based counselling and psychotherapies: Research and applications* (pp. 57–75). London: Routledge.

Persons, J. (1999, Fall). Evidence-based psychotherapy: A graduate course proposal. *Clinical Science, 2,* 12.

Rosen, A., & Proctor, E. (2002). Standards for evidence-based social work practice: The role of replicable and appropriate interventions, outcomes, and practice guidelines. In A. R. Roberts & G. Greene (Eds.), *Social workers' desk reference* (pp. 743–747). New York: Oxford University Press.

Rosenberg, W., & Donald, A. (1995). Evidence-based medicine: An approach to clinical problem-solving. *British Medical Journal, 310,* 1122–1126.

Bruce A. Thyer, PhD, is professor and dean, School of Social Work, Florida State University, Tallahassee, FL 32306-2570.

For further information see
Epistemology; Evidence-Based Practice Guidelines, *2003;* Intervention Research

Key Words

empirical clinical practice	right to effective treatment
evidence-based practice	

Employment and Earnings
Sheldon Danziger

Economic conditions that shaped trends in employment and earnings for American workers over the last three decades of the 20th century are reviewed. Following this, some of the factors that contributed to these trends are discussed and some implications for the future are drawn, concluding with a discussion of public policy options.

Economic Conditions from Early 1970s to Late 1990s

The last quarter of the 20th century was a period of rapid changes in the way the labor market functioned, in part, because of changes that occurred within the United States and, in part, because of technological changes and the globalization of markets that affected labor markets throughout the world. As a result of these changes, growth in real (inflation-adjusted) earnings from the early 1970s to the early 1990s was slow on average for all American workers compared to what it had been in the prior quarter century. Labor market outcomes were particularly problematic for male workers with a high school degree or less—

their employment rates and real earnings were lower at the end of the 20th century than they had been a quarter century earlier.

This recent economic performance stands in stark contrast to "the golden economic age" that characterized the quarter century following World War II. During the postwar period, "a rising tide lifted all boats" and earnings and income gains were rapid and widely shared by the poor, the middle class, and the rich, and by less educated as well as more educated workers. What followed after the early 1970s was two decades of slow economic growth and rising inequalities (Danziger & Gottschalk, 1995).

Although the economy experienced sustained economic recoveries during both the 1980s and the 1990s, economic growth did not trickle down very vigorously to the least advantaged workers. The economic situation for all workers, especially less educated workers, did improve in the late 1990s, as unemployment and inflation rates were low and inflation-adjusted wages rose after 1993. For example, the annual unemployment rate for adult men was below 5.0 percent every year from 1962 to 1974. But in the next 20 years, from 1974 to 1994, it was below 5.0 percent in only four years—1978, 1979, 1988, 1989. The adult male unemployment rate then fell below 5.0 percent in every year from 1995 through 2001; the rate for 2000, 3.3 percent, was the lowest since 1973. The adult female unemployment rate for 2000 was 3.6 percent; the last time the rate for women was this low was 1969 when it was 3.7 percent (U.S. Bureau of Labor Statistics, 2001).

The U.S. economy grew from March 1991 until March 2001, the longest peacetime expansion in history. However, this economic growth, given the current way the labor market functions, did not benefit less educated workers enough to restore their economic standing to where it was in the 1970s relative to that of the average worker. In other words, even though real earnings began to increase and earnings inequality stopped growing at the end of the 1990s, less educated workers were still no better off than they had been a quarter century earlier.

Consider the trend in the average inflation-adjusted hourly wage of private sector nonsupervisory production workers. Their mean wage in July 2001—$14.72 per hour—was 8 percent above the wage of July 1993 but was still 7 percent below the July 1973 level—$15.86 (all figures in constant 2001 dollars; U.S. Bureau of Labor Statistics, 2001).

Simply put, the longest peacetime economic expansion in history managed to restore the unemployment rate and the inflation-adjusted wage rate to about where they stood in the early 1970s. America has never been wealthier as a nation, as real per capita income in the late 1990s was about twice that of the early 1970s, but millions of workers still have difficulty earning enough to support their families.

Even when the economy was booming in the late 20th century, most high school dropouts and single mothers and many high school graduates could not obtain stable employment at wages high enough to allow them to support a family on their own. For example, increased economic incentives to search for work that were part of welfare reform (the Personal Responsibility and Work Opportunity Reconciliation Act of 1996) did contribute to a substantial increase in the work effort and earnings of single mothers. However, poverty rates and experiences of material hardship, even among those who left welfare and found stable employment, remained high (Danziger, Heflin, Corcoran, Oltmans, & Wang, 2002).

Despite a national commitment to providing equal opportunities, the United States has in place a much less effective safety net than that of most other industrialized nations. A review of the economic performance of the last several decades suggests that economic hardship and insecurity will remain problems for millions of workers unless social policies become more responsive to the labor market problems of less skilled workers. If poverty and hardship in America are to be lowered to the levels attained in much of Western Europe, then government will have to do more to supplement the wages of low earners and to provide employment opportunities for those who do not have the skills that employers in today's globalized, technologically sophisticated labor market are demanding.

TRENDS IN EMPLOYMENT AND EARNINGS, 1969–1999

The trends in employment and earnings reviewed here are based on computations from the 1970, 1980, and 1990 Decennial Censuses of Population and the March 1999 and 2000 *Current Population Surveys* (earnings and employment data from the 2000 Census were not available when this entry was completed). Because there are large differences in employment and earnings by race, ethnicity, age, gender, nativity, and education, the data are presented separately for men and women and for the three largest racial and ethnic groups—non-Hispanic whites, non-Hispanic African

Americans, and Hispanics. The data are restricted to people between 25 and 54 years of age, the years during which adults are most attached to the labor force. Data for younger people can be misleading because employment and earnings are affected by school attendance; and data for older people are affected by retirement. The data are also restricted to people born in the United States, as employment and earnings of immigrants are affected by the recency of their arrival, whether they were educated in the United States or in their native country, their English proficiency, and other factors beyond the scope of this entry. Data are shown separately for people with high school degrees or less and for those with college degrees or more. The experience of these two educational groups is highlighted because most people fall into one of them and because the labor market changes of the last quarter century had their largest impacts on these groups.

There is a consensus among labor economists that the main source of labor market problems for less educated workers has been the rising value of workers' skills to employers. For example, in 1979, the median weekly wage of full-time male wage and salary workers with college degrees was 29 percent higher than that of men with high school diplomas only. By 1998 college graduates had a 68 percent edge. Over this period, real wages increased by 8 percent

for male college graduates, but declined by 18 percent for high school graduates. For women, the weekly wage gap between college and high school graduates increased from 43 percent in 1979 to 79 percent in 1998. There was also an increase in the return to labor force experience. The earnings of workers with many years of experience increased relative to those of new labor market entrants (Danziger & Reed, 1999).

Table 1 shows the trend in the employment rate, measured as the percentage of people between the ages of 25 and 54 who had a job in the week before the Census survey. The trends differ most by education and gender; the levels in every year differ substantially by race and ethnicity as well.

There was a sharp decline in the employment rate of men with a high school degree or less, especially for African Americans, but not much change among men who had completed at least a college degree. The decline for the less educated between 1969 and 1989 was steep, with some increase by 1999 due to the economic recovery. The employment decline for less educated men between 1969 and 1999 was 5.9 percentage points for whites, 10.2 percentage points for African Americans, and 8.1 percentage points for Hispanics. As a result, differences between the employment rates of less educated and those of more educated men increased by 1999 to 9.5 percentage points for whites, 17.3 percentage points for African

TABLE 1
Trends in Employment (Percentage of Adults, Ages 25–54, with a Job Last Week)

Population	High School Degree or Less			College Degree or More		
	Non-Hispanic White	Non-Hispanic African American	Hispanic	Non-Hispanic White	Non-Hispanic African American	Hispanic
Native-born men						
1969	91.1	81.5	86.5	95.7	92.2	92.5
1979	86.3	72.6	80.2	95.3	90.1	92.8
1989	83.8	64.1	75.0	95.0	89.6	92.6
1999	85.2	71.3	78.4	94.7	88.6	92.4
Percentage point change, 1969–1999	−5.9	−10.2	−8.1	−1.0	−3.6	−0.1
Native-born women						
1969	44.8	52.5	38.4	57.9	86.1	72.4
1979	55.1	56.2	46.6	72.9	86.7	77.5
1989	63.9	57.2	55.5	82.5	89.9	86.2
1999	70.3	65.8	63.0	84.1	90.2	86.4
Percentage point change, 1969–1999	+25.5	+13.3	+24.6	+26.2	+4.1	+14.0

Source: Computations by author from the public use microdata files from the 1970, 1980, and 1990 *Decennial Census of Population* for 1969, 1979, and 1989; computations by author from the public use microdata files from the combined March 1999 and March 2000 *Current Population Surveys* for 1999.

Americans, and 14 percentage points for Latinos. This large employment differential by education suggests that policies that can effectively raise educational attainment can increase employment and reduce racial–ethnic differences.

Employment trends for women were quite different, as there were dramatic increases in employment over the past 30 years for less educated as well as more educated women. The one exception is that African American women with at least a college degree already had very high employment rates by 1969; in every year, they have the highest female employment rate. The largest increases were among white women in both educational groups. For women with a high school degree or less, employment increased by 25.5 percentage points for whites, by 13.3 percentage points for African Americans, and by 24.6 percentage points for Hispanics; for women with a college degree or more, these percentage point increases were 26.2, 4.1, and 14.0, respectively.

As a result of declining employment among men and increasing employment among women, the gender difference in employment declined rapidly. For example, among white college graduates, the employment rate of men exceeded that of women by 37.8 percentage points in 1969, but by only 10.6 percentage points in 1999. Among African Americans with a high school degree or less, the male–female employment gap fell from 29 percentage points in 1969 to 5.5 points in 1999.

Table 2 presents trends in mean annual earnings for all native-born men and women between ages 25 and 54; persons who did not have earnings during the calendar year are included in these means. The data are adjusted for inflation and presented in constant 1999 dollars for all years. Annual earnings reflect both wage rates—how much someone earns per hour—and employment—how many weeks and how many hours per week someone worked during the calendar year. The patterns are similar to those shown for employment— men with a high school degree or less lost ground relative to men with a college degree or more, and the earnings trend for women was much more favorable than that for men.

For men in each racial and ethnic group, the real earnings of those with a high school degree or less were lower in 1999 than in 1969, whereas those of men with at least a college degree were higher. For example, the educational gap in annual earnings was 74 percent for whites in 1969 (college: $60,252; high school: $34,582), and 120 percent in 1999 (college:

$64,692; high school: $29,455); for African Americans this gap increased from 94 to 130 percent; for Hispanics, from 94 to 135 percent.

Women's annual earnings increased much more than men's earnings because of their large employment increases. For example, mean annual earnings increased by 85.7 percent for whites, 70.6 percent for African Americans, and 95.6 percent for Hispanic women with less than a high school degree, whereas they fell for men in this educational category. Nonetheless, women still earn substantially less than do men, because on average they work fewer hours per year and because they earn less per hour.

Economists typically measure the gender differential in wage rates by comparing the median earnings of men and women who are full-time year-round workers, as this controls for differences in work effort. Over the period from 1969 to 1999, this gender gap also narrowed—a woman earned a median of 59 cents for every dollar earned by a man in 1969, but 72 cents per dollar by 1999 (U.S. Bureau of the Census, 2001).

Racial wage differentials also narrowed over the past 30 years for both men and women. For full-time year-round workers, a black man earned 67 cents for every dollar earned by a white man in 1969, but 81 cents in 1999; the black–white ratio of median earnings for women was 79 percent in 1969 and 91 percent in 1999. Data on Hispanics are available only for the years since 1974. These ratios were 73 percent in 1974 and 62 percent in 1999 for men, and 84 and 73 percent in these years for women (U.S. Bureau of the Census, 2001). The Census Bureau tables are not directly comparable to Tables 1 and 2 shown here because the former include foreign-born, as well as native-born, people and because the categories "white" and "black" in the published tables include people of Hispanic origin.

CAUSES OF LABOR MARKET PROBLEMS FOR LESS EDUCATED WORKERS

There is some disagreement among researchers about the relative importance of various labor market factors that can explain the economic difficulties (declining employment and declining real wages) of less educated male workers over the past 30 years. The factors that have had significant effects on employment and earnings gaps can be categorized into three broad kinds of labor market changes: (1) institutional changes, such as declines in union membership; (2) changes in labor supply, such as increased numbers of workers who are recent immigrants; and (3) changes in employers' labor demand for

TABLE 2
Mean Annual Earnings in Constant 1999 Dollars (All Civilian Adults, Ages 25–54)

Population	High School Degree or Less			College Degree or More		
	Non-Hispanic White ($)	Non-Hispanic African American ($)	Hispanic ($)	Non-Hispanic White ($)	Non-Hispanic African American ($)	Hispanic ($)
Native-born men						
1969	34,582	20,654	25,737	60,252	40,100	50,051
1979	35,307	21,650	25,945	57,088	40,736	46,077
1989	30,835	18,391	23,374	64,434	44,709	51,521
1999	29,455	20,052	23,374	64,692	46,240	54,848
Percent change (%), 1969–1999	−14.8	−2.9	−9.2	+7.4	+15.3	+9.6
Native-born women						
1969	7,891	7,484	6,267	17,393	27,422	21,083
1979	10,442	10,455	8,296	20,426	27,939	22,663
1989	12,710	11,350	10,718	29,662	33,973	32,033
1999	14,650	12,769	12,255	33,383	34,694	34,562
Percent change (%), 1969–1999	+85.7%	+70.6%	+95.6	+91.9	+26.5	+63.0

SOURCE: See Table 1.

less educated workers due to the globalization of markets and rapid technological changes. Many economists have concluded that demand-side factors are the most important ones because they can explain why employer demand for more educated workers increased at the same time as their wages increased relative to the wages of less educated workers (see Danziger & Gottschalk, 1995; Ellwood et al., 2000, for further discussion).

Declines in Union Membership
The percentage of the workforce that is unionized has been falling since the 1950s, but the pace of deunionization accelerated after 1975. Freeman (1993) suggested that in other industrialized countries strong union movements exerted a moderating effect on the declining fortunes of less skilled workers. In those countries, the employment and earnings gaps between less skilled and more skilled workers did not increase as much as they did in the United States. Freeman concluded that the continuing decline in unionization in the United States is likely to further lower the wages of blue-collar workers relative to white-collar workers and less educated workers relative to more educated workers.

Immigration
The supply of less educated workers and hence competition for less skilled jobs is higher in

labor markets where there are more immigrants because a greater percentage of immigrants than native-born workers lack a high school degree. An increased supply of less educated workers can explain some portion of the decline in their real wages. But if only labor supply factors were operative, one would not have expected employment of higher educated workers to increase across all industrial sectors, as has been the case. Also, immigrants are concentrated in a relatively small number of states, whereas falling employment of less educated workers and rising earnings differentials by education can be found over the past 25 years across the country, even in states with few immigrants.

Economic Restructuring
For almost four decades, employment has been shifting out of manufacturing and into the services sector—workers in manufacturing accounted for about 30 percent of all workers in the mid-1960s, but only about 15 percent in the late 1990s. According to the deindustrialization hypothesis, this led to more employment in industries with lower average wages. Deindustrialization can account for some, but not most, of the declining real earnings of male high school graduates and the increased wage gaps by education because these patterns are evident within most industries. Murphy and Welch (1993) documented that employers hired

increasing numbers of college graduates in all industries. This educational upgrading meant that inequality within all industries rose, as there were more highly educated workers whose earnings increased more than those of the average worker in the same industry.

Globalization of the Economy
Increased international trade and global competition have increased worldwide demand for the goods and services produced by skilled American workers in some industries—for example, technology and financial services. In other industries, for example, textiles and shoes, demand has declined for the goods and services produced by lower skilled American workers. In these industries American workers increasingly compete with production workers in developing countries who earn much lower wages. Globalization of markets has increased the availability of imports and the increased outsourcing of production by U.S. firms and has reduced demand for less educated American workers more than it did the demand for higher educated workers. These changes in demand also contribute to the widening wage differential by education.

Berman, Bound, and Griliches (1994) concluded that changes in employment associated with international trade explained only about 10 percent of the decreased demand for production workers in manufacturing. Most of the shift away from production workers is accounted for by the adoption of new technologies that require fewer workers per unit of output. They did find that outsourcing could account for a substantial portion of job loss in some specific industries, such as automotive and semiconductor manufacturing.

Technological Changes
Many economists believe that the adoption of labor-saving technological changes throughout the industrialized world is the primary reason for the employment problems of less skilled workers. The widespread adoption of computers in most industries increased the demand for skilled workers who can run sophisticated equipment and simultaneously reduced the demand for less skilled workers, many of whom had been displaced by automation. Firms have tended to substitute machines and higher skilled workers for lower skilled workers. Technological change, which increases the productivity of more educated workers faster than that of less educated workers, is consistent with both the rise in the wage gap between

college graduates and other workers and the increased employment of college graduates in all industries.

Holzer (1996) provided evidence that employers are demanding labor market skills that many less educated workers do not have. He surveyed 3,200 employers in four metropolitan areas about entry-level jobs available to workers without a college degree. He asked what skills were required, how employers screened workers, and what were the demographic characteristics of recent hires. He measured the kinds of skill requirements that employers reported using by the frequency with which the following tasks—dealing with customers either in person or on the phone, reading paragraphs, writing paragraphs, doing arithmetic, and using computers—were performed.

Most entry-level jobs required several skills and credentials. Each task that Holzer (1996) asked about (with the exception of writing paragraphs) was performed daily in half or more of the entry-level jobs. Employers used several credentials to screen applicants—about three-fourths required a high school diploma, general experience, and references; two-thirds required specific experience; two-fifths, training; over half required applicants to pass a test. Other studies also document skill deficiencies and other barriers to employment for less skilled workers and welfare recipients, including low levels of literacy, health and mental health problems, domestic violence, and family crises (Danziger et al., 2000).

Special Difficulties of Inner-City Residents
Wilson (1987, 1996) has written extensively about the disproportionate effects on African American men of labor market changes from the early 1970s to the early 1990s, especially those living in the nation's inner cities. He recognized the importance of the race-neutral, structural changes that have led to declines in employment for all less educated workers (that is, technological changes, globalization, and so forth). But he emphasized additional factors to explain the larger employment decline for African American men than for whites and native-born Hispanics.

Wilson (1996) documented that many employers attempt to minimize the number of blacks who apply for their job openings by advertising only in neighborhood and ethnic newspapers. Over 40 percent of the firms in his Chicago sample did not advertise entry-level jobs in the city's major daily newspapers. Other firms reported that they did not recruit workers who had attended the Chicago public high schools (they did recruit from Catholic schools) or who were referred to them by welfare programs or state employment agencies.

"Inner-city black men grow bitter and resentful in the face of their employment prospects and often manifest or express these feelings in their harsh, often dehumanizing, low-wage work settings" (Wilson, 1996, p. 144). This leads employers to "make assumptions about the inner-city black workers *in general* and reach decisions based on those assumptions before they have had a chance to review systematically the qualifications of an individual applicant" (1996, p. 137). As a result, many qualified "black inner-city applicants are never given the chance to prove their qualifications on an individual level because they are systematically screened out by the selective recruitment process" (1996, p. 137). Regardless of which came first—the attitudes of inner-city residents toward available jobs or employer prejudices—the result is a downward spiral of joblessness.

The "re-appearance" of some jobs in the inner cities during the economic boom of the 1990s did contribute to increased employment and earnings among African Americans. For example, Table 1 shows that between 1989 and 1999, the employment rate for African American men with a high school degree or less rose by 7.2 percentage points, compared with 1.4 percentage points for white men and 3.4 percentage points for Hispanics. However, Wilson's views provide one possible explanation why the employment decline for African American men from 1969 to 1999 was greater than that for whites or Hispanics.

Taken together, the labor market changes reviewed here have made the economy more efficient, by introducing new products, opening up world markets for some American firms, and lowering the prices of many products through competition with imports. The ability of U.S. firms to respond quickly to these labor market changes contributed to a rapid growth in the number of jobs and the low unemployment and low inflation rates in the last decade of the 20th century. In fact, job growth was higher and unemployment lower in the United States than in most other industrialized countries during this decade. However, these changes have also increased economic hardship and economic insecurity for many American workers. Although it is unlikely that the technological genie or the globalization genie can be put back into the bottle, thoughtful government policies can preserve the efficiency gains and offset the distributional losses that have been caused by these economic changes.

Closing the borders to immigrants and raising protectionist barriers to imports are not likely to deliver higher efficiency and more equality. The United States has pursued policies to promote free trade and technological advancement in the interest of growth and efficiency; in doing so, it has produced winners and losers. Government policies can be modified so that they can better address the economic problems of those who have been adversely affected by economic changes.

IMPLICATIONS FOR THE FUTURE

The employment and earnings gaps between more educated and less educated workers were higher at the turn of the 21st century than they had been a quarter century earlier and the gender and racial–ethnic gaps in economic well-being remain large. The long and robust economic recovery of the 1990s did offset some of the increased hardship of the years between the mid-1970s and mid-1980s when these gaps first began to increase. However, the differentials in employment and earnings remain large primarily because of long-term structural changes in labor markets that are likely to continue in the coming years—especially technological changes and the globalization of markets.

Because the economic returns to education have increased so much, the labor market now provides incentives for workers and young people to upgrade their skills through education and training. Partly in response, the percentage of high school graduates entering college increased in the 1990s. The resulting growth in the future supply of more educated workers should eventually contribute to a reduction in the employment and earnings gaps. However, because new people entering the labor market are only a small portion of the total workforce, it will take many years for such a labor supply adjustment to have a large effect. Thus, the wages of less educated workers are likely to remain much lower than average in the interim.

Furthermore, those still in school and young workers are the most likely to respond to the incentives due to the large educational differential in wages. Prime-age workers who have been hurt by the changes in labor markets over the last quarter century are unlikely to undertake substantial investments in education or training because they have relatively few years of work left before retirement.

In addition, children from the poorest families and racial–ethnic minority children who are concentrated in the inner cities typically attend lower quality schools, are more likely to drop out of high school, and are less likely to attend college than are children from higher income families and from the suburbs. Taken together, the increased labor market inequalities of the last quarter century and pervasive inequalities in school quality suggest that the labor supply responses of disadvantaged young people to the increased educational earnings differential are likely to be smaller than average. Thus, there is an important role for additional governmental policies that operate on both the supply side and the demand side of the labor market.

Some Policy Options

Labor Market Supply-Side Strategies

Over the long run, improving educational attainment and labor market skills offers the best prospects for raising employment and earnings and closing racial–ethnic gaps in socioeconomic status. In the late 1960s, if a young man graduated from high school, he had an excellent chance of finding a job that provided good wages and benefits. In the early 21st century, however, many high school graduates do not earn enough on their own to raise a family above the poverty line. It is critical that we invest more in young people to reduce the high rates of school dropout in the inner city, raise the skills of high school graduates, and increase enrollment of youth from low-income families in junior and four-year colleges.

Unfortunately, many low-income students in public schools are not learning the skills and abilities needed to succeed in today's labor market, especially when those schools are highly segregated. Compared with suburban school districts, central city schools have older buildings that require more maintenance, enroll more disadvantaged students who require additional attention and services, and have difficulty recruiting and retaining qualified teachers. To achieve the same educational outcomes as suburban schools, central city schools would need even greater revenues per student and higher quality teachers than their suburban counterparts.

Apart from finances, bureaucratic inefficiencies and other administrative impediments have plagued central city school districts. Such schools would have great difficulty delivering the educational services needed to prepare their students for the demands of today's workplace even if they received additional funding.

Unfortunately, even though there is great agreement on the goal of improving schools, there are few proven models for achieving results on a large scale. There are promising results in early education programs and after-school mentoring programs that have raised school performance and attendance, but these programs operate outside of the public education system (Karoly, 2002).

Labor Market Demand-Side Strategies

If declining employer demand for less educated workers means that many earn low wages even when unemployment rates are low and the economy is booming, then increased attention should be paid to supplementing low wages and expanding work opportunities. This can be accomplished through social policy changes that would do a better job of "making work pay." Many of the poor want to work and are willing to take minimum wage jobs but do not have the skills or experiences that firms now demand. What is required to raise employment and earnings for the less skilled is an increased willingness to spend public funds to develop a work-oriented safety net. Hence, serious consideration should be given to experimenting with transitional public service jobs of last resort (see Danziger & Gottschalk, 1995; Waller, 2002).

Public service employment programs (PSEs) have a long history in the United States but have not been politically popular since the Great Depression of the 1930s. President Ronald Reagan terminated the last large PSE program when he eliminated the Comprehensive Employment and Training Act in the early 1980s. Following the 1996 federal welfare reform legislation, there is an increased need for PSEs because many single mothers have used up their 60-month lifetime limit on the receipt of cash assistance and are no longer eligible to receive welfare benefits. The labor market experiences in recent years for millions of low-skilled workers suggest that many recipients who are sanctioned for not working and those who reach the time limit may be willing to work but are unable to find an employer to hire them (Danziger, 2002; Waller, 2002).

One possibility is to experiment with a program of subsidized transitional low-wage jobs of last resort for the poor. The federal government, for example, might pay 80 percent of the total costs—but the transitional jobs could be administered by nonprofit or community-based organizations or by local governmental agencies that would have to fund the remainder of the costs. The goal would be to have the workers perform tasks that are socially beneficial but for which there is little effective labor demand in the private or public sectors. PSE workers could provide labor-intensive public services that would be valued in poor communities and which are generally available in more affluent communities—monitoring playgrounds, performing neighborhood maintenance, and assisting the elderly, for example.

Graduated job ladders would provide rewards to workers who succeeded in the PSE position, but wages would be lower than the worker would receive in the private sector, thereby maintaining an incentive for them to take an available job. Employees who failed to meet performance standards would be dismissed. Those hired might be limited to a year to two years of PSE, after which time they should have acquired the experience and skills needed to get a private sector job.

Addressing the labor market problems of less educated workers that were reviewed here requires a movement toward a work-oriented safety net; it does not require a return to the pre-1996 welfare system. The American public is quite pleased with the 1996 welfare reform legislation because it expects adults who are able to work to do so and it enforces those expectations. However, job seekers control only the labor supply component of the labor market; that is, they can take the personal responsibility to look for work, but there is no guarantee that if they diligently search for work they will find an employer who will hire them. If a system of transitional jobs of last resort were put into place, then there would be a labor demand response that could transform a job seeker's willingness to work into an ability to work.

For those who do find jobs, but whose earnings remain low in the current economic context, the key elements of a work-oriented safety net are expanded wage supplements and refundable child care tax credits. The earned income tax credit (EITC), substantially expanded in 1993, has done much to offset the decline in real wages for workers at the bottom of the earnings distribution who work year round and who have children. For example, by 2001, a family with two children in which the head has a year-round full-time job at the minimum wage could receive about $4,000 per year from the EITC. In contrast, most low-wage workers who do not have children and parents who do not have custody of their children can receive an EITC payment of only a few hundred dollars.

The EITC for childless workers and noncustodial parents should be raised substantially. This change would make the federal income tax more progressive and increase their living standards without taking them through the welfare system. Several states have also adopted their own EITCs for families with children, something other states should consider, especially those that continue to impose income taxes on the working poor.

In addition, even though the employment rate and earnings of single mothers have increased substantially in recent decades, especially since the 1996 welfare reform, many have great difficulty working full-time, full-year jobs when their children are young. As a result, many remain poor despite increased earnings and the expanded EITC. An increase in the minimum wage would be particularly beneficial for this group, as would increases in public subsidies for child care, since many of the working poor spend a substantial portion of their earnings on child care.

The dependent care credit (DCC) provides tax relief in the form of a nonrefundable federal income credit that depends on family earnings and the amount spent on child care. However, it currently benefits only families with positive income tax liabilities. If the DCC were made refundable, it would raise the disposable income of low-income working families who spend substantial sums on child care but do not owe federal income taxes. This reform would also make the federal income tax more progressive.

REFERENCES

Berman, E., Bound, J., & Griliches, Z. (1994, May). Changes in the demand for skilled labor within U.S. manufacturing: Evidence from the annual survey of manufacturers. *Quarterly Journal of Economics, 109,* 367–397.

Danziger, S. (2002). Approaching the limit: Early national lessons from welfare reform. In B. Weber, G. Duncan, & L. Whitener (Eds.), *Rural dimensions of welfare reform* (pp. 25–49). Kalamazoo, MI: Upjohn Institute for Employment Research.

Danziger, S., & Gottschalk, P. (1995). *America unequal.* New York & Cambridge, MA: Russell Sage Foundation and Harvard University Press.

Danziger, S., Heflin, C., Corcoran, M., Oltmans, E., & Wang, H.-C. (2002, December). Does it pay to move from welfare to work? *Journal of Public Policy Analysis and Management, 21,* 657–678.

Danziger, S., & Reed, D. (1999). The era of inequality continues. *Brookings Review, 17,* 14–17.

Danziger, S. K., Corcoran, M., Danziger, S. H., Heflin, C., Kalil, A., Levine, J., et al. (2000). Barriers to the employment of welfare recipients. In R. Cherry & W. Rodgers (Eds.), *The impact of tight labor markets on black employment problems* (pp. 245–278). New York: Russell Sage Foundation.

Ellwood, D. T., Blank, R. M., Blasi, J., Kruse, D., Niskanen, W. A., & Lynn-Dyson, K. (2000). *A working nation: Workers, work and government in the new economy.* New York: Russell Sage Foundation.

Freeman, R. (1993). How much has de-unionization contributed to the rise in male earnings inequality? In S. Danziger & P. Gottschalk (Eds.), *Uneven tides: Rising inequality in America* (pp. 133–163). New York: Russell Sage Foundation.

Holzer, H. J. (1996). *What employers want: Job prospects for less-educated workers.* New York: Russell Sage Foundation.

Karoly, L. (2002). Investing in the future: Reducing poverty through human capital investments. In S. Danziger & R. H. Haveman (Eds.), *Understanding poverty* (pp. 314–356). Cambridge, MA: Harvard University Press.

Murphy, K., & Welch, F. (1993). Industrial change and the rising importance of skill. In S. Danziger & P. Gottschalk (Eds.), *Uneven tides: Rising inequality in America* (pp. 101–132). New York: Russell Sage Foundation.

U.S. Bureau of the Census. (1970). *Decennial census of population, 1969* [Public use microdata files]. Available: http://www.census.gov

U.S. Bureau of the Census. (1980). *Decennial census of population, 1979* [Public use microdata files]. Available: http://www.census.gov

U.S. Bureau of the Census. (1990). *Decennial census of population, 1989* [Public use microdata files]. Available: http://www.census.gov

U.S. Bureau of the Census. (1999, 2000). *Current population survey, 1999.* Available: http://www.census.gov

U.S. Bureau of the Census. (2001). *Historic income tables: Current population survey* [Online]. Available: http://www.census.gov/hhes/income/histinc/histinctb.html

U.S. Bureau of Labor Statistics. (2001). *Labor market statistics from the current population survey* [Online]. Available: http://www.bls.gov/cps/home.htm?H4

Waller, M. (2002). *Transitional jobs: A next step in welfare to work policy.* Washington, DC: Brookings Institution, Center on Urban and Metropolitan Policy.

Wilson, W. J. (1987). *The truly disadvantaged: The inner city, the underclass, and public policy.* Chicago: University of Chicago Press.

Wilson, W. J. (1996). *When work disappears: The world of the new urban poor.* New York: Alfred A. Knopf.

Sheldon Danziger, PhD, is professor of public policy and co-director of the National Poverty Research Center, Gerald R. Ford School of Public Policy, University of Michigan, 1015 E. Huron Street, No. 321, Ann Arbor, MI 48104.

For further information see
Employment and Underemployment Measurement; Income Distribution; Income Security Overview; Jobs and Earnings; JOBS Program; Poverty; Rural Poverty; Social Welfare History; Social Welfare Policy; Welfare Employment Programs: Evaluation; Women Overview; Working Poor, *1997*

Key Words

earnings	employment
economic trends	

Empowerment

See Citizen Participation, *Volume 1;* Strengths-Based Practice, *2003*

Empowerment Zone, Microenterprise, and Asset Building

Mizanur R. Miah

This entry underscores some salient features of empowerment zone, microenterprise, and asset-building initiatives as they pertain to social policy and the social work profession. Although the historical background of each initiative is slightly different, all three share the common goals of poverty alleviation, economic and social justice, and empowerment of people and their communities. Each of these goals is also an intrinsic aspect of the mission of the social work profession and is reflected in social work policy, practice, and education.

EMPOWERMENT ZONE AND ENTERPRISE COMMUNITIES

The concept of the empowerment zone has evolved from that of the enterprise zone. The enterprise zone concept was first used by Sir Geoffrey Howe, Prime Minister Margaret Thatcher's foreign secretary, in a speech in 1978 in the British House of Commons. His idea was to set aside about a square mile of land in the cities for free enterprise development where there were no government regulation or taxes involved (Butler, 1991; Green, 1991; Liebschutz, 1995). The British program targeted mostly depopulated abandoned industrial areas to attract new businesses with the aim of economic revitalization.

Early initiatives for empowerment zones in the United States included that of Stuart M. Butler of the Heritage Foundation who basically expanded on the British enterprise idea and proposed it as an urban strategy for America. Later on, in 1980, Jack Kemp, a U.S. House of Representatives member from Buffalo, New York, proposed the very first legislation to create enterprise zones without any success. Later, during the period when Kemp was Secretary of the U.S. Department of Housing and Urban Development (HUD) under President George Bush's administration, he continued his efforts, arguing that enterprise zones should be implemented in inner-city neighborhoods that are heavily blighted and crime ridden. During the 1980s a number of states and the District of Columbia enacted their own statutes for enterprise zones. President Ronald Reagan's tax incentives included in the Consolidated Omnibus Budget Reconciliation Act of 1985 partly propelled this interest by the states. By 1990 there were about 2,000 enterprise zones in 37 states. Three more states enacted similar statutes after 1990 (U.S. Department of Housing and Urban Development, 1995).

It has been suggested that the 1992 riots in Los Angeles rekindled interest in inner-city development by the federal government to create economic opportunities for poor and minority populations (Rich, 1993). In October 1992, as part of the Tax Fairness and Economic Growth Act, Congress passed the Enterprise Zone Bill. The legislation provided $500 million for seed money for 50 enterprise zones along with various other tax incentives (Cowden, 1993; Liebschutz, 1995).

1993 Empowerment Zone Program

On August 10, 1993, Congress passed the Omnibus Budget Reconciliation Act including Title XX, the enterprise zone program, which authorized a specific amount of federal dollars through Title XX social services block grants (SSBGs), tax incentives (such as wage tax credit and new tax-exempt bond financing), and in some cases, economic development initiative (EDI) grants. On December 21, 1994, President Bill Clinton announced the designations of empowerment zones and enterprise communities (EZ–ECs). The first round of urban EZ–ECs included six empowerment zones, two supplemental empowerment zones, four enhanced enterprise communities, and 65 enterprise communities in 42 states that were selected by the Secretary of U.S. Department of Housing and Urban development (see below for lists by location and amount of award):

Empowerment Zones (6):
- Atlanta, GA (received $100 million Title XX SSBG)
- Chicago, IL (received wage tax credits)
- Baltimore, MD (received increased Section 179 funding)
- Detroit, MI (received new tax-exempt bond financing)
- New York, NY (received $100 million Title XX SSBG)
- Philadelphia, PA, and Camden, NJ (received $100 million Title XX SSBG)

Supplemental Empowerment Zones (2):
- Los Angeles, CA (received a $125 million EDI grant)
- Cleveland, OH (received a $87 million EDI grant, a $3 million Title XX SSBG, and new tax-exempt bond financing)

Enhanced Enterprise Community (4):
- Oakland, CA (received a $22 million EDI grant)
- Boston, MA (received a $3 million Title XX SSBG)
- Kansas City, MO, and Kansas City, KS (received new tax-exempt bond financing)
- Houston, TX

Enterprise Community (65):
- For a list, see Riposa (1996; each received a $3 million Title XX SSBG and new tax-exempt bond financing)

Additionally, three rural empowerment zones and 30 rural enterprise communities were designated that were selected by the Secretary of the U.S. Department of Agriculture (for a list of rural EZ–ECs, see U.S. Department of Housing and Urban Development, 1995).

Block grants were earmarked for funding the following:

- economic and community development services (such as transportation subsidies, skills development, and financial management counseling pertaining to business, jobs, and housing) for disenfranchised populations
- programs for low-income groups that promote education, home ownership, and economic self-sufficiency and independence
- community colleges and nonprofit organizations to provide entrepreneurship training for low-income groups aimed at their self-sufficiency
- mentoring programs including after-school programs and weekend study for students.

Additionally, urban and rural EZ–ECs had access to $3 billion in federal resources through programs such as one-stop capital shops, community development banks, and Department of Agriculture grants and loans (Riposa, 1996; Wetherill, 1995).

Taxpayer Relief Act of 1997
The Taxpayer Relief Act of 1997 allowed for the designation of two first-round supplemental enterprise zones into full enterprise zones (Los Angeles and Cleveland), effective January 1, 2000, remaining in effect for the next 10 years. Incentives for these two EZ designations included the wage credit, special tax-exempt financing, additional expenses, as well as the new Brownfields deduction for environmental remediation costs incurred before January 1, 2001, and the public school renovation tax credit. Furthermore, the 1997 Tax Relief Act also authorized an additional 20 EZ designations (15 urban and five rural) from among first-round nonrecipients, qualified rural communities, and Indian nations.

MICROENTERPRISE
The Aspen Institute's Microenterprise Fund for Innovation, Effectiveness, Learning, and Dissemination defines a microenterprise as a partnership or family business with fewer than five employees (Langer, Orwick, & Kays, 1999, p. xii). It is a sole proprietorship with very little access to commercial banking. In fact, loans under $25,000 are common for start-up funds. In most cases, a proprietor runs a microenterprise and generally fewer less than three employees. Grameen Bank in Bangladesh, which serves as a model for microenterprises

throughout the world, organizes borrowers as a group of five members on a voluntary basis who operate on a loan of as little as $25.

The underlying philosophy of a microenterprise is "poverty alleviation" by improving the financial conditions of the poor. Servon (1997) suggested that a microenterprise has a two-pronged agenda: poverty alleviation and economic development. The Grameen Bank philosophy, however, focuses on four issues: poverty alleviation, economic development, social development, and psychological development.

Microenterprise programs clearly complement the mission of the social work profession in that they promote socioeconomic justice for the disadvantaged and seek to empower people socially, politically, and economically. The microenterprise philosophy also emphasizes the social work strengths perspective in that it recognizes a member's inherent aptitude, interest, experience, and skills and builds on those to promote individual or group initiatives (Edgcomb, Klein, & Clark, 1996). According to Raheim (1996) a microenterprise essentially fulfills the social work profession's concern by "promoting human capital formation through building interpersonal skills and enhancing family and community strengths" (p. 69).

Origin and Background of Microenterprise as Self-Employment Initiative
No single program can be clearly identified that marks the beginning of microenterprise programs. Raheim (1996) noted that a 1972 International Labor Organization study in Nairobi, Kenya, first underscored the value of self-employment as a strategy for economic development. Later, in 1978, as a strategy for microenterprise development, the U.S. Agency for International Development (USAID) sponsored a program for self-employment in 16 different countries of Africa, Asia, and Latin America, known as the Program for Investment in the Small Capital Enterprise Sector (PISCES). Based on insights gained from the first phase of PISCES, a number of microenterprise projects were launched in Egypt, Costa Rica, Kenya, and the Dominican Republic (Ashe, 1985; Raheim, 1996). Other USAID initiatives for microenterprise development included the Assistance to Resource Institutions for Enterprise Support Project (ARIES) launched in 1985 and the Growth and Equity through Micro-Enterprise Investments and Institutions (GEMINI). Although ARIES provided technical, research, and project management assistance

to governments, banks, and nongovernmental voluntary organizations and cooperatives, and GEMINI was essentially a continuation of ARIES after it ended.

On the European front, microenterprise self-employment initiatives included France's experimental program of 1980 to finance the creation of small businesses known as Chômeurs Createurs (meaning unemployed entrepreneurs). In 1982 a pilot project in Britain called the Enterprise Allowance Scheme followed suit, offering technical assistance and an allowance to the unemployed for a year to help them establish their own businesses (Puls, 1988; Raheim, 1996).

The Grameen Bank of Bangladesh, which started as a demonstration project in 1974 and was established as a full-fledged bank in 1983, provided much of the impetus for a global movement for microenterprise development, including activities in the United States. The creation of economic opportunities for unemployed and low-income populations through U.S. microenterprise programs has proved to be significantly viable (Clark & Kays, 1999; Raheim, 1996; Raheim & Bolden, 1995). Some of the early U.S. microenterprise initiatives included:

- self-employment programs for low-income groups in New York and Vermont run by community action agencies, with financial support from the demonstration partnership program of the Office of Community Services of the U.S. Department of Health and Human Services
- small enterprise development programs for low-income people by some community development corporations, which were originally formed as part of the War on Poverty programs in the 1960s, with funding from the same sources as above
- access to credit, technical assistance, and business training provided to women during the 1980s by a number of women's organizations (most of these were supported by funding from corporations and private foundations), such as Women's Self-Employment Project founded in 1986 in Chicago; Women Venture founded in 1983 in St. Paul, Minnesota; Women's Initiative for Self-Employment in San Francisco; Coalition for Women's Economic Development founded in 1989 in Los Angeles; and the Entrepreneurial Center for Women in Hartford, Connecticut
- the Good Faith Fund established in 1988 in Pine Bluff, Arkansas, by the Southern Development Bancorporation, following the peer

lending model of Grameen Bank; the bank funds the groups for small businesses, including training
- the Institute for Social Economic Development established in 1988 in Iowa City, Iowa, which provides training to the poor to start businesses
- the Portable Practical Education Program/ Micro Industry Rural Credit Organization established in 1987 following the ACCION International model mainly to serve the Hispanic population in the border areas of California and Arizona
- the Rural Economic Development Center's Microenterprise Loan program founded in 1989 in Raleigh, North Carolina, which extends loans as well as training assistance to low-income borrowers
- the Self-Employment and Enterprise Development Demonstration (SEED) program in Washington State to fund self-employment using income maintenance payments (the success of SEED programs in Washington State and Massachusetts provided positive legislative responses in terms of changing the unemployment insurance regulations)
- the Self-Employment Investment Demonstration (SEID) program for microenterprise development for Aid to Families with Dependent Children (AFDC) recipients, although managed by the Corporation for Enterprise Development, SEID was implemented in Maryland, Michigan, Minnesota, Mississippi, and Iowa between 1988 and 1990. Under this program local organizations or institutions (such as community colleges, small business incubators, community action organizations, and self-employment development organizations) provided contractual services (such as counseling, self-employment training, direct loans or help to access loans, and technical assistance).

Growth of Microenterprise Programs in the United States and Elsewhere

The growth of microenterprise programs in the United States in the last decade or so has been phenomenal. The Aspen Institute's *1999 Directory of U.S. Microenterprise Programs* (Langer et al., 1999) listed 341 U.S. microenterprise programs in 46 states and the District of Columbia, a 4 percent increase since the 1996 report and a 72 percent increase since the 1994 report. The Aspen Institute's 1996 and 1994 reports profiled 328 and 195 programs, respectively.

Globally, the Grameen Bank model in Bangladesh is being replicated in 58 other countries, including Canada, France, the Netherlands, Norway, United Kingdom, and the United States. Presently, Grameen has a total of 143 branches that serve over 2 million borrowers in 39,635 villages. Its current membership totals 2,352,867, of which about 94 percent (2,229,765) are women; there are only 123,102 male members in Grameen (Yunus & Shams, 2000). Ninety-two percent of the bank is owned by the rural poor borrowers, and the other 8 percent is owned by the government.

Types of Microenterprise Programs and Program Strategies

Edgcomb and associates (1996, p. 2) classified microenterprise programs into three major types:

1. credit individual loan programs (training and technical assistance provided)
2. group lending programs (follows Grameen or ACCION International models of group formation and lending where peer groups of clients guarantee loans with no collateral needed)
3. training-led strategies (only business management training is offered with an option for access to credit).

Strategies used in the microenterprise programs are as diverse as the populations they serve, even though all mainly serve low-income populations. Edgcomb and associates (1996, p. 2) identified these common features from the seven agencies they evaluated:

- focus on poverty alleviation
- emphasis on client's choice and self-selection
- commitment to help develop client "incrementally"
- employment of a business approach rather than a charity approach (uses market interest rates and strict repayment schedule and program standards)
- emphasis on the significance of training and technical assistance, offered on an as-needed basis.

Microenterprises and Global Response

As the microenterprise programs are growing at a rapidly increasing rate, so are the commitments from the global communities and their leaders. In 1997 at the first Microcredit Summit held in Washington, DC, the organizers and participants launched a campaign to reach 100 million of the world's poorest families by the year 2005, especially the women, with credit for self-employment and small businesses (Microcredit Summit Campaign, 1999). At this first summit, only 30 institutional action plans were submitted out of a membership of 1,700 council members. In 1999 more than 1,200 institutions submitted over 2,100 institutional action plans. This clearly signals a global movement toward increasing microenterprise program development aimed at poverty alleviation and social development.

ASSET BUILDING

Kretzmann and McKnight (1993) offered a very broad definition of asset building that includes an extensive array of community resources such as financial, personal (individual talents and skills), physical (buildings and facilities), organizational (capacity), and political (connections) resources. Such a definition is all-inclusive but essentially elusive and vague and, hence, is of little assistance to guide social work practice (Page-Adams & Sherraden, 1997). Sherraden (1988, 1990, 1991) proposed a more succinct and specific definition of asset building that implies accumulation of wealth in terms of financial resources and property ownership (by savings, investment, and accumulation).

Owning wealth and property has significant positive effects on personal well-being, civic participation, and social status in America (Yadama & Sherraden, 1996). This may hold true globally as well. These ideas have roots in the thinking and philosophy of Alexis de Tocqueville and Thomas Jefferson and have affected the orchestration of social policies in America, such as home mortgage lending programs, the Homestead Act, employee stock ownership plans, and public housing ownership.

Clearly, asset building is more than earning an income or income maintenance. Sherraden (1988) asserted that poverty, measured by levels of income, is not only misleading, but also inadequate as an explanation. Any social welfare policy measured or defined by the concept of income is also inadequate. Asset building includes endeavors such as savings, education, investment in microenterprises, ownership of homes, and other community revitalization activities (safer streets, drug abuse prevention, and so forth). To Sherraden, wealth or assets are more appropriate indicators of social justice (see also Stoesz & Saunders, 1999).

Asset Accumulation Process: Individual Development Account

Sherraden's pioneering work on the asset-building concept was given concrete shape in his book *Assets and the Poor* (1991), in which he proposed an individual development account (IDA) for poor and marginalized people to help them own homes, get an education, and start small businesses. This involved matched savings by individuals with the government or the employer sharing the match. States and community-based organizations that started IDA programs after passage of the Personal Responsibility and Work Opportunity Reconciliation Act of 1996 encouraged a savings of from $5 to $20 by account holders, which was matched by between $0.50 to $4 for every dollar of earned income (Stoesz & Saunders, 1999). The IDA is a tax-exempt fund if used for one of the following four purposes: (1) buying a home, (2) completing college or vocational school, (3) launching a business, or (4) providing a pension supplement.

Sherraden (1991) believed that assets have multiple positive effects on an individual:

- increase confidence and expectations about the future
- increase protective and prudent personal behavior
- make more specific plans with family and work
- increase social connectedness with neighbors, organizations, and relatives.

Legislative Support for Asset Building in the United States

In 1994 President Clinton's welfare reform proposal asked for increasing asset limits and creating IDAs. His proposal received bipartisan support in Congress from the House of Representatives and the Senate. This dimension of bipartisan support ushered in a new era of legislative reform to eradicate poverty and promote asset building for an impoverished and disenfranchised class that was historically denied the status of "owners" of assets or wealth. Congressional bills for IDA demonstration projects such as the 1998 Assets for Independence Act (Corporation for Enterprise Development, 1998a) had also received bipartisan support (cosponsored by Sen. Dan Coates, R–IN, and Sen. Carol Mosley-Braun, D–IL). The largest funding support for IDA demonstration projects came from the Ford Foundation, which set up a separate division known as Asset Building and Community Development (Page-Adams & Sherraden, 1997).

Today, the idea of an IDA has gained new momentum at the federal, state, and local levels. Although the 1996 welfare reform had

provisions for IDAs, there was no money authorized for the purpose. Consequently, implementation required support from state and local governments and nongovernmental private organizations. As a demonstration project known as Downpayments on the American Dream, the IDA concept is now being pilot tested in 14 program sites in the United States with $15 million in funding from a consortium of foundations (see Corporation for Enterprise Development, 1998b). The impetus for the initiative comes from passage of the Assets for Independence Act of 1998 that authorized $125 million for IDA demonstrations nationally. The act is an outgrowth of persistent advocacy by the Washington University Center for Social Development and the Corporation for Enterprise Development (Stoesz & Saunders, 1999). On January 27, 2000, President Clinton, in his State of the Union Address, endorsed the IDA as a matched-savings program for asset building as a national policy. A recent evaluation of the American dream demonstration project shows that IDA participants have mean savings of $33 per month and median savings of $23. This report clearly documented that the poorest participants of IDA are saving at a much higher rate than all other groups (Sherraden et al., 2000).

CONCLUSIONS

The EZ–EC initiatives are witnessing an increased vitality in many urban and rural communities and are seen as a new opportunity for community revitalization with active involvement of people and government. Insofar as its key goals are concerned, such as creating and strengthening economic opportunities, the initiatives in many areas have been able to enlist major commitments from the private sector to invest and create employment within the zones. The areas of sustainable community development, such as promotion of education, support for families, and creation of opportunities for personal growth of adult populations, has remained a little fuzzy. This is because it is very hard to measure success in this area. Also, planning and efforts in this area have not been operationally well-defined, and they have also varied from zone to zone.

Evaluation studies show mixed results in the areas of community-based partnerships and increased community capacity (Gittell, 1995; Gittell, Newman, Bockmeyer, & Lindsay, 1998). Gittell and associates' (1998) study of six urban EZ areas showed that community capacity has not achieved the desired expansion in terms of development of the networks and strength of participation, largely owing to the control of the process by the mayors. There are also variations in capacity levels among these six sites. Apart from the mayoral control of the process, capacity of the community was stunted due to the reuse of the existing networks rather than the creation of new ones. Also, there has been a limited role of community organization at the local levels. Gittell (1995) noted that the politics of control and token participation seem to characterize EZ–EC efforts at this time. It is, however, too early to evaluate the full impact of the EZ in all the areas of its set goals.

In the area of microenterprise, self-employment and microcredit initiatives have witnessed a phenomenal growth both at home and abroad (Langer et al., 1999; Yunus & Shams, 2000). Findings from the Self-Employment Learning Project, a five-year survey of micro-enterprises in America, show that about three-fourths (72 percent) of the microentrepreneurs in the sample (N = 405) have gained an average of $8,484 in their household income over a five-year period. More than half of this sample (53 percent) has moved out of poverty largely due to income gained from microenterprises. More importantly, in a majority of these families, household income has almost doubled in five years (Clark & Kays, 1999). There has also been a substantial decrease (61 percent) in the reliance on governmental assistance by poor microentrepreneurs, especially AFDC recipients. In terms of growth of assets over five years, an average household gained an asset value of nearly $16,000. In a majority of the cases, these gains were in housing assets.

Microenterprise programs have been seen as an integral part of the "social capital" model (Putnam, 2000) in the social work and social development field that offers a positive alternative to remedial and maintenance-oriented social welfare models (Midgley, 1995, 1997, 2000; Midgley & Sherraden, 2000; Page-Adams & Sherraden, 1997; Sherraden, 1991). Social workers see this as an opportunity to initiate economic development and asset accumulation. Microenterprises also accrue a number of social benefits, such as an increase in self-confidence, self-esteem, and abilities that essentially lead to self-empowerment (Raheim, 1996, 1997).

Furthermore, although Banerjee (1998) found microenterprise development as "a viable response to poverty" (p. 63), Yunus (1987) strongly believed that "credit is a fundamental human right" (p. 6) and if poor people are given access to credit, such as microloans, they would be able to get involved in viable income-generating activities and, thereby, will be able to get out of poverty (see also Counts, 1996; Mizan, 1994).

Despite these noted gains and optimism, microenterprise programs have really done poorly in advancing health insurance for people who are poor. A recent evaluation report shows that about one-half of the poor entrepreneurs surveyed did not have any health insurance and those who did were receiving it through a government assistance program (Clark & Kays, 1999). The extent to which microenterprise helps low-income people to exit poverty has remained questionable. Servon and Bates (1998), among others, doubted that a small loan alone would help poor people to succeed in business. Besides, they opined that microenterprise should not be seen as a panacea for poverty alleviation. Lindenfeld (1998) argued that "by itself microenterprise development is hardly a cure for mass poverty and unemployment. It is, however, potentially part of an answer" (p. 420). Ehlers and Main (1998) pointed out another significant dimension of its limitations. From their research on MicroFem, they concluded that as a strategy for poverty alleviation and economic development this urban microenterprise program has had a negative impact on welfare-dependent mothers and low-income women. Overall, they find microenterprise development for women not only problematic, but also detrimental. Earlier, Adams and Pischke (1992) had criticized microenterprise credit programs for contributing to the increase in debt of poor participants and argued that "debt is not an effective tool for helping most poor people to enhance their economic conditions, be they operators of small farms or microenterprises" (p. 1463).

However, Servon (1997) had emphasized that microenterprise initiatives clearly shifted the focus of policy from maintenance orientation to investment (see also Midgley, 1995, 1997, 2000; Sherraden, 1991; Yadama & Sherraden, 1996). Servon's case studies of three microenterprise programs in the United States showed positive results in terms of economic benefits to the participants. It is, however, more beneficial for those who were marginally placed in the mainstream economy than those who were completely excluded from it (Servon, 1997).

Recently, asset-building initiatives as an exit route from poverty have gained much popularity in political circles as well as among policy researchers and social workers. Their appeal for bipartisan political support comes from their emphasis on reduced dependency on public welfare and government spending. Policy researchers and social workers (especially the neoinstitutionalists such as James Midgley and Michael Sherraden) support them due to their productiveness and asset-building appeal that counteracts much criticized remedial, maintenance-oriented, and consumption-based social welfare programs (Midgley & Sherraden, 2000).

In conclusion, it can be said that although numerous positive effects of asset building have been noted, including its social and psychological effects, the reciprocal effects of these variables on asset building should also be examined (Page-Adams & Sherraden, 1997; Yadama & Sherraden, 1996). This kind of examination will require the use of advanced multivariate analyses. Moreover, in-depth qualitative data will be needed to identify and describe the psychological impact of asset building on various aspects of well-being of the individual and the family. Evaluation of these initiatives must go beyond counting simple asset accumulation (Page-Adams & Sherraden, 1997).

The relationships between the effects of asset building on the psychological, social, and community dimensions and vice versa must be theoretically linked and understood. Otherwise, the results of the initiatives, whether they are EZ–EC, microenterprise, or asset building, will remain fragmented and compartmentalized, leading to inadequate integrated knowledge. Attempts must be made to put these results into a coherent whole by building some middle-range theories at a minimum or using these data to test or validate existing theories in the field. This, however, remains a task for the scientific researchers rather than the policymakers. For that matter, as Page-Adams and Sherraden (1997) succinctly put it, "more collaborative work between traditional poverty researchers and evaluators of asset-based community strategies would be highly desirable" (p. 432).

REFERENCES

Adams, D. W., & Pischke, J.D.V. (1992). Microenterprise credit programs: Deja vu. *World Development, 20*(10), 1463–1470.

Ashe, J. (1985). *The PISCES II experience: Local efforts in micro-enterprise development.* Washington, DC: Agency for International Development.

Banerjee, M. M. (1998). Micro-enterprise development: A response to poverty. *Journal of Community Practice, 5*(1–2), 63–83.

Butler, S. M. (1991). The conceptual evolution of enterprise zones. In R. E. Green (Ed.), *Enterprise zones: New directions in economic development* (pp. 27–40). Newbury Park, CA: Sage Publications.

Clark, P., & Kays, A. (1999). *Microenterprise and the poor.* Washington, DC: Aspen Institute.

Corporation for Enterprise Development. (1998a). *Assets for independence act.* Washington, DC: Author.

Corporation for Enterprise Development. (1998b). *Reclaiming the American dream.* Washington, DC: Author.

Counts, A. (1996). *Give us credit.* New Delhi, India: Research Press.

Cowden, R. (1993). *Enterprise zone: Case study in American urban policy.* Washington, DC: American Association of Enterprise Zones.

Edgcomb, E., Klein, J., & Clark, P. (1996). *The practice of microenterprise in the U.S.: Strategies, costs, and effectiveness.* Washington, DC: Aspen Institute.

Ehlers, T., & Main, K. (1998). Women and the false promise of microenterprise. *Gender and Society, 12*(4), 424–440.

Gittell, M. (1995). Growing pains, politics beset empowerment zones. *Forum for Applied Research and Public Policy, 10,* 107–111.

Gittell, M., Newman, K., Bockmeyer, J., & Lindsay, R. (1998). Expanding civic opportunity: Urban empowerment zones. *Urban Affairs Review, 33*(4), 530–558.

Green, R. E. (Ed.). (1991). *Enterprise zones: New directions in economic development.* Newbury Park, CA: Sage Publications.

Kretzmann, J. P., & McKnight, J. L. (1993). *Building communities from the inside out: A path toward finding and mobilizing a community's assets.* Evanston, IL: Northwestern University, Center for Urban Affairs and Policy Research.

Langer, J. A., Orwick, J. A., & Kays, A. J. (Eds.). (1999). *1999 directory of U.S. microenterprise programs.* Washington, DC: Aspen Institute.

Liebschutz, S. F. (1995). Empowerment zones and enterprise communities: Reinventing federalism for distressed communities. *Publius: Journal of Federalism, 25*(3), 117–132.

Lindenfeld, F. (1998). Possibilities and limits of U.S. microenterprise development for creating good jobs and increasing the income of the poor. *Humanity and Society, 22*(4), 411–421.

Microcredit Summit Campaign. (1999, June 24–26). *Final report.* 1999 Meeting of Councils of the

Microcredit Summit Campaign, Abidjan, Cote D'Ivoire. Washington, DC: Author.

Midgley, J. (1995). *Social development: The development perspective in social welfare*. Thousand Oaks, CA: Sage Publications.

Midgley, J. (1997). Social work and international social development: Promoting a developmental perspective in the profession. In M. C. Hokenstad & J. Midgley (Eds.), *Issues in international social work: Global challenges for a new century* (pp. 11–26). Washington, DC: NASW Press.

Midgley, J. (2000). The institutional approach to social policy. In J. Midgley, M. B. Tracey, & M. Livermore (Eds.), *The political economy of social policy* (pp. 365–376). Washington, DC: NASW Press.

Midgley, J., & Sherraden, M. (2000). The social development perspective in social policy. In J. Midgley, M. B. Tracy, & M. Livermore (Eds.), *The handbook of social policy* (pp. 435–446). Thousand Oaks, CA: Sage Publications.

Mizan, A. N. (1994). *In quest of empowerment: The Grameen Bank impact on women's power and status*. Dhaka, India: University Press.

Page-Adams, D., & Sherraden, M. (1997). Asset building as a community revitalization strategy. *Social Work, 42*, 423–434.

Puls, B. (1988). *From unemployed to self-employed: A program analysis*. Washington, DC: National Conference of State Legislators.

Putnam, R. D. (2000). *Bowling alone: The collapse and revival of American community*. New York: Simon & Schuster.

Raheim, S. (1996). Micro-enterprise as an approach for promoting economic development in social work: Lessons from the self-employment investment demonstration. *International Social Work, 39*(1), 69–82.

Raheim, S. (1997). Problems and prospects of self-employment as an economic independence option for welfare recipients. *Social Work, 42*, 44–53.

Raheim, S., & Bolden, J. (1995). Economic empowerment of low-income women through self-employment. *Affilia, 10*(2), 138–154.

Rich, M. J. (1993). Riot and reason: Crafting an urban policy response. *Publius: Journal of Federalism, 23*, 115–134.

Riposa, G. (1996). From enterprise zones to empowerment zones: The community context of urban economic development. *American Behavior Scientist, 39*, 536–551.

Servon, L. J. (1997). Microenterprise programs in U.S. inner cities: Economic development or social welfare? *Economic Development Quarterly, 11*(2), 166–180.

Servon, L. J., & Bates, T. (1998). Microenterprise as an exit route from poverty: Recommendations for programs and policy makers. *Journal of Urban Affairs, 20*(4), 419–441.

Sherraden, M. (1988). Rethinking social welfare: Toward assets. *Social Policy, 18*(3), 37–43.

Sherraden, M. (1990). Stakeholding: Notes on a theory of welfare based on assets. *Social Service Review, 64*, 580–601.

Sherraden, M. (1991). *Assets and the poor: A new American welfare policy*. New York: M. E. Sharpe.

Sherraden, M., Johnson, L., Clancy, M., Beverly, S., Schreiner, M., Zhan, M., et al. (2000). *Saving patterns in IDA programs: Downpayments on the American Dream Policy demonstration*. St. Louis: Washington University, Center for Social Development.

Stoesz, D., & Saunders, D. (1999). Welfare capitalism: A new approach to poverty policy? *Social Service Review, 73*(3), 380–400.

U.S. Department of Housing and Urban Development. (1995). *Urban empowerment zones and enterprise communities* (HUD-1551-CPD). Washington, DC: Author.

Wetherill, G. R. (1995). Empowerment holds key to rural revitalization. *Forum for Applied Research and Public Policy, 10*, 117–120.

Yadama, G. N., & Sherraden, M. (1996). Effects of assets on attitudes and behaviors: Advance test of a social policy proposal. *Social Work Research, 20*, 3–11.

Yunus, M. (1987). *Credit for self-employment: A fundamental human right*. Dhaka, Bangladesh: Grameen Bank, Al-Falah Printing Press.

Yunus, M., & Shams, K. (Eds.). (2000, January). *Grameen dialogue*. Dhaka, Bangladesh: Grameen Trust.

FURTHER READING

Boshara, R., & Friedman, R. (1997). *Twenty promising ideas for savings facilitation and mobilization in low-income communities in the U.S.* Washington, DC: Corporation for Enterprise Development.

Clark, P., & Huston, T. (1993). *Assisting the smallest businesses: Assessing micro-enterprise development as a strategy for boosting poor communities*. Washington, DC: Aspen Institute

Danziger, S., & Gottschalk, P. (1986). Work, poverty, and the working poor: A multifaceted problem. *Monthly Labor Review, 109*, 17–21.

Dignard, L., & Havet, J. (1995). *Women in micro- and small-scale enterprise development*. Boulder, CO: Westview Press.

Ehlers, T. (1998). Women and the false promise of microenterprise. *Gender and Society, 12*(4), 424–440.

Else, J. F., & Raheim, S. (1992). AFDC clients as entrepreneurs: Self-employment offers an important option. *Public Welfare, 50*(4), 36–41.

Fairley, J. (1998). New strategies for microenterprise development: Innovation, integration, and the trickle up approach. *Journal of International Affairs, 52*(1), 340–350.

Gaventa, J., Morrissey, J., & Edwards, W. R. (1995). Empowering people: Goals and realities. *Forum for Applied Research and Public Policy, 10,* 116–121.

Green, R. K., & White, M. J. (1997). Measuring the benefits of home owning: Effects on children. *Journal of Urban Economics, 41,* 441–461.

Haveman, R. (1992). Review of M. Sherraden, assets and the poor. *Journal of Economic Literature, 30,* 1520–1521.

Hill, M. S., & Duncan, G. J. (1987). Parental family income and the socio-economic attainment of children. *Social Science Research, 16,* 39–73.

Hyman, E. L. (1998). Comprehensive impact assessment systems for NGO microenterprise development programs. *World Development, 26*(2), 261–276.

Meyerhoff, D. (1997). Federal funding opportunities for microenterprise programs. *Journal of Developmental Entrepreneurship, 2*(2), 99–109.

Midgley, J. (1999). Growth, redistribution, and welfare: Toward social investment. *Social Service Review, 77*(1), 3–21.

Morris, R. (1986). *Rethinking social welfare: Why care for the stranger?* New York: Longman.

Morrisson, C., Lecomte, H.-B.S., & Oudin, X. (1994*). Micro-enterprises and the institutional framework in developing countries.* Paris: Organization for Economic Co-operation and Development.

Mosley, P. (1998). Microenterprise finance: Is there a conflict between growth and poverty alleviation? *World Development, 26*(5), 783–790.

Moynihan, D. (1987, February 15). It's time to replace AFDC. *St. Louis Post-Dispatch,* p. 3C.

Naparstek, A. J., & Dooley, D. (1997). Countering urban disinvestment through community-building initiatives. *Social Work, 42,* 506–514.

Piven, F., & Cloward, R. (1982). *The new class war: Reagan's attack on the welfare state and its consequences.* New York: Pantheon.

Prugl, E., & Tinker, I. (1997). Microentrepreneurs and homeworkers: Convergent categories. *World Development, 25*(9), 1471–1482.

Rohe, W. M., & Stegman, M. A. (1994). The impact of home ownership on the social and political involvement of low-income people. *Urban Affairs Quarterly, 30,* 152–172.

Schuler, S. R., & Hashemi, S. M. (1994). Credit programs, women's empowerment, and contraceptive use in rural Bangladesh. *Studies in Family Planning, 25,* 65–76.

Sherraden, M. (1986). School dropouts in perspective. *Educational Forum, 51*(1), 15–31.

Sherraden, M., Page-Adams, D., Emerson, S., Beverly, S., Scanlon, E., Cheng, L., et al. (1995). *IDA evaluation handbook: A practical guide and tools for evaluation of pioneering IDA projects.* St. Louis: Washington University, Center for Social Development.

Sherraden, M., Page-Adams, D., & Yadama, G. (1995). Assets and the welfare state: Policies, proposals, politics, and research. *Research in Politics and Society, 5,* 241–268.

Spalter-Roth, R., Soto, E., Zandniapour, L., & Braunstein, J. (1994). *Microenterprise and women.* Washington, DC: Institute for Women's Policy Research.

Stoesz, D. (1997). Welfare behaviorism. *Society, 34*(3), 68–75.

U.S. Bureau of the Census. (1986). *Household wealth and asset ownership, 1984: Current Population Reports, Household Economic Studies* (Series P-70, No. 7). Washington, DC: U.S. Government Printing Office.

Wagner, A. (1995). Reassessing welfare capitalism. *Journal of Community Practice, 2*(3), 45–63.

Whitbeck, L. B., Simons, R. L., Conger, R. D., Lorenz, F. O., Huck, S., & Elder, G. H., Jr. (1991). Family economic hardship, parental support, and adolescent self-esteem. *Social Psychology Quarterly, 54,* 353–363.

Yunus, M. (1987). The poor as the engine of development. *Washington Quarterly, 10*(4), 139–145.

Yunus, M. (1995). Grameen Bank: Experiences and reflections. *Impact, 30*(3/4), 13–25.

Mizanur R. Miah, PhD, is director and professor, School of Social Work, Southern Illinois University, Carbondale, Carbondale, IL 62901-4329.

For further information see
Community Building, *1997;* Jobs and Earnings; Working Poor, *1997*

Key Words

asset building	enterprise communities
empowerment zone	microenterprise

Evidence-Based Practice Guidelines

Matthew O. Howard
John Bricout
Tonya Edmond
Diane Elze
Jeffrey M. Jenson

Evidence-based guidelines have proliferated widely over the past decade. This review examines the nature and methods of current guideline development activities in medicine and allied health professions, factors contributing to the rapid growth of guidelines, desirable attributes of practice guidelines, guideline effectiveness, dissemination and implementation issues, strengths and limitations of guidelines, and barriers to guideline development in social work.

The notion that professional interventions should be justified by a supportive body of empirical findings has only recently gained widespread acceptance in medicine, psychology, and allied health care and social services professions (Gambrill, 1999; Howard & Jenson, 1999b, 2000; Pearson, 1998; Persons, 1995). Within social work the past quarter century has been marked by a series of controversial initiatives, each promising to foster more intimate and fruitful relations between knowledge development and its professional applications (Kirk, 1999; Klein & Bloom, 1995). Proponents of the "scientist–practitioner" model of professional training contended that student practitioners could be taught to critically appraise knowledge gained from research and judiciously apply it to their practice endeavors (Turnbull & Dietz-Uhler, 1995). Systematic program evaluation methods were developed in response to early summative reviews that called the efficacy of social casework interventions seriously into question (Fischer, 1976). Advocates of single-subject research methods (Bloom, Fischer, & Orme, 1995) and research and development type intervention efforts (Rothman & Thomas, 1994) also sought, in disparate ways, to create stronger links between research and practice within social work.

There are few indications that previous attempts to promote evidence-based practice have, individually or in toto, exerted an even modest effect on the daily practices of most social workers (Howard & Lambert, 1996; Rosen, Proctor, Morrow-Howell, & Staudt, 1995). Practitioners rarely use single-case research designs, administer standardized instruments to assess intervention effects, or avail themselves of other widely endorsed evaluation approaches (Richey, Blythe, & Berlin, 1987). Furthermore, as Wakefield and Kirk (1996) aptly observed, "ironically, the scientist–practitioner model, which was designed as a method of integrating practice and research, may have exacerbated the tension between practitioners and researchers" (p. 94). Clearly, new approaches to practice and research integration are needed to improve the effectiveness of social work interventions.

Many of the factors accounting for the failure of previous efforts to significantly increase evidence-based social work practice are circumvented by guideline development. Unlike earlier approaches, clinical guideline utilization requires neither that practitioners become researchers nor even expert consumers of research findings (Howard & Jenson, 1999a). Instead, guidelines offer practitioners explicit recommendations for client care and "support scientifically-based decision-making in a manner that reduces clinical uncertainty and otherwise assists social workers in their day-to-day activities" (Howard & Jenson, 1999b, p. 284). If disseminated appropriately, guidelines are more accessible to practitioners than research findings, which are typically published in scientific journals primarily for other researchers.

Professionals in other fields have increasingly turned to guidelines as the exponential growth of the scientific literature has made it nearly impossible to remain apprised of practice-relevant research advances in more than a few areas. In addition, the methodological and analytical approaches used in social and health services research have become highly sophisticated, further complicating efforts to translate research findings into practice directives. Social workers, like practitioners in other services professions, would benefit from clearly written, evidence-based guidelines for client care. Guidelines for social workers should, of course, reflect the traditional concerns and outcomes of interest to social workers and their clients. Furthermore, guideline development within social work might also provide the basis for a rapprochement between social work researchers and practitioners that would serve the profession and its clients well.

Guideline development to date has primarily occurred within medicine and allied health professions. Thus, our discussion of definitional, historical, procedural, and evidentiary considerations relating to practice guidelines will, of necessity, draw heavily on the findings of research in these areas. The strengths and limitations, desirable attributes, and effectiveness of guidelines are examined briefly below, and potential barriers to guideline development within social work are identified.

TERMINOLOGY

More than a decade ago, the Institute of Medicine (IOM) defined practice guidelines as "systematically developed statements to assist practitioner and patient decisions about appropriate health care for specific clinical circumstances" (1990, p. 1). This influential characterization emphasized the formal process by which guidelines are developed and the central role that guidelines play in helping clients, as well as practitioners, to make more informed health care decisions. Shapiro, Lasker, Bindman, and Lee (1993) described guidelines as "statements of approaches to care for particular clinical situations" (p. 223). Proctor and Rosen (2000) referred to guidelines as sets of "systematically compiled and organized knowledge statements that are designed to enable practitioners to find, select, and use the interventions that are most effective and appropriate" (p. 1).

A number of closely related terms are often used synonymously with the concept of "practice guidelines." Practice options are intervention recommendations similar to guidelines, but less prescriptive because they derive from less abundant or convincing scientific evidence than guidelines. Conversely, practice standards are more prescriptive than guidelines and should be adhered to in most cases, because they rest on a large body of persuasive scientific findings (Eddy, 1990). Few standards are found in medicine, and virtually no practice standards would be available to social workers. Practice parameters was the phrase originally preferred by the American Medical Association, because it highlighted the flexibility of guideline recommendations and the need for practitioners' decisions to be tailored to the unique needs of individual clients. Other groups have referred to preferred practice patterns, emphasizing that excessively rigid practice recommendations cannot ensure quality because clients' needs are never identical (Sommer, Weinter, & Gamble, 1990). Critical pathways and practice algorithms generally refer to graphical depictions of clinical care in relation to the treatment of clients sharing a common disorder or life problem. Highlighted in these linear representations are decision nodes, which are points in the client care process where one or a combination of alternative assessment or treatment approaches is selected from available options.

All of the terms discussed above refer to codified "recommendations for clinical care based on research findings and the consensus of experienced clinicians with expertise in a given practice area" (Howard & Jenson, 1999b, p. 285). Although guidelines are characterized in many ways, most definitions emphasize their common aim of improving practitioner and client decision making by describing appropriate indications for specific intervention approaches.

PRACTICE VARIATION AND GUIDELINE DEVELOPMENT

Although rudimentary guidelines have been published for more than 50 years, the origin of the modern guideline development movement is traceable to Wennberg's seminal studies of "small area" variations in physicians' professional practices (Wennberg, Blowers, Parker, & Gittelsohn, 1977; Wennberg, Freeman, & Culp, 1987; Wennberg & Gittlesohn, 1973). Wennberg and colleagues found significant, and seemingly inexplicable, local variations in the medical treatments physicians provided to patients presenting with similar health problems. For example, Wennberg and associates (1977) noted a 13-fold difference between the lowest and highest age-adjusted per capita rates of tonsillectomy across 13 hospital services areas in Vermont.

Many health care analysts argued that the significant unexplained practice variation identified by Wennberg and colleagues (1977, 1987) reflected inappropriate under- or overutilization of selected medical interventions (IOM, 1992). Unjustifiably low or excessive rates of health care technology utilization were, in turn, believed to result from physicians' uncertainties about the appropriate indications and support for various health care interventions. Policymakers promoted practice guidelines as one promising means by which practitioner uncertainty could be reduced, medical interventions standardized, and the processes and outcomes of client care thereby improved (Walker, Howard, Lambert, & Suchinsky, 1994).

With the establishment of the Agency for Health Care Policy and Research (now the Agency for Health Care Research and Quality) in 1989, the federal commitment to guideline development was formalized.

Evidence-based practice guidelines were subsequently incorporated into many of the health care reform proposals floated in the 1990s. Perhaps the most contentious issue to arise in early policy discussions of guidelines concerned the extent to which guidelines were primarily health care cost-containment mechanisms vis-à-vis instruments to improve the quality of client care. Although optimal methods for guideline development and dissemination had not been established and guideline effectiveness remained much in dispute, guideline development efforts, notwithstanding, were vigorous during the 1990s.

GUIDELINE DEVELOPMENT IN MEDICINE AND ALLIED PROFESSIONS

Practice guidelines have proliferated ever more widely in recent years. Woolf (1998) estimated that more than 26,000 such guidelines had been developed. The American Medical Association's (AMA) *Clinical Practice Guidelines Directory* (2000) listed over 2,000 guidelines developed by more than 90 organizations. By any reckoning, it is clear that the development of evidence-based guidelines has been a growth industry within medicine over the past two decades, and there is no indication that the rate of guideline development has begun to slow.

Other developments during the 1990s possibly reflected growing practitioner interest in evidence-based practice—new journals commenced publication, including *Evidence-Based Medicine, Evidence-Based Nursing, Evidence-Based Mental Health,* and *Abstracts of Clinical Care Guidelines,* all offering critical digests of the best available scientific findings in practitioner-friendly formats. Comprehensive reports examining guidelines were also published, including IOM's *Clinical Practice Guidelines: Directions for a New Program* (1990) and *Guidelines for Clinical Practice: From Development to Use* (1992). A special series of articles addressing evidence-based practice and clinical guidelines was published in the *Journal of the American Medical Association* (*JAMA*) and the *British Medical Journal* (Churchill, 1998). *JAMA's Users' Guide to the Medical Literature* (Guyatt & Rennie, 2002) currently includes more than 20 reports providing physicians with state-of-the-art recommendations for finding, evaluating,

and applying scientific information to their practices. New Web sites and CD-ROMs offer health care workers ready access to directories of practice guidelines (Bell, 1999). Also, excellent reviews of the many Web sites providing links to evidence-based practice guidelines are available in Morris (1999) and Owens (1998). Some of the most important Web sites are the National Guideline Clearinghouse (http://www.guideline.gov), the National Library of Medicine's Health Services/Technology Assessment Text (http://text.nlm.nih.gov/), and McMaster University's Guideline Appraisal Project (http://hiru.mcmaster.ca/cpg/default.htm).

Although guidelines are most abundant in medicine, they are increasingly found in dentistry (Shugars & Bader, 1995), nursing (Thomas, McColl, Cullum, Rousseau, & Soutter, 1999), pharmacy (Kirk, Michael, Markowsky, Restino, & Zarowitz, 1996), and other health care professions. Guideline development has proceeded much more slowly in clinical and counseling psychology and has taken a substantially different tack. Members of the American Psychological Association chose to publish a template for constructing and evaluating guidelines designed to be used by various programs and organizations, rather than develop guidelines themselves (Howard & Jenson, 2000). The American Psychological Association has also conducted reviews to identify empirically supported treatments and disseminated knowledge of efficacious treatments to practitioners (Chambliss & Hollon, 1998; Chambliss et al., 1996).

In addition to professional groups, organizational and governmental bodies actively involved in guideline development include individual hospitals and hospital networks; health maintenance organizations; insurance and utilization review companies; voluntary organizations such as the American Cancer Society; federal agencies, including the National Institutes of Health, Food and Drug Administration, Centers for Disease Control and Prevention, and Congressional Office of Technology Assessment; state governmental bodies; and various research organizations and policy "think tanks" (Howard & Jenson, 1999b).

Undoubtedly, many practicing social workers would benefit from reading guidelines developed by other professional groups. For example, the American Psychiatric Association (APA) has developed excellent guidelines for assessment and treatment of nicotine dependence, substance abuse, and major mental disorders including schizophrenia and depression (for example, APA, 1993, 1995). The Department of Veterans Affairs recently published guidelines for clinical work with clients living with bipolar affective disorder (Bauer et al., 1999). Useful guidelines for practitioners conducting child custody evaluations, assessing children who may have been physically or sexually abused, or treating youth with attention, hyperactivity, or conduct problems have been developed, for example, by the American Academy of Child and Adolescent Psychiatry (1997). Although these and other guidelines are of some utility to social workers, guidelines developed by and for social workers are needed, given that the clients, practice contexts, and intervention goals and outcomes of social work practice often differ from those of other helping professions (compare Thyer, 2000, for a dissenting view).

As the number of organizations creating guidelines and the intensity of guideline development efforts continue to grow, it is inevitable that intra- and interprofessional disputes will arise over guideline recommendations. Clinical psychologists and psychiatrists, for example, argued vehemently about the relative roles accorded pharmacotherapy and psychotherapy in APA's (1993) guideline for the treatment of major depression (McIntyre & Zarin, 1996). Scant experience has been gained to date with methods that might forestall or help resolve these conflicts, but multidisciplinary guideline development panels might serve a useful function in this regard.

Guideline Development Methods
Most early guideline development efforts were conducted by small, homogeneous groups of experts who achieved some poorly specified level of consensus regarding treatment recommendations following a desultory review of the pertinent scientific evidence (Walker & Howard, 1996; Walker, Howard, Walker, Lambert, & Suchinsky, 1995). Guideline development currently is often a complex and costly enterprise involving scores and sometimes hundreds of professionals, laypersons, and members of key affected groups.

Initially, guideline development panels (usually from 12 to 20 members) are composed by the sponsoring professional or governmental organizations, and panel chairpersons are selected. Little is known presently about optimal protocols for panel constitution (IOM, 1992). Special care is then taken to identify and collect all of the scientific evidence bearing on the practice issue of interest (often with the aid of a National Library of Medicine literature search and ancillary efforts to identify important unpublished reports). Scientific findings are abstracted from the obtained reports and explicitly weighted by reviewers on the basis of their likely validity, which is a function of the methodological rigor of the studies reporting them. Meta-analytic techniques are used, when possible, to quantitatively summarize the findings of relevant studies in select areas. The intervention recommendations constituting the guidelines are assigned confidence or validity ratings on the basis of the strength of the evidence supporting them. Guideline recommendations supported by a number of large, randomized clinical trials receive the highest ratings, whereas the lowest ratings are assigned to guidelines based only on expert consensus.

Successive rounds of reviews by representatives of client groups, professional organizations, and practice and research experts in the area of interest help further refine the guidelines. Initial guideline development often requires several years to complete. Review and revision of guidelines should then be undertaken every three to five years and on an ad hoc basis in response to important scientific advances (APA, 2000).

Published guidelines vary greatly in quality. Shaneyfelt, Mayo-Smith, and Rothwangl (1999) evaluated 279 guidelines published between 1985 and 1997 and found that, on average, they met fewer than 11 of the 25 standards recommended by a group of guideline development experts. For example, relatively small proportions of guidelines described formal methods for combining scientific evidence and expert opinion (7.5 percent), attempted to quantify intervention costs (14.3 percent), or discussed how patient preferences were incorporated into guideline recommendations (21.5 percent). Shaneyfelt and colleagues (1999) identified some improvement in guideline quality over time, although even recently developed guidelines generally met fewer than half of the criteria experts believed they should. Ward and Grieco (1996) found that only a few of the 34 Australian guidelines they examined met a majority of the 18 criteria across which they were assessed.

In an effort to improve guideline quality, several attempts have been made to develop "guidelines for guidelines." The AMA instituted a guideline recognition program to promote rigorous guideline development methods and published a document articulating standards for AMA guideline certification (AMA, 2000). The IOM (1992) also published a useful instrument for assessing clinical practice guidelines.

Clearly, much has been learned in medicine about optimal approaches to guideline development and dissemination. Social work should likewise employ the best available methods to develop its guidelines. Through implementation of rigorous protocols for social work guideline development, many of the potentially deleterious effects of guidelines could be avoided altogether and their salubrious effects enhanced.

Desirable Attributes of Practice Guidelines

Although many extant guidelines are of poor quality, general agreement has recently been reached regarding the characteristics that guidelines should possess (Howard & Jenson, 1999b). Most observers agree that guidelines should be developed by a public process that is

- open to critical scrutiny based on scientific evidence of the highest quality—randomized clinical trials and other controlled studies
- comprehensive—including all indications for an intervention
- specific—explicitly describing the contexts in which an intervention is recommended
- inclusive—addressing all considerations relevant to the treatment of a given client problem
- reliable—largely reproducible given the same data and development methods
- valid—leading to the practice and cost outcomes projected for them (IOM, 1990, 1992).

Guidelines should also be easy to understand and use, developed by a multidisciplinary process including client representatives, undergo regular revision, and be widely and effectively disseminated as described below. Guidelines should also be explicit regarding the cross-cultural relevancy of treatments and interventions. Given that many studies have excluded women and people of color, guidelines should clearly state with whom the treatments and interventions were empirically tested. Further, existing guidelines do not specify culturally sensitive treatment modifications (Videka-Sherman, 2000) or needed modifications in practitioner and setting characteristics (Zayas, 2000). With the profession's commitment to cultural competency in services delivery, social work is uniquely positioned to address these gaps in guideline development.

As stated previously, relatively few guidelines evidence even a majority of the desirable features experts believe they should. Nonetheless, social workers should ensure that the guidelines they create meet basic standards for guideline quality. To this end, they may choose to use one of the instruments developed by the AMA (2000) or IOM (1992) to guide and evaluate their developmental efforts. Although the guidelines developed by other professions have generally failed to address the roles that gender, social class, and ethnicity should play in shaping treatment decisions, social workers will undoubtedly pay particular attention to these considerations.

Guideline Effectiveness

Recent reviews from medicine indicate that practice guidelines can significantly influence practitioner behavior and improve client outcomes. Grimshaw and Russell (1993) evaluated 59 methodologically sound investigations, noting that only four studies failed to report statistically significant positive effects of guidelines on the processes of client care. Although only 11 studies had examined whether guidelines exerted beneficial effects on the outcomes of care, nine of these studies reported significant positive findings. More recently, Worrall, Chaulk, and Freake (1997) found that of the 13 studies they identified that examined guidelines' effects on patients' outcomes in primary care settings, five reported significant positive findings. We are aware of no evaluations of guideline effectiveness in psychology or social work. However, findings in medicine clearly indicate that guidelines can increase the effect of professional interventions. Therefore, it seems reasonable to think that guidelines could have a similarly positive effective on social work practice. Thus, it is our opinion that social work guidelines should be developed and evaluated to determine whether they promote more effective social and human services interventions.

Guideline Dissemination and Implementation

Prior research suggests that passive diffusion of practice guidelines via publication of guidelines in professional journals or through mass mailings to members of professional organizations is largely ineffective (Gates, 1995). Dissemination methods actively involving professionals in guideline promotion have proved substantially more effective than passive approaches. Active dissemination strategies include use of local practitioner opinion leaders to direct guideline implementation efforts (Cohen, Halvorson, & Gosselink, 1994), local adaptation of guidelines developed nationally (Puech, Ward, Hirst, & Hughes, 1998), interactive workshops (Borduas, Carrier, Drouin, Deslauriers, & Tremblay, 1998), small-group consensus building (Karuza, Calkins, & Feather, 1995), and clinical auditing and practitioner profiling, which provide practitioners with systematic feedback about their practice behaviors (Eagle et al., 1990). Financial incentives in the form of reduced malpractice premiums for practitioners who adhere to guidelines have also been effective under some conditions (Pierce, 1990). Although social workers have not often been the subject of malpractice actions, there is evidence that suits against social workers are increasingly common (Reamer, 1995).

Oxman, Thomson, Davis, and Haynes (1995) reviewed 102 studies of interventions designed to change practitioners' behaviors such that clients' outcomes were improved. They concluded that passively disseminated intervention recommendations were ineffective, whereas actively disseminated interventions were associated with a range of outcomes, including strong positive findings. If social workers develop practice guidelines, they should disseminate them using one or more of the active dissemination methods mentioned above.

Strengths and Limitations of Evidence-Based Guidelines

Prior experience in medicine and allied fields suggests that practice guidelines have a range of potentially positive and deleterious effects (Walker et al., 1994). Among the positive consequences of guidelines, proponents contend that guidelines empower clients to make more informed health care decisions; help increase practitioners' use of effective and comparatively cost-effective interventions; assist third-party payers in utilization review, performance rating, and reimbursement determinations; facilitate the development of measurable clinical indicators that can be used to assess organizational quality; and serve important didactic functions, including the provision of state-of-the-art practical intervention recommendations that can be incorporated into more traditional instructional approaches.

Chief among the many concerns raised with regard to guidelines is that they might promote formulaic or "cookbook" practices if they were made the legal standard of care or were otherwise rigidly implemented. Guideline opponents also argue that the cost savings associated with guidelines would not likely be substantial, given the costs that their development and implementation entail. Some critics contend that guidelines might even *increase* the costs of care by identifying service interventions that are currently underutilized. Practitioners are also concerned that guidelines might be used against them for inculpatory purposes in malpractice litigation, diminish interest in practice careers if they overly constrain clinical work, and discourage additional research activity if they are taken as the "final word" in a given practice area. In addition, practitioners are concerned that guidelines might serve to decrease the use of clinical techniques that appear to be effective but have not yet been empirically validated, and lead to diminished practitioner creativity. These and other criticisms of guidelines have been examined in detail elsewhere (Howard & Jenson, 1999a, 1999b, 2000).

Perhaps the fairest summary of the evidence to date is that is known very little about the long-term consequences of practice guidelines. Additional empirical work is needed to assess the full range of effects guidelines might exert on professional social work practice. In medicine, early reports suggested that physicians generally viewed guidelines as threats to professional autonomy that were primarily developed for cost-containment purposes. Recent surveys indicate that physicians now see many advantages to guidelines, although they continue to express some ambivalence in relation to guidelines (Carrick et al., 1998; James, Cowan, Graham, & Majeroni, 1997). It is likely that social work practitioners will also greet practice guidelines with cautious skepticism, if not overt hostility, at least until they gain some experience with their use and perceive them as beneficial to their clients. If guidelines help make practice easier and more effective, as they appear to have done in medicine, and are not unduly rigid, social workers may well also come to view them favorably.

BARRIERS TO GUIDELINE DEVELOPMENT IN SOCIAL WORK

At least six potential barriers to social work guideline development have been identified (Howard & Jenson, 1999a). These include (1) paucity of the social work scientific literature, (2) high costs associated with guideline development and dissemination, (3) perceived ineffectiveness of guidelines, (4) multiple roles, diverse settings, and agency-based nature of social work practice, (5) practitioners' resistance to and (6) ethical concerns about guidelines.

Limited Breadth and Depth of Social Work Research

Kirk (1999) argued that the social work research database is "too thin" to support an ambitious guideline development effort. Although this observation is clearly true if the "social work literature" is narrowly defined, it is also true that research findings are abundant in some practice areas. For example, more than 500 alcohol-dependent treatment outcome studies had been published by 1980 (Hester & Miller, 1995; Walker & Howard, 1996; Walker et al., 1995). Although virtually none of these studies was conducted by a professional social worker or published in a social work journal, the findings of these investigations are indisputably germane to social work practitioners working in the chemical dependency area. There are other practice domains of central importance to social work, such as delinquency and youth violence, that have received significant research attention (Jenson & Howard, 1999), demonstrating the efficacy of particular interventions, such as multisystemic therapy with juvenile offenders and substance-abusing youth. Social work contributes significantly to practice in the chemical dependency and juvenile justice areas; thus, these and other reasonably well-developed research areas would be logical foci for early guideline development efforts within social work.

High Costs of Guideline Development and Dissemination

The high costs of guideline creation, which currently range from thousands to millions of dollars, may pose the greatest challenge to guideline development within social work. It is unlikely that social work can mount a serious guideline development effort unless social work researchers, practitioners, and professional organizations are willing to donate significant quantities of time and other resources to their development. Thyer (2000) contended that it would be preferable, from a cost-effectiveness perspective, for social workers to sit on the guideline development panels of other professions rather than develop profession-specific guidelines. The former approach might increase the extent to which social work knowledge is incorporated into the practice guidelines of other fields, at a relatively low cost to the profession. Proctor and Rosen (2000) have argued compellingly for profession-specific guidelines and have outlined a research agenda critical to the development, dissemination, and application of social work guidelines. Given the unique treatment populations and intervention outcomes of interest to social workers, we believe that profession-specific guidelines should be developed. Such guidelines could do much to increase the effectiveness of social work practice and enhance the perceived credibility of the profession. Of course, efforts to develop profession-specific guidelines would in no way prevent social workers from contributing to the guideline creation efforts of other professions. The exigencies of guideline development within social work require that vigorous lobbying efforts be undertaken so that funds can be garnered from public and private sources to support the development and testing of pilot social work practice guidelines.

Perceived Ineffectiveness of Guidelines

Several other perceptions may undermine guideline development in social work. Some theorists question the potential utility of guidelines, asking whether it is reasonable to expect that practitioners will read, remember, and use guidelines (Kirk, 1999). Others doubt whether guidelines will contribute to improved client outcomes, even if they are widely adopted (Wambach, Haynes, & White, 1999). On the basis of accumulated findings in the health professions, properly constructed and disseminated guidelines could be easy to use and would improve practice effectiveness. However, questions regarding the utility and efficacy of social work guidelines can be resolved only with further research.

Multiple Roles, Diverse Settings, and Agency-Based Nature of Social Work Practice

Another concern raised by some social workers is that the complex institutional and organizational contexts of social work practice, and the many professional roles that social workers play, may complicate efforts to develop guidelines (Jackson, 1999). Noting that social work often takes place in a multidisciplinary context, Jackson (1999) suggested that the agreement and support of other professionals in the agency are important to the successful implementation of practice guidelines. We concur with Jackson that the potential for cross-disciplinary disagreements and conflicts must be addressed (see Howard & Jenson, 1999a, for a detailed discussion). However, the implications of the environmental context for practice guidelines are substantially greater than considered heretofore.

Agency practices, structural characteristics, and values influence the attitudes, perceptions, and behaviors of social workers and other professionals in their employ (Cherin, 2000; Jinnett & Alexander, 1999; Kirsh, 2000). They can also influence the quality of services that social workers and other human services workers provide (Glisson & Hemmelgarn, 1998). Even the exercise of expertise in an organization is mediated by the context of organizational routines and values (Mueller & Dyerson, 1999). Thus, we anticipate that key characteristics of the agency will mediate the implementation of social work practice guidelines. Before practice guidelines are implemented in an agency or other institutional context, it is important to evaluate the "fit" of practice guidelines with current policies and practices, and then make facilitative changes accordingly at the organizational, departmental, and work group levels.

Practitioner Resistance

As has been true for other professions, resistance to social work guidelines will likely be substantial, particularly early in the guideline development enterprise. However, findings in the health professions suggest that practitioners' acceptance of guidelines grows as they gain experience with them. For example, a recent survey of 2,000 physicians found that a majority strongly agreed that guidelines were convenient sources of information and important educational tools (Hayward, Guyatt, Moore, McKibbon, & Carter, 1997). Efforts to promote guidelines within social work will be enhanced by the involvement of practitioners at every level of development, dissemination, and evaluation. Furthermore, the flexible nature of guideline recommendations and the primacy of practitioner judgment in individualizing clinical decision making should be emphasized.

Ethical Concerns

Practitioners in social work and other helping professions generally object to guidelines created primarily to contain costs rather than to improve client care (Wambach et al., 1999). Even when they are developed solely to improve the quality of care, clinicians' ethical perspectives influence their acceptance of guidelines. Clinicians who embrace utilitarianism generally support guidelines, whereas those holding deontological ethical views tend to reject systematic treatment recommenda-

tions that might lead to less than optimal care for any given client. Guidelines are generally designed with the average or prototypical client in mind, offering intervention recommendations that produce the greatest good for the largest number of clients. On occasion, however, guidelines may suggest treatments that are less than ideal given the particular circumstances of the case at hand.

We believe that useful guidelines are not rigidly prescriptive and that practitioners should always make individualized treatment decisions on the basis of their consideration of guideline recommendations, patient preferences, and other relevant sources of information. The existence of guidelines does not obviate the need for, or overriding importance of, informed practitioner judgments in client care.

EVIDENCE-BASED SOCIAL WORK PRACTICE: RECENT DEVELOPMENTS

Practice guidelines have proliferated widely in recent years. A wealth of findings indicates that guidelines promote evidence-based practice and enhance client outcomes. Unlike previous efforts to foster scientifically rationalized practice methods, which required that practitioners become researchers or expert consumers of research knowledge, guideline implementation does not constitute as significant an additional burden to busy practitioners. Of course, practitioners will expend time accessing, reading, and learning to apply guidelines. However, evidence-based guidelines should increase practice effectiveness, as they reduce practitioners' uncertainties about preferred treatment approaches to given client problems. Guidelines might also promote "more informed client decision-making, improve clinical training in schools of social work, encourage more cost-effective and accountable practice, and help codify current knowledge in controversial practice areas" (Howard & Jenson, 1999a, p. 350).

Although social work has been slow to develop guidelines, there is emerging support for evidence-based practice within the profession. The George Warren Brown School of Social Work at Washington University, St. Louis, Missouri, recently became the first school within the profession to formally adopt evidence-based practice as one of the core principles guiding its capacity-building efforts with students. The publishers of *Social Services Abstracts* began compiling "best practices" for social workers in their *Social Services InfoNet* Web site (www.socservices.com), which they hope will "represent excellent guidelines for those engaged in direct practice, program planning, and policy making" (*Social Services Abstracts,* 2000, p. 1).

With respect to guidelines specifically, two developments are noteworthy. In 1999 a special issue of *Research on Social Work Practice,* the official journal of the Society for Social Work and Research, addressed basic questions related to clinical practice guideline development in social work (Howard & Jenson, 1999a, 1999b). A far broader set of concerns related to social work guideline development was subsequently examined in a national conference convened at Washington University (Proctor & Rosen, 2000).

Although the dissemination of intervention guidelines and related efforts to promote evidence-based practice should do much to enhance the effectiveness and credibility of social work, there are many remaining issues to be resolved. It is currently unclear, for example, who should develop social work guidelines, which practice areas should be the foci of early guideline development efforts, how the best social work guidelines might be developed, and how clients' preferences and cost considerations will be incorporated into guidelines. Guidelines could significantly shape social work practice in the approaching years, but only time, additional resources, and well-planned development, implementation, and evaluation efforts will make evidence-based guidelines a reality in social work.

REFERENCES

American Academy of Child and Adolescent Psychiatry. (1997). Practice parameters for the forensic evaluation of children and adolescents who may have been physically or sexually abused. *Journal of the American Academy of Child and Adolescent Psychiatry, 36,* 423–442.

American Medical Association. (2000). *Clinical practice guidelines directory.* Chicago: Author.

American Psychiatric Association. (1993). Practice guidelines for the treatment of patients with major depressive disorder. *American Journal of Psychiatry, 150*(Suppl.), 1–26.

American Psychiatric Association. (1995). Practice guideline for the treatment of patients with substance use disorders: Alcohol, cocaine, opioids. *American Journal of Psychiatry, 152*(Suppl.), 30–50.

American Psychiatric Association. (2000). Practice guideline for the treatment of patients with major depressive disorder (rev.). *American Journal of Psychiatry, 157*(Suppl.), 1–45.

Bauer, M. S., Callahan, A. M., Jampala, C., Petty, F., Sajatovic, M., Schaefer, V., et al. (1999). Clinical practice guidelines for bipolar disorder from the Department of Veterans Affairs. *Journal of Clinical Psychiatry, 60,* 9–21.

Bell, C. C. (1999). Electronic DSM-IV plus, version 3.0. *Journal of the American Medical Association, 282,* 387.

Bloom, M., Fischer, J., & Orme, J. G. (1995). *Evaluating practice: Guidelines for the accountable professional* (2nd ed.). Needham Heights, MA: Allyn & Bacon.

Borduas, F., Carrier, R., Drouin, D., Deslauriers, D., & Tremblay, G. (1998). An interactive workshop: An effective means of integrating the Canadian Cardiovascular Society clinical practice guidelines on congestive heart failure into Canadian family physicians' practice. *Canadian Journal of Cardiology, 14,* 911–916.

Carrick, S. E., Bonevski, B., Redman, S., Simpson, J., Sanson-Fisher, P., & Webster, F. (1998). Surgeons' opinions about the NHMRC clinical practice guidelines for the management of early breast cancer. *Medical Journal of Australia, 169,* 300–305.

Chambliss, D. L., & Hollon, S. D. (1998). Defining empirically supported therapies. *Journal of Consulting and Clinical Psychology, 66,* 7–18.

Chambliss, D. L., Sanderson, W. C., Shoham, V., Bennett-Johnson, S., Pope, K. S., Crits-Christoph, P., et al. (1996). An update on empirically validated therapies. *Clinical Psychologist, 49,* 5–18.

Cherin, D. A. (2000). Organizational engagement and managing moments of maximum leverage: New roles for social workers in organizations. *Administration in Social Work, 23,* 29–46.

Churchill, R. (1998). Critical appraisal and evidence-based psychiatry. *International Review of Psychiatry, 10,* 344–352.

Cohen, S. J., Halvorson, H. E., & Gosselink, C. A. (1994). Changing physician behavior to improve disease prevention. *Preventive Medicine, 23,* 284–291.

Eagle, K. A., Mulley, A. G., Skates, S. J., Reder, V. A., Nicholson, B. W., Sexton, J. O., et al. (1990). Length of stay in the intensive care unit: Effects of practice guidelines and feedback. *Journal of the American Medical Association, 264,* 992–997.

Eddy, D. M. (1990). Designing a practice policy: Standards, guidelines, and options. *Journal of the American Medical Association, 264,* 992–997.

Fischer, J. (1976). *Effectiveness of social casework.* Springfield, IL: Charles C Thomas.

Gambrill, E. (1999). Evidence-based practice: An alternative to authority-based practice. *Families in Society, 80,* 341–350.

Gates, P. E. (1995). Think globally, act locally: An approach to implementation of clinical practice guidelines. *Journal of Quality Improvement, 21,* 71–85.

Glisson, C., & Hemmelgarn, A. (1998). The effects of organizational climate and interorganizational coordination on the quality and outcomes of children's service systems. *Child Abuse & Neglect, 22,* 401–421.

Grimshaw, J. M., & Russell, I. T. (1993). Effect of clinical guidelines on medical practice: A systematic review of rigorous evaluations. *The Lancet, 242,* 1317–1322.

Guyatt, G., & Rennie, D. (Eds.). (2002). *Users' guides to the medical literature: Essentials of evidence-based clinical practice.* Chicago: AMA Press.

Hayward, R. S., Guyatt, G. H., Moore, K. A., McKibbon, K. A., & Carter, A. O. (1997). Canadian physicians' attitudes about and preferences regarding clinical practice guidelines. *Canadian Medical Association Journal, 156,* 1715–1723.

Hester, R. K., & Miller, W. R. (1995). *Handbook of alcoholism treatment approaches* (2nd ed.). Needham Heights, MA: Allyn & Bacon.

Howard, M. O., & Jenson, J. M. (1999a). Barriers to development, utilization, and evaluation of social work practice guidelines: Toward an action plan for social work. *Research on Social Work Practice, 9,* 347–364.

Howard, M. O., & Jenson, J. M. (1999b). Clinical practice guidelines: Should social work develop them? *Research on Social Work Practice, 9,* 283–301.

Howard, M. O., & Jenson, J. M. (2000, May 3–5). *Clinical guidelines and evidence-based practice in medicine, psychology, and allied professions.* Paper presented at the Developing Practice Guidelines for Social Work Interventions: Issues, Methods, and Research Agenda Conference, George Warren Brown School of Social Work, Washington University, St. Louis.

Howard, M. O., & Lambert, M. D. (1996). The poverty of social work: Deficient production, dissemination, and utilization of practice-relevant scientific information. In P. R. Raffoul & C. A. McNeese (Eds.), *Future issues for social work practice* (pp. 270–292). Boston: Allyn & Bacon.

Institute of Medicine. (1990). *Clinical practice guidelines: Directions for a new program.* Washington, DC: National Academy Press.

Institute of Medicine. (1992). *Guidelines for clinical practice: From development to use.* Washington, DC: National Academy Press.

Jackson, V. H. (1999). Clinical practice guidelines: Should social work develop them? A response to Howard & Jenson. *Research on Social Work Practice, 9,* 331–337.

James, P. A., Cowan, T. M., Graham, R. P., & Majeroni, B. A. (1997). Family physicians' attitudes about and use of clinical practice guidelines. *Journal of Family Practice, 45,* 341–347.

Jenson, J. M., & Howard, M. O. (Eds.). (1999). *Youth violence: Current research and recent practice innovations.* Washington, DC: NASW Press.

Jinnett, K., & Alexander, J. A. (1999). The influence of organizational context on quitting intention: An examination of treatment staff in long-term mental health settings. *Research on Aging, 21,* 176–204.

Karuza, J., Calkins, E., & Feather, J. (1995). Enhancing physician adoption of practice guidelines: Dissemination of influenza vaccination guideline using a small-group consensus process. *Archives of Internal Medicine, 155,* 625–632.

Kirk, J. K., Michael, K. A., Markowsky, S. J., Restino, M. R., & Zarowitz, B. J. (1996). Critical pathways: The time is here for pharmacist movement. *Pharmacotherapy, 16,* 723–722.

Kirk, S. A. (1999). Good intentions are not enough: Practice guidelines for social work. *Research on Social Work Practice, 9,* 302–310.

Kirsh, B. (2000). Organizational culture, climate and person–environment fit: Relationships with employment outcomes for mental health consumers. *Work, 14,* 109–122.

Klein, W. C., & Bloom, M. (1995). Practice wisdom. *Social Work, 40,* 799–807.

McIntyre, J. S., & Zarin, D. A. (1996). The role of psychotherapy in the treatment of depression: Review of two practice guidelines. *Archives of General Psychiatry, 53,* 291–293.

Morris, K. (1999). Virtual guiding lights. *The Lancet, 353,* 1450–1451.

Mueller, F., & Dyerson, R. (1999). Expert humans or expert organizations. *Organization Studies, 20,* 225–256.

Owens, D. K. (1998). Use of medical informatics to implement and develop clinical practice guidelines. *Western Journal of Medicine, 168,* 166–175.

Oxman, A. D., Thomson, M. A., Davis, D. A., & Haynes, R. B. (1995). No magic bullets: A systematic review of 102 trials of interventions to improve professional practice. *Canadian Medical Association Journal, 153,* 1423–1431.

Pearson, K. C. (1998). Role of evidence-based medicine and clinical practice guidelines in treatment decisions. *Clinical Therapeutics, 20,* C80–C81.

Persons, J. B. (1995). Why practicing psychologists are slow to adopt empirically-validated treatments. In S. C. Hayes, V. M. Follette, R. W. Dawes, & K. E. Grady (Eds.), *Scientific standards of psychological practice* (pp. 141–157). Reno, NV: Context Press.

Pierce, E. C. (1990). The development of anesthesia guidelines and standards. *Quality Review Bulletin, 16,* 16–64.

Proctor, E., & Rosen, A. (2000, May 3–5). *The structure and function of social work practice guidelines.* Paper presented at the Developing Practice

Guidelines for Social Work Interventions: Issues, Methods, and Research Agenda Conference, George Warren Brown School of Social Work, Washington University, St. Louis.

Puech, M., Ward, J., Hirst, G., & Hughes, A. (1998). Local implementation of national guidelines on lower urinary tract symptoms: What do general practitioners in Sydney, Australia, suggest will work? *International Journal for Quality in Health Care, 10,* 339–343.

Reamer, F. G. (1995). Malpractice claims against social workers: First facts. *Social Work, 40,* 595–601.

Richey, C., Blythe, B., & Berlin, S. (1987). Do social workers evaluate their practice? *Social Work Research & Abstracts, 23,* 14–20.

Rosen, A., Proctor, E., Morrow-Howell, N., & Staudt, M. (1995). Rationale for practice decisions: Variations in knowledge use by decision task and social work service. *Research on Social Work Practice, 5,* 501–523.

Rothman, J., & Thomas, E. (Eds.). (1994). *Intervention research: Design and development for human services.* New York: Haworth.

Shaneyfelt, T. M., Mayo-Smith, M. F., & Rothwangl, J. (1999). Are guidelines following guidelines? The methodological quality of clinical practice guidelines in the peer-reviewed medical literature. *Journal of the American Medical Association, 281,* 1900–1905.

Shapiro, D. W., Lasker, R. D., Bindman, A. B., & Lee, P. R. (1993). Containing costs while improving quality of care: The role of profiling and practice guidelines. *Annual Review of Public Health, 14,* 219–224.

Shugars, D. A., & Bader, J. D. (1995). Practice parameters in dentistry: Where do we stand? *Journal of the American Dental Association, 126,* 1134–1143.

Social Services Abstracts. (2000). Bethesda, MD: CSA.

Sommer, A., Weinter, J. P., & Gamble, L. (1990). Developing specialty-wide standards of practice: The experience of ophthalmology. *Quality Review Bulletin, 16,* 65–70.

Thomas, L. H., McColl, E., Cullum, N., Rousseau, R., & Soutter, J. (1999). Clinical guidelines in nursing, midwifery, and the therapies: A systematic review. *Journal of Advanced Nursing, 30,* 40–50.

Thyer, B. (2000, May 3–5). *Social work should not develop practice guidelines: A response to Proctor and Rosen.* Paper presented at the Developing Practice Guidelines for Social Work Interventions: Issues, Methods, and Research Agenda Conference, George Warren Brown School of Social Work, Washington University, St. Louis.

Turnbull, J. E., & Dietz-Uhler, B. (1995). The Boulder model: Lessons from clinical psychology for social work training. *Research on Social Work Practice, 5,* 411–429.

Videka-Sherman, L. (2000, May 3–5). *Accounting for variability in client, population and setting charac-*

teristics: Moderators of intervention effectiveness. Paper presented at the Developing Practice Guidelines for Social Work Interventions: Issues, Methods, and Research Agenda Conference, George Warren Brown School of Social Work, Washington University, St. Louis.

Wakefield, J. C., & Kirk, S. A. (1996). Unscientific thinking about scientific problems: Evaluating the scientist–practitioner model. *Social Work Research, 20,* 83–95.

Walker, R. D., & Howard, M. O. (1996). The American Medical Association's guideline for primary care physicians—Alcoholism in the elderly: Diagnosis, treatment, prevention. *Abstracts of Clinical Care Guidelines, 7,* 1–3.

Walker, R. D., Howard, M. O., Lambert, M. D., & Suchinsky, R. (1994). Medical practice guidelines. *Western Journal of Medicine, 161,* 39–44.

Walker, R. D., Howard, M. O., Walker, P. S., Lambert, M. D., & Suchinsky, R. T. (1995). Practice guidelines in the addictions: Recent developments. *Journal of Substance Abuse Treatment, 12,* 63–73.

Wambach, K., Haynes, D. T., & White, B. (1999). Practice guidelines: Rapprochement or estrangement between social work practitioners and researchers. *Research on Social Work Practice, 9,* 322–330.

Ward, J. E., & Grieco, V. (1996). Why we need guidelines for guidelines: A study of the quality of clinical practice guidelines in Australia. *Medical Journal of Australia, 165,* 574–576.

Wennberg, J. E., Blowers, L., Parker, R., & Gittelsohn, A. M. (1977). Changes in tonsillectomy rates associated with feedback and review. *Pediatrics, 6,* 821–826.

Wennberg, J. E., Freeman, J. L., & Culp, W. J. (1987). Are hospital services rationed in New Haven or overutilized in Boston? *The Lancet, 1,* 1185–1189.

Wennberg, J. E., & Gittelsohn, A. M. (1973). Small-area variations in health care delivery. *Science, 182,* 1102–1108.

Woolf, S. H. (1998). Do clinical practice guidelines define good medical care? The need for good science and the disclosure of uncertainty when defining "best practices." *Chest, 113,* 116S–171S.

Worrall, G., Chaulk, P., & Freake, D. (1997). The effects of clinical practice guidelines on patient outcomes in primary care: A systematic review. *Canadian Medical Association Journal, 156,* 1705–1712.

Zayas, L. H. (2000, May 3–5). *Educational, research, and service-delivery factors in the implementation of practice guidelines: Response to Videka-Sherman paper.* Paper presented at the Developing Practice Guidelines for Social Work Interventions: Issues, Methods, and Research Agenda Conference, George Warren Brown School of Social Work, Washington University, St. Louis.

Matthew O. Howard, PhD, John Bricout, PhD, Tonya Edmond, PhD, and **Diane Elze, PhD,** are professors, George Warren Brown School of Social Work, Campus Box 1196, One Brookings Drive, Washington University, St. Louis, MO 63130-4899; **Jeffrey M. Jenson, PhD,** is professor, Graduate School of Social Work, 2148 South High Street, University of Denver, Denver, CO 80208.

For further information see
Empirically Based Interventions, *2003;* Expert Systems

Key Words

| clinical guidelines | evidence-based practice |
| empirical practice | practice guidelines |

F

The Future of Social Work Practice
Elizabeth J. Clark

The coming decade looks very promising for the future practice of social work. In 2001 *U.S. News and World Report* listed social work as one of the 21 best career choices for the decade (Spake, 2001). Similar reports were issued by *Ebony* magazine ("Best Jobs," 2002) and *Time* magazine ("The Coming Job Boom," 2002). Perhaps more important, the U.S. Bureau of Labor Statistics, based on the 2000–2010 National Employment Matrix, which collects information from employers, predicts that the need for social workers will increase at two times the rate of the need for other professions (U.S. Bureau of Labor Statistics, 2000). That translates into a need for 30 percent more social workers in 2010 than in 2000.

NASW frequently receives inquiries about the current number of practicing social workers. The total number is elusive because available data sets are inadequate to answer the question authoritatively. To complicate matters further, individuals who lack any formal social work training identify themselves as social workers. In 2000 the U.S. Bureau of the Census reported that 845,000 respondents self-identified as social workers (Barth, 2001). Yet, nearly 280,000 of these persons have less than a bachelor's level education. Of the 354,000 with bachelor's degrees who self-identify as social workers, it is not possible to tell whether they hold social work degrees.

The figure most often used is that there are 604,000 professionally trained social workers practicing in the United States (U.S. Bureau of Labor Statistics, 2000). The Association of Social Work Boards (ASWB) reported that 320,000 social workers hold licenses (ASWB, 2001). That means over 200,000 practicing social workers are not licensed or work in positions not requiring a social work license. While licensing has helped to separate professionally trained social workers from others, the legal protection of the use of the title of "social worker" is limited.

According to the Bureau of Labor Statistics projections, the number of professionally trained social workers will increase to 822,000 in 2008 (U.S. Bureau of Labor Statistics, 2000). Major growth areas include child and school social work (27 percent increase), medical and public health social work (31 percent increase), and mental health–substance abuse social work (39 percent; O'Neill, 2002a).

DEFINITION OF SOCIAL WORK PRACTICE
In 1973 NASW adopted a current definition of social work practice that is still quite relevant today:

> Social work practice consists of the professional application of social work values, principles, and techniques to one or more of the following ends: helping people obtain tangible services; counseling and psychotherapy with individuals, families, and groups; helping communities or groups provide or improve social and health services; and participating in legislative processes. The practice of social work requires knowledge of human development and behavior; of social, economic, and cultural institutions; and the interaction of all these factors. (NASW, 1973, pp. 4–5)

The profession of social work clearly dominates the field of mental health (O'Neill,1999b). In a study conducted by the U.S. Substance Abuse and Mental Health Services Administration, there were more clinically trained social workers than the combined totals of the other three core mental health professions—psychiatrists, psychologists, and psychiatric nurses (see Figure 1). Social workers often are the only mental health professionals available in some rural areas.

Other characteristics of the profession include the facts that social work is still predominately female (72 percent; Barth, 2001) and still predominately white. If one believes that the characteristics of the profession should somewhat model the gender and ethnic makeup of its clients, the demographics would be 40 percent

FIGURE 1
Social Workers Provide Mental Health Services

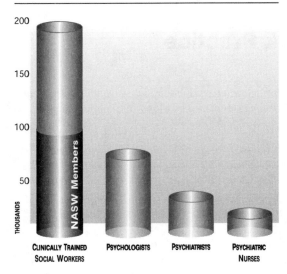

SOURCE: *Mental Health, United States, 1998,* U.S. Substance Abuse and Mental Health Services Administration.

males and 40 percent ethnic minorities (Sheafor, 2001). Clearly, the profession has a long way to go to meet these diversity goals.

ISSUES FACING THE PROFESSION TODAY

Public Image
The centennial of social work was celebrated in 2000. Despite these years of service and commitment, the profession of social work lacks a coherent public image. Burrelle's Information Services (2002) regularly identifies between 1,500 to 2,000 mentions of social work in the media each month, and an analysis by the Public Affairs Office of NASW noted that 80 percent of these articles are positive.

Many of the remaining 20 percent identify problems in the child welfare system. All too often individuals identified in these stories are not professionally trained social workers. Instead, they are performing in a social work capacity or hold a social work title without appropriate training or professional social work supervision.

Some of the difficulty in establishing an acceptable public image may be the result of the breadth of the profession and the diversity of the field. For example, there are more than 40 professional organizations of social work in the United States. Many of these groups represent areas of practice such as group work,

administration, or clinical social work. Other groups focus on specialty areas such as oncology, genetics, or home care social work. Still other groups are bounded by ethnic background or a common identity (National Association of Black Social Workers, National Association of Puerto Rican/Hispanic Social Workers) or by a commonality or viewpoint such as a religious preference (National Association of Christians in Social Work).

Although diversity of practice specialties is an exciting part of the profession, it can lead to confusion in public understanding of what the profession of social work entails, or what social workers do, or why social workers should be reimbursed for their services. This has consequences for how social work is viewed by employers, by third-party payers and legislators, and by the public.

Although social work competencies by educational degree have been identified (Morales & Sheafor, 1997), a lack of clear differentiating criteria for levels of practice is another area of divisiveness within the field. Recent data from the Council on Social Work Education (CSWE) indicated that there were 417 baccalaureate programs, 131 master's programs, and 62 doctoral programs in social work (Lennon, 2001). It is sometimes difficult to demonstrate boundaries or discrete areas of social work practice based on educational levels. This issue has been a particular area of contention in some state licensing laws and in some agency hiring practices.

Every state now has some licensing or state regulation for social workers; yet, licensing, too, lacks uniformity. In 2001 the ASWB identified 24 different titles for licensed social workers in the United States (ASWB, 2001). This adds further confusion to the field.

Another concern for the profession is that state licensing fees can be costly, and as a result some social workers are discontinuing their memberships in their professional associations, citing competing expenses as a deciding factor. This again may lead to less cohesiveness of the profession.

Other professions are broad based and have many specialty areas. Medicine, law, nursing, and teaching are such examples. When people are asked what doctors or lawyers or nurses or teachers do, they seem comfortable with their understanding of these professions. Social work needs to be able to provide a similar understanding of the profession to the general public.

In 1998 NASW convened a summit of social work organizations (NASW, 1998) with the goal of strengthening communication and coalescing the power of the social work profession into a more effective catalyst for change. A second summit of the same group was held in late 2002 with the goal of discussing the image and influence of the profession. Participants agreed to explore forming a social work coalition to advance the field and set a collaborative advocacy agenda. One outcome was to determine the feasibility of a national and coordinated public image campaign for the social work profession.

Salary Issues

Another serious issue facing social workers today is the salary structure of the profession. One recent report by economist Michael Barth (2001) noted that social work salaries have been essentially flat for the past decade. When compared with salaries of other counseling professions, social workers are the lowest paid of the professions. Similarly, increases in social work salaries have not kept pace with other professions such as teaching and nursing.

While recent comprehensive salary surveys are not available, a Practice Research Network survey completed by NASW in 2000 does provide some information about the salaries of NASW members. The median salary for members employed full time in a social work position was $45,600. (NASW, 2000c). This varied by gender; men had a median salary of $54,290 compared with women, who had a median salary of $43,510 (NASW, 2002b). Differences in median income were also noted across different types of organizations. Income for practitioners in solo practice was the highest at $62,500. Outpatient mental health agencies and nursing home–hospice settings had the lowest median salaries at $38,610 and $38,500, respectively. While these salaries may appear respectable, it should be noted that the average number of years of practice for respondents in the NASW survey was 16 years. Entry-level positions generally are much lower than the median.

Despite lower than desired salaries, the need for social work services continues to rise. Some geographic and practice areas are already reporting a social work shortage, especially in the areas of child welfare and geriatric social work (Deichert, 2002). There also is concern about the possible retirement of a large cohort of experienced social workers that will be concomitant with the aging of the baby boom generation. While we are graduating record numbers of social work professionals, new graduates naturally lack the years of experience of the retiring cohort.

Managed Care and Reimbursement Issues

The shift since the late 1980s from a largely fee-for-service system to a managed care–dominated system "has resulted in revolutionary changes in the organization, accessibility, and delivery of health and mental health services in the United States" (Roberts, 1998, p. 506). The changes have been so sweeping that while the main concern has been health and mental health virtually all social work specializations, all social work students, and all social work practitioners have been directly or indirectly affected (CSWE/NASW, 1996), including child welfare and juvenile justice. From a macro perspective managed care's stringent cost-cutting efforts have had a more negative result for mental health services than for general medicine. For instance, the Hay Group's 1999 analysis of trends in employer health care expenditures found that from 1988 to 1997 general health care benefits declined 7 percent while behavioral health care benefits dropped 54 percent. Behavioral health as a percent of the total health care benefit from employed people plummeted from 6.2 percent in 1988 to 3.1 percent in 1997 (O'Neill,1999a).

For social workers in various work settings, the results of managed care vary. For those in clinical practice or wishing to start a clinical practice, managed care has been a mixed blessing. In the 1980s only a handful of insurance companies reimbursed individual social workers for clinical work. Now virtually all reimburse individual practitioners. However, managed care has brought with it a large hassle factor: difficulty and delays in getting treatment approved, in getting reimbursed, and in demands for confidential patient information to justify treatment that raise ethical questions. Reimbursement rates have been flat for years while costs have increased. Some social workers have fled private practice or moved to self-pay practices.

Approximately half of Medicare recipients, who comprise a major portion of social workers' clients, are enrolled in managed behavioral health care plans (Rosenbaum, 2002). Many Medicaid recipients receive care in community health and mental health programs converted to managed care. Problems arising as public systems have converted to managed care include inadequate care coordination, slight knowledge of special populations, and insufficient coverage. In some cases managed care only reimburses social workers for time spent with clients, leaving community support programs without a funding source. Much has been written in the social work literature regarding managed care services—issues of quality, access, and community networks; regarding values—adherence to ethical standards, advocacy for marginalized peoples, and cultural competence; regarding professionalism—supervision and graduate education; and regarding issues of professional status—good faith working relations with managed care companies, morale, career development, job satisfaction, and retention (Davidson, Davidson, & Keigher (1999).

The social work literature abounds with admonitions for social workers to enhance their business expertise to demonstrate outcomes and cost savings lest they be marginalized or eliminated in the profit-driven managed care environment. A new mind-set needs to be established in which each psychosocial service is related to income generated and cost savings in which services that do not generate income are valued on the preventive costs they save the organization (Dziegielewski & Holliman, 2001). Managed care has demonstrated beyond doubt that to thrive social workers need to find ways to translate their interventions into cost savings and articulate them in ways that managed care can understand.

CHALLENGES FOR FUTURE SOCIAL WORK PRACTICE

In addition to professional social work issues such as image, salaries, and reimbursement, other challenges face the practice of social work in the future.

- Social workers need to be able to identify and react to new needs in a timely fashion, which requires that they stay aware of societal trends and political decisions. Social workers are adept in the person-in-environment approach to interventions (Karls & Wandrei, 1994) but sometimes are not as familiar with state and national policy decisions that can have an impact on the well-being of their clients. Social work practice has always been grounded in activism, and in times of conservative government and limited resources for the general good, social work activism will need to be increased.

- Another challenge may be serving the same populations, but the populations will have more intense needs. School violence and gang behavior are examples of the increasing intensity of needs of the adolescent population. Similarly, as people live to older ages, the need for expanded health and mental health services is guaranteed. The increase in the number of elderly will also require creative approaches to home care, nursing home care, and end-of-life care.

- The increased need for health and mental health services is coupled with increasing disparities in access to care. There now are 42 million people in the United States who are uninsured (U.S. Senate Committee on Finance, 2001). There are many more who are underinsured. Also, as former Surgeon General David Satcher noted in his mental health report (1999), the mental health needs of racial and ethnic populations are not being addressed by our current mental health system. Disparities in mental health services create significant challenges for African Americans, Hispanic Americans, Asian Americans, and Native Americans. In general, persons from minority groups are less likely to seek or receive outpatient mental health treatment. Cost is a major barrier, and it is made worse by the lack of parity coverage for mental health services. Social work will need to redouble efforts to effect universal health insurance coverage and national mental health parity.

- As federal, state, and local funding continues to be limited or decreased for service agencies, agency staff will have to assume more of a development role. Agency fundraising activities may compete with social work service delivery. Responsibility for fundraising can add to the stress level of the workplace. It is difficult for staff to live with uncertainty, and downsizing of staff and limited services may result if the agencies are unsuccessful in their development efforts.

- Information and technology are transforming how social workers and other health–mental health professionals are practicing. As McCarthy and Clancy (2002) noted most things social workers do face-to-face, including counseling, home visits, supervision, consultation, research, and tracking, can now be done electronically.

There is much debate about how one can maintain an adequate professional–client relationship online. The Clinical Social Work Federation has taken a position firmly in opposition to Internet-based practice (ASWB, 2002). Others such as Giffords (1998) see potential benefits to the possibilities of electronic counseling, including equalization of power and socially unstratified relationships. Still others see legal, regulatory, and ethics issues that need to be resolved. For example, Sowers and Ellis (2001) identifed technological development as one of the major future challenges for the social work profession and noted that it may represent an important departure from the ethical foundation of social work. Especially troubling may be shared client databases that are limited to standardized variables. This may result in a loss of individuality and inadequate biopsychosocial evaluations. Other issues related to expanding technology that need more study include licensing, liability, privacy, consent, and reimbursement.

- In recent years there has been a trend away from single profession service delivery to integrated services delivery networks and interprofessional practice. This trend can be seen clearly in health care, case management, and in school systems (Franklin, 2000). Multidisciplinary collaboration can strengthen an agency or program and can provide more comprehensive services for clients. On the other hand, this type of practice can lead to deprofessionalization, downsizing, lowered professional competency requirements, and ethical conflicts. Cross-training alone is insufficient. Successful interprofessional practice requires that professionals from different disciplines have clarification of each other's roles, open communication, a shared language, shared goals, shared decision making, and shared accountability (Berkman & Volland, 1997). In addition, differences in ethical standards and professional regulations will need to be discussed and resolved.

- The need for social work research and evidence-based practice has never been greater. In this age of professional encroachment, downsizing, and managed care, social work must be able to substantiate effectiveness of its interventions and its outcomes. Although social work has made progress in evidence-based practice (O'Neill, 2002b), other professions such as medicine and nursing are further advanced in this area.

- In 1991 a task force report on social work research was released from the National Institute of Mental Health (NIMH). The report noted that there was a crisis in the current development of research resources in social work and that little research was being conducted to improve effectiveness of social work services (Zlotnik, Biegel, & Solt, 2002). One outgrowth of the NIMH report was the development of the Institute for the Advancement of Social Work Research (IASWR), formed in 1993. The goal of IASWR is threefold: developing the research capacity of the profession; bridging research and practice; and informing policymaking with research (Vallianatos, 2001).

- In 1994, a second important group, the Society for Social Work and Research (SSWR), was formed. Together IASWR and SSWR have moved forward a national social work research agenda. Yet, for the profession of social work to succeed and be competitive with other helping professions, social workers from agencies and academia and from the baccalaureate to the postdoctoral level must make research and evidence-based practice a priority.

AREAS OF GROWTH FOR SOCIAL WORK PRACTICE

As noted previously practice areas such as clinical social work, health care social work, and school social work will continue to be in demand in the next decade. There are some additional growth areas that deserve special mention.

Forensic Social Work

While the term "forensic social work" is relatively new, social workers have been engaged in corrections or "correctional social work" since the 1800s. Today, however, a specialization in forensics has developed among various professional groups including nursing, psychology, psychiatry, and social work.

Many professional social workers engage in forensic social work. Barker (1995, p. 140) defines forensic social work as "the practice specialty in social work that focuses on the law and educating law professionals about social welfare issues and social workers about the legal aspects of their objectives." Roberts and Brownell (1999, p. 360) operationally define forensic social work as "policies, practices, and social work roles with juvenile and adult offenders and victims of crime."

The potential scope of forensic social work practice is broad, and many areas of intervention could come under these headings. These include family violence; child, partner, and elder abuse; substance abuse; juvenile justice; and adult corrections. Also, areas such as health/mental health care in jails and prisons, probation and parole, and community-based corrections can be considered forensic social work.

Some social workers are working as expert witnesses and as court-appointed mediators. Others work in interdisciplinary teams in law practices, in legal aid, in public defenders' offices, or as court staff (Pierce, Gleason-Wynn, & Miller, 2001). Some may term this subspecialty "judicial social work" (Lynch & Mitchell, 1995) or social work practice in a law environment.

Only a few social work graduate programs offer a specialization in forensic social work. However, more than a dozen schools of social work have developed interdisciplinary programs with law schools as well as joint degree programs in social work and law (Roberts & Brownell, 1999).

As crime and violence continue to increase in our society, more social work services will be required. Social workers who practice in the criminal justice or legal system may not self-identify as forensic or judicial social workers, but, taken collectively, this area of practice is an important growth area for the profession.

Corporate Social Work
The social work profession has long been concerned about the conditions of employment and the impact of work for individuals. Occupational social work is the field of practice serving individuals, families, groups, and managers related to a work setting. It also covers organizational developments, training, policy formulation, and administration.

Perhaps the best-recognized activities in occupational social work are employee assistance programs (EAPs). This direct practice with individuals, families, and special populations includes areas such as crisis intervention, assessment of personal problems, counseling for substance abuse, retirement counseling, and relocation counseling (NASW, 2000b).

In addition to direct practice in EAPs, other social work roles in the corporate sector are developing (Mor-Barak & Bargal, 2000). For instance, an increasing number of social workers direct or work in foundations. Since foundations generally have educational and service missions, this is an easy fit for social workers. Other areas such as fundraising, contract management, marketing, public affairs, or media management are newer uses of social work skills.

Social work ownership of either for-profit or not-for-profit human service businesses is increasing. According to the U.S. Census Bureau service industries data, the percentage of day care, home health care, and other social service facilities that were for-profit grew rapidly during the last decade (Frumkin & Andre-Clark, 1999).

For-profit firms have become dominant in day care and home health care, and there is much growth in ownership of case management and welfare-to-work human services firms. Social workers with an expertise in relevant areas are moving into these ownership roles and may be referred to as entrepreneurial social workers. Also, social workers may be outstanding marketers for advertising human services firms.

Working in a corporate setting requires that social workers have a clear understanding of their code of ethics. This will be necessary to resolve conflicts that may arise with the corporate agenda.

National and International Practice
The profession of social work has played an important role in shaping the social and economic fabric of the United States. Social workers have been on the forefront of the civil rights movement, the women's movement, and the antipoverty movement. Social workers have worked hard for social security, Medicare, disability rights, the humane treatment of persons affected by mental illness, and children's rights. They have had an impact on reducing domestic violence, substance abuse, and discrimination in many forms. Today, they are working on important issues such as welfare reform, disparities in health and mental health care, and employment nondiscrimination.

These are not issues specific only to our country. Social work is a multifaceted profession that recognizes the interrelated needs of individuals, communities, countries, and societies. The military and economic upheavals throughout the world affect many of the clients social workers serve. For example, the terrorist attacks in New York, Washington, DC, and Pennsylvania on September 11, 2001, will have repercussions for years, even decades, to come. Although many social workers were in the forefront of the disaster response and provided services for persons directly affected by the terrorists' attacks, the need for social work intervention will continue for many years.

September 11 also pointed out the need for more and better disaster preparedness for social work and other professional groups. Social workers have important skills needed during large-scale natural or man-made emergencies and disasters. These include crisis intervention, bereavement counseling, posttraumatic stress management, resource identification, and community organizing.

Social workers also have skills applicable to international affairs and international activities. Civil rights are the bedrock of the social work profession, and issues in this country and abroad, including areas of displacement, immigration, forced migration, and the effects of war, all have implications for social work practice.

On the international front, social workers around the world are concerned for the poor and vulnerable populations of all countries. The growing social and economic disparities surrounding quality of life must be addressed. Added to this is the overarching challenge of violence worldwide. Social workers are committed to preventing war and to opposing violence in all forms. They will need to work with other professions to find constructive and nonviolent means to deal with international conflicts.

Social work has an inherent international quality. There are social workers and social work organizations around the world. As noted by the NASW Task Force on International Development, social workers have skills, knowledge, and training applicable to international development. These include the ability (NASW, 2000a, p. 1):

- to understand political realities and the relationship of economic development to social well-being or to social disruption
- to translate policy into workable projects
- to set goals and establish objectives
- to understand the potential effects of policies on individuals, groups, and communities
- to mobilize local communities to engage in activities that enhance their well-being
- to be sensitive and to work effectively with cultural influences on behavior and values within and between cultures and societies
- to facilitate discussions, to analyze, and to solve problems, and engage in collaborative projects
- to understand and analyze organizational structures and communities and their effects on individuals.

The profession of social work has much to offer on both the national and international fronts. Social workers will need to become more active partners in the search for solutions to problems not only in the United States, but around the globe.

Political Social Work

Social workers have always been activists who bring about social change to enhance the lives of their clients and for the betterment of society. The *NASW Code of Ethics* (NASW, 1999, section 6.04) requires social workers to engage in social and political action to foster social justice, to be aware of the impact of politics on practice, and to act to prevent and eliminate discrimination in all forms.

Federal, state, and local politics all contribute to creating the context in which social workers practice. Over a decade ago, Figueira-McDonough (1993) outlined four primary methods of policy practice: social policy analysis, social action, social reform through litigation, and legislation advocacy.

An example of effective policy analysis is the Blue Ribbon Panel on Economic Security established by NASW in 2002 to work on welfare reauthorization concerns. It was decided that NASW would advocate through priority goals for welfare reauthorization: reducing poverty, increasing assistance to families with barriers such as mental illness or domestic abuse, and enhancing the capacity of the welfare workforce. Resulting policy analysis was translated into advocacy efforts and lobbying strategies. An NASW lobbyist and panel members have met with legislators and legislative staff and participated in press conferences. Additionally, letters to editors of newspapers around the country have been written (Stoesen, 2002).

Engaging in social action for policy development and change has been a long tradition for the profession of social work. This includes coalition building to increase public awareness and to effect social change at all levels. In the current conservative context, social workers will need to have an even stronger voice to identify and rectify the important social and economic issues of the times (Brill, 2001).

Social work through litigation is a growing area for NASW. This includes working with NASW chapters to identify test cases, preparing supporting documentation, and monitoring court decisions (Hagen, 2002). Recent topics addressed by NASW include client confidentiality for social workers, protection from sexual harassment, and rights of gay and lesbian parents.

Social workers nationwide continue to play an important role in legislative activity, with legislative advocacy as the most frequently used method of policy practice. NASW and most state chapters have legislative networks and political action arms to support political candidates who support social work values. For the 2002 elections, eight field organizations were hired by NASW in states with important federal Senate races. Their primary role was to acquire voter support for these candidates in their respective states.

Another important goal for the profession is to endorse and support social work candidates for election. Currently, there are six social workers in Congress. Additionally, it is estimated that 166 social workers hold elected political office around the country. Many more social workers are employed as legislative aides and lobbyists (NASW, 2002a).

The activities of social workers in the political arena are critical to ensure that the voice of social work is heard in all aspects of the policymaking process. Whether social workers are doing coalition work; performing policy analysis, development, and advocacy; lobbying; or holding political office, the profession of social work must be well represented to shape a better future for the nation.

Gerontology Social Work

For many years the helping professions have been aware of the "graying of America" and of its potential impact on social service agencies. The first of the baby boomers are only a decade away from reaching age 65, and both the health and mental health communities are ill-prepared to handle the increased need for services (CSWE, 2001).

The disconnect between the need and supply of gerontology social workers is well documented. The National Institute on Aging (1987) projected a need for 50,000 social workers trained in gerontology in 2000 and 70,000 by 2010. Less than 10 percent of that number are currently available.

An added concern is that social workers lack the formal training they need to provide quality care for older persons (CSWE, 2001). Additionally, few social work degree programs offer direct gerontology content (Scharlach, Damron-Rodriguez, Robinson, & Feldman, 2000). Without a trained and adequate cadre of professionals dedicated to gerontology, appropriate services simply will not be available as needed.

Areas for social work intervention with the elderly are broad and diverse. On the health side there are issues surrounding adaptation to chronic illness, adjustment to disability and physical limitations, end-of-life concerns, compliance with medical regimens, long-term care, wellness, and quality of life.

On the mental health side are issues related to loss, cognitive deficits, depression, substance abuse, chronic mental illness, and suicide prevention. These health and mental health issues are further complicated by economic and social issues such as poverty, inadequate housing, isolation, elder abuse, transportation issues, lack of access to care, lack of adequate insurance, and age discrimination.

Gerontology social workers are needed in agency settings, nursing homes, hospitals, and hospices. They are needed in community centers, in case management programs, in community development that targets the elderly, and in resource development. They also need to be in research programs that study issues of aging and the needs of the elderly, and at the policy table where state and national decisions affecting the elderly are made.

Social workers can choose to work in gerontology at any level of practice from the micro to the macro. There are abundant opportunities for individuals with bachelor's, master's, and doctoral degrees in social work. In the future, almost all social workers will be required to have basic competencies in gerontology. Gerontology social work is not just a potential growth area for social work practice; it is becoming a practice imperative.

CONCLUSION

The profession of social work has a long and illustrious tradition. For over a century, social workers have been present in times of crisis and in times of relative calm. They have brought about positive change on many levels and have contributed greatly to the betterment of society. There is no reason to think that this social work tradition will not continue. To the contrary, there is every reason to believe that the need for social work services and the role of the social work profession will only increase in the future.

This growth will not be without challenges and pitfalls. Despite these, there is great opportunity. There are new practice areas to explore and new fields of expansion for the profession. Students are entering the field in record numbers. Other individuals are choosing social work as a second career. Social work skills are broad and applicable in many occupational settings, and social workers' competencies are transferable from the micro to the macro level. Most important, social workers' core values and ethical base remain strong, central, and essential for the practice of social work in the future.

REFERENCES

Association of Social Work Boards. (2001). New reporting gives ASWB real count of social workers. *ASWB Association News*, pp. 1, 3.

Association of Social Work Boards. (2002). E-therapy questions remain from 2001. *ASWB Association News*, pp. 3, 5.

Barker, R. L. (Ed.). (1995). *The social work dictionary* (4th ed.). Washington, DC: NASW Press.

Barth, M. C. (2001). *The labor market for social workers: A first look*. New York: John A. Hartford Foundation.

Berkman, B., & Volland, P. (1997). Health care practice overview. In R. L. Edwards (Ed.-in-Chief), *Encyclopedia of social work* (19th ed., 1997 Suppl., pp. 143–149). Washington, DC: NASW Press.

Best jobs and best moves for 2002. (2002, January). *Ebony, 57*(3), 56.

Brill, C. K. (2001). Looking at the social work profession through the eye of the NASW Code of Ethics. *Research on Social Work Practice, 11*(2), 223–234.

Burrelle's Information Services Forecast Report. (2002, June 11). Correspondence with the National Association of Social Workers. Livingston, NJ: Author.

The coming job boom. (2002, May 6). *Time, 159*(18), 41.

Council on Social Work Education/National Association of Social Workers. (1996). *CSWE/NASW managed care and workforce/training: Social work strategic action plan*. Funded by SAMHSA/CMHS, No. 95MF269421.

Council on Social Work Education/SAGE–SW. (2001*). A blueprint for the new millennium*. Funded by the John A. Hartford Foundation of New York City.

Davidson, T., Davidson, J. R., & Keigher, S. M. (1999). Managed care: Satisfaction guaranteed . . . not! *Health & Social Work, 24*(3), 163–168.

Deichert, K. (2002). Social work education and the social work shortage. *NASW California News*, pp. 1, 24.

Dziegielewski, S. F., & Holliman, D. C. (2001). Managed care and social work: Practice implications in an era of change. *Journal of Sociology and Social Welfare, 28*(2), 125–139.

Figueira-McDonough, J. (1993). Policy practice: The neglected side of social work intervention. *Social Work, 38,* 179–188.

Franklin, C. (2000). Predicting the future of school social work practice in the new millennium. *Social Work in Education, 23*(1), 3–7.

Frumkin, P., & Andre-Clark, A. (1999). The rise of the corporate social worker. *Social Science and Public Policy, 36*(6), 46–52.

Giffords, E. D. (1998). Social work on the Internet: An introduction. *Social Work, 43,* 243–251.

Hagen, J. L. (2002). *Engaging in policy practice. NASW New York State Chapter update* (Vol. 26, No. 5, pp. 1, 9). Albany, NY: NASW–NYS.

Karls, J. M., & Wandrei, K. E. (Eds.). (1994). *Person-In-Environment system: The PIE classification system for social functioning problems*. Washington, DC: NASW Press.

Lennon, T. M. (2001). *Statistics on social work education in the United States: 1999*. Alexandria, VA: CSWE.

Lynch, R. S., & Mitchell, J. (1995). Judicial social worker practice model: Paradigm for a specialty and curricula enhancement. *Journal of Law and Social Work, 5*(1), 25–40.

McCarthy, D., & Clancy, C. (2002). Telehealth: Implications for social work practice. *Social Work, 47*(2), 153–161.

Morales, A. & Sheafor, B. W. (1997). *Social work: A profession of many faces*. Boston: Allyn & Bacon.

Mor-Barak, M. E., & Bargal, D. (2000). Human services in the context of work: Evolving and innovative roles for occupational social work. *Administration in Social Work, 23* (3/4), 1–11.

National Association of Social Workers. (1973). *Standards for social service manpower*. Washington, DC: Author.

National Association of Social Workers. (1998). Summary and recommendations. In *Social work summit: A historic convening of the profession*. Washington, DC: Author.

National Association of Social Workers. (1999). *NASW Code of Ethics*. Washington, DC: Author.

National Association of Social Workers. (2000a). *A framework for the social work profession in international development*. Washington, DC: National Presidential Initiative Task Force.

National Association of Social Workers. (2000b). Occupational social work. In *Social Work Speaks* (5th ed., pp. 229–233). Washington, DC: NASW Press.

National Association of Social Workers. (2000c). Social work income. In *Practice research network: Informing research and policy through social work practice* (Vol. 1, No. 1). Washington, DC: Author.

National Association of Social Workers. (2002a). Selected characteristics of social workers in elected offices [Online]. Available: http://www.socialworkers.org/pace/characteristics.asp

National Association of Social Workers. (2002b). Social work income 2. In *Practice research network: Informing research and policy through social work practice* (Vol. 1, No. 6). Washington, DC: Author.

National Institute on Aging. (1987). *Personnel for health needs of the elderly through the year 2020*. Bethesda, MD: U.S. Department of Health and Human Services, Public Health Service.

O'Neill, J. V. (1999a, April). At managed care's table, physical care takes lion's share. *NASW News*, p. 3.

O'Neill, J. V. (1999b, June). Profession dominates in mental health. *NASW News*, pp. 1, 8.

O'Neill, J. V. (2002a, May). Better labor data on social work sought. *NASW News*, pp. 1, 8.

O'Neill, J. V. (2002b, April). Evidence for practice is readily available. *NASW News*, p. 9.

Pierce, C. T., Gleason-Wynn, P., & Miller, M.G. (2001). Social work and law: A model for implementing social services in a law office. *Journal of Gerontology Social Work, 34*(3), 61–71.

Roberts, A. R. (1998). Epilogue: Inhumane versus humane managed care. In G. Schamess & A. Lighthouse (Eds.), *Humane managed care?* Washington, DC: NASW Press.

Roberts, A. R., & Brownell, P. (1999). A century of forensic social work: Bridging the past to the present. *Social Work, 44*(4), 359–369.

Rosenbaum, J. D. (2002). Health policy report: Medicaid. *New England Journal of Medicine, 346*(8), 635–640.

Satcher, D. (1999). *1999 mental health: A report of the surgeon general* [Online]. Available: http://www.surgeongeneral.gov/library/mentalhealth/cre/default.asp

Scharlach, A., Damron-Rodriguez, J., Robinson, B., & Feldman, R. (2000). Educating social workers for an aging society: A vision for the 21st century. *Journal of Social Work Education, 36*(3), 521–538.

Sheafor, B. W. (2001). Three decades of baccalaureate social work: A grade card on how professionalization of the BSW has played out. *The Journal of Baccalaureate Social Work, 6*(21), 25–43.

Sowers, K. M., & Ellis, R. A. (2001). Steering currents for the future of social work. *Research on Social Work Practice, 11*(2), 245–254.

Spake, A. (2001). Social work returns to its roots. In *Best graduate schools*. U.S. News & World Report [Special edition].

Stoesen, L. (2002, July). House vote doesn't stem welfare push. *NASW News*, p. 4.

U.S. Bureau of Labor Statistics. (2000). *Occupational outlook handbook, 2000–2001 edition*. Available: http://www.umsl.edu/services/govdocs/ooh20002001/8.htm

U.S. Senate Committee on Finance. (2001). *Living without health insurance: Hearings before the Committee on Finance, United States Senate* [Online]. Available: http://finance.senate.gov/72189.pdf

U.S. Substance Abuse and Mental Health Services Administration. (1999). *Mental health, United States, 1998*. Washington, DC: Author.

Vallianatos, C. (2001, November). Stronger partnership on research emerges. *NASW News*, p. 5.

Zlotnik, J. L., Biegel, D. E., & Solt, B. E. (2002). The Institute for the Advancement of Social Work Research: Strengthening social work research in practice and policy. *Research on Social Work Practice, 12*(2), 318–337.

Elizabeth J. Clark, PhD, ACSW, MPH, is executive director of the National Association of Social Workers.

For further information see

Clinical Social Work; Direct Practice Overview; Ethics and Values; Generalist and Advanced Generalist Practice; International and Comparative Social Welfare; Long-Term Care; Prevention and Wellness; Primary Prevention Overview; Progressive Social Work; Social Work Practice: History and Evolution; Social Work Profession: History; Social Work Profession Overview

---

Key Words

gerontology social work	political social work
managed care	social work practice

H

Harassment

See Sexual Harassment, *Volume 3*

Hate Crimes

Nancy A. Humphreys

Attacks motivated by hatred, known as hate crimes, have always been part of the fabric of human culture; yet recent events in the United States have focused public attention on this phenomenon. As is true for many social issues, hate crimes are complex and create a variety of dilemmas for social workers. They are the nexus of prejudice, which we abhor, and freedom, which we esteem. When bigotry underlies a violent act, the two are inexorably linked, particularly when recognized as a separate category of crime. The perpetrators of violent hate crimes are considered not just for their acts, but also for their thoughts. Although social workers are fundamentally committed to ending oppression in all its forms, and the violence to which it can lead, "criminalizing hate" is not without consequences that should be of concern to those in the field. In his classic *Nineteen Eighty-Four* (1949), George Orwell questioned the notion of "thought crimes" and considered the potential consequences of government regulation of thought and speech. Jacobs and Potter (1998) asked whether it is appropriate to make hate a crime. Many wonder whether highlighting bias as the motivation for certain criminal acts will bring about a "Balkanization" of America.

Hate crimes not only affect their immediate victims but also, by creating fear and insecurity, often victimize all the members in the group of which the target is a member. In addition to their psychological impact, hate crimes often lead to retaliation and counterretaliation, which can lead to large-scale social unrest and even civil war, as with the ethnic cleansing in the former Yugoslavia. Because of the potential consequences, the American Civil Liberties Union has, for example, maintained that crimes motivated by hate should carry greater penalties than do other types of crimes.

For social workers, addressing hate crimes is not an easy undertaking, for it represents a clash of equally important social work values: condemning bias and promoting the freedoms of thought, speech, and choice. Because of their unique position in the field of direct services, however, social workers have much to contribute to the debate regarding how best to respond to hate crimes.

In many ways, it is counterproductive to punish those who have acted out of bias or the fear that motivates bias. Social workers in general are uncomfortable with the profound irony inherent in punishment—if you kill, we will punish you by killing you—and generally prefer treatment to punishment. They are also aware

that punishing those who act out of hate may, in fact, fuel the hatred of like-minded people. Social workers are likely to become involved with victims of hate crimes who seek help in dealing with the trauma, and, occasionally, social workers are even called on to provide counseling services for perpetrators.

McPhail (2000) noted that social workers must educate themselves about hate crimes and conduct the research that informs the current social debate if they wish to help shape policy about this important topic. The *NASW Code of Ethics* (1999) requires all social workers to endeavor to eliminate oppression of vulnerable and disadvantaged populations, and hate crimes, in many respects, are the ultimate form of oppression. These crimes target oppressed individuals and often are designed to inflict terror on a whole group.

Intergroup tensions, rivalries, bias, and hate—from the persecution of Christians by the Romans through the Nazi Holocaust, the genocide in Rwanda, or other recent efforts at "ethnic cleansing"—have shaped and sometimes defined the human experience. As McPhail (2000) has noted, hate crimes have a "long past but a short history" (p. 636). In the United States, the public has begun to take greater notice of hate crimes. The Southern Poverty

Law Center (SPLC), a leading advocacy group, report that hate crimes are committed every hour in the United States alone, and the SPLC has done much to publicize them because it views them not as isolated incidents but as "eruptions of a nation's intolerance" (SPLC, 1999, p. 1). Most important, President Bill Clinton signaled his clear support for sweeping federal hate crime legislation when in 1997 he convened the White House Conference on Hate Crimes, prompted, perhaps, by recent incidents of domestic terrorism, such as the bombing of the Federal Building in Oklahoma City and the growing number of underground militias, as well as by the two particularly brutal bias-motivated murders of Matthew Shepard, a young gay man, and James Byrd, an African American. These incidents received considerable attention in the media and were widely condemned by the public and officials alike.

This entry will examine how hate crimes are defined in federal, state, and local legislation and the controversies that complicate efforts to define, categorize, and respond to these crimes. It will also discuss ways in which social workers can influence how society, communities, and victims cope with hate crimes, treat perpetrators, and prevent or reduce the overall climate of hate.

WHAT CONSTITUTES A HATE CRIME?

A hate crime (also referred to as a bias crime or bias-motivated crime) is a criminal offense committed against a person or property that is motivated in whole or in part by the offender's bias. The Hate Crime Statistics Act (HCSA) of 1990, which asks states to report the incidence of hate crimes, defines protected classes to include race, religion, disability, sexual orientation, and ethnicity and national orientation; it does not include gender, age, class, political belief, or less common prejudices, such as style of dress.

Current legislation defines hate crimes according to certain criteria. First, hate, bias, or prejudice must have been a motivating factor in carrying out the criminal act. Second, the victim must belong to a legislatively protected group; race, for example, is a protected class in all hate crime legislation, whereas gender and sexual orientation are not. Third, there must be a process by which the act is deemed to be a hate crime. In this regard, the Federal Bureau of Investigation (FBI) urges local law enforcement to follow a two-tiered decision-making process. The first tier requires that a review be conducted by the official at the scene of the crime to determine whether

- the motive of the perpetrator is bias
- the victim perceived the bias
- there were other motivating factors
- the incident occurred on or near a religious or cultural celebration
- there are relevant demographic factors that might have created resentment or bias
- symbols were involved in the incident that are associated with hate, such as a swastika.

The second tier, which takes place away from the crime scene, is a review conducted by a larger group that analyzes the answers to these questions and determines whether the crime qualifies as a hate crime.

Levin and McDevitt (1993) proposed dividing hate crimes into three distinct types: *thrill seeking*, *reactive*, and *mission*. Thrill-seeking hate crimes do not necessarily involve a precipitating event. Acts of vandalism and desecration are typical examples, when "groups of bored young men [are] looking for a thrill" (p. 70)—violence against gays frequently falls into this category. Reactive hate crimes occur when the perpetrator perceives a personal threat and reacts to it. Unlike traditional notions of what constitutes self-defense, however, reactive hate crimes involve the perception that a specific individual is a threat to the perpetrator or to members of his or her social group. Mission hate crimes, which are rare, occur when a perpetrator tries to rid society of a perceived evil by eliminating the "offending" group altogether.

According to studies by the Bureau of Justice Assistance (U.S. Department of Justice, 1997), hate crimes are significantly more likely than other crimes to lead to injury or to the death of the victim. Whereas 11 percent of all categories of crimes involve physical assault of the victim, over 30 percent of all hate crimes involve such assaults. This percentage could be much higher, as it is generally accepted that incidents of hate crimes are underreported. Because the nature of hate crimes is to intimidate, many victims and family members do not report the crime to authorities. In fact, victims of hate crimes often face socially accepted forms of discrimination or oppression. Some fail to report because they perceive the authorities to be as biased as the perpetrator of the crime. Mistrust of those in authority is reinforced when police are accused of or are known to have violated the civil rights of members of these groups.

Another problem for gays, lesbians, and transgendered individuals in reporting they have been victims of hate crimes frequently means they must "out" themselves, with all of the attendant consequences (Cramer, 1999). Illegal aliens will rarely report a hate crime for fear of being deported. And all victims want to avoid the further humiliation that recounting the incident carries with it. Individuals who come from other countries and cultures are often the targets of hate crimes, and language problems and different cultural expectations can make it difficult for them to handle the legal procedures of prosecution. Some victims cope with the trauma of attack by denying that it happened at all or, more often, by denying that it was a hate crime. Many feel responsible, believing that their behavior caused the crime—that is, had they behaved differently, the attack would not have occurred. And there are some who simply lack the energy, or whose lives are so filled with stress and deprivation that they do not notice, or hardly notice, that the attack was motivated by hate.

Criminalizing the violent actions of bigots is not the best way to reduce or eliminate prejudice in society. It is difficult to fix motivation for a crime. In addition, a crime can be committed as a result of hatred of a person, but not necessarily because the person is a member of a hated group. Is it possible for a prejudiced individual to commit a crime against a member of a group toward which the prejudice is directed and it is not a hate crime? Is it possible to envision a situation in which such a crime might, in fact, be a crime of passion more than a hate crime?

PUBLIC POLICY AND LEGISLATION

Most crime is legislated and punished at the state and local levels. Ever since the Reconstruction period following the Civil War, however, certain acts based on racial prejudice or other forms of invidious discrimination have been criminalized in federal law, although such legislation has been limited to crimes motivated by racial or ethnic bias. Federal legislation known as the Hate Crime Prevention Act of 1969 currently requires the federal government to prosecute as a hate crime any assault based on race, religion, or national origin in which the assailant sought to prevent an individual from exercising a federally protected right, such as voting or attending school, or in which the assault occurred on federal property, such as a national park, or on an Indian reservation. Despite the mandate, the law is rarely used—there have never been more than 10 prosecutions in a single year.

A poll in 2000 by the Garin-Hart-Yang Research Group (Human Rights Campaign, 2001) showed that hate crime legislation is widely supported by the voting public, almost 66 percent of whom say they would be less likely to vote for a candidate who voted against hate crime legislation. In a study by Penn, Schoen, and Berland Associates conducted in April 1999, it was found that 91 percent of young people believe that hate crimes are "a serious national problem," and 95 percent support expanding federal law to include sexual orientation, gender, and disability as protected classes (Human Rights Campaign, 1999).

In 1990 Congress enacted the HCSA, which requires the Department of Justice to acquire data on crimes motivated by race, religion, sexual orientation, or ethnicity from law enforcement agencies across the country and to publish an annual summary of the findings. (In 1994 Congress expanded the scope of the HCSA to require the FBI to report on crimes based on "disability"; see Violent Crime Control and Law Enforcement Act of 1994.) An obvious advantage of this implementation strategy is that hate crime data are more likely to be reported as part of a mandatory report, and thereby the process eases administration at the local, state, and federal levels.

Even those who opposed federal prosecution of hate crimes supported this legislation as a way to get more reliable data concerning incidents of hate crimes. But in order to gain sufficient legislative support for the bill, it was necessary to make state and local reporting voluntary, and, not surprisingly, voluntary reporting has been uneven. Eight years after implementation, Sloan, King, and Shepard (1998) conducted a national telephone survey of local law enforcement agencies and found that states with laws requiring local authorities to report hate crimes have higher compliance rates than states where laws make reporting voluntary.

Statistics are collected on the 11 offenses that currently constitute hate crimes: murder and nonnegligent manslaughter, forcible rape, robbery, aggravated assault, burglary (breaking and entering), larceny and theft, motor vehicle theft, arson, simple assault, intimidation, and destruction, damage, and vandalism of property. It is questionable whether these criteria capture the full extent of the problem. Forcible rape, for example, is usually not reported as a hate crime (of the 89,107 forcible rapes reported in 1999, only six were classified as hate crimes; see U.S. Department of Justice, 2000), although it could be argued that, because they involve intent to control women, most rapes should be classified as such.

Following enactment of the HCSA, two additional pieces of federal legislation regarding hate crimes were passed. The first was the Violent Crime Control and Law Enforcement Act of 1994, which provides for tougher sentencing when hate can be proved (beyond a reasonable doubt, the highest standard of proof) as the motivating factor behind the commission of a crime. This legislation is limited to federal crimes, however, and typically only those that take place on federal property. Despite this obvious shortcoming, it has established solid precedent for future legislation.

The second piece of federal legislation addressing hate crimes is the Church Arson Prevention Act of 1996, which passed the U.S. Senate by a remarkable margin of 98 to 0. Enacted in response to a rash of church burnings in the rural South, most with black congregations, this law not only makes church burning a federal offense, but also increases penalties for damaging religious properties and provides compensation for rebuilding.

A growing consensus about the nature and extent of hate crimes led to increased efforts to pass federal legislation in the 106th Congress, and President Clinton's support of such legislation was a major impetus. Several bills were introduced in Congress—the Hate Crimes Prevention Act of 1999, for example, was sponsored by Representative John Conyers (D-MI) and had over 100 cosponsors. The act was intended to give the federal government power to assist state and local law enforcement in the investigation and prosecution of hate crimes. The legislation would have authorized funding to states in order to help offset the costs associated with investigating and prosecuting hate crimes. It would also have provided funding to support state and local programs designed to combat and prevent hate crimes committed by juveniles. Most important, the legislation would have made it a federal offense to commit any crime based on actual or perceived race, religion, color, national origin, gender, sexual orientation, or disability—in short, the most comprehensive list of protected classes ever proposed.

To avoid the federal government becoming the primary arbiter of hate crimes, certain restrictions were included in the legislation: The federal government could become involved in the investigation or prosecution of a particular hate crime only when the crime involved interstate commerce or when state authorities specifically requested federal involvement—and only the Attorney General or designee could authorize federal prosecution. The legislation died in committee.

In 2000, legislation was reintroduced as the Local Law Enforcement Enhancement Act and included all of the provisions of the 1999 proposal. After extensive debate and political maneuvering, the Senate eventually incorporated hate crime legislation into an amendment to a U.S. Department of Defense (DOD) authorization bill. The DOD bill was then sent to a congressional conference committee. Many advocacy groups, including the Action Network for Social Work Education and Research—a coalition of national social work organizations including the Association of Baccalaureate Social Work Directors, Council on Social Work Education, Group for the Advancement of Doctoral Education in Social Work, Institute for the Advancement of Social Work Research, National Association of Deans and Directors of Schools of Social Work, and NASW—lobbied hard for the amendment. Despite clear bipartisan support, however, the legislation again died in committee. Supporters of hate crime legislation immediately mobilized in the 107th Congress and introduced the Local Law Enforcement Enhancement Act of 2001 in the Senate. Companion legislation was introduced in the House. Both bills died in committee. In January 2002, Representative Sheila Jackson of Texas introduced HR 80, successor legislation to the 2001 bills. HR 80 was referred to the House Judiciary Committee, where, to date, no action has been taken.

Forty-five states and the District of Columbia currently have some form of hate crime legislation; Arkansas, Indiana, New Mexico, South Carolina, and Wyoming do not. State laws vary greatly in scope and are unevenly enforced. At least half do not include crimes based on sexual orientation, gender, or disability in definitions of what constitute hate crimes. The District of Columbia has the most comprehensive statute: In addition to including race, color, religion, national origin, gender, and sexual orientation, it also protects physical disability, age, personal appearance, family responsibility, marital status, political affiliation, and matriculation (Jacobs & Potter, 1998).

Several states modeled their legislation after the Anti-Defamation League's model statute (1994), which calls for two types of hate crime legislation. The first, "intimidation," includes any criminal act that is motivated by bias or prejudice based on race, color, religion, national origin, or sexual orientation and allows for "enhancing the maximum possible sentence when the offender is motivated by . . . bias"

(Jacobs & Potter, 1998, p. 33). The second is "institutional vandalism," which covers the destruction of any property belonging to religious groups.

State and local law enforcement authorities are hampered in their enforcement of state hate crime laws by a lack of resources. Yet lack of willingness on the part of the police and other law enforcement officials poses a particular problem to certain groups—gays, lesbians, and transgendered individuals, for example, who report that authorities are often virulently homophobic. Without federal oversight, local prejudices frequently remain unchallenged.

The matter of enforcement is "further muddied," as McPhail (2000) noted, by the fact that one must assess the amount of bias involved before the crime can be considered a hate crime. For an act to be considered a hate crime by the FBI, it must have been motivated "in whole or in part" by the bias of the offender against members of a protected group—leaving the degree to which the crime was motivated by bias open to interpretation. A primary example of this is the issue of assault against women. It is now generally accepted that both battery and rape are motivated by a desire to have power and control over women; therefore, these crimes could be considered as motivated by bias and fall within the hate crime category. Defining such assaults against women as hate crimes would shift the focus of responsibility for the problem from an individual to society as a whole. By the same token, it could be argued that *any* crime by a member of the majority against a member of a racial or ethnic minority could be classified as a hate crime.

Another source of ambiguity is the "but for" criterion—that is, but for the hate, the crime would not have occurred. For example, when anyone argues with a member of a protected class and the argument escalates into violence, the violent act could conceivably be classified as a hate crime. A prejudicial statement about a person's membership in a protected class would usually carry with it a presumption that bias was the motivating factor and, therefore, that a hate crime had been committed. The line between hate speech and free speech (and free thought) can be very difficult to determine, and the but for criterion opens a Pandora's box of interpretations and potential misuse.

SPECIAL ISSUES REGARDING HATE CRIMES

Except under a very narrow set of circumstances, the prosecution and punishment of criminals is the responsibility of state and local law enforcement. Any effort to expand federal police power is usually met with considerable resistance, and, as a result, every effort to add to the short list of federal crimes involves considerable controversy. Others argue that it is the responsibility of the federal government to ensure equal treatment for all U.S. citizens and that this mandate has led to placing certain civil rights crimes within the purview of the federal government; they would argue that hate crime protection is equally important.

Another source of controversy is determining which classes should be afforded protection. The inclusion of women, gays, lesbians, and transgendered individuals has been especially controversial. Federal legislation could put an end to the controversy by providing a "national definition," thereby offering protection to groups not currently recognized in state and local laws.

Referring to the complexities associated with hate crime legislation, McPhail (2000) stated, "defining, criminalizing, and punishing hate is a slippery slope which makes policy formulation, implementation, and analysis all the more difficult" (p. 640). The paramount issue is how to protect the civil rights of certain groups of people without unconstitutionally restricting the civil rights (specifically, freedom of speech) of others. In analyzing the free speech issue, Appleby and Anastas (1998) concluded that "antilocution"—verbal attacks against a group that promote discrimination—could lead to violence. The American Civil Liberties Union, a longtime defender of First Amendment rights and advocate of the rights of oppressed groups, has struggled to craft a distinction between legislation that unconstitutionally restricts free speech and legislation that legitimately punishes conduct that threatens or harms. The American Civil Liberties Union argues that this delicate balance can be maintained through enhancement of penalties for crimes that are motivated by bias (U.S. Department of Justice, 1997).

CLASSIFICATIONS OF SPECIAL CONCERN TO SOCIAL WORKERS

In 1997 the Bureau of Justice Assistance, an arm of the U.S. Department of Justice, released *A Policymaker's Guide to Hate Crimes*, in which it reported:

> While there has been a concerted effort to establish a statistical baseline of hate crimes at the national level, uncertainty still exists about whether the "hate crime rate" is rising or

falling. Nationally, the volume of hate crime incidents *seems* to have increased dramatically in 1992, stabilized and dipped during the following 2 years, then increased again in 1995. According to the FBI, State and local law enforcement agencies in 1991 reported 4,755 bias-motivated crimes. The number of reported hate crimes rose to 7,466 incidents in 1992 and to 7,581 incidents in 1993. Reported hate crimes dropped nearly 30 percent to 5,852 incidents in 1994, then increased in 1995 to 7,947 incidents. . . . However, because many agencies do not submit hate crime data or have not recorded hate crime incidents, these statistics are suspect. (p. xi)

In 2000, five states did not collect or report hate crime data. It also must be noted that there is a great disparity between official law enforcement data and data compiled by private organizations. Private organizations, particularly those that use their data to advocate for stronger hate crime legislation and protection, often include incidents that do not rise to the level of a criminal offense (U.S. Department of Justice, 1997). This is in part because these groups often hear about incidents of bias, discrimination, or actual hate crimes that have not been reported to law enforcement. This is especially true for gays, lesbians, and transgendered individuals, among the more prominent unprotected groups, who are often reluctant to go to authorities but who might be willing to cooperate with organizations that represent or are sensitive to their interests. Appleby and Anastas (1998), using both official data and data drawn from advocacy groups, reported that gays and lesbians are the most frequent victims of bias-motivated violence, although to argue over who is the most seriously affected by hate crimes keeps the focus away from the real enemy—hate and violence—and serves to foster divisiveness rather than uniting groups to work toward changing the social climate that contributes to hate in the first place.

Considerable controversy exists over whether women should be included as a protected class in terms of hate crimes. The issue poses an interesting set of problems that social workers can help address. Assault and rape can be hate crimes, but when committed against women are not usually classified as such. The resistance to including violent acts against women as hate crimes speaks to the extent to which society is committed to treating assault, battery, and rape as isolated acts against individuals rather than as an expression of bias

against women as a class. Yet there is clear evidence that discrimination against women is an important factor in the perpetuation of violence against women. Title IV of the Violence Against Women Act of 1994 includes in its definition of hate crimes assaults against women that are motivated by bias against women. However, because crimes against women are not included in the HCSA reporting criteria, it is impossible to know how many bias-motivated attacks on women have occurred.

Treating attacks against women as hate crimes would expand the options available to law enforcement and require it to take a more active role. Many studies have documented the fact that crimes against women are treated less harshly than are crimes against men, particularly heterosexual men (Wolfe & Copeland, 1994). The failure to include gender as a protected class in current federal law and much of state hate crime legislation maintains the myth that crimes against women are not bias-motivated but rather individual in nature. Enacting federal hate crime protection would strengthen the civil rights of women and reduce the laxity with which the criminal justice system sometimes approaches crimes against women. Classifying assault and rape as hate crimes could also improve victim reporting, improve law enforcement response, and, perhaps, act as a deterrent (Levin, 1999). It would also elevate such crimes from the realm of individual acts to community and social problems.

Although women have been included as a protected class in recent legislative proposals, it is not clear whether states and localities will pass such laws. The issue has been plagued by all the same reasons that have made passing hate crime legislation difficult in the first place. Angelari (1994) noted that including crimes against women could increase the controversy associated with hate crime legislation and thereby make passage of hate crime laws that much more difficult. In other words, persistent sexism and discriminatory attitudes, so evident in those opposed to the development of laws protecting women, make it difficult to sell the idea that crimes against women qualify as hate crimes.

Furthermore, the requirement of interchangeability—that is, other members of the protected class must feel threatened by each instance of a crime for it to be counted as a hate crime—would not, in the eyes of many, apply to battering between intimate partners, because not all women share the same fear that their partners will batter them. What is lost in this analysis is the fact that an effort to control even one woman fuels the overall perception that women are acceptable targets of violence and abuse.

Many believe that another factor that fuels hatred is hate groups. Social workers are also professionally involved with the perpetrators of hate crimes. Although most people associate hate crimes with so-called hate groups, in fact most perpetrators are not members of such groups; most hate crimes are committed by young white males, about one-fourth of whom are juveniles (U.S. Department of Justice, 1997). Some perpetrators act in response to their perception of being personally threatened by the success of another group, especially when that group is the target of social stereotyping and oppression—for example, anti-Semitism being fueled by the perception that Jews control money and commerce. Growing economic and political power or social status by a so-called minority group can often make that group vulnerable to those who feel threatened by its success. The term "minority" is often a misnomer. Women, for example, are included in references to minorities even though they are the numerical majority of the U.S. population. Furthermore, in some areas of the United States, European whites have become the numerical and proportional minority, even though they typically are accepted as comprising the majority. Traditionally, the term "minority" has been used to characterize ethnic and racial groups. In order to have their issues considered, women have had to act like a minority group even though they are not.

Many feminists maintain that attacks on women reflect a backlash against the growing power and independence of women and the overall success of the women's movement (Faludi, 1991). Harway and O'Neil (2000) analyzed the complex set of factors that lead men to commit violence against women (and presumably other victims)—some relate to the ways boys are socialized to manhood, which includes rigid adherence to gender roles and an inability to express or process feelings well. They suggested that an inability to empathize contributes to a tendency to dehumanize others and to act in violent and controlling ways. By encouraging men to violence—albeit controlled violence, as when men are trained for soldiering or encouraged to participate in physical and competitive sports—and at the same time requiring women to be submissive associates manliness with violence and femininity with helplessness and a need for protection.

These role prescriptions create fertile ground for an outbreak of violence against women. Yet these prescriptions, and their consequences, run parallel to the experience of all oppressed groups (Gross, 1999).

Although the vast majority of hate crimes are the acts of individuals, hate groups do play an important role in creating a climate of violence and hatred. Following the conflagration at the Branch Davidian Compound in Waco, Texas, a great deal of attention has been paid to the cults and groups that have come to be known as "hate groups." Jacobs and Potter (1998) have found that this designation might be a misnomer because the ideologies of these groups are often idiosyncratic and confused and because members of these groups have been linked to few actual hate crimes. However, this finding must be questioned in light of the evidence that many hate crimes go unreported and, therefore, that the group affiliation of the perpetrator is unknown.

The SPLC, an acknowledged excellent source for data about hate groups, has reported a dramatic decline in the number of "patriot groups," from a high of 858 in 1996 to 194 in 2000 (SPLC, 2001). Lawrence (1999), however, pointed out that it is difficult to track membership levels in these groups because individuals often leave one group and join another. And even though some hate crime perpetrators are not "officially" members of a particular group—for example, Timothy McVeigh and Terry Nichols, the convicted bombers of the Federal Building in Oklahoma City—they often are inspired by militia ideologies (D'Angelo, 1998).

IMPLICATIONS FOR SOCIAL WORKERS

The field of social work is committed to addressing the causes and consequences of oppression, and has contributed several important concepts that could offer new insights about hate crimes. Abramovitz (1991) developed the notion of "doublespeak," which involves benign-sounding terms that contain buried negative metaphors about women, race, and poverty, and how these terms have found their way into everyday speech. For example, Abramovitz argued that although the often used phrase "feminization of poverty" has brought much needed attention to the economic plight of women, the phrase "povertization of women" more accurately defines the problem. These terms desensitize us to subtle forms of bias and prejudice, but understanding their hidden meanings can help us avoid their use.

Van Soest and Bryant (1995) have developed an innovative paradigm for understanding and responding to violence that would be useful to social workers as well as inform the social debate about hate crimes and other forms of violence. The paradigm equates harmful acts against individuals with more prevalent institutional violence, which includes harmful actions by social institutions. Common examples of institutional violence include (1) poverty when it is enforced by public policy and (2) gross disparities in sentences handed out in the criminal justice system (Kilty & Joseph, 1999; Sachs & Newdom, 1999). The most prevalent form of institutional violence is generated by the structural–cultural arena, that is, when violence becomes normative and ideological.

These innovative concepts are helpful to social workers and can also inform the social debate surrounding hate crimes and other forms of violence. Social workers have a direct services interest in working with people who have been affected by hate crimes, whether as victims or as perpetrators, and there are many practical ways in which social workers can be involved (1) by evaluating and treating perpetrators of hate crimes; (2) by assisting communities to prevent hate crimes and to deal with the effects of them; and (3) by working to achieve stronger public policy regarding hate crimes. These contributions can lead to specific recommendations regarding how social workers can best respond to issues of hate crimes.

Most social workers practice in direct services jobs and in these positions are likely to encounter both victims and perpetrators of hate crimes. Greater attention has been paid to the direct services needs of victims of hate crimes than to the needs of perpetrators, who require counseling and therapy if they are to learn how to control their hateful impulses. Social work educators Arnold Barnes and Paul Ephross are among only a few social workers who have taken an interest in hate crimes and victims. In 1994, they published a study of 59 victims of hate crimes and found that more than half of the victims reported experiencing a series of attacks rather than a single episode. They also found that the attacks left the victims feeling overwhelmed, angry, fearful, and sad. About one-third of the victims reported making a significant life change, such as moving or buying a gun. Barnes and Ephross (1994) concluded that the services needs of hate crime victims are similar to the services needs of other crime victims, and that short-term interventions are best suited to meeting the intense emotional reactions of victims of hate crimes. Interestingly, they also found that in their sample a major difference between the victims of hate crimes and other crime victims is that hate crime victims do not evidence reduced self-esteem in the wake of the attack. They postulate that this may be because the motivation of the perpetrators, that is, the bias, is so clear. The victim does not have to wonder "Why me?" or "What could I have done to prevent this?"

As with all crime victims, and others who require services because of their victimization, group services can be especially helpful and effective because they enable victims to understand their shared position with others and can reinforce their sense of personal power and mastery over the events associated with the crime. Some highly traumatized victims will require long-term, individual psychotherapy to fully recover from the trauma of being attacked.

As with all direct services intervention, social workers can be an important element in helping communities cope with hate in general and with specific incidents of hate crimes and other forms of violence, and they have a responsibility to do so. The ideal social work intervention program would combine direct services with community outreach. Social workers can mobilize existing community groups as well as organize new community initiatives to involve local resources. In 1999 the SPLC released *Ten Ways to Fight Hate: A Community Response Guide,* which are as follows:

1. act, do something—apathy is interpreted as acceptance
2. unite, organize group of allies—getting others involved can empower the community
3. support victims—who often feel alone and unsupported
4. do homework—accurate information is necessary for an effective strategy
5. create alternative and do not attend hate rally—find another way to oppose viewpoints expressed
6. speak up—present balanced and in-depth analysis and avoid getting trapped into debating hate mongers in conflict-driven talk shows that tend to foment hate
7. lobby leaders
8. look long range—create ongoing mechanisms that celebrate diversity and harmony
9. teach tolerance—create programs that target children and youth who may be influenced by hate or hate groups

10. dig deeper—attack underlying issues and work to change individual prejudices.

Social workers can make use of any or all of these strategies, most of which fit in with what they are likely to be doing with community groups anyway.

The Bureau of Justice Assistance (U.S. Department of Justice, 1997) has identified several successful community models for combating hate and hate crimes, including community-based response networks, continuing education, racial and ethnic reconciliation initiatives, and improved systems for obtaining local community data on violence and hate crimes. In the opinion of the justice bureau, the most innovative approach to community problem solving involves a local or regional "hate crimes response network," which serves as an information clearinghouse on rights and services. To be successful, however, the network requires a central authority—such as a human rights commission—to coordinate the work of all the regional networks. Better data would help pinpoint the precise nature of the problem and catalog innovative community approaches to mediating the effects of hate and violence: Social workers and social work organizations can contribute to all of these efforts.

The SPLC has employed a very successful legal strategy against hate groups by filing suits against them in order to obtain financial settlements for victims and their families. In two recent cases, *Donald v. United Klans of America* (1987) and *Seraw v. Metzger* (1990), the SPLC won judgments in civil courts of $7 million and $12 million against the White Aryan Resistance and the Ku Klux Klan, respectively, for killing two African American men. An important aspect of this strategy is to deprive the organizations of their financial resources, leading them toward bankruptcy. In future cases, social workers and social work organizations can file amicus curiae briefs and serve as expert witnesses.

Other important community-based approaches are those that involve education. The SPLC has developed an innovative curriculum, *Teaching Tolerance*, which has been made widely available to schools and community groups. The Anti-Defamation League of B'nai B'rith offers the *Juvenile Diversion Program: Learning about Difference,* one of only a few programs targeted to perpetrators, especially juvenile offenders. It is a 10-week, 30-hour program of instruction, counseling, and sensitivity training. Programs that address and seek to reduce school violence have become commonplace. A study of school social workers by Astor, Behre, Wallace, and Fravil (1998) revealed that more than 60 percent of the schools represented in the sample had some form of program for violence prevention or management. Most services concentrated on skill-building activities such as anger management, whereas only 50 percent involved counseling. Only 40 percent of school social workers were involved in these school violence programs, however, and had minimum involvement in community-oriented programs that addressed community violence. Schools and school social workers working with community groups are a natural linkage and could be one way to provide violence and hate prevention interventions.

Proponents of violence prevention and other programs argue persuasively that rigorous diversion programs are more effective than imprisonment. Prisons are notorious for racial gang violence and homosexual rapes, which intensify feelings of hate and prejudice, especially in juveniles and first-time offenders.

It is undisputed that better training of law enforcement personnel is an essential component of any successful community-based effort to mitigate an atmosphere of hate and the incidence of hate crimes. After all, law enforcement personnel become involved whenever a hate crime is reported. And local law enforcement is often the community institution most knowledgeable about intergroup tensions, hostility, and potential violence. Sloan et al. (1998) surveyed a number of state and local law enforcement officials. They found that federal uniform crime reporting officers have conducted training in hate crime investigating and reporting for a large number of law enforcement officials in all 50 states as well as in the District of Columbia. Advocates for gays and lesbians have urged that, given the homophobia and heterosexism that pervade law enforcement in many communities, special content about sexual orientation be included. Sloan and colleagues (1998) also found:

> Although more than half of the training programs included sections on identifying and investigating, criminal and civil statutes, reporting, and community issues, fewer than half addressed victim impact prejudice and discrimination or cultural diversity or sensitivity. (p. 37)

Social workers can assist in training law enforcement officials as well as contributing to strengthening content in these areas.

At present, NASW lacks a policy statement covering hate crimes, although social workers have much to contribute to the debate. To play an important and significant role in the debate, they must move beyond rhetoric. They must analyze the issue more systematically, and they must seek innovative ways of dealing with hatred, violence, bias prejudice, and oppression. Social workers can play a constructive role in implementing community programs as well as developing other innovative approaches for individual, small groups, communities, and organizations to deal with violence and hate crimes. They can develop new knowledge and contribute to the systematic evaluation of antiviolence programs. A useful first step in this process would be to have serious discussions on the issue of hate crimes and to develop a position statement for the social work profession regarding this important subject. A policy statement would guide the profession's efforts to influence public policy as well as highlight how social workers and social work organizations, especially undergraduate and graduate schools of social work, could contribute and, where appropriate, direct the growing social response to violence and hate crimes. Society's concern about and attention to hate crimes would be enriched by the social work perspective.

REFERENCES

Abramovitz, M. (1991). Putting an end to doublespeak about race, gender and poverty: An annotated glossary for social workers. *Social Work, 36,* 380–384.

Angelari, M. (1994). Hate crimes statutes: A promising tool for fighting violence against women. *American University Journal of Gender & the Law, 2,* 63–105.

Anti-Defamation League of B'nai B'rith. (1994). *Hate crimes laws: A comprehensive guide.* New York: Freeman.

Appleby, G. A., & Anastas, J. W. (1998). *Not just a passing phase: Social work with gay, lesbian, and bisexual people.* New York: Columbia University Press.

Astor, R. A., Behre, W. J., Wallace, J. M., & Fravil, K. A. (1998). School social workers and school violence: Personal safety, training, and violence programs. *Social Work, 43,* 223–232.

Barnes, A., & Ephross, P. H. (1994). The impact of hate violence on victims: Emotional and behavioral responses to attacks. *Social Work, 39,* 247–251.

Church Arson Prevention Act of 1996, P.L. 104-155.

Cramer, E. P. (1999). Hate crime laws and sexual orientation. *Journal of Sociology and Social Welfare, 26,* 5–24.

D'Angelo, L. (1998). *Hate crimes.* Philadelphia: Chelsea House Publishers.

Donald v. United Klans of America, 84 S.D. Ala. 725 (1987).

Faludi, S. (1991). *Backlash: The undeclared war against American women.* New York: Crown Publishers.

Gross, E. (1999). Hate crimes are a feminist concern. *Affilia, 14,* 141–143.

Harway, M., & O'Neil, J. (2000). *What causes men's violence against women?* Thousand Oaks, CA: Sage Publications.

Hate Crimes Prevention Act of 1969, 18 U.S.C.A. § 245.

Hate Crime Statistics Act of 1990, 28 U.S.C. § 534, H.R. 1048 (1990).

Human Rights Campaign. (1999, April). *Public polling shows strong support for the local Law Enforcement Enhancement Act* [Online]. Available: http://www.hrc.org/issues/federal_leg/lleea/background/polling.asp

Human Rights Campaign. (2001, March 27). *HRC begins push to pass local Law Enforcement Enhancement Act as key members of Congress unveil measure* [Press release; online]. Available: http://www.hrc.org/newsreleases/2001/010327lleea.asp

Jacobs, J. B., & Potter, K. (1998). *Hate crimes: Criminal law and identity politics.* New York: Oxford University Press.

Kilty, K. M., & Joseph, A. (1999). Institutional racism and sentencing disparities for cocaine possession. *Journal of Poverty, 3,* 1–17.

Lawrence, F. M. (1999). *Punishing hate: Bias crimes under American law.* Cambridge, MA: Harvard University Press.

Levin, B. (1999). Hate crimes: Worse by definition. *Journal of Contemporary Criminal Justice, 15,* 6–21.

Levin, J., & McDevitt, J. (1993) . *The rising tide of bigotry and bloodshed.* New York: Plenum Press.

McPhail, B. A. (2000). Hating hate: Policy implications of hate crime legislation. *Social Service Review, 74,* 635–653.

National Association of Social Workers. (1999). *NASW code of ethics.* Washington, DC: NASW Press.

Orwell, G. (1949). *Nineteen eighty-four.* London: Secker & Warburg.

Sachs, J., & Newdom, F. (1999). *Clinical work and social action: An integrative approach.* New York: Haworth Press.

Seraw v. Metzger (Multnomah County Cir. Ct. 1990), 850 P.2d 373.

Sloan, L. M., King, L., & Shepard, S. (1998). Hate crimes motivated by sexual orientation: Police reporting and training. *Journal of Gay & Lesbian Social Services, 8,* 25–39.

Southern Poverty Law Center. (1999). *Ten ways to fight hate: A community response guide.* Montgomery, AL: Author.

Southern Poverty Law Center. (2001, Summer). *Intelligence report: Memories of "patriotism."* Montgomery, AL: Author.

U.S. Department of Justice, Bureau of Justice Assistance. (1997). *A policymaker's guide to hate crimes* [Online]. Available: www.fas.org/irp/agency/doj/162304.htm

U.S. Department of Justice, Federal Bureau of Investigation. (2000). *Uniform crime reports 1999.* Washington, DC: Author.

Van Soest, D., & Bryant, S. (1995). Violence reconceptualized for social work: The urban dilemma. *Social Work, 40,* 549–557.

Violence Against Women Act of 1994, 42 U.S.C. 13981.

Violent Crime Control and Law Enforcement Act of 1994, P.L. 103-322, H.R. 3355 (1994).

Wolfe, L., & Copeland, L. (1994). Violence against women as bias motivated hate crime: Defining the issues in the U.S.A. In M. Davies (Ed.), *Women and violence* (pp. 200–213). Atlantic Highlands, NJ: Zed.

FURTHER READING

Jenness, V., & Broad, K. (1997). *Hate crimes: New social movements and the politics of violence.* New York: Aldine de Gruyter.

Weiss, J. C. (1986). Group work approaches to "hate violence" incidents. *Social Work, 31,* 132–136.

Nancy A. Humphreys, DSW, ACSW, is professor and director, Institute for the Advancement of Political Social Work Practice, University of Connecticut School of Social Work, 1798 Asylum Avenue, West Hartford, CT 06117.

For further information see

Gay and Lesbian Adolescents; Gay Men: Direct Practice

Key Words

bias	hate crimes
civil rights	

History of Research in Social Work
David M. Austin

The development of research in social work in the United States during the past century and a half has been shaped by an uneasy alliance between social work and the social sciences. The development of social work and social science in the United States began together in the mid-19th century. As each field of work began to develop in more specific and specialized forms, there was a process of separation between the two fields. In the mid-20th century, these two fields began to come together again as social work looked to the social sciences for tools for assessing the effectiveness of social work interventions. The development of doctoral programs in schools of social work brought a new emphasis on research training using tools from the social sciences as part of the social work curriculum. In the 1980s a collaboration began between social work and the National Institute of Mental Health (NIMH). This led to the establishment of the Task Force on Social Work Research in 1988, followed by the creation of the Institute for the Advancement of Social Work Research (IASWR), NIMH funding for social work research development centers, and the development of programs of interdisciplinary research to strengthen social work practice.

In 1865 Franklin Sanborn, general secretary of the Massachusetts Board of Charities, organized the first meeting of what became the American Social Science Association (ASSA). In 1874 he invited members of state boards of charities to meet together in conjunction with the annual ASSA meeting (Bruno, 1948). Initially, members of the state boards of charities and social scientists had a shared concern with social policy and social reform, particularly with regard to the persistent problem of family poverty (MacIver, 1933). However, in 1878 members of several state boards of charities decided to establish their own organization—the National Conference of Charities and Correction. A movement to organize local charities through the creation of Charity Organization Societies (COS) in major cities had begun in the 1870s and the National Conference soon included COS leaders (Bruno, 1948). The organizers of the National Conference viewed social scientists as too preoccupied with descriptions of general social conditions and development of social theory and not sufficiently concerned with the practical management issues facing social welfare leaders (Broadhurst, 1971).

During the remaining years of the 19th century, a process of specialization developed among ASSA social scientists, leading to the creation of separate associations for historians, economists, political scientists, and sociologists (Broadhurst, 1971). ASSA held its last meeting in 1909 (Broadhurst, 1971). Within each of these social science fields, there were debates about the balance to be struck between objective, detached theory building and the application of social science interpretations to societal problems. In general, it was the emphasis on formal research and value-neutral theory building that ultimately dominated in academic social science departments. During the same period, the meetings of the National Conference of Charities and Correction reflected the steady expansion of a mixed system of social welfare in the United States. This system included philanthropic, nongovernmental social welfare organizations that focused on the problems of urban poverty and related issues, such as orphaned and abandoned children, as well as a network of state-administered institutions for orphaned children; for people with chronic disabilities, including mental illness, mental retardation, blindness, and deafness; and for "correctional" institutions (Leiby, 1978).

STUDIES OF THE CAUSES OF POVERTY

Social welfare leaders of the National Conference of Charities and Correction were concerned with discovering causes of household poverty and, particularly, of "pauperism," that is, chronic dependency. The Charity Organization Societies were concerned with applying scientific principles to the treatment of household poverty, much like early biological scientists were translating scientific knowledge about the causes of contagious diseases into treatment of those diseases. This concern for "scientific philanthropy" was a major dynamic in the development of social welfare during the latter part of the 19th century (Zimbalist, 1977).

The search for the causes of poverty was based initially on analyses of COS case records. The most important analysis was *American Charities: A Study in Philanthropy and Economics* by Amos G. Warner (1894). Warner was a graduate of the first program of graduate studies in social science in the United States, at Johns Hopkins University, initiated in 1874. He served as general secretary of the Baltimore Charity Organization Society while completing his doctoral studies. Warner's analysis drew on COS case records from Boston, New York, and Baltimore. At the center of Warner's analysis (cited in Zimbalist, 1977) was the issue of distinguishing between broad, objective, deductive explanations of poverty

based on theories about social and economic forces in society (economic crises, inadequate education, and capitalist exploitation of workers) and individual, subjective, inductive explanations of poverty based on the study of individual charity cases (laziness, drunkenness, illness, and industrial injury).

The inductive analysis of individual cases focused on the problems of the male breadwinner in the household because it was primarily the lack of adequate financial support from the earnings of the husband and father that resulted in household poverty. Although Warner recognized both social causes and individual causes of poverty, his preference was ultimately for individual explanations, on the grounds that even if there were broad social conditions that contributed to poverty, it was individual characteristics that determined how particular individuals responded to those conditions. "But even when environment is the primary cause of poverty, the immediate cause or coordinate result is often deterioration of character" (Zimbalist, 1977, p. 53).

Mary Richmond, first employed at the Baltimore COS when Warner was general secretary and then appointed general secretary when he left, used a "medical model" (Broadhurst, 1971) that included a combination of individual factors and social factors in analyzing problems in individual households (Richmond, 1917). However, in her model, individual and household factors were the focus of the work of charity workers, or social workers, who dealt primarily with women and children in a household. It was the responsibility of COS board members and other civic leaders to address the social problem issues identified through examination of COS case records (Pittman-Munke, 1999).

Early social welfare leaders were also concerned with measuring the extent of poverty and related social problems, in part influenced by the 17-volume report of Charles Booth on *The Life and Labour of the People of London*, completed in 1902 (Zimbalist, 1977). In 1909 the Russell Sage Foundation published *The Standard of Living Among Workingmen's Families in New York City*, a report by Robert Coit Chapin. The establishment of the Children's Bureau in 1912, with Julia Lathrop of Hull House (a Chicago social work center for community research) as the first director, was followed by the first national effort to gather comprehensive statistics on infant mortality, viewed as being largely a consequence of family poverty

(Zimbalist, 1977). This led, in turn, to a nation-wide effort to establish systematic birth records in every community. The Children's Bureau also published statistical reports on the number of children in gainful employment, information used in the national effort to enact an amendment to the Constitution restricting the use of child labor (Zimbalist, 1977).

Although COS records were being analyzed to identify the need for social reform measures directed at individual and household problems, in the 1890s and early 20th century social scientists like Clarence Ely of the Johns Hopkins University faculty were promoting the concept of public funding for "outdoor relief" for households in poverty, and "Christian socialism" (Broadhurst, 1971). This approach led later to advocacy by social scientists for social insurance as a universal approach to dealing with poverty. The social insurance proposals were based, in part, on experience with social insurance initiatives in Germany (Lubove, 1968). This was a social welfare approach to problems of poverty that was connected to the workplace and the economic position of the industrial worker rather than the privately funded "scientific philanthropy" approach to dealing with poverty conditions in individual households.

By the end of the 19th century, social scientists were based primarily in colleges and universities. Their concerns with poverty were often focused on social and economic reforms at a societal level, influenced, in part, by the theories of Adam Smith and Karl Marx. Social welfare leaders based in community agencies were primarily concerned with dealing with individual households with specific problems and with specific, but limited, reform proposals intended to assist with those problems, without changing the basic social and economic system of the United States.

THE RUSSELL SAGE FOUNDATION

The establishment by prominent social welfare leaders of the Russell Sage Foundation in 1907 aided the development of social welfare research in the early part of the 20th century (Glenn, Brandt, & Andrews, 1947). John M. Glenn, a social welfare leader from Baltimore, was selected as the first general director of the foundation.

One of the earliest projects of the foundation was funding support for the Pittsburgh Survey, beginning in 1907. The Pittsburgh Survey was directed by Paul Kellogg, the managing editor of *Charities and the Commons* (later titled *The Survey*) published by the New York Charity Organization Society (NYCOS). The Pittsburgh Survey, publicly identified as a "social work" study, moved from a focus on individual household poverty to a concern with social problems at the community level that were associated with massive immigration, rapid industrialization, and urban congestion (Kellogg, 1910; Zimbalist, 1977).

The Pittsburgh Survey involved six nationally recognized social welfare specialists, each of whom studied a particular aspect of the community, primarily focusing on the steel industry and steelworker families and neighborhoods. The survey included both quantitative studies of the occurrence of social problems and qualitative individual case studies concerned with causative factors. The primary objective of the Pittsburgh Survey was to provide information for civic leaders and for legislative reform initiatives intended to address the social problems that were identified. The Pittsburgh Survey contributed directly to the development of workers' compensation legislation intended to deal with what was identified in the survey as a major cause of household poverty—industrial accidents (Kellogg, 1910).

Following the publication of *The Pittsburgh Survey* were requests from other cities for assistance in carrying out communitywide studies of social conditions. The Russell Sage Foundation established a Department of Surveys and Exhibits that provided consultations to local communities. However, as the number of community surveys increased, problems arose from the lack of consistent methods of investigation and from recognition that study conclusions depended more on the opinions of the survey consultants than on the information gathered. Over time community surveys shifted from a comprehensive examination of the community context of social welfare problems to more specialized studies of the local organization of particular types of social services (Zimbalist, 1977). By the late 1920s, such studies were being carried out under local auspices, including the newly organized Community Chests and Community Welfare Councils. During the same period, social scientists were developing technical survey research methodologies that were increasingly being used for gathering and analyzing information from systematic samples of individuals or households, not only on social and economic conditions, but also on political opinions and buying preferences.

The social survey movement moved the focus in studies of poverty from individual household dynamics to community-level factors. However, social scientists such as John Common, originally from Johns Hopkins University, continued to advocate for social insurance. He and Clarence Ely became members of the faculty at the University of Wisconsin after leaving Johns Hopkins. Common played a key role in the development of the first social insurance legislation in the form of the Wisconsin workers' compensation law. Later the Wisconsin experience with social insurance would have an important role in the development of national proposals for social insurance under President Franklin D. Roosevelt.

Hull House in Chicago was the other major social work center of community-level social research. Hull House residents established a tradition of social investigation. This included the publication in 1895 of *Hull House Maps and Papers: A Presentation of Nationalities and Wages in a Congested District of Chicago* (Zimbalist, 1977), and studies of women's working conditions in Illinois by Florence Kelley, later the executive director of the National Consumers League. Edith Abbott emphasized social research in developing the academic program at the School of Social Service Administration at the University of Chicago, the second school of social work to include a doctoral program. She and Sophonisba Breckinridge initiated the journal *Social Service Review* in 1927 to publish scientific information about social welfare problems (Diner, 1977).

The early days of the Russell Sage Foundation coincided with the initial development of organized social work education. In 1907 the foundation sought to join its concerns for improving social welfare with an interest in stimulating the development of social research in schools of social work. The Russell Sage Foundation made grants to social work education programs in Boston, New York, Chicago, and St. Louis (Glenn et al., 1947). The objective of the foundation was to support the development of departments of social investigation by supporting the employment of a research specialist at each school, as well as research fellowships for students (Diner, 1977). In turn, the fellows might assist the foundation with its studies. However, by 1915, when the grants ended, the Russell Sage Foundation had determined that its research could be carried out more effectively by researchers directly under its own direction, although it was noted that research publications dealing with local issues

had been prepared in each school (Glenn et al., 1947).

SOCIAL SCIENCE AND SOCIAL WORK

In 1915 Abraham Flexner in his address "Is Social Work a Profession?" said that professions must be "learned," that is, "they need to resort to the laboratory and the seminar for a constantly fresh supply of facts; and it is the steady stream of ideas, emanating from these sources, which keeps professions from degenerating into mere routine, from losing their intellectual and responsible characters" (p. 579). In response to this element of the Flexner challenge, social work turned to the psychological theories of Sigmund Freud in the 1920s as an intellectual base for professional practice rather than theories and research coming from the new social sciences. This was consistent with the preference of Mary Richmond to turn to the diagnostic procedures in medical practice, rather than to social science research, as the source of guidance for designing the methods of professional assessment/diagnosis in social work (Broadhurst, 1971).

During the first two decades of the 20th century, a separation took place between professional education for social work and academic social sciences. This separation was foreshadowed by the statement by Mary Richmond in 1897 in which, in describing her concept of a "training school in applied philanthropy," she warned, "it should never be forgotten that the emphasis is to be placed on practical work rather than on academic requirements" (p. 186). In 1905 Edward Devine, general secretary of NYCOS, selected Samuel McCune Lindsey, an economist from Columbia University, to be the director of the New York School of Philanthropy when it became a one-year program of professional education rather than a summer institute. Lindsey was one of the founders of the American Association for Labor Legislation, advocates of social insurance as the answer to household poverty (Lubove, 1978). In 1910 Lindsey returned to Columbia, citing differences of opinion with the advisory committee for the School of Philanthropy (Meier, 1954). Specifically, John M. Glenn, director of the Russell Sage Foundation, and Mary Richmond, by then a member of Russell Sage Foundation's staff, had addressed a letter to Devine protesting the direction being taken in the curriculum of the School of Philanthropy under Lindsey.

Following the departure of Lindsey, the curriculum of the New York School of Social Work (formerly the School of Philanthropy) was changed from a program organized around a series of required academic social science classes with only electives in social casework practice to a program that included hands-on training in community agencies and made teaching about social casework practice central to the curriculum (Meier, 1954). At the 1915 National Conference of Charities and Correction, Devine stated that social work education includes "a course which deals with individuals and families and their complicated disabilities. . . . Next in importance to the study of the principles and techniques of family rehabilitation, I would place acquaintance with the history and nature of social movements" (p. 609).

In 1916 all-male Harvard University withdrew from the Boston School of Social Work that had been jointly created by Simmons College and Harvard. The president of Harvard stated that the training was appropriate for women for altruistic social service but inappropriate for training men for careers of public service and public leadership (Shoemaker, 1998). Later, Harvard created its own academic program of social ethics to prepare men for careers in social research, social reform, and government (Shoemaker, 1998). In Chicago individual members of the Department of Sociology had worked closely with social researchers at Hull House. However, in 1920 when the Graduate School of Social Service Administration was established at the University of Chicago, it was distinctly separate from the male-dominated Department of Sociology (Costin, 1983; Gordon, 1994). The faculty of the sociology department was committed to a model of objective and detached investigation of social phenomena, whereas leaders of the graduate school program were committed to a model of social investigation specifically directed to the solution of practical problems (Diner, 1977).

Gender distinctions were part of the issue in each of these developments separating professional education from academic social science. In New York social work students were predominantly women seeking employment as frontline workers in social services agencies, rather than the academic or civic leadership careers that men in graduate social science programs at Columbia University and other private universities normally pursued. In Boston the issue was specifically identified as a gender issue. In Chicago the male-dominated Department of Sociology chose not to employ Abbott and Breckinridge who were the leaders in

the development of the plans for the university-based school of social work (Gordon, 1994). In turn, they insisted on creating a totally separate academic department (Costin, 1983).

With the formation in 1919 of the Association of Training Schools for Professional Social Work (later the American Association of Schools of Social Work), a national framework was established for the development of social work education separate from academic social science departments. Although most of the undergraduate social work education programs that started in the 1920s began within undergraduate sociology departments as one or two courses, often involving practical experience in the community, they evolved into an undergraduate major and then a separate academic program.

EVALUATING SOCIAL CASEWORK

Studies of the social work curriculum during the 1920s and 1930s reported that social casework was at the core of the social work curriculum (Brown, 1942). The development of a theoretical framework for social casework was shaped in part by the influence of the theories of Sigmund Freud. This contributed to the establishment of a psychological, individual, mental health focus for casework (Jarrett, 1919) rather than the sociological focus on problems of household poverty set forth by Mary Richmond. It also broadened the focus of social casework beyond individuals and families in economic distress.

The development of social casework was also shaped by the report of the Milford Conference defining social casework as a generic professional procedure rather than as a series of specialized procedures defined by setting (American Association of Social Workers, 1929). Brown, in a report funded by the Russell Sage Foundation, noted that social work curriculums in the 1920s included one or two courses on research, generally dealing with social statistics. She also stated, "in a few schools the faculties are doing a considerable amount of research. The total publications within a year of all the schools, however, probably do not exceed those of the departments of social science of any one of several universities" (Brown, 1942, p. 66).

By the end of the 1920s, questions were being asked about the ability of social workers to demonstrate the effectiveness of social casework (Zimbalist, 1977). Richard Cabot, president of the 1931 Conference of Social Work (and earlier the initiator at Massachusetts General

Hospital of the first medical social work program), challenged the members of the conference: "I appeal to you—social workers of the country. . . . Measure, evaluate, estimate, appraise your results" (p. 21). This was part of the process through which the primary research focus within social work and social work education shifted from the study of social problems and social welfare institutions to the study of social work practice. Jeter in the 1937 *Social Work Year Book* made an explicit distinction between "social research" and "social work research." "Research in social work is inquiry into the techniques used by social workers in meeting certain human problems, whether these be individual or community-wide" (p. 420).

In the 1920s Sophie van Senden Theis carried out a study of children who had been in foster care under the auspices of the State Charities Aid Association of New York (Zimbalist, 1977). She reported that 77 percent were judged as being "capable in their adjustment" as adults. In 1939 Cabot initiated the Cambridge–Somerville Youth Study as a research project dealing with one of the recurrent social welfare concerns of the social work community—juvenile delinquency (Zimbalist, 1977). The study was also an early effort to use a control group as part of a large-scale community intervention research demonstration. An original group of 650 young boys, referred to the study by schools and community agencies, was divided into matched pairs and then individual members of each pair were randomly assigned to a "service" group or a "control" group.

Members of the service group were each assigned an individual counselor. There was no effort to define or control the methods or the intensity of activity used by each counselor. The service program continued until 1945, and the statistical analysis of the results was published in 1951 (Powers & Witmer, 1951). The results were inconclusive with only 19 percent of the boys in the treatment group being judged to have received definite benefits. Moreover, a qualitative analysis of the individual records indicated that it was particular combinations of the characteristics of the boy and of the counselor that produced the most definite benefits rather than any particular service methodology (Witmer, 1952). In spite of the inconclusive outcomes, the Cambridge–Somerville Study contributed to the concept of designing large-scale social work research demonstration projects at a community level.

Beginning in the 1920s and extending into the 1960s, there was a series of efforts to use the case records of social agency social workers to analyze "movement," or change in individual social work cases over time. These studies included measurement of changes in problem conditions (Reed, 1931) and changes in personal adjustment, or discomfort relief (Dollard & Mowrer, 1947). The experience with these studies led to the development of the Hunt–Kogan Movement Scale (Hunt & Kogan, 1950) that was used in additional studies. As Kahn (1999) pointed out, the "judges" and "raters" in these studies were social work practitioners, but the instrument designers were social scientists. Several of these evaluative research projects were supported by the Russell Sage Foundation and based in community agencies, in particular the Community Service Society of New York (originally the New York Charity Organization Society). In 1952 French, a member of the School of Social Work at the University of Michigan, prepared *An Approach to Measuring Results in Social Work* to answer questions from leaders of the Michigan Welfare League as to whether people were being benefited by social services and whether the community investment in such services was producing results (Kahn, 1999).

A community-level research effort to understand the impact of individual and household problems on community service resources was carried out by Bradley Buell and Associates in St. Paul, Minnesota, in the 1950s. Entitled *Community Planning for Human Services,* the study reported that some 6 percent of the families in the city were "absorbing well over half of the combined services of the community's dependency, health and adjustment services" (Buell & Associates, 1952, p. 9). One result of the study was a focus on the dynamics of the "multiproblem family" rather than on the problems of individual family members. A follow-up service project in St. Paul involved the concept of multiagency coordination through a single service worker, consistent with what later became identified as "case management" and the concept of "assertive casework" (Overton & Tinker, 1957). However, there was no systematic effort to evaluate the results of these service procedures. Another outcome of the St. Paul study was the development of the Geismar Scale of Family Functioning (Geismar, 1971) that was used in later studies of social casework services for multiproblem households.

In 1972, 13 direct services social work research projects carried out during the 1960s were reviewed at a Fordham University symposium (Mullen, Dumpson, & Associates, 1972).

Most of the studies involved social casework services, although a limited number also included group services and some form of control group comparison in order to compensate for methodological limitations of many earlier studies. Among these studies the one in Chemung County focused specifically on multiproblem families, based on the concepts of the St. Paul study. The services users included in the research studies were from lower income households. Several of the studies were designed to test the effectiveness of social casework services for households receiving public assistance payments. This followed the passage of the 1962 Amendments to Title IV(A) of the Social Security Act providing for federal/state funding for social casework services for households receiving Aid to Families with Dependent Children (AFDC) payments.

Overall, the results from the several studies as to the effectiveness of social casework with low-income, economically dependent households were inconclusive. There were research design problems in many of the studies, including the absence of clear definitions of the service methods actually used. Several of the analyses emphasized that the studies pointed to the significance of both community-level factors and social policy factors in the problems faced by the participating poverty households, problems that social casework services could not affect (Mullen et al., 1972). Among the 13 studies was the Casework Methods Project. This was the first of what later became an ongoing series of studies intended to test the effectiveness of "planned short-term services" in comparison to traditional open-ended or "continued services" (Reid & Shyne, 1969). This study did produce statistically positive differences in outcomes among services users favoring the planned short-term services, although there was no true, no-services control group.

These studies during the 1960s marked the end of the role of the Russell Sage Foundation as a major funder of research on social work practice. It also marked the end of major studies on casework effectiveness carried out under social services agency auspices, rather than academic auspices. Moreover, changes in the federal AFDC program beginning in 1967 led to a policy shift away from an emphasis on the use of social casework for AFDC households to an emphasis on directly promoting a transition to employment for AFDC parents. This change in federal policy coincided with a shift of focus

within social work education and social work practice from serving only economically dependent households to serving a more inclusive cross section of the community within a broadly defined concept of psychological or mental health counseling services.

COMMUNITY-LEVEL RESEARCH

The concept of comprehensive community-level research demonstration projects that focused on interrelated problems of poverty and juvenile delinquency in central-city communities received increased attention during the 1950s. Many of these communities were also affected by pervasive economic and social discrimination against African American households that had moved in large numbers from the rural South to the urban North during the late 1940s and early 1950s. In 1957 the Henry Street Settlement on the lower east side of New York initiated planning for Mobilization for Youth. The initial proposal was influenced by earlier efforts of the New York City Youth Service Board to deal with juvenile gang violence. Richard Cloward and Lloyd Ohlin (1960) created a theoretical community change model that focused on increasing economic opportunities for youths as an alternative to delinquency and crime in order to apply to the National Institute of Mental Health to fund the Mobilization for Youth as a research-based project. The research plan involved the Columbia University School of Social Work as a mobilization partner. In the early 1960s, the Ford Foundation began funding Grey Areas Projects, which were ultimately established in six cities and North Carolina (Marris & Rein, 1969). Although the Grey Areas Projects were identified as "demonstration" projects, there was not a requirement for a specific research design.

The example of these community-level demonstration projects, in turn, contributed to the passage of the 1961 legislation establishing the President's Committee on Juvenile Delinquency and Youth Crime. The committee's objective was to fund a limited number of comprehensive community intervention juvenile delinquency control demonstration research projects (Marris & Rein, 1969; Matusow, 1984). In order to assure that these projects had a significant evaluation research design, a national research advisory panel was established chaired by the executive director of the Russell Sage Foundation (Matusow, 1984). The first project to be funded by the President's committee was the Community Action for Youth project in Cleveland for which the author of this entry was the planning director (Matusow, 1984). Mobilization for Youth and the President's committee projects were the first time that substantial federal funds were used to support large-scale demonstration projects based on combining a diverse mixture of social services programs with a research-based knowledge-building objective.

These demonstration research projects generally involved some combination of community mobilization initiatives, services for individuals and households, and group services for adolescents. Social workers were often involved in the design of the projects or as administrators and services personnel. However, it soon became evident that it was impossible to establish and maintain a controlled, experimental research model for a multi-program, comprehensive, locally directed program in a period of maximum community and political turmoil. Irresolvable conflicts developed among local governmental bodies, community-based governance bodies for the projects, and university-based researchers responsible for creating the research design and gathering information consistent with that design (Marris & Rein, 1969; Matusow, 1984).

The War on Poverty was launched in 1964, including Community Action Programs (CAPs) that had a priority emphasis on "action," not on outcome evaluation research. In some communities, CAPs absorbed services programs initiated under the President's Committee on Juvenile Delinquency and Youth Crime. However, neither the President's committee projects nor CAPs actually dealt with the fundamental social and economic realities of the "poverty" communities that were "targeted." The overall evaluation of CAPs ultimately took the form of a political assessment that they had failed, an assessment made by two political science writers, Daniel Patrick Moynihan in *Maximum Feasible Misunderstanding* (1969) and Edward Banfield in *The Unheavenly City* (1970). With the beginning of the 1970s and the presidency of Richard M. Nixon, efforts to change poverty and delinquency dynamics in central-city neighborhoods through federally funded comprehensive services interventions came to an end.

INSTITUTIONAL DEVELOPMENT OF SOCIAL WORK RESEARCH

The development of social work research following the 1950s was centered primarily in schools of social work rather than in community agencies. Before 1950 only two schools of social work included doctoral programs, Bryn

Mawr and the University of Chicago. Beginning in the 1950s, a number of schools began to establish doctoral programs, in part, to respond to requirements by colleges and universities that faculty members in schools of social work must have a doctorate. Initially, many existing faculty members completed doctoral studies in a social science department, primarily sociology or psychology. That, in turn, made it possible for schools of social work to establish their own doctoral programs. The faculty leaders selected to head such doctoral programs were often those who were particularly knowledgeable about research methodology.

In 1975 the directors of doctoral programs in schools of social work formed a national association—the Group for the Advancement of Doctoral Education in Social Work. Their annual meeting provided an opportunity to address issues related to the development of research resources in social work education. Because the doctorate in social work was not defined as an entry-level practice degree, doctoral programs were not subject to accreditation by the Council on Social Work Education (CSWE). The result was a diversity of focus among doctoral programs, some focusing on developing specialized social work researchers, some on preparing social work educators with basic research competency, and some on preparing advanced clinical practitioners.

The Social Work Research Group (SWRG) was organized in 1948 (Graham, Al-Krenawi, & Bradshaw, 2000; Kahn, 1999). It included faculty members in schools of social work and researchers in community agencies, community planning councils, and federal agencies. It included individuals with social science research training as well as those with a social work background. SWRG became one of the participating organizations in the creation of the National Association of Social Workers (NASW) in 1955. Consistent with the original merger understandings, SWRG continued in the form of a specialty section within NASW that in 1963 became the Council on Social Work Research (Graham et al., 2000). However, NASW membership requirements meant that after 1955 individuals with a graduate social science degree rather than a graduate professional social work degree would not be eligible for new membership in the research section (Kahn, 1999), although there was a modification in 1969 recognizing individuals with a social science doctorate who were employed by a social agency (Graham et al., 2000).

Under the auspices of the NASW Council on Social Work Research the first social work research textbook was published in 1960, edited by Norman Polansky. The concern with expanding the research base for practice was reflected in NASW's publication of the first of a series of three social work research reviews by Maas (1966, 1971, 1978). However, in 1974 the Council on Social Work Research disappeared when reorganization within NASW eliminated all of the specialty groups in favor of a definition of social work as a single unified profession. There was no national association of social work researchers for 20 years until the Society for Social Work and Research was established in 1994. Without a national association or regular meetings, a separation developed between social work researchers in federal, state, and local social welfare agencies and those in academic settings.

In 1956 the Committee on the History of Social Welfare (later the Social Welfare History Group) met for the first time. It was organized with a dual affiliation with CSWE and with the American Historical Association (Fisher, 1999) and initially held alternate meetings in connection with their annual conferences. It included researchers interested in studies of social welfare history and social work history. Over time, however, the participation of social science historians diminished: "Professional boundaries and disciplinary divisions were too great, and interdisciplinary effort received little payoff in the disciplines" (Fisher, 1999, p. 201). The social work history researchers preferred to emphasize historical developments explicitly identified with social work and those reflective of the value commitments associated with the profession. The social science historians were interested in refining historical research methodology and in an inclusive concept of social welfare history without a specific value orientation. The Social Work History Group has continued to the present with an annual symposium associated with CSWE's annual program meeting and an annual bibliographical publication.

During the 1980s the Quantitative Methods Interest Group was organized to sponsor an annual symposium on the teaching of research methods at the annual program meeting of CSWE. Although a number of professional journals in social work, including NASW's *Social Work*, published research reports together with other professionally relevant articles, there was not a journal explicitly committed to research publications until the 1960s. In 1965 NASW initiated the publication of *Research and Ab-*stracts combining research-based articles and abstracts of professional and social science publications relevant to social work practice. In 1994 the publication was divided with *Social Work Research* becoming a separate publication. In 1977 the *Journal of Social Service Research* was initiated by the George Warren Brown School of Social Work at Washington University. In 1991 the publication of *Research on Social Work Practice* was initiated by the University of Georgia.

RESEARCH DEVELOPMENT IN SCHOOLS OF SOCIAL WORK

Research was a minor element in the graduate social work curriculum through the 1940s. In research courses, emphasis was on learning basic social statistic analytic procedures. In 1952 the accreditation criteria of the American Association of Schools of Social Work included a research thesis in the standards for master's degree programs. One of the major themes of the report of the 1959 Social Work Curriculum Study Project, directed by Warner Boehm, was an emphasis on the importance of research in the curriculum. Research was presented as both a commitment to a scientific orientation and as one of five social work practice methods (Dinerman & Geismar, 1984).

However, in actual practice, schools of social work often borrowed faculty members from psychology or sociology to teach a required course in research methods and to supervise thesis preparation. There was little connection made between research methods and professional practice courses (Dinerman & Geismar, 1984). The result frequently was that more attention was given to the statistical analysis procedures in the thesis report than to the social work practice significance of the research question being asked.

There was little change through the 1970s in the perception within schools of social work that research was a topic separate from the other parts of the curriculum (Dinerman, 1981) or that it was dealt with in depth only in the doctoral programs. It was notable that although the 1977 publication by Zimbalist, *Historic Themes and Landmarks in Social Welfare Research*, makes reference to individual researchers who are faculty members in schools of social work, there is no reference at all to schools of social work as a primary setting for doing social work research.

There was a growing concern about the extent to which the social work curriculum included contemporary information from the social sciences, particularly as faculty members increasingly held doctorates from schools of social work rather than from social science departments. The Russell Sage Foundation granted funds in the 1950s to several schools of social work to establish closer connections between social science and the social work curriculum. However, the interdisciplinary social work/social science doctoral program at the University of Michigan was the only one of the special initiatives that continued after the Russell Sage funding ended.

The 1981 publication of "The Obsolete Scientific Imperative in Social Work Research" by Heineman highlighted a growing controversy within social work and social work education about the nature of the knowledge base underlying social work practice. Heineman questioned the assumptions of "logical empiricism" that there is ultimately one "correct" or "true" scientific explanation of events and that the application of traditional scientific methods and quantitative statistical analyses are the most appropriate methods for identifying such truths. She took the position that there cannot be any single "objective" research result because the researcher is always, in some form, part of any research result.

Heineman proposed that a variety of research procedures should be used to achieve heuristic understandings of a problem rather than focusing on a single, "scientific" model of research construction (Heineman-Pieper, 1989). This criticism challenged not only the design of research, but also the traditional technical content of research training in social work, content largely borrowed from psychology and sociology. Other social work researchers responded with defenses of traditional scientific research methods (Hudson, 1982). The debates over the assumptions of logical empiricism and empirical research, and over the place of qualitative as well as quantitative research methods, continued throughout the rest of the 20th century (Reid, 1994; Rubin, 2000).

Two specialized forms of research dealing with social work practice, rather than with discovering basic social science principles, developed during the period following the 1960s (Kahn, 1999). One was single-system research, drawn originally from the field of behavioral psychology. The other was intervention research or developmental research. Single-system design research, also identified as "empirical practice," involved time-series experiments in which individual treatment interventions were measured over time by the practitioner (Briar, 1990). The concept of a practitioner-based form of practice research contributed to the inclusion by CSWE (1984) of an accreditation requirement that students be prepared to "systematically evaluate their own practice." Intervention research, also known as "design and development" research, involved a system of developing program design innovations, testing those interventions in practice, and using the results of those tests to modify the innovations (Reid, 1995; Rothman & Thomas, 1994).

As schools of social work, in particular schools with doctoral programs, became the location for the development of social work research designs and for the initiation of studies of social work practice and of the problems addressed by social work practitioners, there was a growing concern about a gap between research and the professional practice of social work practitioners (Briar, Weissman, & Rubin, 1981; Grasso & Epstein, 1992; Task Force on Social Work Research, 1991). Research-oriented professional journals reporting specialized and discrete research studies served primarily as publication outlets for faculty members in schools of social work, with very limited circulation in the professional practice community. National practitioner conferences were primarily organized around immediate practice concerns; researchers met in specialized conferences presenting research results to other researchers.

NIMH AND THE DEVELOPMENT OF RESEARCH RESOURCES IN SOCIAL WORK

The establishment of the National Institute of Mental Health (NIMH) in 1949 set in motion the most important developments in social work research during the second half of the 20th century. The initial NIMH mission concentrated heavily on the training of mental health clinical specialists in medicine, psychology, nursing, and social work. The expanded professional resources in mental health made it possible to initiate a national program of publicly funded community mental health centers by the end of the 1960s. During this period, NIMH became the single most important source of external funding support for social work education, particularly after the elimination, at the end of the 1970s, of the preferential funding provisions for schools of social work under Title XX of the Social Security Act Amendments of 1975, funding that was directed primarily at the training of personnel for public social services programs.

The NIMH mission also included support of research on the causes and treatment of mental illness. By the 1970s NIMH began giving increased attention to the training of research specialists as well as clinicians in each of the mental health professional fields, including social work. In the 1970s NIMH funded two national conferences dealing with social work research, the 1977 conference sponsored by CSWE (Rubin & Rosenblatt, 1979) and the 1978 conference sponsored by NASW (Fanshel, 1980). These conferences were, in part, a response to the continuing issue of the outcome effectiveness of social casework that was raised by Fischer (1973) in an article entitled "Is Casework Effective? A Review." These two conferences documented the gap that existed between the level of social work involvement in mental health services and the research-tested base for such practice.

These conferences also highlighted the limitations of the existing level of support for the training of social work research specialists. NIMH research training funds went largely to departments of psychiatry and psychology that had existing programs of research and research training. The field of nursing, which had many of the same limitations in research training as social work, initiated a successful legislative effort by the mid-1980s to establish a National Center for Nursing Research within the National Institutes of Health.

By the end of the 1980s, NIMH ended its funding support for the training of clinical practitioners in social work. Emphasis in NIMH funding was placed on creating a scientific base for the treatment of mental illness. Resources were shifted to the support of research on causes and treatment of mental health conditions and to training of mental health researchers. Concerned about the financial implications for social work education, leaders of CSWE and NASW met with Lewis Judd, director of NIMH, in 1988. He proposed the establishment of a task force to examine current research resources in social work and to develop recommendations for strengthening those resources. The 13-member Task Force on Social Work Research was appointed in the fall of 1988, chaired by the author of this entry, and submitted its report, *Building Social Work Knowledge for Effective Services and Policies: A Plan for Research Development*, in 1991.

A major theme in the report was the urgency of expanding research that dealt directly with social work practice in mental health. Two of the major recommendations in the task force

report led to action by NIMH to create a national program for the competitive funding of Social Work Research Development Centers, and to action by five national associations in social work and social work education to establish the Institute for the Advancement of Social Work Research (IASWR). NIMH funded eight Social Work Research Development Centers in schools of social work during the 1990s. A program of research consultation and research workshops and training institutes with NIMH funding, together with national representation of social work research concerns, was carried out by IASWR. In 1994 social work researchers created the Society for Social Work and Research as an international professional association with an ongoing series of annual research conferences and sponsorship of the journal *Research on Social Work Practice*—by 2001, the society had 900 members.

AT THE END OF THE 20TH CENTURY
By the end of the 1990s, the federal government, primarily through NIMH, had become the major funding source for ongoing programs of research dealing with social work practice, although foundations and state governments also provided funding grants for problem-focused research and program evaluation studies. Federal research requirements in particular emphasized the importance of interdisciplinary participation in the development of research designs, requiring social work researchers to reach out to develop collaborations with social scientists. Although social work researchers provided leadership in defining professionally relevant research issues, social work practice research studies relied primarily on the work of social scientists in the development of research instruments, technical research design models, and research analysis procedures, including computerized quantitative and qualitative data analysis procedures.

In addition to the NIMH-supported research development centers, several other schools of social work created similar research centers with funding from other sources. The establishment of such research centers represented a shift from a traditional academic model of individual research projects carried out by individual faculty members toward a model of systematic, knowledge-building programs of interdisciplinary research directed at specific social and behavioral problems. In 1999 congressional legislation, sponsored by a coalition of national social work associations, was filed to establish a National Center for Social Work

Research. In 2000 the National Institute on Drug Abuse announced the creation of a Social Work Research Development Program and in 2001 the first grants were made under this program.

In 1998, *A Report on Progress in the Development of Research Resources in Social Work* was published by IASWR (Austin, 1998). The report summarized the significant developments in practice-relevant research during the 1990s, particularly with regard to social work practice in mental health, and stressed the urgent necessity of similar developments in other areas of social work practice, in particular the field of child welfare services. The report also noted that the ethical responsibilities for providing effective services have been reinforced by the demands of managed health care for demonstrated effectiveness. "The most important issue for the immediate future is to bring the practice effectiveness concerns of social work practitioners together with the resources represented by social work researchers" (Austin, 1998, p. 27). The report also noted that although the number of social work doctoral programs had increased, there was no significant increase overall in the number of doctoral graduates and that, moreover, not all doctoral programs were designed to prepare social work researchers.

REFERENCES

American Association of Social Workers. (1929). *The Milford Conference report: Social casework: Generic and specific.* New York: Author.

Austin, D. M. (1998). *A report on progress in the development of research resources in social work.* Washington, DC: Institute for the Advancement of Social Work Research.

Banfield, E. C. (1970). *The unheavenly city: The nature and future of our urban crisis.* Boston: Little, Brown.

Briar, S. (1990). Empiricism in clinical practice: Present and future. In L. Videka-Sherman & W. J. Reid (Eds.), *Advances in clinical social work practice* (pp. 1–7). Silver Spring, MD: NASW Press.

Briar, S., Weissman, H., & Rubin, A. (1981). *Research utilization in social work education.* New York: Council on Social Work Education.

Broadhurst, B. P. (1971). *Social thought, social practice and social work education: Sanborn, Ely, Warner, Richmond.* Unpublished doctoral dissertation, Columbia University School of Social Work, New York.

Brown, E. L. (1942). *Social work as a profession* (4th ed.). New York: Russell Sage Foundation.

Bruno, F. J. (1948). *Trends in social work.* New York: Columbia University Press.

Buell, B., & Associates. (1952). *Community planning for human services.* New York: Columbia University Press.

Cabot, R. C. (1931). Presidential address. In *Proceedings of the National Conference of Social Work, Minneapolis* (pp. 3–24). Chicago: University of Chicago Press.

Chapin, R. C. (1909). *The standard of living among workingmen's families in New York City.* New York: Russell Sage Foundation.

Cloward, R., & Ohlin, L. (1960). *Delinquency and opportunity: A theory of delinquent gangs.* Glencoe, IL: Free Press.

Costin, L. B. (1983). *Two sisters for social justice: A biography of Grace and Edith Abbott.* Urbana: University of Illinois Press.

Council on Social Work Education. (1984). *Handbook of accreditation standards and procedures.* New York: Author.

Devine, E. (1915). Education for social work. In *Proceedings of the National Conference of Charities and Correction* (pp. 606–610). Chicago: Hildmann.

Diner, S. J. (1977). Scholarship in the quest for social welfare: A fifty-year history of the Social Service Review. *Social Service Review, 51,* 1–66.

Dinerman, M. (1981). *Social work curriculum at the baccalaureate and master's levels.* New York: Lois & Samuel Silberman Fund.

Dinerman, M., & Geismar, L. L. (Eds.). (1984). *A quarter-century of social work education.* Silver Spring, MD: National Association of Social Workers.

Dollard, J., & Mowrer, O. H. (1947). A method of measuring tension in written documents. *Journal of Abnormal and Social Psychology, 42,* 3–32.

Fanshel, D. (1980). *Future of social work research.* Washington, DC: National Association of Social Workers.

Fischer, J. (1973). Is casework effective? A review. *Social Work, 18,* 5–20.

Fisher, R. (1999). Speaking for the contribution of history: Context and the origins of the Social Welfare History Group. *Social Service Review, 73,* 191–217.

Flexner, A. (1915). Is social work a profession? In *Proceedings of the National Conference of Charities and Correction, 1915* (pp. 576–590). Chicago: Hildmann.

French, D. G. (1952). *An approach to measuring results in social work.* New York: Columbia University Press.

Geismar, L. L. (1971). *Family and community functioning: A manual of measurement for social work practice and policy.* Metchuen, NJ: Scarecrow Press.

Glenn, J. M., Brandt, L., & Andrews, F. E. (1947). *Russell Sage Foundation, 1907–1946.* New York: Russell Sage Foundation.

Gordon, L. (1994). *Pitied but not entitled: Single mothers and the history of welfare*. Cambridge, MA: Harvard University Press.

Graham, J. R., Al-Krenawi, A., & Bradshaw, C. (2000). The Social Work Research Group/NASW Research Section/Council on Social Work Research 1949–1965: An emerging research identity in the American profession. *Research on Social Work Practice, 10,* 622–643.

Grasso, A. J., & Epstein, I. (Eds.). (1992). *Research utilization in the social services*. New York: Haworth Press.

Heineman, M. B. (1981). The obsolete scientific imperative in social work research. *Social Service Review, 55,* 371–397.

Heineman-Pieper, M. B. (1989). The heuristic paradigm: A unifying and comprehensive approach to social work research. *Smith College Studies in Social Work, 60,* 8–34.

Hudson, W. W. (1982). Scientific imperatives in social work research and practice. *Social Service Review, 56,* 246–258.

Hunt, J. M., & Kogan, L. S. (1950). *Measuring results in social casework: A manual on judging movement*. New York: Family Service Association of America.

Jarrett, M. (1919). The psychiatric thread running through all social case work. In *Proceedings of the National Conference of Social Work, 1919* (pp. 587–592). Chicago: Rogers & Hall.

Jeter, H. R. (1937). Research in social work. In *Social work year book, 1937* (pp. 419–426). New York: Russell Sage Foundation.

Kahn, A. (1999). The social work research domain in historical perspective: The first 100 years. In M. Potocky-Tripodi & T. Tripodi (Eds.), *New directions for social work practice research* (pp. 9–38). Washington, DC: NASW Press.

Kellogg, P. U. (Ed.). (1910–1916). *The Pittsburgh Survey* (6 Vols.). New York: Russell Sage Foundation.

Leiby, J. (1978). *A history of social welfare and social work in the United States*. New York: Columbia University Press.

Lubove, R. (1968). *The struggle for Social Security, 1900–1935*. Cambridge, MA: Harvard University Press.

Maas, H. S. (Ed.). (1966). *Five fields of social service: Review of research*. New York: National Association of Social Workers.

Maas, H. S. (Ed.). (1971). *Research in the social services: A five-year review*. New York: National Association of Social Workers.

Maas, H. S. (Ed.). (1978). *Social service research: Review of studies*. Washington, DC: National Association of Social Workers.

MacIver, R. M. (1933). Sociology and social work. In *Social work year book* (pp. 497–500). New York: American Association of Social Workers.

Marris, P., & Rein, M. (1969). *Dilemmas of social reform: Poverty and community action in the United States*. New York: Atherton Press.

Matusow, A. J. (1984). *The unraveling of America: A history of liberalism in the 1960s*. New York: Harper & Row.

Meier, E. (1954). *A history of the New York School of Social Work*. New York: Columbia University Press.

Moynihan, D. P. (1969). *Maximum feasible misunderstanding*. New York: Free Press.

Mullen, E. J., Dumpson, J. R., & Associates. (Eds.). (1972). *Evaluation of social intervention*. San Francisco: Jossey-Bass.

Overton, A., & Tinker, K. (1957). *Casework notebook*. St. Paul, MN: Greater Saint Paul United Fund & Council.

Pittman-Munke, P. (1999). Bridging the divide: The casework policy link. *Sociology and Social Welfare, 26,* 203–216.

Polansky, N. A. (1960). *Social work research*. Chicago: University of Chicago Press.

Powers, E., & Witmer, H. (1951). *An experiment in the prevention of delinquency: The Cambridge–Somerville youth study*. New York: Columbia University Press.

Reed, E. F. (1931). A scoring system for the evaluation of social case work. *Social Service Review, 5*(2), 214–236.

Reid, W. J. (1994). Reframing the epistemological debate. In E. Sherman & W. J. Reid (Eds.), *Qualitative research in social work* (pp. 464–480). New York: Columbia University Press.

Reid, W. J. (1995). Research overview. In R. L. Edwards (Ed.-in-Chief), *Encyclopedia of social work* (19th ed., Vol. 3, pp. 2040–2054). Washington, DC: NASW Press.

Reid, W. J., & Shyne, A. W. (1969). *Brief and extended casework*. New York: Columbia University Press.

Richmond, M. E. (1897). The need of a training school in applied philanthropy. In *Proceedings of the National Conference of Charities and Correction, 1897* (pp. 181–187). Boston: George E. Ellis.

Richmond, M. E. (1917). *Social diagnosis*. New York: Russell Sage Foundation.

Rothman, J., & Thomas, E. J. (Eds.). (1994). *Intervention research*. New York: Haworth Press.

Rubin, A. (2000). Social work research at the turn of the millennium: Progress and challenges. *Research on Social Work Practice, 10,* 9–14.

Rubin, A., & Rosenblatt, A. (Eds.). (1979). *Sourcebook on research utilization*. New York: Council on Social Work Education.

Shoemaker, L. M. (1998). Early conflicts in social work education. *Social Service Review, 72,* 182–191.

Task Force on Social Work Research. (1991). *Building social work knowledge for effective services and policies: A plan for research development.* Austin: University of Texas, School of Social Work.

Warner, A. G. (1894). *American charities: A study in philanthropy and economics.* New York: Crowell.

Witmer, H. (1952). An analysis of "an experiment in the prevention of delinquency." In D. French (Ed.), *An approach to measuring results in social work* (pp. 155–160). New York: Columbia University Press.

Zimbalist, S. E. (1977). *Historic themes and landmarks in social welfare research.* New York: Harper & Row.

David M. Austin, PhD, is emeritus professor, School of Social Work, University of Texas at Austin.

For further information see

African American Pioneers in Social Work; Archives of Social Welfare; Economic Analysis; Intervention Research; Qualitative Research; Research Overview; Social Work Practice: History and Evolution; Survey Research

---

Key Words

evaluation	quantitative research
history	research
mental health	social casework

HMOs

See Health Care: Financing, *Volume 2;* Managed Care, *Volume 2;* Primary Health Care, *Volume 3*

I

Industrial Social Work

See Occupational Social Work, *Volume 2*

Issues of Multiculturalism: Multicultural Practice, Cultural Diversity, and Competency

Sadye M. L. Logan

The predominant worldview in the United States and many other countries is based on a dualistic or dichotomous paradigm. From birth to death, human beings are taught how to think, act, and speak dichotomously. They are not taught to view and experience their worlds with equanimity. The most used framework by humans for describing group interactional patterns is "them and us." This orientation to the world not only creates, but also perpetuates feelings of separateness and distrust. Even the most well-intentioned individual gets trapped in a mind-set of viewing multiculturalism as inclusive of so-called minorities in this society as well as people who are oppressed in some form or fashion.

This pervasive mind-set begs the question of whether a multicultural world can be created in this society, the academic community, and the social work profession. It is, therefore, the intent of this entry to examine the issues reflected in the concept of multiculturalism. In this process, multiculturalism and other related terms—multicultural practice, cultural diversity, and cultural competency or responsiveness—will be defined. These definitions will serve to bridge a discussion on the roles and perspectives assumed by the social work profession in fostering a multicultural world. The discussion addresses practice, education, and research implications. Finally, an expanded framework is discussed for conceptualizing and experiencing multiculturalism.

DEFINITIONS, ASSUMPTIONS, AND EMERGENT ISSUES

The umbrella concept for multicultural practice, cultural diversity, and cultural competency or responsiveness is "multiculturalism," a complex term and quite paradoxical in its theoretical conceptualization. It is sometimes referred to in the literature as a social movement, and other times as an educational strategy or an approach or perspective. As an approach or perspective, it affirms the reality of cultural diversity, the need for tolerance and appreciation of different cultures, and the importance of understanding the dynamics of cultural diversity and interactions in work with people (Sanders, 1980). As an edu-

cational strategy, it is intended to support individuals in their own ethnic identities as well as expose them to a variety of other cultures and enhance their capacity to adapt (Bateson, 1994). As a social movement, the intent is to make society a place in which people from all cultures have equal respect and equal voice and equal influences in shaping larger community values (Markowitz, 1994).

Indeed, multiculturalism incorporates all of these factors, but it is even more important to view and experience this concept as depicting a way of living or being in the world. It is not something to do but a way of being. Simon (1994) suggested that multiculturalism is not only an expression of chic postmodern relativism, as some contemporary authors might suggest, but also an age-old longing for an all-inclusive human community. This longing, however, is influenced by contemporary realities in the global marketplace, the political arena, and a deep-seated morality fueled by ideologies of fairness and respect. This concept along with diversity came into existence during the late 1980s and early 1990s. It is important, however, to identify some critical issues that shroud the conceptualization of multiculturalism. Although the issues identified here are not intended to be inclusive but overarching, they will clarify and extend the definition of multiculturalism. The first issue concerns the dynamics and usage of language. The second issue is multifaceted—it is concerned with experiencing the unfamiliar as separate and different from oneself at the same time believing Americans are a single people of diverse backgrounds. The third issue is concerned with teaching and learning about diverse cultures from a unidimensional approach.

A brief story about a wise man from the East giving a lecture on the power of words ("mantra" in Sanskrit) will serve to place this issue in perspective:

> As the wise man was saying, "Mantra is great. Mantra takes us to God." Someone shouted from the back of the room. "How can you say that a mantra takes us to God? If I say, 'Bread, bread, bread,' will that get me bread?" "Sit down, you bastard!" the wise man shouted. When the man heard this, he became furious. He began to shout and his hair stood on end. Even his necktie began to vibrate. He shouted, "you call yourself a saint, yet you use such filthy words for me?" "I am sorry, sir," the wise man said, "please be calm and tell me what happened." "You have the audacity to ask me what happened! Don't you realize how you have insulted me?" "I used just one abusive word," the wise man said, "and it has had such a, powerful effect on you! When this is the case with an abusive term, what make[s] you think the name of God, who is the Supreme Truth, does not have its own power and will not also affect you?" (Muktananda, 1991, p. 30).

Therefore, the way in which we put words together, the manner or context in which these words are expressed, conveys powerful messages that are often easier to go along with than to raise questions about the message or about those for whom the words are intended. For the purpose of this discussion references are made concerning those words that are used to describe nonwhite or specific situations related to nonwhites in society—for example, minorities, ethnic minorities, racial minorities, minority groups, minorities of color, disadvantaged minorities, deprived minorities, and so forth. These words among many others serve to perpetuate, albeit unconsciously, the implied differences between nonwhites and whites in this society. These terms, especially minorities, have become so inculcated in our language usage that the so-called minorities refer to themselves in this manner. Minorities, in popular usage, refer to the limited or nonexistent opportunities (social, economic, and political) available to African Americans, Asian Americans, Latin Americans, and Native Americans in this

country (Lum, 1996). From another perspective, minority status also suggests a numerically smaller or politically powerless group in relation to a larger, dominant majority. Whites are viewed as the majority and nonwhites as minorities. Generally, in the minds of many, a majority–minority label implies a superiority–inferiority distinction (Devore & Schlesinger, 1999; Lum, 1996). Referring to nonwhites as minorities not only denies their ethnicity, but also ignores our multicultural world; it would be just as easy to write in the names of the groups in question.

Within this context, it is important to be cognizant of Hartman's (1991) observations about how words create worlds. She reminded practitioners and educators to never discount the power of language. The belief that evolves out of postmodern theory is that words not only reflect but also shape our world. She stated that "names" or "naming" can inflict irreparable harm—a process that marginalizes or subjugates those in our society who are considered minorities, at risk, or oppressed. We must be reminded words carry intentionality, and we must work to create words that can be used by nonwhites in our society in ways that are respectful and uplifting.

At the root of the second issue is fear, an old enemy that masquerades in so many different ways. In our society, it appears to be synonymous with any situation related to "race." It is common knowledge that anything that appears to be different or unfamiliar is met with suspicion and distrust. This fear is manifested in a variety of ways related to the conceptualization of multiculturalism in American society. The fear permeates all aspects of our lives, but especially our educational system—a system that is still perhaps the most "segregated" in America.

In the early 1990s, a fear-based discourse that evolved out of Stanford University's attempt to define its content for the core curriculum on Western Civilizations riveted the attention of the academic community. The fallouts from this unfriendly discourse reverberated far beyond the boundaries of the university to the wider community, including popular magazines and the media (D'Souza, 1992). Coupled with this acrimonious dialogue was the much-cited trend reflected in the 1990 census that the racial and ethnic composition of the American population changed more dramatically in the past decade than at any other time in the 20th century (Barringer, 1991). Further, in recent years, more than four in five legal immigrants to the United States have been of non-European ancestry.

Due to these changes in racial and ethnic makeup in the United States, a more culturally diverse population was perceived as a threat to the American identity. These differences were met with fear and hostility from factions in our society described as neoconservatives (Van Soest, 1995). Within this context many assumptions about multiculturalism emerged or resurfaced along with the term "political correctness" (Hartman, 1991; Markowitz, 1994). One of the protagonists in this discourse suggested that eventually one of the many special interest groups would want to take over and dominate all of the other groups (Cheney, 1992). Further, it was thought that speech and behavior codes addressing racism by academics and affirmative action programs were forms of a double standard and intimidation that increased racial tension and separatism (Bloom, 1987; D'Souza, 1992).

Another assumption held that greater ethnic and racial inclusiveness would automatically result in either lowering standards or no standards at all. Finally, the political correctness perspective emerged as a derisive term for describing the various stances on the rights and protections of nonwhite people and other disenfranchised groups (Hartman, 1991). Lawrence (1992), not unlike others (Cheney, 1992; D'Souza, 1992), used political correctness to describe courses in social justice, racism, and women's issues and viewed these courses "as a lot of propaganda designed to make approved minority students feel good and everyone else feel guilty" (p. 384). Therefore, a multicultural agenda, in part, is seen as politicizing the academic curriculum and stifling freedom of thought and expression.

The third and final issue flows naturally from the preceding issues. Essentially, the implications to be drawn from these issues are that it is extremely difficult if not impossible to teach that which one does not understand or one is committed to. Despite the social work profession's history and current mandate "to prepare competent and effective social work professionals who are committed to a practice that includes services to the poor and oppressed, and who work to alleviate poverty, oppression and discrimination" (Council on Social Work Education [CSWE], 1994, p. 134), questions have been raised and continue to be raised about the profession's level of commitment to and interpretation and implementation of CSWE's current curriculum policy statement

(CPS) on diversity, promotion of social and economic justice, and populations at risk (Gould, 1995; Hartman, 1991; Van Soest, 1995). Although these concepts suggest multiculturalism, the concept itself has not been used to date in CSWE standards. Nevertheless, the challenge to develop and implement a multicultural curriculum and culturally competent or responsive practice persists. The struggle continues to be greatly influenced by a prevailing ideology that denies that the cultures of people of color have the equivalent values as that of the culture of white people. According to Gould (1995), the social stratification of the United States implicitly endorses the value of "Anglo conformity," a concept coined by Gordon (1964).

Therefore, for white America, no intrinsic or long-term commitment is connected to the process necessary for creating and sustaining a multicultural world. As a result, the change process inherent in education and practice, at best, is rote and mechanical. Educators and students began to view and experience the learning process as an imposition—something to tolerate and be done with so that one can get to the important task of learning how to "do" therapy. From this perspective, learning about cultural diversity becomes one dimensional. Multiculturalism and ethnic minorities become synonymous. Consequently, instead students learn to view themselves as people without ethnic or racial identities and cultures and view nonwhite people as the other—people whose cultures they are required to learn about and who are in many ways different from themselves (Gould, 1995).

This approach to multiculturalism has left many members of the social work community somewhat bewildered. For example, following the issuing of CSWE's policy statement in 1992, a study of 118 social workers on how content on special populations guided their practice behaviors and professional values in relation to oppressed populations resulted in very disappointing findings. Workers showed awareness for sensitivity to the needs of nonwhite clients and also confusion as to who were special populations or what their needs were (Van Soest, 1995). In 1992 the Council's Commission on Educational Policy conducted an assessment of the CPS. According to Sheridan (2000), 50 percent of the deans and directors interviewed reported that their programs had strengthened content in one or more of their mandated content areas, whereas 30 percent reported that these areas were the most difficult to apply or interpret. Sheridan (2000) further reported that this finding was supported by the sample of site team visitors that was also included in the assessment.

These study participants agreed that not being able to differentiate among mandated content areas of diversity, populations at risk, and promotion of social and economic justice was the primary issue. It appears that this challenge to implementing and interpreting these mandated areas is precisely the crux of this discussion: that the narrowly focused conceptualization of multiculturalism misconstrues the intent of multicultural social work practice and education.

CULTURAL DIVERSITY, MULTICULTURAL PRACTICE, AND CULTURAL COMPETENCE

Speaking of social work practice and education from a multicontextual perspective acknowledges and affirms that we live in a culturally diverse world, that is, recognition that dictates that our practice and education be conceptualized as a multicultural practice. It follows that if our practice is multicultural, then practice cannot be effective unless practitioners are culturally competent. So what is meant by these terms: cultural diversity, multicultural practice, and cultural competence or responsiveness?

Cultural diversity or cultural pluralism is an inclusive term that defines the complexity of how humans live in transactions with their environments. It captures groups distinguished by race, ethnicity, class, gender, sexual orientation, religion, spirituality, physical or mental ability, age, and national origin (CSWE, 1992, 2001). The CSWE curriculum policy statement mandates that each social work program include content on human diversity in order to prepare students to understand and appreciate human diversity. This content is expected to include information about differences and similarities in the experiences, needs, and beliefs of people. It also affirms that practitioners who serve diverse populations must be trained in the use of differential assessment and intervention skills. Additionally, "cultural diversity captures a set of common adaptive behaviors and experiences derived from memberships in a variety of different contexts . . . and or values derived from partaking of similar historical moments or particular ideologies" (Falicox, 1988, p. 236).

This broad-based definition with its contextual and ecological orientation requires that understanding and appreciation of diversity include self and are not limited to ethnic groups. Certainly, for practitioners valuing, understanding, and appreciating the tenets of

multiculturalism dictate a multicultural practice. A multicultural practitioner embodies specific characteristics and is expected to be culturally competent.

Sanders (1980) described a multicultural person as an individual whose identification and loyalties transcend the boundary of nationalism and whose commitments are based on a vision of the world as a global community. Other characteristics include:

- ability to be "psycho-culturally" adaptive; in other words, the person has an open, fluid frame of reference and is situational in relating to others and in connecting to culture
- personal transitions that reflect a worldview where values, attitudes, and belief systems are in the process of ongoing change; such a person is a transformer, courageous, evolutionary, and appropriate.

Overall, the multicultural person is a bridge builder (Logan, 2000). She or he is open to new ideas, people, places, and situations and is willing to put himself or herself in the role of learner.

Cultural competency reflects the current practice style or orientation for social work practitioners. However, it is important to note at the onset that cultural competency is an inclusive term. It extends beyond people of color to include all the characteristics and dynamics reflected in cultural diversity. General consensus defines the culturally competent social worker as a practitioner who can effectively apply social work skills within a context that reflects knowledge of and respect for the client's way of being in the world. Cultural competence or cultural responsiveness may be conceptualized as having three components that imply the cultural context of any given individual must be recognized and assessed before planning interventions:

1. knowledge base—begins with information about human development and the social environment and extends to include history, worldview, and experiences of being in the world
2. self-awareness and self-understanding—takes into consideration assumptions, biases, values, strengths, and one's own cultural history and stories
3. intervention strategies and skills—are concerned with selecting, modifying, and assessing appropriateness of available practice strategies and ability to differentiate and effectively apply these strategies.

The practitioner's role and responsibilities are reflected in these three components:

1. knowledge of particular content of many different cultures, including one's own (McGoldrick, Pearce, & Giordano, 1982; Sue, Arredondo, & McDavis, 1992; Weaver, 1997); although not expected to know every thing, a practitioner or educator is expected to put himself or herself in the position of learner
2. awareness of differences within different size client systems, between client systems and social worker, and between different client systems and larger societal systems (Falicox, 1983; Imber-Black, 1988; McGill, 1992)
3. ability to apply appropriate intervention and skills with diverse client groups (Browne, Broderick, & Fong, 1993; Weaver & Wodarski, 1995).

The preceding discussion serves as a framework for subsequent discussions. The following section presents a literature overview, which creates historical contexts for the evolution of multiculturalism in the social work profession.

LITERATURE OVERVIEW

There is growing recognition that the United States is by its very nature multicultural. In recent times, scientists have shown that America was a mosaic of people and cultures even 11,000 years ago (Begley & Murr, 1999). However, despite this awareness, the American people continue to struggle with how to live in a world that is multiethnic.

The social work profession has played and continues to play a key role in defining as well as creating multicultural practice and education. Although the complex subtitles of multiculturalism did not emerge in the social work literature, the process had its origin in the profession's cross-cultural work with immigrants during the late 19th and early 20th centuries. This work with immigrant families gave rise to the social reform movement that later came to be known as the Progressive Era of social work (Ehrenreich, 1985). Contemporary social work also evolved out of this progressive era. The diverse groups of immigrants arriving in mass in the United States required early social workers to address, even if indirectly, issues of cultural diversity in their work with poor immigrant families.

The approach to helping immigrant families was influenced by two divergent schools of thought: the assimilation approach and the pluralist approach. As discussed earlier, assimilation was the primary approach used to integrate immigrants into American society and was employed by the Charity Organization Societies, social workers that provided direct services to immigrant families and children. They served with the intent of helping families to rise out of poverty by teaching them moral ways of living (Landon, 1980). However, they also believed that most people who were poor were responsible for their impoverished condition. Social workers in the settlement house movement, which began as a response to the impoverished conditions of immigrants in Chicago, employed the pluralist approach, which was based on the belief that all cultures are equally valued. This belief was affirmed by encouraging immigrants to develop exhibits of their cultural traditions.

It is important to note that the early social work community essentially ignored people of color. Although some scholars such as Osofsky (1971) and Spears (1967) contended that settlement house workers were the first major group since the abolitionist era to show concern for racial inequalities in U.S. society, others such as Jackson, Rhone, and Saunders (1978) and Philpott (1991) expressed the belief that the settlements houses deliberately excluded African Americans. According to Berman-Rossi and Miller (1994), "the record of the settlements on the matter of race, simply does not justify the comparison [with the abolitionist]. Mitigating factors and difficulties imposed by the social context, while understandable, do not obviate a history of acts of commission and omission" (p. 89). They go on to describe the contributions of some of the settlement leaders in the founding of the National Association for the Advancement of Colored People (NAACP) as acts of decency and grace that do not constitute absolution.

During the early 19th century, E. Franklin Frazier, then dean of the Atlanta School of Social Work, was a strong advocate for racial equality. In fact, his outspoken stance against institutional racism resulted in him and his family fleeing Atlanta in fear for their lives (Platt & Chandler, 1988).

In large part, during the 1920s, the social work profession's interest in cultural pluralism was abandoned for its emerging interest in psychodynamic theory. In its thrust forward, the profession adapted a psychiatric model based on Sigmund Freud's dynamic psychiatry. This development led to a Freudian diagnostic school of thought that dominated social work from the 1920s to the 1940s. Potocky (1995) noted that the surge of national pride during the Depression of the 1930s, the Second World War, and the Cold War revived society's interest in applying the assimilation approach to people of color.

During the 1960s and 1970s, multicultural curricula in social work were influenced by many factors: the civil rights movement and ethnic pride movement, and the CSWE curriculum policy statement that mandated curricula requirements for all accredited schools of social work (Bisno, 1984). Since the mid-1970s, both undergraduate and master's level programs have been required to include content on ethnic and racial groups of color and women (Dinerman, 1981). Despite restrictions and the conservative climate of the 1980s, the profession attempted to extend its focus on diversity to include the faculty and student bodies of schools of social work. In this regard, the CSWE Commission on Accreditation, which develops standards by which social work education programs are evaluated for accreditation, adopted its first mandatory nondiscrimination standard in 1954 (Reichert, 1970). This was followed by the 1988 CSWE accreditation standards, which prohibited schools of social work from discriminating on the basis of race, color, creed, gender, age, or sexual orientation (CSWE, 1988). Enforcement of these standards as well as aggressive faculty and student recruitment allow the social work profession to hold the distinction of being the only profession in which African Americans have attained parity of access and equity in graduation rates (Blackwell, 1981).

Although in recent years the professional literature has increased with respect to education and practice with diverse populations, and CSWE's standards, guidelines, and policies on diversity continue to expand, concern exists for what is described as silence or lack of consensus on some educational policies and practices that promote multicultural curricula (Van Soest, 1995). Others believe that many in social work education have compartmentalized and ignored curricula content on issues of diversity because they thought it pertained only to students of color and contained "a lot of propaganda" (Lawrence, 1992, p. 384). Gould (1995) contended that the situation did not change substantially even with the supposed integration of ethnically sensitive content into the total curricula.

In addition to what appears to be mixed messages from the profession, ethnic relations in the United States continue to deteriorate. Racism is alive and doing well. Hate crimes and racially motivated violence have increased dramatically (Weiss & Ephross, 1986). Judicial decisions on civil rights have been overturned, civil rights legislation vetoed (Hopps, 1988), and affirmative action policies attacked (Chestang, 1996).

It is somewhat ironic that, on the one hand, the profession struggles with developing and teaching a multicultural curriculum and, on the other hand, the suggestion that all "social workers should understand culture and its function in human behavior and society, should obtain education about and seek to understand the nature of social diversity and oppression and should not practice, condone, facilitate, or collaborate with any form of discrimination" (NASW, 1996, p. 9). In addition to the irony of mandating an understanding of the nature of social diversity and oppression with respect to race, ethnicity, national origin, color, sex, sexual orientation, age, marital status, political belief, religion, and mental or physical disability, social workers are given limited or no information about what is meant by "white." Limited attempts are being made to research and understand white identity development (Thandeka, 1999) as well as to devise strategies to combat individual racism (Garcia & Swenson, 1992; Morrison, Dorcey, Sylvester, & Wade, 1988; Weiss & Ephross, 1986).

However, it is becoming increasingly evident, albeit a slow process, that true multiculturalism is a movement for a just and equal world, and that we must work to transform the individual self and institutional structures to create this world as well as our group identities. The years since the early 1980s also provided some important lessons about culture. It has become increasingly clear that we carry several cultures within us at once. These cultures may be grouped into two broad categories: inherited and acquired. Our inherited cultures are the most obvious: ethnicity, nationality, religion, the generation into which we are born, gender, class, and sexual orientation. All these attributes and more are mutable, as they change our realities of who and what we are. Not unlike inherited cultures, acquired cultures are multifaceted. These include the culture of our profession and our group identities.

Markowitz (1994) spoke about the power of group identities and the extraordinary influence they have on defining our communities—places where we feel most at home. She went on to say that because our society is not one that values every group equally, we are often forced to sacrifice parts of ourselves that seem most deeply "us" in order to fit. A multiculturalist, however, would argue that cutting off one's significant cultural legacy results in internalized shame and low self-esteem. This shaming process is even more pronounced for those who come from cultures already in a one-down economic position—such as refugees, people from developing nations, those whose cultures include a history of colonization or persecution, or descendants of African slaves. This ambivalence about themselves comes not simply from trying to fit in, but also from rampant stereotypes about their culture, which become the seeds of self-hate (Markowitz, 1994).

Clearly, culture provides us with a sense of belonging, of being part of a larger picture—part of the larger sense of "we" that has been passed down as part of what it means to be human. As a resource, culture allows us to visualize ourselves as part of a timeless existence. It becomes a powerful tool that heals external barriers as well as internal suffering. The multiculturalism of the 1990s was a challenge to the status quo because it highlighted the undeniable link between people's culture and their economic status and position in society (Markowitz, 1994).

Not unlike the multiculturalism of the 1990s, the multiculturalism of the 21st century will and must continue to challenge the status quo. As we work to create a society of true equality, it is imperative that we recognize as have leaders in the multicultural movement that the mainstream, heterosexual white culture controls the money and the power to define for society what is acceptable and not acceptable, valuable, and useless; and to impose those definitions through school curricula, the media, and the justice system or simply all venues of life (Markowitz, 1994).

COMPETING IDEOLOGIES AND SOCIAL POLICY ISSUES

How we define ourselves, how we live, and how we come to live together as a nation are becoming increasingly complex. Assimilation has been, in the minds of many, and continues to be the process through which newly arrived ethnic groups become a part of U.S. society. Generally, an immigrant was expected to melt into a new society; "divest[ing] himself at once of the culture of his homeland, . . . ceas[ing] to speak its language, . . ." (Gordon, 1964, p. 136). Essentially, this newly transformed person learned to regard others with the same suspicions and

hostility as his/her attackers, he/she became closely identified with and supported by familiar and psychologically satisfying ethnic institutions and organizations. That people of color, particularly African Americans and a small number of people from the Orient, were all but ignored by this process, speaks volumes about the tacit policies and programs that systematically denied the presence of people of color in this country (Devore & Schlesinger, 1999). This denial of presence is explicitly evident in social policy related to all aspects of our lives: health, housing, education, and welfare. People of color and others suffering some form of oppression experience these policies through limited or no health care (Logan & Freeman, 2000), substandard or no housing (Freeman, 2000), poor quality of education (Caple, 1990), and punitive social welfare programs (Ginsberg, 1999). Intersecting these issues are increasing concerns about foster care placements and adoptions of children that are from mixed ethnic groups who are being placed or adopted by caretakers or parents that are from different ethnic groups.

These competing ideologies are directly related to the debates about what is affirmative action and who benefits (Bloom, 1987; Chestang, 1996; D'Souza, 1992). These struggles have moved American society further away from the concept of assimilation toward a more peaceful coexistence of the various ethnic groups. The heated discussion about multicultural education during the mid-1990s, however, has highlighted the many unacknowledged facets of this peaceful coexistence or cultural pluralism. This conflict has been referred to as a "culture war" and placed in a broader context (Hunter, 1991). For example, the old conflicts of the 19th and early 20th centuries that took place along religious and ethnic lines are today reflecting sharp polarization on program and policy issues related to abortion, gay rights, health care, education, housing, affirmative action, quotas, as well as multiculturalism. This sharp polarization, which fosters the competing ideologies, is based on many lifetimes of tension that are deeply imbedded in the psyche of the American people. This polarization is also reflected in dualistic thinking and a dichotomous way of being. This dichotomous, dualistic thinking may be viewed from two perspectives: conformist or traditionalist and transformer or progressivist. The traditionalists include groups of people who are outer directed and look outside of themselves for answers. They are committed to an external authority that provides a consistent unchangeable definition of what is true and good. The transformers include those groups of people who are guided by an inner mission of what is real, good, and unchanging. This inner authority reflects an internal vision that is new and constantly unfolding.

It is within this context that the challenge for social work in this century is to find a common ground from which a healing vision will evolve. Through this healing vision of unity we will come to see that these competing ideas about what and how the American society should look and be are more about our spiritual identity than our national identity. Our attempt, as a nation, as a world to answer these age-old questions of who am I, where did I come from, where am I going, and how will I get there is what will sustain and move us to our highest potential in the 21st century.

EXPANDED FRAMEWORK FOR CONCEPTUALIZING MULTICULTURALISM

The social work literature on multiculturalism has expanded since the mid-1980s. This expansion represented a variety of ways to provide racial, ethnic, and cultural diversity in the education and practice arenas. In recent times, there have been calls for paradigmatic shifts in conceptualizing multiculturalism (Gould, 1995) and in the extension of antiracist strategies beyond institutional racism to include individuals, small groups, and communities. The intent of Gould's reconceptualization of multiculturalism is fivefold:

1. to assist all of society to orient its thinking at the transcultural level
2. to emphasize society's prescriptive nature that provides guidelines for dealing with issues of diversity
3. to build a multicultural identity for all people
4. to create a cultural dialogue
5. to interpret in contextual terms the actions of people who do not reflect only one culture, thereby eliminating forced conformity.

The bottom line in expanded conceptualization is building a multicultural identity for all groups. This is by no means an easy feat in that it requires, as suggested throughout this entry, a new social order; Table 1 captures the essence of this expanded conceptualization. The intent is to extend the transcultural to an adaptive transcendent approach or orientation for social work education and practice. This approach reconnects the profession with its mission and its belief in helping all human beings reach their highest potential.

IMPLICATIONS FOR SOCIAL WORK PRACTICE AND RESEARCH

This expanded approach views multiculturalism as adaptive and transcendent. According to Bateson (1994), adaptive multiculturalism is used to increase tolerance and civility, but more important, it offers multiple ways of viewing and experiencing the world. This view may be applied to social work's focus, target of change, goals, and intervention strategies (see Table 1). As suggested by Gould (1995), "a paradigm that informs thinking at a transcultural level and not just a model that provides specific strategies for ethnic-sensitive practice . . . replace[s] rather than preserve[s] the color lines that have divided social work faculty and students" (p. 204). Incorporating the adaptive transcendent perspective moves us into one community that does not exclude anyone. Instead, it allows for everyone to be treated equitably and with respect.

Although the focus changes, the issues are the same in conceptualizing multicultural research as in conceptualizing multicultural practice and education. For example, in conducting culturally competent or culturally responsive research the practitioner not only incorporates the principles of multiculturalism, but also uses culturally sensitive methodologies and direct and ongoing involvement of study participants in planning and implementing the research (Davis, 1986; Freeman & Logan, 1999; Weaver, 1997). Further, when conducting multicultural research, especially with people of color, four factors are important:

1. to acknowledge and address negative images of study participants that have been perpetuated by racially based research
2. to work to gain community access through appropriate community representatives
3. to involve the community from inception to completion of the research
4. to involve the study participants in dissemination of the study findings.

CONCLUSION

This entry discusses the challenges encountered by the social work profession in its attempt to celebrate and embrace differences rather than fear or feel threatened by them. There is no doubt that the profession has made progress in understanding multicultural

TABLE 1
Adaptive Transcendent Approach of Multicultural Social Work for the 21st Century

Solution-Focused, Compassion-Based[a]	Target of Change	Social Work Goals	Intervention Strategies
To create a world in which people from all cultures have equal respect, equal voice, and equal influence in shaping larger community values based on the belief that all things are possible and that everything can and will change	The hearts and minds of all human beings	Work to uplift all of humanity through spiritual, social, cultural, economic, educational, and political action	• Teach compassionate listening, helping • Teach dynamics of white identity development • Oppose and work to change all "isms" of domination and oppression • Eradicate dualism between humans and nature • Put more love and caring in what we do

[a]*Compassion-based helping* is based on the spiritual consciousness of another person's pain and a feeling of unselfish tenderness directed toward the person.

practice, cultural diversity, and cultural competence. However, much serious work remains as we struggle to implement the concept and to rise above our dualistic thinking and the vision of a multicultural world that excludes white people. It suggests, instead, the creation of a world in which equality pervades all aspects of our lives. Such a world requires a high level of responsibility and is supported in the context of an adaptive transcendent perspective.

As we move to embrace and define the "new" in this millennium, it is suggested that researchers, practitioners, and educators equip themselves and their students with a broader knowledge of human potential and possibilities, with greater abilities for reflective, critical thinking, and with the courage to evolve a compassion-based approach to social work practice and education.

REFERENCES

Barringer, F. (1991, March 11). Census shows profound change in racial makeup of nation. *New York Times,* pp. A1, A12.

Bateson, M. C. (1994). *Peripheral visions: Learning along the way.* New York: HarperCollins.

Begley, S., & Murr, A. (1999, April 26). The first Americans. *Newsweek,* pp. 50–57.

Berman-Rossi, T., & Miller, I. (1994). African Americans and the settlements during late nineteenth and early twentieth centuries. *Social Work with Groups, 17,* 77–95.

Bisno, H. (1984). Conceptualizing social work practice in social work education. In M. Dinerman & L. L. Geismar (Eds.), *A quarter-century of social work education* (pp. 47–89). Silver Spring, MD: National Association of Social Workers.

Blackwell, J. E. (1981). *Mainstreaming outsiders: The production of black professionals.* Bayside, NY: General Hall.

Bloom, A. (1987). *The closing of the American mind.* New York: Simon & Schuster.

Browne, C., Broderick, A., & Fong, R. (1993). Lessons from the field: Social work practice with multicultural elders. *Educational Gerontology, 19*(6), 511–523.

Caple, F. S. (1990). The black family and the school. In S.M.L. Logan, E. M. Freeman, & R. G. McRoy (Eds.), *Social work practice with black families: A culturally specific perspective* (pp. 115–132). New York: Longman.

Cheney, L. V. (1992, September). *Telling the truth: A report on the state of the humanities in higher education.* Washington, DC: National Endowment for the Humanities.

Chestang, L. W. (1996). Is it time to rethink affirmative action? No! *Journal of Social Work Education, 32,* 12–18.

Council on Social Work Education. (1988). *Handbook of accreditation standards and procedures.* New York: Author.

Council on Social Work Education. (1992). *Curriculum policy statement M.3.1.* Alexandria, VA: Author.

Council on Social Work Education. (1994). Curriculum policy statement for master's degree programs in social work education. In *Handbook on Accreditation Standards and Procedures.* Alexandria, VA: Author.

Council on Social Work Education. (2001). *Educational policy and accreditation standards,* Alexandria, VA: Author.

Davis, L. V. (1986). A feminist approach to social work research. *Affilia, 1,* 32–47.

Devore, W., & Schlesinger, E. G. (1999). *Ethnic-sensitive social work practice* (5th ed.). Boston: Allyn & Bacon.

Dinerman, M. (1981). *Social work curriculum at the baccalaureate and master's levels.* New York: Lois and Samuel Silberman Fund.

D'Souza, D. (1992). *Illiberal education: The politics of race and sex on campus.* New York: Vintage Books.

Ehrenreich, J. (1985). *The altruistic imagination: A history of social work and social policy in the U.S.* Ithaca, NY: Cornell University Press.

Falicox, C. (1983). *Cultural perspective in family therapy.* Rockville, MD: Aspen Press.

Falicox, C. (1988). Learning to think culturally in family training. In H. Liddle, D. Breunlin, & D. Schwartz (Eds.), *Handbook of family therapy training and supervision* (pp. 232–247). New York: Guilford Press.

Freeman, E. (2000). Homelessness among African American families. In S. Logan (Ed.), *The black family: Strengths, self-help and positive change* (2nd ed., pp. 67–82). Boulder, CO: Westview Press.

Freeman, E., & Logan, S. (1999, February). *Culturally sensitive research with people of color.* Paper presented at the 3rd annual conference of the Society for Social Work Research, Austin, TX.

Garcia, B., & Swenson, C. (1992). Writing the stories of white racism. *Journal of Teaching in Social Work, 6,* 3–17.

Ginsberg, L. (1999). *Understanding social problems, politics, and programs* (3rd ed.). Columbia: University of South Carolina Press.

Gordon, M. M. (1964). *Assimilation in American life: The role of race, religion and national origins.* New York: Oxford University Press.

Gould, K. H. (1995). The misconstruing of multiculturalism: The Stanford debate and social work. *Social Work, 40,* 198–204.

Hartman, A. (1991). Words create worlds [Editorial]. *Social Work, 36,* 275–276.

Hopps, J. G. (1988). "Dé jà vu" or new view? *Social Work, 33,* 291–292.

Hunter, J. D. (1991). *The culture wars: The struggle to define America.* New York: Basic Books.

Imber-Black, E. (1988). *Families and large systems: A therapist's guide through the labyrinth.* New York: Guilford Press.

Jackson, W. S., Rhone, J. V., & Saunders, C. L. (Eds.). (1978). *Social service delivery systems in the black community during the antebellum period, 1619–1860* (Alton M. Child series). Atlanta: Atlanta University School of Social Work.

Landon, J. W. (1980). *The development of social welfare.* New York: Human Sciences Press.

Lawrence, H. (1992). Do "words create worlds?" [Reader response letter]. *Social Work, 37,* 384.

Logan, S. (2000, February). *Bridging the gap.* Columbia: South Carolina Chapter, National Association of Social Workers.

Logan, S., & Freeman, E. (Eds.). (2000). *Health care in the black community: Empowerment, knowledge, skills, and collectivism.* New York: Haworth Press.

Lum, D. (1996). *Social work practice and people of color: A process-stage approach.* Pacific Grove, CA: Brooks/Cole.

Markowitz, L. M. (1994, July/August). Beyond politically correct: The cross currents of multiculturalism. *Family Therapy Networker, 18,* 18–27, 69.

McGill, D. W. (1992). The cultural story in multicultural family therapy. *Families in Society: Journal of Contemporary Human Services, 3,* 339–349.

McGoldrick, M., Pearce, J. K., & Giordano, J. (1982). *Ethnicity and family therapy.* New York: Guilford Press.

Morrison, J. D., Dorcey, S., Sylvester, S., & Wade, J. (1988). Using a social work campus-wide racism awareness training. *Journal of Continuing Social Work Education, 4,* 14–20.

Muktananda. (1991). *Meditate* (2nd ed.) Albany: State University of New York Press.

National Association of Social Workers. (1996). *NASW code of ethics.* Washington, DC: NASW Press.

Osofsky, G. (1971). *Harlem: The making of a ghetto* (2nd ed.). New York: Harper & Row.

Philpott, T. L. (1991). *The slum and the ghetto: Immigrants, blacks, and reformers in Chicago, 1880–1930.* Belmont, CA: Wadsworth.

Platt, T., & Chandler, S. (1988). Constant struggle: E. Franklin Frazier and black social work in the 1920s. *Social Work, 33,* 293–297.

Potocky, M. (1995). Multiculturalism social work in the United States: A review and critique. *International Social Work, 40,* 315–326.

Reichert, K. (1970). Survey of nondiscriminatory practices in accredited graduate schools of social work. In C. Scott (Ed.), *Ethnic minorities in social work education* (pp. 39–51). New York: Council on Social Work Education.

Sanders, D. S. (1980). Multiculturalism: Implications for social work. *International Social Work, 23,* 9–16.

Sheridan, M. (2000, February). *Teaching social justice: Becoming vulnerable vs. being informed.* Invitational presentation at the 46th annual program meeting, Council on Social Work Education, New York.

Simon, R. (1994, July/August). From the editor. *Family Networker, 18,* 2.

Spears, A. (1967). *Black Chicago: The making of a Negro ghetto.* Chicago: University of Chicago Press.

Sue, D. W., Arredondo, P., & McDavis, R. J. (1992). Multicultural counseling competencies and standards: A call to the profession. *Journal of Counseling and Development, 70,* 477–486.

Thandeka. (1999). *Learning to be white: Money, race, and God in America.* New York: Continuum Publishing Company.

Van Soest, D. (1995). Multiculturalism and social work education: The non-debate about competing perspectives. *Journal of Social Work Education, 31,* 55–66.

Weaver, H. N. (1997). The challenges of research in Native American communities: Incorporating principles of cultural competence. *Journal of Social Service Research, 23*(2), 1–15.

Weaver, H. N., & Wodarski, J. S. (1995). Cultural issues in crisis intervention: Guidelines for culturally competent practice. *Family Therapy, 22*(3), 213–223.

Weiss, J. C., & Ephross, P. H. (1986). Group work approaches to hate violence incidents. *Social Work, 31,* 132–136.

FURTHER READING

Anderson, M. L., & Collins, P. H. (Eds.). (1998). *Race, class, and gender: An anthology* (3rd ed.). Belmont, CA: Wadsworth.

Aguirre, A., & Turner, J. H. (1998). *American ethnicity: The dynamics and consequences of discrimination* (2nd ed.). New York: McGraw-Hill.

Chau, K. L. (1990, Spring/Summer). A model for teaching cross-cultural practice in social work. *Journal of Social Work Education, 26,* 124–133.

Chidvilasananda. (1999). *My Lord loves a pure heart: The yoga of divine virtues.* New York: SYDA Foundation.

Fong, R., Spickard, P., & Ewalt, P. (1996). A multiracial reality: Issues in social work. In P. L. Ewalt, E. M. Freeman, S. A. Kirk, & D. L. Poole (Eds.), *Multicultural issues in social work practice* (pp. 21–28). Washington, DC: NASW Press.

McMahon, A., & Allen-Meares, P. (1992). Is social work racist? A content analysis of recent literature. *Social Work, 37,* 533–539.

Nakanishi, M., & Rittner, B. (1992). The inclusionary cultural model. *Journal of Social Work Education, 28,* 27–35.

Rodwell, M. K., & Blankebaker, A. (1992). Strategies for developing cross-cultural sensitivity: Wounding as metaphor. *Journal of Social Work Education, 28,* 155–165.

Rothenberg, P. S. (1998). *Race, class, and gender in the United States: An integrated study* (4th ed.). New York: St. Martin's Press.

Swignoski, M. E. (1996). Challenging privilege through Afrocentric social work practice. *Social Work, 41,* 141–153.

Taki, R. (1994). *From different shores: Perspectives on race and ethnicity in America* (2nd ed.). New York: Oxford University Press.

Tator, C. (1996). Anti-racism and the human service delivery system. In C. E. James (Ed.), *Perspectives on racism and the human services sectors: A case for change* (pp. 152–170). Toronto: University of Toronto Press.

Warren, K. J. (Ed.). (1997). *Ecofeminism: Women, culture and nature.* Bloomington: Indiana University Press.

Sadye M. L. Logan, DSW, ACSW, is professor of social work at the University of South Carolina, Columbia, SC 29208.

For further information see

Adoption; Ethnic-Sensitive Practice; Families: Direct Practice; Family Preservation and Home-Based Services; Management: Diverse Workplaces; Management Overview; Supervision and Consultation; White Ethnic Groups

Key Words

cultural competency	social diversity
cultural diversity	spirituality
multiculturalism	

M

Medicare and Medicaid: Health Policy
Janet D. Perloff

Passed as Titles XVIII and XIX of the Social Security Act Amendments of 1965 (known as Health Insurance for the Aged Act), Medicare and Medicaid are the cornerstones of health policy in the United States. Medicare was intended to increase access to medical care and to reduce the financial burden of the high costs of medical care for elderly people. Medicaid was intended to improve access to medical care for poor people. A basic description of Medicare and Medicaid is provided in this entry. Evidence is presented about the impact of each program, and some of the central policy issues presently facing Medicare and Medicaid are described.

MEDICARE
Medicare is the largest public payer for health care, financing 19 percent of all health spending in 1998 (Health Care Financing Administration [HCFA], 2000a). Medicare covers 95 percent of the nation's elderly population, as well as many people on social security because of disability. Total disbursements for Medicare in 1999 were $213 billion (HCFA, 2000c).

Medicare consists of two primary parts: hospital insurance, known as Part A, and supplementary medical insurance, known as Part B. Today, Medicare Parts A and B are sometimes referred to as the original or traditional Medicare plan. A third part of Medicare, known as Part C, is the Medicare + Choice program that was established by the Balanced Budget Act of 1997 and began providing services January 1, 1998. Beneficiaries must have Parts A and B in order to enroll in Part C. In 2000, about 40 million people were enrolled in one or both Parts A and B of the Medicare program, and 6.4 million of them have chosen to participate in a Medicare + Choice plan (HCFA, 2000c). Medicare Parts A, B, and C are described more fully below.

In general, individuals are eligible for Medicare if they or their spouses worked for at least 10 years in employment covered by social security and Medicare taxes, and if they are 65 years of age and citizens or permanent residents of the United States. Individuals under age 65 also may be eligible if they have received social security or Railroad Retirement Board disability benefits for 24 months, or if they have end-stage renal disease requiring continuing dialysis or kidney transplant. Also eligible for Medicare are certain noncovered people over 65 years of age who can enroll in Part A by paying a monthly premium, for example, those with little or no labor force attachment or those who have immigrated to the United States from other countries and lived here for at least five years (Waid, 1998).

Medicare Part A
Medicare Part A is generally provided automatically to those who are eligible. For the roughly 300,000 individuals not automatically eligible but who enrolled in Part A by paying a monthly premium, the Part A premium was $301 per month in 2000 and $166 per month for those with at least 30 quarters of employment in jobs covered by social security (Koski & Sacks, 2000).

Medicare Part A provides substantial coverage for medically necessary hospital care. In 2000, for example, Medicare paid for all but a $776 deductible per spell of illness for the first 60 days of hospitalization (an amount equal to about one day of hospital care); all but $194 per day for Day 61 to Day 90; and all but $388 per day for 60 lifetime reserve days that can be used only once (Koski & Sacks, 2000). Medicare Part A also provides more limited coverage for skilled nursing facility (SNF) care, home health services, and hospice services (Bodenheimer & Grumbach, 1998). In 2000, for example, Medicare Part A paid for SNF care following hospitalization. The beneficiary paid no deductible and no coinsurance for SNF care from Day 1 through Day 20. From Day 21 through Day 100, the beneficiary paid for coinsurance, or $97 per day in 2000 (Koski & Sacks, 2000).

Medicare Part A is financed almost entirely by a 1.45 percent tax on earnings assessed on both employees and on employers for each employee (and thus a 2.9 percent tax on overall payroll). Self-employed people pay a 2.9 percent tax on earnings. Unlike social security, there is no limit on the amount of earnings subject to

Medicare's tax. Under Medicare law, Part A payments are made only so long as there is a positive balance in the Federal Hospital Insurance Trust Fund. This provision periodically results in the need for legislative changes to Medicare Part A aimed at restoring the positive balance in the Part A trust fund (Moon, 1996).

In 1999 Medicare Part A covered about 39 million people (34 million aged and 5 million disabled enrollees), and Part A benefit payments totaled $129 billion (HCFA, 2000c). In any given year, however, Part A benefits are used by only a fairly small proportion of those who are covered. For example, only 22 percent of Part A beneficiaries required services covered by Part A during 1997 (Waid, 1998).

Medicare Part B
Medicare Part B is available to almost all U.S. resident citizens over 65 years of age and to disabled beneficiaries eligible for Part A. Part B coverage is optional and requires a monthly premium. In 2000 Part B cost the beneficiary $45.50 each month, and in many states premiums were paid on behalf of low-income elderly and disabled people (HCFA, 2000e). Most but not all who are eligible enroll in Part B because the premium is generously subsidized. In 1994 over 96 percent of elderly beneficiaries and 90 percent of disabled Part A beneficiaries elected Part B coverage (Moon, 1996). In 1999 Part B covered about 37 million people, and benefit payments totaled $80.7 billion (HCFA, 2000c). In contrast with Part A benefits, which are used by only about one-fifth of those covered, some 87 percent of Part B beneficiaries received covered services during 1997 (Waid, 1998).

Medicare Part B helps to pay the costs of medically necessary doctor's care as well as the costs of certain nonphysician services, including emergency and outpatient hospital services; physical, occupational, and speech therapy; laboratory tests; clinical social work services; clinical psychologist services; medical equipment; most supplies; diagnostic tests; ambulance services; and some other preventive, health, and therapeutic services (Bodenheimer & Grumbach, 1998). Part B also pays for some home health care services for which Part A does not pay. Medicare Part B pays 80 percent of approved charges for most covered services. The beneficiary is responsible for paying a $100 deductible per calendar year and the remaining 20 percent of the Medicare-approved charge.

Part B is funded in part from premium contributions of beneficiaries and in part from general revenue contributions by the federal government. Although there is a Medicare Part B trust fund, its solvency is not an issue because, by law, the U.S. Treasury must contribute the difference between premium contributions and Part B spending. As a result, financing for Part B seldom provokes a crisis, although the high rate of growth of Part B expenditures has raised financial concerns for this part of Medicare as well (Moon, 1996).

Medicare Part C
Established as part of the Balanced Budget Act of 1997, Medicare Part C (known as Medicare + Choice) enables beneficiaries enrolled in Medicare Parts A and B to choose to receive their Medicare benefits through a wide variety of health plans. Depending on the options available in a beneficiary's community, these may include Medicare managed care plans, private fee-for-service plans, Medicare medical savings account plans, or religious fraternal benefit plans. These plans provide services covered by Parts A and B, and many offer additional benefits (such as preventive care, prescription drugs, dental care, hearing aids, or eyeglasses) not covered by traditional Medicare (HCFA, 2000e).

Impacts and Gaps
Medicare is a very popular social insurance program. Some of its popularity stems from the fact that in their lifetimes, most Americans will receive Medicare services with a dollar value far greater than what they paid in Medicare payroll taxes and premiums (Iglehart, 1999b). Medicare Part B offers a particularly good dollar value. Although beneficiaries pay a premium, federal tax revenues pay 75 percent of the program's actuarial costs, so those with coverage are paying only 25 percent of what the coverage is worth (Katzenstein, 2000).

Some of Medicare's popularity stems from the program's significant accomplishments. Medicare is credited with having drastically reduced uninsurance and impoverishment among older people (Vladeck, 1999). The program also is credited with having improved the lives of elderly and disabled adult beneficiaries (National Academy of Social Insurance, 1999) and, although disparities persist, with having narrowed disparities in health status and use of services between minority and nonminority elderly people (Moon, 1996).

Despite Medicare's many strengths, concerns often are raised about access problems experienced by some of the program's beneficiaries and about gaps in Medicare's coverage that result in the unmet needs and high costs borne by beneficiaries. Surveys find that some Medicare beneficiaries are particularly vulnerable to being unable to access the services they need, including those who are African American, Hispanic, functionally disabled, in poor health, poor, or those lacking in additional health insurance that supplements the coverage available through Medicare (Medicare Payment Advisory Commission, 2000). Also problematic is the fact that traditional Medicare does not cover many health services. These include long-term nursing care, custodial care, and certain other needs such as denture and dental care, eyeglasses, and hearing aids. The lack of prescription drug coverage under traditional Medicare is regarded as particularly troublesome because the costs of prescription drugs have been rising rapidly (Davis, Poisal, Chulis, Zarabozo, & Cooper, 1999) and because elderly people, with their multiple chronic illnesses, have a much greater need for prescription drugs than does the population as a whole (Lagnado, 1998). Finally, observers note that the structure of Medicare benefits discourages management and coordination of health care; tends to favor acute care over interventions aimed at improving functional status; and generally has not kept pace with advances in areas such as the treatment of sensory impairment and psychiatric conditions (Cassel, Besdine, & Siegel, 1999).

Financial Woes and Proposals for Reform
The 1990s brought many concerns about Medicare's financial condition. In mid-1995 the Medicare trustees forecast the "insolvency" of the program's Part A trust fund by 2002. The predicted troubles of the Part A trust fund, along with concerns about the demands that will be placed on the program by aging baby boomers, led to the passage of the Balanced Budget Act of 1997 and the Balanced Budget Refinement Act of 1999, legislation that enacted what some regard as the most far-reaching changes in the program since its inception (Medicare Payment Advisory Commission, 2000). The laws included provisions to slow the growth in payments to Medicare providers; increase beneficiary premiums; shift the financing of many home health services from the Part A to the Part B trust fund; expand coverage of several preventive services; and authorize the offering of several new types of managed care products by creating the Medicare + Choice program as Part C (Medicare Payment Advisory Commission, 2000). In addition to these major Medicare reforms, the Balanced Budget Act of 1997 authorized the creation of a

Bipartisan Commission on the Future of Medicare. The work of this group of experts and political leaders ended in March 1999 without a formal recommendation to Congress for further Medicare reform, reflecting the deeply divided views among Republican and Democratic commission members about future Medicare reforms.

Medicare's fiscal pressures eased toward the end of the 1990s. The rate of growth of Medicare spending slowed considerably, and in 1999 the Medicare trustees reported that the Part A trust fund would remain solvent until 2015. Nonetheless, average annual spending increases of 6 percent to 7 percent are forecast between 2000 and 2010, and even sharper increases are expected once the first of the baby boomers become eligible for Medicare in 2010 (Medicare Payment Advisory Commission, 2000). As a result, pressures for further Medicare reform are likely to continue.

As the work of the Bipartisan Commission on the Future of Medicare indicated, there is considerable disagreement about the next steps needed to further stabilize Medicare's financing and to ensure that the program has resources sufficient to meet the needs of future elderly and disabled beneficiaries. Indeed, Medicare scholar Ted Marmor (2000) observed that at the end of the 20th century "there remain deep divisions over the purpose, structure, and future of the program" (pp. 180–181). Proposals for strengthening Medicare's solvency tend to fall into three categories: (1) those that would shift risks onto beneficiaries, perhaps through the use of vouchers or by requiring enrollment in managed care; (2) those that would reduce coverage of services, perhaps by making Medicare the payer of last resort, substantially increasing premiums, or by taxing the value of Medicare benefits; and (3) those that would limit eligibility, perhaps by increasing the age of eligibility or by making eligibility subject to a means test (Moon, 1996).

Health policy expert John Iglehart (1999b) predicted a Republican-favored voucher plan will receive serious consideration in the coming years. This controversial proposal would replace Medicare's commitment to provide a defined set of benefits to all beneficiaries with a "premium support" system under which all beneficiaries would receive a predetermined amount (vouchers) to be applied to the purchase of a health plan providing defined benefits. Premium support, a form of managed competition for Medicare, would limit and make more predictable federal expenditures for Medicare. But unlike Medicare historically, such a voucher system would shift the risk of additional spending to beneficiaries and to the plans they chose (Marmor, 2000).

At the same time that Congress considers various strategies to improve Medicare's financial condition and prepare the program for the aging of the baby boom generation, it will also need to improve the program's benefit package to better meet the needs of beneficiaries. Prominent among the changes being considered is the addition of prescription drug coverage to traditional Medicare, the absence of which has become even more conspicuous because some Medicare beneficiaries now have this coverage through Medicare + Choice plans.

MEDICAID

Medicaid is the largest health plan in the United States, covering some 40 million people in 1998. In 1998 approximately 51 percent of Medicaid-eligible people were low-income children, 20 percent were low-income adults, 18 percent were low-income disabled people, and some 11 percent were low-income elderly people (HCFA, 2000b). Total disbursements for Medicaid in 1999 were $180.9 billion, or $102.5 billion in federal and $78.4 billion in state funds (HCFA, 2000b).

Overview

Medicaid is a complex federal–state grant-in-aid program. The program makes federal matching payments available to states to help cover the costs of delivering services to eligible individuals. Federal law and regulations outline broad national guidelines for Medicaid. Within these guidelines each state administers its own program and is free to establish its own eligibility standards, covered services, and provider payment rates. As a result of its federal–state structure, Medicaid varies widely from state to state. State discretion over Medicaid policy was increased through provisions of the 1997 Balanced Budget Act, and interstate variation in Medicaid can be expected to increase in the future (Boyd, 1998).

To receive federal Medicaid matching payments, states must cover certain categories of individuals including, for example: (1) those eligible for Medicaid because they meet the requirements for Aid to Families with Dependent Children that were in effect in their state on July 16, 1996; (2) pregnant women and children under six years of age whose family income is at or below 133 percent of the federal poverty level; (3) Supplemental Security Income recipients in most states—recipients

of Title IV (Grants To States For Aid and Services To Needy Families With Children and For Child Welfare Services, P.L. 100-485), all children born after September 30, 1983, who are under 19 years of age and living in families with incomes at or below the federal poverty level—and (4) certain Medicare beneficiaries (HCFA, 2000b).

States also have the option of covering many other categories of people, but states vary considerably in the extent to which they do so. Among the groups that can be covered at state option are the "medically needy," that is, people who would be eligible for Medicaid under one of the mandatory or optional categories except that their income or resources are above the state eligibility level. These individuals may qualify for Medicaid by "spending down"—that is, by incurring medical expenses that reduce their income to or below a medically needy protected income level set by the state. The medically needy provisions of Medicaid provide especially valuable protection against impoverishment for elderly people, the chronically ill, and other low-income people who incur high medical expenses.

In general, individuals must be American citizens in order to qualify for Medicaid. Illegal aliens who would otherwise be eligible for Medicaid can qualify only for emergency care. Legal immigrants can qualify under certain circumstances primarily related to their date of entry into the United States (Kaiser Commission on Medicaid and the Uninsured, 1999).

State Medicaid programs provide coverage that extends well beyond the services covered either by Medicare or by most employer-sponsored health insurance plans. Federal law requires that certain services be covered by state Medicaid programs, although states have leeway in deciding the "amount, scope, and duration" of the coverage. Mandatory services include inpatient services; outpatient services; physician services; prenatal care; vaccines for children; nursing facility services for people 21 years of age or older; family planning services; rural health clinic services; home health care for people eligible for skilled nursing care; laboratory and x-ray services; pediatric nurse practitioner, family nurse practitioner, and nurse midwife services; services provided in a federally qualified health center; and early and periodic screening, diagnosis, and treatment for children under 21 years (HCFA, 2000b).

In addition to the mandatory services, states have the option of covering some 34 other services. Among the most commonly covered optional services are diagnostic services, clinic services, intermediate care facilities for mentally retarded people, prescribed drugs and prosthetic devices, optometrist services and eyeglasses, and home and community-based services to certain people with chronic illnesses. The 1997 Balanced Budget Act added a new option known as Programs of All-Inclusive Care for the Elderly. These programs enable states to provide alternatives to institutional care for those people 55 years or older requiring a nursing facility level of care (HCFA, 2000b).

Medicaid is primarily financed through federal and state general tax revenues. On average, the federal government pays 57 percent of the program's costs (Kaiser Commission on Medicaid and the Uninsured, 1999). The size of the federal government's contribution to a state's Medicaid program can vary from 50 percent to 83 percent and is determined by a formula that compares the state's per capita income level with the national average. States with a higher per capita income level are reimbursed a smaller share of their Medicaid costs. States may impose nominal cost sharing for some services, although federal law requires that cost sharing not be placed on certain services, including those for pregnant women, children under 18 years, emergencies, or family planning services.

Although adults and children in low-income families comprise nearly three-fourths of Medicaid-eligible people, their medical care accounts for less than 30 percent of program expenditures. Elderly, blind, or disabled recipients, although only about one-fourth of eligible recipients, account for most of the program's expenditures because of their greater reliance on acute and long-term care services (Iglehart, 1999a). Acute care services accounted for just over half of all Medicaid spending in 1997, and long-term care accounted for an additional 37 percent (Kaiser Commission on Medicaid and the Uninsured, 1999). Indeed, Medicaid is the nation's major payer for long-term care services; in recent years, Medicaid has paid for almost 45 percent of the total cost of care for people using nursing facility or home health services (HCFA, 2000b).

Impact and Gaps

Medicaid is often credited with having improved the health of low-income Americans; having improved access to care and satisfaction with care for low-income Americans; and having helped to reduce (although not eliminate) differentials in access related to income and race (Lillie-Blanton, 1999). People who are poor and enrolled in Medicaid are more likely than people with no insurance to have a usual source of medical care, a higher number of physician visits, and a higher rate of hospitalization. Such findings provide strong support for the view that Medicaid has improved access to care for the populations it covers (Berk & Schur, 1998).

Despite its many achievements, Medicaid—a public assistance program—has never enjoyed the popularity of the U.S. social insurances, that is, social security and Medicare. Objections to Medicaid have periodically focused on concerns about fraud and abuse or other types of program mismanagement. But by far the most serious and consistent objections have been aimed at the program's high and sometimes seemingly uncontrollable costs. Between 1988 and 1993, federal Medicaid spending grew at an average annual rate of 19.6 percent, wreaking havoc with federal and state budgets. Various pieces of legislation were enacted throughout the 1990s aimed at slowing the rate of growth of Medicaid costs. These cost containment initiatives, along with welfare reform and low unemployment rates, led to a rate of growth in Medicaid spending in 1997 of only 3.9 percent. According to the Congressional Budget Office, the rate of growth in Medicaid spending is not expected to return to double digits (Kaiser Commission on Medicaid and the Uninsured, 1999).

In addition to concerns about costs, critics have often raised serious concerns about the quantity and quality of care to which Medicaid recipients have access. Historically, Medicaid has been committed to ensuring access to "mainstream" medical care—that is, care from the same private physicians and hospitals used by patients who are privately insured. In reality, however, the range of providers available to Medicaid patients has often been considerably more limited than this, both because Medicaid patients tend to reside in "underserved" communities with few medical providers and because the proximate providers often do not accept Medicaid patients into their practices (Fossett & Perloff, 1999; Perloff, 1996; Perloff, Kletke, Fossett, & Banks, 1997). As a result, Medicaid patients (like other low-income, high-risk, or uninsured patients) have tended to delay seeking care and to rely on hospital emergency rooms as a major source of their care. They also have tended to obtain care from the limited number of physicians accepting Medicaid patients and from "safety net" providers— community health centers, public health clinics, and hospital outpatient clinics.

In an effort to expand access and contain Medicaid costs, states have increasingly enrolled Medicaid patients in managed care plans. Until recently, states could offer managed care plans but could not require Medicaid-eligible people to enroll in managed care plans unless the state had obtained a waiver from the federal agency administering Medicaid—the Health Care Financing Administration. The 1997 Balanced Budget Act eliminated the waiver requirement except as it applies to certain high-risk groups, including those dually eligible for Medicare and Medicaid, children with special needs, and Native Americans. This new provision makes it considerably easier for states to require that Medicaid-eligible individuals participate in managed care plans.

Under Medicaid managed care, health maintenance organizations, prepaid health plans, or comparable entities agree to provide a specific set of services to Medicaid enrollees, usually in return for a predetermined periodic payment per enrollee. The proportion of Medicaid beneficiaries in managed care plans has increased dramatically, from 2 percent in 1981, to 9.5 percent in 1991, to 48 percent in 1997, and to 54 percent in 1998 (HCFA, 2000b; Iglehart, 1999a). Until recently, the population enrolled in managed care has been comprised primarily of children and adults in low-income families. However, some states are contemplating enrolling higher cost Medicaid patients, such as elderly and disabled people and those with specific conditions—AIDS, high-risk pregnancies, substance abuse, mental illness, and diabetes (Iglehart, 1999a).

According to Fossett and Perloff (1999), the recent slowdown in Medicaid costs has slowed some of the pressures to enroll Medicaid-eligible people in managed care plans and has largely removed Medicaid managed care from the policy limelight. Nonetheless, advocates remain concerned about aspects of enrolling them in managed care plans. There are concerns about whether enrollees fully understand and can make the most effective use of their managed care plans; about the adequacy of the provider networks to which Medicaid managed care enrollees have access; about the adequacy of provisions for care for the chronically ill; about whether states are setting capitation rates at a level sufficient to keep commercial plans interested in enrolling Medicaid patients; and about the ability of states to provide the oversight needed to ensure that managed care plans provide services that are efficient and effective (Perloff, 1996).

Policy analysts and policymakers also question whether Medicaid will be able to bear the growing costs of long-term care for the growing numbers of elderly and disabled Americans. As previously noted, more than one-third of Medicaid's dollars presently go toward long-term care (both nursing home services and home and community-based services), and the pressure on Medicaid to pay for more long-term care is likely to grow in the future. Given their significance in the Medicaid program, long-term care services and the people who rely on them will play an important role in future debates about Medicaid policy (Feder, Lambrew, & Huckaby, 1997).

Finally, one of the most serious concerns raised about Medicaid is its inability to cover all those individuals who are poor or uninsured. Although Medicaid aims to help them, it does not provide medical assistance for them. Low incomes and limited resources are among Medicaid's eligibility criteria, but someone who is poor must also be a member of one of the groups covered by his or her state Medicaid program. As a result of Medicaid's income, resource, and categorical eligibility requirements, the program covered only 44 percent of the nation's nonelderly poor population in 1997 (Iglehart, 1999a).

To make matters even worse, Medicaid is not helping all those that it could. There is a growing awareness that many people who presently are among the uninsured are actually eligible for Medicaid. Factors that cause eligible families not to enroll in Medicaid are not well-understood. Some of the reasons are thought to include: (1) Medicaid's lack of outreach and resulting lack of awareness within families of potentially eligible members; (2) families' desires to avoid the stigma of Medicaid; and (3) the sometimes daunting complexity of Medicaid. In addition, there is considerable evidence that as the 1996 welfare reform law has been implemented and families have made the transition away from cash assistance, growing numbers of people—although often still eligible for Medicaid—are inadvertently disappearing from the Medicaid rolls (Perloff, 1999).

Platform for Incremental Expansion of Health Insurance Coverage

Although Medicaid falls short of providing health care coverage for all people who are poor and even for all those who are eligible for its benefits, the program has frequently served as a vehicle for helping to increase the proportion of Americans with health care coverage. For example, federal legislation adopted during the mid-1980s and early 1990s dramatically expanded Medicaid eligibility for low-income pregnant women and children. As a result of such initiatives, between 1986 and 1995 the number of low-income children served by Medicaid grew from 10 million to more than 17 million. Today, as a result of these laws, states are phasing in Medicaid eligibility to all resident children younger than 19 years living in families with incomes below the federal poverty level (and below 133 percent of poverty for children younger than six years) by the year 2002 (Newacheck, Pearl, Hughes, & Halfon, 1998).

More recently, in 1997 Congress created Title XXI of the Social Security Act, known as the State Children's Health Insurance Program (SCHIP). This legislation provides federal block grant funds so that states can provide health insurance to uninsured children below 19 years of age with family incomes up to 200 percent of the federal poverty level. In this legislation, Congress once again gave states the opportunity to use Medicaid as a platform for expanding health insurance coverage—states were given the option of using SCHIP funds to expand coverage under the state's existing Medicaid program, provide coverage under a separate state child health assistance program, or both (Perloff, 1999). As of July 1, 2000, all 50 states, the District of Columbia, and five U.S. territories had implemented SCHIP: 15 states had created separate child health programs, 23 states had expanded Medicaid, and 18 states had done both. To date, it is estimated that SCHIP has brought health care coverage to some 2 million children (HCFA, 2000d).

CONCLUSION

Medicare and Medicaid have had a significant impact on access to and use of health services by elderly, disabled, and poor populations. Gaps in eligibility and coverage persist and improvements in the performance of these programs continue to be needed. Medicare and Medicaid are likely to undergo significant changes in the coming years. Social workers will need to be knowledgeable about proposals to reform these programs, able to gauge their likely impact; and ready to undertake advocacy at both the state and federal levels with the goal of shaping these programs to best serve the interests of the populations they serve.

REFERENCES

Balanced Budget Act of 1997, P.L. 105-33.

Berk, M. L., & Schur, C. L. (1998). Access to care: How much difference does Medicaid make? *Health Affairs, 17,* 169–180.

Bodenheimer, T. S., & Grumbach, K. (1998). *Understanding health policy: A clinical approach.* Stamford, CT: Appleton & Lange.

Boyd, D. J. (1998). Medicaid devolution: A fiscal perspective. In F. J. Thompson & J. J. DiIulio (Eds.), *Medicaid and devolution: A view from the states* (pp. 56–105). Washington, DC: Brookings Institution Press.

Cassel, C. K., Besdine, R. W., & Siegel, L. C. (1999). Restructuring Medicare for the next century: What will beneficiaries really need? *Health Affairs, 18,* 118–131.

Davis, M., Poisal, J., Chulis, G., Zarabozo, C., & Cooper, B. (1999). Prescription drug coverage, utilization, and spending among Medicare beneficiaries. *Health Affairs, 18,* 231–243.

Feder, J., Lambrew, J., & Huckaby, M. (1997). Medicaid and long-term care for the elderly: Implications of restructuring. *The Milbank Quarterly, 75*(4), 425–459.

Fossett, J. W., & Perloff, J. D. (1999). The "new" health reform and access to care: The problem of the inner city. In D. Rowland, S. Rosenbaum, A. Salganicoff, & M. Lillie-Blanton (Eds.), *Access to health care: Promises and prospects for low-income Americans* (pp. 97–121). Washington, DC: Kaiser Commission on Medicaid and the Uninsured.

Health Care Financing Administration. (2000a). *Highlights, national health expenditures, 1998* [Online]. Washington, DC: Author. Available: http://www.hcfa.gov/stats/nhe-oact/hilites.htm

Health Care Financing Administration. (2000b). *Medicaid: A brief summary* [Online]. Washington, DC: Author. Available: http://www.hcfa.gov/pubforms/actuary/ormedmed/DEFAULT4.htm

Health Care Financing Administration. (2000c). *Medicare: A brief summary* [Online]. Washington, DC: Author. Available: http://www.hcfa.gov/pubforms/actuary/ormedmed/DEFAULT3.htm

Health Care Financing Administration. (2000d). *The state children's health insurance program: Preliminary highlights of implementation and expansion* [Online]. Washington, DC: Author. Available: http://www.hcfa.gov/init/wh0700.pdf

Health Care Financing Administration. (2000e). *What is Medicare?* [Online]. Washington, DC: Author. Available: http://www.medicare.gov/whatis.html

Health Insurance for the Aged Act of 1965, P.L. 89-97, 79 Stat. 290.

Iglehart, J. K. (1999a). Medicaid. *New England Journal of Medicine, 340,* 403–408.

Iglehart, J. K. (1999b). Medicare. *New England Journal of Medicine, 340,* 327–332.

Kaiser Commission on Medicaid and the Uninsured. (1999). *Medicaid: A primer.* Washington, DC: Author.

Katzenstein, L. (2000, February 16). Making your way through the maze of Medicare options. *New York Times,* p. H19, Col. 1.

Koski, A., & Sacks, D. (2000). *Medicare*. New York: Hunter College, Samuel Sadin Institute on Law of the Brookdale Center on Aging.

Lagnado, L. (1998, November 17). Hard to swallow: Drug costs yield grim choice of medicines over necessities. *Wall Street Journal*, pp. A1, A15.

Lillie-Blanton, M. (1999). *Access to health care: Promises and prospects for low income Americans*. Washington, DC: Kaiser Commission on Medicaid and the Uninsured.

Marmor, T. R. (2000). *The politics of Medicare*. Hawthorne, NY: Aldine de Gruyter.

Medicare Payment Advisory Commission. (2000). *Report to the Congress: Medicare payment policy*. Washington, DC: Author.

Moon, M. (1996). *Medicare now and in the future*. Washington, DC: Urban Institute Press.

National Academy of Social Insurance. (1999). *Medicare and the American social contract* [Online]. Washington, DC: Health Care Financing Administration. Available: http://www.nasi.org/publications2763/publications_show.htm?doc_id=54378

Newacheck, P. W., Pearl, M., Hughes, D. C., & Halfon, N. (1998). The role of Medicaid in ensuring children's access to care. *Journal of the American Medical Association, 280,* 1789–1793.

Perloff, J. (1996). Medicaid managed care and the urban poor: Implications for social work. *Health & Social Work, 21,* 189–195.

Perloff, J. (1999). Insuring the children: Obstacles and opportunities. *Families in Society, 80,* 516–525.

Perloff, J., Kletke, P., Fossett, J., & Banks, S. (1997). Medicaid participation among urban physicians. *Medical Care, 35,* 142–157.

Vladeck, B. C. (1999). The political economy of Medicare. *Health Affairs, 18,* 22–36.

Waid, M. O. (1998). Overview of the Medicare and Medicaid programs (1998 statistical supplement). *Health Care Financing Review,* 1–19.

Janet D. Perloff, PhD, is professor, School of Social Welfare and School of Public Health, University at Albany, State University of New York, 135 Western Avenue, Albany, NY 12222.

For further information see

Aging: Public Policy Issues and Trends; Federal Social Legislation from 1961 to 1994; Health Care: Financing; Health Care: Policy Development, *1997;* Health Care: Reform Initiatives; Health Services Systems Policy; Long-Term Care; Managed Care; Social Security

Key Words	
health care	Medicaid
financing	Medicare

Mental Illness

See Mental Health Overview, *Volume 2;* Serious Mental Illness: A Biopsychosocial Perspective, *1997;* Treatments for People with Severe and Persistent Mental Illness, *2003*

P

Participatory and Stakeholder Research
Lorraine Gutiérrez

Social workers have involved community members in research since the beginning of the 20th century. However, within recent years there has been an expansion of interest in a number of fields of research that are conducted in collaboration with community constituents (Ansley & Gaventa, 1997). Various terms have been used to describe this research, including participatory research (Bailey, 1992; Brown & Tandon, 1983; Hick, 1997), empowerment research (Fetterman, Kaftarian, & Wandersman, 1996; Gutiérrez, 1997; Maton & Salem, 1995; Ristock & Pennell, 1996; Zimmerman, Ramirez-Valles, Suarez, de la Rosa, & Castro, 1997), action research (Chesler, 1990; Medvene, Mendoza, Lin, Harris, & Miller, 1995), participatory action research (Sohng, 1992; Wang & Burris, 1997), multicultural research (de Anda, 1997; Gutiérrez, 1997), community-based research (Hatch, Moss, & Saran, 1993; Israel, Schulz, Parker, & Becker, 1998), and feminist research (Maguire, 1987; Ristock & Pennell, 1996). The development of participatory approaches is motivated by an interest in grounding our questions, methods, and analyses in the experiences of stakeholders to develop knowledge that can be directly useful for practice and ultimately for stakeholders themselves (Hick, 1997; Israel et al., 1998; Rist, 1994). As this field grows and our public and private funding organizations call for this work, social work researchers will need to develop skills for maintaining scholarly integrity while using collaborative research methods (Lather, 1986; Nyden & Weiwel, 1992). This entry identifies the ways in which participatory and stakeholder research has evolved and how it has contributed to our social work knowledge base. It also identifies the methods that are currently evolving in other disciplines and fields—such as public health, education, feminist studies, and sociology—that can inform our own field. Examples of "best practices" are used to demonstrate these methods, and conclusions are discussed for future participatory and stakeholder research.

WHAT IS PARTICIPATORY AND STAKEHOLDER RESEARCH?

Participatory and stakeholder research refers to methods in which individuals, families, or community members study issues or conditions that directly affect their lives (Nyden, Figert, Shibley, & Barrows, 1997). Unlike other forms of research, the purpose, structure, and outcome are focused on constituents' needs and resources. The goal of this research is toward action ranging from program development and implementation to confrontational social action (Ristock & Pennell, 1996). The involvement of academic researchers in these projects is related to the degree to which they will meet the community's goals. Many terms have been used to describe participatory and stakeholder research and although the differences can appear to be inconsequential, they can be useful in distinguishing between the different purposes of this work and degree of stakeholder participation.

With its focus on developing knowledge for practical use, most participatory and stakeholder-based research can be considered a form of action research. Action research was developed in the 1940s by Kurt Lewin and other social and organizational psychologists interested in developing research methods that could both address the needs of organizations and develop basic knowledge (Green et al., 1995). These methods have a strong tradition in Europe and in the area of educational and organizational studies and have been instrumental in changing our understanding of workplace behavior (Brown & Tandon, 1983). Much of social work research, with its emphasis on informing policy and practice, can be considered a form of action research. Action research, however, is not by definition activist research, as in many cases the focus is on maintaining power relationships. It is also not inherently participatory, as action researchers may be outside consultants who do research on workers or community members without their direct involvement (Brown & Tandon, 1983; Stoeker, 1999).

Participatory research is also focused on action and the creation of knowledge, but it is characterized by extensive collaboration between the investigator and the stakeholders, or beneficiaries, of the research (Brown & Tandon, 1983; Green et al., 1995; Hick, 1997). This form of research requires that all interested partners come to the table to work together on all aspects of the research process (Israel et al., 1998; Nyden et al., 1997; Ristock & Pennell, 1996). The focus is on conducting research that will build knowledge and make positive community change. Participatory research reflects a social justice perspective that takes a critical view of community and social structures and recognizes conflicts between elite individuals and those with less power (Stoeker, 1999). The goal of this work is social transformation and the improvement of the lives of stakeholders through research, education, and action (Yeich & Levine, 1992).

In much of the literature, the boundaries between participatory research and participatory action research can be unclear. Participatory action research (PAR)—with its reference both to participation and action—is most descriptive of much of the participatory and stakeholder research that social workers do. PAR also places equal value on participation of community members and facilitating action as a result of the knowledge gained (Nyden et al., 1997; Sohng, 1992). Much of the work on PAR places a high priority on the empowerment of community members through collaboration and knowledge development, and through the skills gained from participation. Community members and researchers are partners in the research and the boundaries between the two groups are blurred (Bailey, 1992). The goals of PAR are to make research more relevant to stakeholders, to share ownership of the data collected, to motivate community members toward change, and to inform social action (Chataway, 1997).

Further distinctions have been made within the field of participatory and stakeholder research. The term community-based research (CBR) has been used to describe research conducted by, with, or for communities or community groups (Israel et al., 1998). The level of community involvement in CBR will vary by its form. Research *by* communities is research that is conducted independently by an organization in order to reach its goals. University researchers are rarely involved in these activities and the results are rarely represented in our scholarly journals (Nyden & Weiwel, 1992). Research *with* communities refers to PAR methods used with community groups. Research conducted *for* communities occurs when a community group hires or otherwise involves an outside

researcher to conduct research that will meet its needs. This form of CBR places the outside researcher in the role of consultant or employee of the community organization (Hick, 1997; Nyden & Weiwel, 1992; Singer, 1993).

The involvement of community members in CBR will vary depending on the needs, desires, and resources of the group. Often, the information gathered through this process is for the sole benefit of the organization and may not contribute directly to the social work knowledge base. Research *by* communities requires a high level of involvement by the members, whereas research *for* communities may require a low level of involvement. Research *with* communities will require a moderate or high level of residents' involvement, depending on the project.

The literature on feminist research indicates that participatory methods are often incorporated. Feminist research is focused on scholarship that addresses issues of gender, sexism, and other forms of inequality. The purpose of feminist research is to contribute to a more just society (Gold, 1998; Maguire, 1987; Ristock & Pennell, 1996). Although feminist research literature has focused more on perspectives than on methods, current scholarship has emphasized a constructivist and participatory perspective that shares many characteristics of PAR (Maguire, 1987; Ristock & Pennell, 1996). Uncovering the voices of stakeholders and other less powerful groups is a critical aspect of a feminist research perspective.

Multicultural or culturally relevant research also often calls for participatory methods. Multicultural social work research has been described as a process, not a method, of research that reflects our professional values of cultural competence and social justice (Uehara, Sohng, Bending, & Seyfried, 1996). Collaboration with stakeholders is necessary for this work, as the members of ethnic and racial communities are the experts of the social meaning of the issues they face and the interventions that they find acceptable and effective (Hatch et al., 1993; Uehara et al., 1996). This form of collaboration requires private and public reflection on the research process and how it relates to inequality, collaboration across different groups, and community empowerment and social transformation (Uehara et al., 1996). Like other participatory methods, it decenters the role and power of the investigator and calls for true collaboration.

Another similar trend is the development of participatory evaluation methods that involve all stakeholders in the process of an evaluation project. Two models for participatory evaluation have been described as fourth generation evaluation (Guba & Lincoln, 1989) and empowerment evaluation (Fetterman et al., 1996; Worthington, 1999). Both approaches argue that evaluation can be a tool to improve organizational functioning if stakeholders are actively involved in its design, implementation, and interpretation. These methods call for more process-oriented methods of research and methods that bring together the different constituencies and stakeholders within an organization. In this way, evaluation methods can be a tool for empowerment (Fetterman et al., 1996; Guba & Lincoln, 1989).

SOCIAL WORK PERSPECTIVES ON PARTICIPATORY AND STAKEHOLDER RESEARCH

Participatory and stakeholder research is not new to social work. For over a century, social workers have endeavored to develop knowledge that can improve programs and communities and inform social policy. For example, neighborhood-focused research was a central activity of Jane Addams and other settlement workers at Hull House. *Hull-House Maps and Papers* ([1895] 1970), was an investigation by settlement workers in the neighborhood in which Hull House was located. The papers included maps and descriptions of the demographic and social characteristics of neighborhood residents. Hull House then used the data in its reform activities (Harkavy & Puckett, 1994).

These types of activities continued to be an integral part of social work practice throughout the 20th century. The field of community planning has as one of its cornerstones the collection of neighborhood-based data to identify community resources and issues. For example, in the early 1950s, the Los Angeles Youth Project brought together group workers, ministers, case workers, and community leaders to analyze census data, interview key informants, and map youth resources, such as parks and community centers in "high-risk" areas of the city (Los Angeles Youth Project, 1953). These findings led to recommendations for program coordination, services, and new social policies. These types of community planning methods have been used to address issues such as gang involvement (Gold & Winter, 1961; Spergel, 1999), health and mental health services (Bailey, 1992; Barry, 1999), child welfare (Day, Robison, & Sheikh, 1998), and neighborhood stabilization (Turner, 1999).

The interest of social workers in participatory and stakeholder methods has grown in the latter quarter of the 20th century and the beginning of the 21st century. This reflects trends in social work practice toward empowerment and consumer-driven paradigms overall (Sohng, 1992). In the past decade, interest in participatory research, PAR, CBR, and other methods in social work research has grown (see Bailey, 1992; Hick, 1997; Sohng, 1992; Uehara et al., 1996). This is paralleled in other fields such as public health, which has contributed much to our understanding of CBR (Hatch et al., 1993; Israel et al., 1998; Wallerstein, 1993; Wang & Burris, 1997), community psychology (Medvene et al., 1995; Yeich & Levine, 1992; Zimmerman et al., 1997); and education (Delgado-Gaitan, 1995; Sagor, 1992). Although many of the concepts and methods of PAR are not yet represented in social work research literature, they represent a growing force within the field.

CHARACTERISTICS OF PARTICIPATORY AND STAKEHOLDER RESEARCH

An extensive body of literature, primarily in the social sciences, has worked to define and delineate methods for participatory and stakeholder research. Although some of this literature attempts to distinguish between these models, there are common themes and principles across them in relation to the processes used and the perspective on research. The following discussion identifies these common attributes.

Most participatory research, particularly recent models, reflects a postmodern and constructivist perspective to knowledge development. This perspective recognizes that knowledge is socially constructed and that all individuals can be engaged in the construction of knowledge (Israel et al., 1998; Lather, 1986). It critiques models for research that are focused on notions of objectivity and the separation of "researchers" and "subjects" for simplifying social reality and being less conducive to action (Sohng, 1992; Yeich & Levine, 1992). The collaboration of stakeholders in the process ensures that new and different perspectives are represented in the process and outcome.

This interpretive method has led some to represent PAR as less "scientific" than more conventional research (Lather, 1986). However, PAR must be rigorous in order to collect valid information that is useful for the community (Nyden et al., 1997). Although it has been commonly associated with qualitative and interpretive methods, there are many examples of PAR that use quantitative methodologies (Nyden et al., 1997). The choice of research method should be tailored to the purpose of the research, the context, and the nature of the project (Israel et al., 1998). The triangulation of research methods, in which data from different sources are combined and compared, is often used in order to reflect the multiple perspectives in a community (Lather, 1986). Validity in participatory research is based primarily on construct and face validity, triangulation of different research methods, and catalytic validity—the degree to which the results can be translated into action (Lather, 1986).

PAR methods recognize that access to knowledge, and the ability to define legitimate knowledge, can be a critical tool for empowerment. Linkages between PAR and empowerment have been drawn both to the process of research and to the outcome of projects (Hick, 1997; Park, 1993; Sarri & Sarri, 1992; Yeich & Levine, 1992). Participatory approaches to research make explicit the linkages between development and access to knowledge in our information-based society (Park, 1993). Practitioners of PAR approaches have identified ways in which community involvement in the research processes can develop the critical awareness and skills that can be the basis of the members' empowerment (Lather, 1986; Sarri & Sarri, 1992; Yeich & Levine, 1992). PAR projects can also contribute to empowerment by bringing to the forefront the concerns and perspectives of stakeholders and citizens (Navarro, Prevost, & Romero, 1995; Reardon, 1998). Participation in PAR can empower stakeholders to develop ongoing projects to investigate issues that affect their lives (Hick, 1997).

PAR values can link the research process to an outcome of action or practice that informs theory. The goal of PAR for stakeholders is to be involved in the creation of knowledge that will be useful to them (Bailey, 1992; Fox, McDermott, Hamilton, & Toumbourou, 1996; Hatch et al., 1993; Sarri & Sarri, 1992; Schulz et al., 1998). The knowledge gained can contribute to planning processes at the community and organizational levels (Gold, 1998; Schulz et al., 1998; Singer, 1993) or in evaluation of programs and policies (Bailey, 1992; Fox et al., 1996; Guba & Lincoln, 1989). In addition, this should be a cyclical process in which action and practice inform theory (Bailey, 1992; Hatch et al., 1993; Turnbull, Friesen, & Ramirez, 1998).

These linkages require some level of collaboration in all aspects of the research process that break down traditional hierarchies between the "researched" and the "researchers." PAR projects have used a range of participatory methods to link stakeholders and researchers (Hatch et al., 1993; Hick, 1997; Sarri & Sarri, 1992; Turnbull et al., 1998). Hick (1997) has identified two dimensions—involvement and decision making—that can be used to analyze the collaborative process. The most collaborative methods are those in which there is a high level of community involvement and a high level of community decision-making power. Less collaborative processes would be those with lower community involvement but high community decision making or high involvement but low community decision making. Noncollaborative methods are those with low community involvement and low community decision making. The level and type of involvement used should be determined by the nature of the research activity, the researchers, and the groups involved (Alvarez & Gutiérrez, 2001; Turnbull et al., 1998).

Participatory and stakeholder research should include methods that are sensitive to multicultural perspectives and that build on the strengths of disenfranchised communities. With its focus on empowerment, PAR is most often used with disenfranchised and disempowered individuals, families, and communities. Multicultural methods must be used to involve communities of color in PAR projects. These have included partnering with community-based or culturally oriented organizations (Grinstead, Zack, & Faigeles, 1999; Navarro et al., 1995), reflecting by the research team on how multicultural issues are affecting the project (Uehara et al., 1996), and engaging community residents in research (Delgado, 1997, 1999) in order to use research methods that are culturally congruent. Use of these methods has been effective with other less powerful groups such as children and youth (Harper & Carver, 1999; Hill, 1997; Penuel & Freeman, 1997), communities of color (Delgado, 1997, 1999; Hatch et al., 1993; Navarro et al., 1995), prison inmates (Grinstead et al., 1999), and people with psychiatric disabilities (Townsend, Birch, Langley, & Langille, 2000; Yeich & Levine, 1992).

PAR methods are consistent with social work values of self-determination, social justice, and cultural competence (NASW, 1996). A central social work value is the recognition of the importance of self-determination for consumers and community members. PAR methods, by involving stakeholders in the research processes, recognize the ability of individuals and communities to understand, change, and address their own needs. NASW's current code of ethics also emphasizes the importance of developing cultural competence for practice that is sensitive to issues of social diversity and oppression. As discussed previously, PAR methods should be enacted in culturally competent ways and by reflecting the experiences of less powerful groups; therefore, this research has great potential to enhance overall cultural competence within the social work field. Through the processes of empowerment, PAR methods can also be a tool for social justice. Just as the *Code of Ethics* emphasizes social justice work that is collaborative, PAR is particularly appropriate for social work researchers and practitioners.

EXAMPLES OF PARTICIPATORY AND STAKEHOLDER RESEARCH

Although much of the literature on PAR is theoretical and conceptual, there is a growing body of literature that describes ways in which these methods have been implemented in the field. These examples of PAR are illustrative for identifying methods for PAR and for discussing challenges and how they can be overcome. They are also useful resources for thinking about how PAR methods can be used for research with systems of different sizes. This section discusses examples of PAR that have been used with different levels of analysis and change.

In their article on research with families, Turnbull and colleagues (1998) argued that PAR could be invaluable for improving the validity and rigor of research findings while enhancing the empowerment of participants. This article proposes a continuum of family participation in research that can range from very low levels, in which families are research participants or contribute to an advisory board, to very high levels, in which families and researchers are co-researchers or in which families direct the research activity. Turnbull and colleagues' work has focused primarily on what they term "level four" in which families collaborate as ongoing advisors to the research team and as active members of a PAR committee that oversees the project. By involving families in this way, teams have been able to learn firsthand about living with children with disabilities and about important research issues and questions. Family members have also been invaluable in educating researchers about the best ways to reach families of children with disabilities and to translate research findings into policy and practice. These researcher–stakeholder teams have been most useful when they spell out how decisions will be made and what decisions will be made so that they can collaborate most productively.

Harper and Carver (1999) described an innovative collaboration between university-based researchers and a community-based clinic that was focused on improving HIV education and interventions for high-risk street youth. The community-based clinic had a long history of reaching this population effectively. This positive reputation with "out of the mainstream youth" made it possible for researchers to involve these young people as advisory board members and research assistants. The project the youth were involved in was conducting focus groups, advising researchers on issues, and providing information on where and how to reach other youth. These methods gave voice to the experiences of young people and led to developing specific programs such as street-based outreach, reality-based workshops, and a drop-in center. This project required that researchers devote time to developing relationships and common understandings with the youth. In some cases, this involved pizza parties and other informal activities to break down community youth–researcher boundaries. In other cases, this required spending time working directly with youth in the field-based research office. Although this approach required more and different types of efforts on the part of researchers, the quality of outcomes was worth this investment.

Photovoice is a PAR method developed by public health researchers that has considerable potential for social work (Wang & Burris, 1997; Wang, Yi, Tao, & Carovano, 1998). This method involves community members in documenting their experiences through the use of photography. Members of a community research team are provided with inexpensive cameras and asked to take photographs that are on a theme of the project, such as "community assets," "health issues," "dangers in our environment," and so forth. When the photos are developed, they can then be used as the focus of discussion for grouping and identifying larger issues in the community. For example, in a Photovoice project in a rural Chinese village, a participant photographed a family planning class meeting outdoors. Through the discussion, participants identified many issues, including the large size of the group, the large range of ages, and the lack of males involved. This led to suggestions of how family planning education could be more relevant to community members. The use of Photovoice has been effective as a means of involving stakeholders in research *and* as a means for community organizing and influencing public policy. Photos from the project in rural China were used to provide data about the need for improved health resources in the villages that led to specific policy and program changes.

These are only three examples of PAR from the human services field. Although they had different foci and methods, together they suggest that PAR can be a powerful tool for creating useful knowledge and empowerment. In all three examples, members of disenfranchised groups were able to use participation in research to change the programs, policies, and conditions that have direct effects on their lives. Collaboration with researchers required deliberate work and attention to ensure that community members' participation was genuine and useful. Researchers benefited by developing knowledge with good external validity for reaching communities that they knew little about. Therefore, in all of these cases, the collaborative work was productive to both researchers and community members.

CONCLUSION

Through the use of PAR, social workers and social work researchers can work toward developing knowledge that can be useful for policy, program development, and practice. Social workers practice on the boundary between theory and practice. Professional ethics emphasize the importance of using methods that are effective and appropriate for the population (NASW, 1996), but social workers often lack knowledge regarding specific stakeholder groups, their needs, and their resources. PAR methods have the potential for generating knowledge that is directly relevant to practice and that spans the boundary between "theory" and "practice" (Reisch & Rivera, 1999; Singer, 1993).

In order to ensure that social workers' use of PAR methods are effective, they must understand what this type of research is and how it is practiced. The literature on stakeholder and participatory methods for research provides useful discussions for analyzing and understanding the meanings of participation, action, and research. In developing collaborative research, social workers must examine these terms and determine the degree to which they will engender participation, work toward action, and develop their knowledge base. For example, within any situation there are many potential stakeholders (Perkins & Wandersman, 1990; Turnbull et al., 1998). Research teams must determine who to involve, under what circumstances, and how. These discussions are best conducted

collaboratively so that all participants will have a common understanding of the process and goals of the activity (Israel et al., 1998).

A significant challenge to all PAR work is *how* to build collaborative partnerships across what are often substantial differences in power resources, goals, and interests. The literature on PAR has identified many barriers to this collaboration, such as mutual mistrust, additional amount of time required to build relationships, lack of academic rewards for PAR, lack of interest in research by community members, inability of many researchers to communicate effectively, and lack of adequate funding for PAR projects (see Cancian, 1993; Chataway, 1997; Chesler & Flanders, 1967; Stoeker, 1999; Turnbull et al., 1998). However, this literature has also identified methods that have been useful in overcoming some of these challenges such as hiring community workers to contribute to projects, partnering with community-based organizations, setting explicit research principles and ground rules for collaboration, ensuring informal interaction between community members and research team members, and seeking alternative forms of funding (see Ansley & Gaventa, 1997; Bailey, 1992; Israel et al., 1998; Perkins & Wandersman, 1990; Stoeker, 1999). These challenges should be seen as opportunities for creativity in the pursuit of activist research.

Social workers involved in PAR must also attend to the unique ethical issues involved in this work (Reisch & Rivera, 1999). Although this method is consonant with social work ethics, there are also issues involved in working in community contexts where researchers have not been invited to participate and where they may represent organizations that have been oppressive to community members. Issues also arise in respect to the "ownership" of raw data and findings, particularly when they do not reflect community expectations or when community members participate in projects with "hidden agendas" to enhance their organizations (Perkins & Wandersman, 1990). PAR, as is the case with all research, should always be conducted in ways that reflect our ethics and values. Many of the methods for collaboration discussed above can be ways to address potential ethical problems and concerns.

Although this entry has argued that PAR fits well with the needs of social workers and social work researchers, it is not for every situation, researcher, or community. Just as the interventions of social workers must reflect what is most appropriate for the population, issue, and social worker, the research project should be created to best fit with the researcher, community, topic, organizational context, and constraints (Alvarez & Gutiérrez, 2001). This literature has identified a range of participatory strategies that can ensure that there is some stakeholder involvement regardless of the project (Hick, 1997; Turnbull et al., 1998). When stakeholders cannot be actively involved in every aspect of the research process, it is still imperative that social work researchers consider how their "voices" or perspectives can be included. The PAR methods can be a tool for enhancing any form of social work research or practice.

REFERENCES

Alvarez, A., & Gutiérrez, L. (2001). Choosing to do participatory research: An example and issues of fit to consider. *Journal of Community Practice, 9,* 1–20.

Ansley, F., & Gaventa, J. (1997). Researching for democracy and democratizing research. *Change, 29,* 46–53.

Bailey, D. (1992). Using participatory research in community consortia development and evaluation: Lessons from the beginning of a story. *American Sociologist, 23,* 71–82.

Barry, M. (1999). Service and cause—Both sides of the same coin. In J. Rothman (Ed.), *Reflections on community organization: Enduring themes and critical issues* (pp. 136–148). Itasca, IL: F. E. Peacock Publishers.

Brown, L., & Tandon, R. (1983). Ideology and political economy in inquiry: Action research and participatory research. *Journal of Applied Behavioral Sciences, 19,* 277–294.

Cancian, F. (1993). Conflicts between activist research and academic success: Participatory research and alternative strategies. *American Sociologist, 24,* 92–106.

Chataway, C. (1997). The examination of the constraints on mutual inquiry in a participatory action research project. *Journal of Social Issues, 53,* 747–765.

Chesler, M. (1990). Action research in the voluntary sector: A case study of scholar–activist roles in self-help groups. In S. Wheelan, E. Pepitone, & V. Abt (Eds.), *Advances in field theory* (pp. 265–279). Newbury Park, CA: Sage Publications.

Chesler, M., & Flanders, M. (1967). Resistance to research and research utilization: The death and life of a feedback attempt. *Journal of Applied Behavioral Sciences, 3,* 469–487.

Day, P., Robison, S., & Sheikh, L. (1998). *Ours to keep: A guide to building a community assessment strategy for child protection.* Washington, DC: CWLA Press.

de Anda, D. (Ed.). (1997). *Controversial issues in multiculturalism.* Boston: Allyn & Bacon.

Delgado, M. (1997). Interpretation of Puerto Rican elder research findings: A community forum of research respondents. *Journal of Applied Gerontology, 16,* 317–332.

Delgado, M. (1999). Involvement of the Hispanic community in ATOD research. *Drugs and Society, 14,* 93–105.

Delgado-Gaitan, C. (1995). Researching change and changing the researcher. *Harvard Educational Review, 63,* 389–411.

Fetterman, D., Kaftarian, S., & Wandersman, A. (1996). *Empowerment evaluation: Knowledge and tools for self-assessment and accountability.* Thousand Oaks, CA: Sage Publications.

Fox, A., McDermott, F., Hamilton, M., & Toumbourou, J. (1996). Insider/partnership evaluation: Approach and concept development. *Evaluation and Program Planning, 19,* 199–207.

Gold, M., & Winter, J. (1961, October). *A selective review of community-based programs for preventing delinquency.* Chicago: Chicago Youth Development Project.

Gold, N. (1998). Using participatory research to help promote the physical and mental health of female social workers in child welfare. *Child Welfare, 77,* 701–724.

Green, L., George, M., Daniel, M., Frankish, C., Herbert, C., Bowie, W., et al. (1995). *Study of participatory research in health promotion: Review and recommendations for the development of participatory research in health promotion in Canada.* Ottawa: Royal Society of Canada.

Grinstead, O., Zack, B., & Faigeles, B. (1999). Collaborative research to prevent HIV among male prison inmates and their female partners. *Health Education and Behavior, 26,* 225–238.

Guba, E., & Lincoln, Y. (1989). *Fourth generation evaluation.* Newbury Park, CA: Sage Publications.

Gutiérrez, L. (1997). Multicultural community organizing. In M. Reisch & E. Gambrill (Eds.), *Social work in the 21st century* (pp. 249–259). Thousand Oaks, CA: Pine Forge Press.

Harkavy, I., & Puckett, J. (1994). Lessons from Hull House for the contemporary urban university. *Social Service Review, 68,* 299–321.

Harper, G., & Carver, L. (1999). "Out-of-the-mainstream" youth as partners in collaborative research: Exploring the benefits and challenges. *Health Education and Behavior, 26,* 250–265.

Hatch, J., Moss, N., & Saran, A. (1993). Community research: Partnership in black communities. *American Journal of Preventive Medicine, 9*(Suppl.), 27–31.

Hick, S. (1997). Participatory research: An approach for structural social workers. *Journal of Progressive Human Services, 8,* 63–79.

Hill, M. (1997). Participatory research with children. *Child and Family Social Work, 2,* 171–183.

Hull-House maps and papers [by] residents of Hull-House. ([1895] 1970). New York: Arno Press.

Israel, B., Schulz, A., Parker, E., & Becker, A. (1998). Review of community based research: Assessing partnership approaches to improve public health. *Annual Review of Public Health, 19,* 173–202.

Lather, P. (1986). Research as praxis. *Harvard Educational Review, 56,* 21–42.

Los Angeles Youth Project. (1953, October). *Juvenile delinquency: A cooperative plan for prevention.* Los Angeles: Welfare Council of Metropolitan Los Angeles.

Maguire, P. (1987). *Doing participatory research: A feminist approach.* Amherst, MA: Center for International Education.

Maton, K. I., & Salem, D. A. (1995). Organizational characteristics of empowering community settings: A multiple case study approach. *American Journal of Community Psychology, 23,* 631–656.

Medvene, L. J., Mendoza, R., Lin, K.-M., Harris, N., & Miller, M. (1995). Increasing Mexican-American attendance of support groups for parents of the mentally ill: Organizational and psychological factors. *Journal of Community Psychology, 23,* 307–325.

National Association of Social Workers. (1996). *NASW code of ethics* [Online]. Available: http://www.naswdc.org/Code/ethics.htm

Navarro, R., Prevost, T., & Romero, C. (1995). Padres unidos: Grassroots researchers. *Educator, 9,* 16–19.

Nyden, P., Figert, A., Shibley, M., & Barrows, D. (1997). *Building community: Social science in action.* Thousand Oaks, CA: Pine Forge Press.

Nyden, P., & Wiewel, W. (1992, Winter). Collaborative research: Harnessing the tensions between researcher and practitioner. *American Sociologist, 23,* 43–55.

Park, P. (Ed.). (1993). *Voices of change: Participatory research in the United States and Canada.* Toronto: Ontario Institute for Education.

Penuel, W., & Freeman, T. (1997). Participatory action research in youth programming: A theory in use. *Child and Youth Care Forum, 26,* 175–185.

Perkins, D., & Wandersman, A. (1990). "You'll have to work to overcome our suspicions": The benefits and pitfalls of research with community organizations. *Social Policy, 21,* 32–41.

Reardon, K. (1998). Enhancing the capacity of community-based organizations in East St. Louis. *Journal of Planning Education and Research, 17,* 323–333.

Reisch, M., & Rivera, F. (1999). Ethical and racial conflicts in urban-based action research. *Journal of Community Practice, 6,* 49–63.

Rist, R. (1994). Influencing the policy process with qualitative research. In N. K. Denzin & Y. S. Lincoln (Eds.), *Handbook of qualitative research* (pp. 545–557). Thousand Oaks, CA: Sage Publications.

Ristock, J. L., & Pennell, J. (1996). *Community research as empowerment: Feminist links, postmodern interruptions.* Toronto: Oxford University Press.

Sagor, R. (1992). *How to conduct collaborative action research.* Alexandria, VA: Association for Supervision and Curriculum Development.

Sarri, R., & Sarri, C. (1992). Organizational and community change through participatory action research. *Administration in Social Work, 16,* 99–123.

Schulz, A., Parker, E., Israel, B., Becker, A., Maciak, B., & Hollis, R. (1998). Conducting a participatory community-based survey for a community health intervention on Detroit's eastside. *Journal of Public Health Management Practice, 4,* 10–24.

Singer, M. (1993). Knowledge for use: Anthropology and community-centered substance abuse research. *Social Science and Medicine, 37,* 15–25.

Sohng, S. (1992). Consumers as research partners. *Journal of Progressive Human Services, 3,* 1–14.

Spergel, I. (1999). Gangs and community organization. In J. Rothman (Ed.), *Reflections on community organization: Enduring themes and critical issues* (pp. 150–173). Itasca, IL: F. E. Peacock.

Stoeker, R. (1999). Are academics irrelevant? Roles for scholars in participatory research. *American Behavioral Scientist, 42,* 840–854.

Townsend, E., Birch, D., Langley, J., & Langille, L. (2000). Participatory research in a mental health clubhouse. *Occupational Therapy Journal of Research, 20,* 18–44.

Turnbull, A., Friesen, B., & Ramirez, C. (1998). Participatory action research as a model for conducting family research. *The Journal of the Association for Persons with Severe Handicaps, 23,* 178–188.

Turner, J. (1999). Neighborhood organization: How well does it work? In J. Rothman (Ed.), *Reflections on community organization: Enduring themes and critical issues* (pp. 122–135). Itasca, IL: F. E. Peacock.

Uehara, E., Sohng, S., Bending, R., & Seyfried, S. (1996). Toward a values-based approach to multicultural social work research. *Social Work, 41,* 613–623.

Wallerstein, N. (1993). Empowerment and health: The theory and practice of community change. *Community Development Journal, 28,* 218–227.

Wang, C., & Burris, M. A. (1997). Photovoice: Concept, methodology, and use for participatory needs assessment. *Health Education & Behavior, 24,* 369–387.

Wang, C., Yi, W., Tao, Z., & Carovano, K. (1998). Photovoice as a participatory health promotion strategy. *Health Promotion International, 13,* 75–85.

Worthington, C. (1999). Empowerment evaluation: Understanding the theory behind the framework. *Canadian Journal of Program Evaluation, 14,* 1–28.

Yeich, S., & Levine, R. (1992). Participatory research's contribution to a conceptualization of empowerment. *Journal of Applied Social Psychology, 22,* 1894–1908.

Zimmerman, M. A., Ramirez-Valles, J., Suarez, E., de la Rosa, G., & Castro, M. A. (1997). An HIV/AIDS prevention project for Mexican homosexual men: An empowerment approach. *Health Education & Behavior, 24,* 177–190.

Lorraine Gutiérrez, PhD, is professor of social work and psychology at the School of Social Work, University of Michigan, 1080 S. University, Ann Arbor, MI 48109.

For further information see

Agency-Based Research; Citizen Participation; Survey Research

Key Words

community participation	research
empowerment	

Practice Guidelines

See Ethical Standards in Social Work: The *NASW Code of Ethics, 2003;* Evidence-Based Practice Guidelines, *2003*

Public Assistance

See Conservatism and Social Welfare, *2003;* General Assistance, *Volume 2;* Temporary Assistance for Needy Families, *2003;* Temporary Assistance to Needy Families, *1997*

R

Radical Social Work

See Progressive Social Work, *Volume 3*

Retirement, Private Pensions, and Individual Retirement Accounts

Robert B. Hudson

One of the major developments of the past century has been the institutionalization of retirement as a stage in the life process. There have always been individuals who could not work due to the infirmities of old age or who were not required to work given particular economic or social status afforded them in old age. However, over the last few decades, retirement has increasingly become a normatively sanctioned or institutionalized role rather than largely an exclusionary or residual one. The majority of contemporary retirees are in relatively good health, enjoy extensive social security and potentially considerable private pension protection, and have been able to choose retirement as an option rather than having been forced into it due to ill health or disability. Nonetheless, there remain significant numbers of older Americans—principally women and people of color—who either continue to work for reasons of economic necessity or who are "retired" by virtue of being unable to work or find employment. Retirement is important from a number of perspectives. The decision to retire or to cease to work for monetary compensation has enormous consequences for the individuals involved, both the worker and immediate family members. The role of retirement is important to the larger society, which is directly affected by the leisure, volunteer, or part-time employment choices that retirees from full-time work may make. And retirement is of great consequence to public and private sector decision makers who must wrestle with how to accumulate and distribute the resources required for economically sustaining the growing numbers of people in late middle age and old age who are no longer working.

UNDERSTANDING RETIREMENT

As straightforward as it might first appear, retirement is not easily conceptualized or defined. At its most basic, retirement is withdrawal from the labor force (with the important presumption that one had, in fact, participated in the labor force), but a young or middle-aged worker who stopped working—either voluntarily or through a layoff—would likely not be considered retired (O'Grady-LeShane, 1995; Quinn, Burkhauser, & Meyers, 1990). Henretta (2001) suggested an admittedly truncated definition: "retirement is a shorthand term to refer to a labor force exit that is not reversed for a substantial period of time" (p. 256). Broader definitions add receipt of some form of pension or deferred earnings to the labor force withdrawal element (Gendell & Seigel, 1992).

Beyond the economic understanding of retirement built around work and income maintenance, it can also be understood in social terms. Here, retirement is more about assuming new roles than about leaving old ones. As health and well-being of older adults have improved in recent years, retirement is less centered on the inability to work than it is on the ability and desire to assume social roles outside of the labor force (Atchley, 2000). Older cohorts no longer retire largely because they must (due to health or mandatory retirement practices) or even simply because they are able to (a sufficient pension). Rather, today large numbers of older people retire because they believe it to be a status legitimated by a range of age-related public benefits (principally social security), including coverage for workers, spouses, and survivors (O'Rand, 1990).

The joining of these two understandings of retirement—established exit from the labor force and normatively sanctioned assumption of new roles outside of the labor force—has together created the indisputable "institutionalization of retirement," which is found today throughout the industrial world. Extending

Wilensky and Lebeaux's (1965) well-known distinction between residual and institutional policies, both the retirement role (today increasingly involving individuals voluntarily leaving the labor force who are in good health) and retirement policy (today centered on social insurance rather than public assistance) are no longer residual; they have become fully institutional. Morgan and Kunkel (2000) effectively bring these developments together in enumerating the four core elements of retirement as a social institution: (1) society is able to produce an economic surplus; (2) it has devised a mechanism for diverting this surplus to the needs of the currently nonproducing; (3) there are established positive attitudes about not working; and (4) people live long enough to accumulate an acceptable number of productive years to warrant support.

A final way of understanding retirement centers neither on an event nor status but on function. In this understanding, retirement and retirement policies are seen as an important means of controlling the size and composition of the labor force. At times when employers or government wish to limit the supply of older workers, they liberalize retirement policies, thereby encouraging older workers to exit the labor market. In the United States, it is widely acknowledged that both social security and traditional pensions were long designed in such a way as to encourage older workers to retire (Graebner, 1980; Schulz, 1988). This function of retirement policy continues to be more pronounced in European nations, where concern has long centered on youth unemployment and the severe political and economic consequences it can bring (Kohli, Rein, Guillemard, & van Gunsteren, 1991). At least in the United States, however, there has recently been an important reversal in emphasis, with the introduction of changes in both social security and private pension policy now intended to encourage extended labor force participation among older workers (Henretta, 2001).

PATTERNS OF RETIREMENT

Historical Developments

As the preceding material strongly suggests, one of the major demographic and economic trends of the 20th century was the decline in labor force participation among older workers, a large majority of whom historically were men. In 1900 roughly two-thirds of men 65 years of age and older were in the labor force; by 1950 that number was less than one-half, and by

1985 only 16 percent of men 65 years old and above were at work (U.S. Bureau of the Census, 1992). Burtless and Quinn (2001), compiling participation data on five cohorts of older men leaving the labor force between 1910 and 1999, found (1) employment declines for each of the cohorts, (2) the sharpest drops in participation in the men's early to mid-60s, (3) more pronounced declines among more recent cohorts of men, and (4) the suggestion of a leveling off in the retirement trend of older men within the most recent cohort.

Although until recently most labor force studies included only men (Szinovacz, 1982), it is known that the historical labor force patterns of older women have differed from those of older men in important ways. Women's overall labor force participation rates have historically been lower than those of men—only an estimated 17 percent of women were in the labor force in 1890. Yet, those rates have risen noticeably since World War II and trail men's by far less a margin than was historically the case. Partially because of this populationwide employment increase among women, there is no evidence of the dramatic falloff in older women's workforce effort that there has been among older men. Labor force participation rates of women 60 to 64 years of age increased from 33.2 percent in 1975 to 38.8 percent in 1999 and for women 65 to 69 years increased from 14.5 to 18.4 percent (Henretta, 2001). Weaver (1994), comparing successive birth cohorts of women born at five-year intervals between 1915 and 1930, reported notable increases for women from their mid-50s until their mid-60s, with a mixed but essentially flat pattern for women 65 years and above. That older women's labor force effort has been increasing modestly while older men's has been falling is a function of two conflicting, contrary currents: the long-term secular trend of greater labor force participation among recent cohorts of adult women versus older workers, including married couples, in general seeking retirement opportunities.

Recent Developments

Since roughly 1985, however, there has been some coalescing of the retirement patterns of men and women. Most noticeably, the historical trend of men retiring earlier has at least flattened out and may have reversed. Between 1985 and 1999, the labor force participation rates of men at ages 62, 65, and 70 have increased, if only marginally. At the same time, older women's employment rates at these ages have increased between 0.4 and 1.0 percent annually (Burtless & Quinn, 2001). Given the long time periods in which older men's presence in the workforce was declining and older women's was rising only modestly, the reversal for men and the marked increase in participation for women are significant. Whether these trends are permanent is not yet known because the shifts have been relatively recent. Whatever the ultimate outcome, these trends will be critical for the larger economy (the number and proportion of the adult population in the workforce), for public policy (strains on public and private pensions), and informal social networks (household makeup, nuclear and extended family responsibilities). Of particular importance will be determining the degree to which older people, especially divorced and widowed women, continue to work at later ages out of necessity as opposed to better-off elders who continue to work largely out of preference (Uchitelle, 2001).

A second recent trend around work and retirement centers on an erosion in the traditional understanding of individuals transitioning from full-time work into full-time retirement. Increasing numbers of people may be moving into part-time or self-employed situations or leaving the labor market for short periods of time only to later return on some basis. In these ways, the traditional work–retirement distinction may be becoming less discrete and more continuous, a pattern that Mutschler, Burr, Pienta, and Massaghi (1997) referred to as a transition that is "blurred" rather than "crisp" and into what Ruhm (1989) and Quinn and Burkhauser (1990) first labeled "bridge jobs."

Data from the Health and Retirement Study from the 1970s showed that even then roughly one-fourth of workers leaving full-time jobs engaged in work of some other kind (Quinn, 1997). More recent data analyzed by Ruhm (1995) found that one-third of men ages 58 to 63 were engaged in some kind of "postcareer" job. Using data sets from the 1992 and 1994 waves of the Health and Retirement Study, Quinn (1997) found that 50 percent of male workers in their mid- to late-50s were still in a career job, that 20 percent were in a bridge job (defined as a part-time job or a full-time job expected to last less than 10 years), and that 30 percent were no longer working. Of this last group, fully one-third had themselves retired from a bridge job. Of the women in the sample, 30 percent were in a bridge job, and those who were retired were more likely to have retired from a bridge job. As these data suggest, patterns of

retirement may become more diverse and will also have important consequences for the economy, public policy, and families.

Accounting for Retirement Patterns

Reasons for retirement have been clustered in various ways. Atchley (2000) spoke of employment problems, disability issues, and desire. Villani and Roberto (1997) noted the interplay of employment issues (layoffs, forced retirement, age discrimination) and personal preferences (income or leisure). Placed in somewhat sharper relief, Kohli and colleagues (1991) spoke of the "push" factors (those that make work difficult or unattractive) and "pull" factors (those that make retirement a desirable alternative to work) that create different "pathways" to retirement. Quadagno and Hardy (1996) captured the micro and macro level complexities that surround patterns around leaving the workforce, observing that

> what has become increasingly apparent is that retirement decisions are shaped by individual preferences, but that individual choices are made relative to the opportunities and constraints that workers encounter. (p. 326)

At the individual level, relevant factors may include economic well-being; health status; attitudes toward one's work situation; preferences of a spouse concerning work and retirement; obligations to spouse, children, or others; and one's preference for leisure over work. At the aggregate level, the constraining effects include labor market opportunities, public and private pension provisions, and availability of health insurance. Together, these individual-level and aggregate characteristics may combine either to push people out of the workforce into retirement or to pull people into retirement by rendering it, on balance, preferable to working.

Push Factors

In historical context two major push factors— poor health and loss of work—forced men out of the labor force. In a remarkable study using archival data on northern Civil War veterans, Costa (1996) found changes in health status to be a much greater contributor to retirement and pension eligibility than she found in a sample of men a century later. Indeed, push factors seemed very disproportionately responsible for retirement decisions at least through the 1950s. Studies of people retiring in the 1940s and 1950s found ill health and layoffs cited by over 80 percent of respondents as the reasons for retirement, with only about 5 percent in the 1950s and 20 percent in the 1960s citing a desire to retire as the reason (Quinn & Burkhauser, 1990). Packard and Reno (1989) found that men leaving the workforce even without pensions cited poor health as the principal reason.

The job layoffs that push older workers out of the labor force may be ascribed to factors that do not necessarily tie to a worker's age, such as an economic recession, structural unemployment, or inadequate job skills. However, an important factor that has targeted older workers is age discrimination. Here, workers are denied employment on the basis of their chronological age, appearance, and age-based assumptions about their work-related abilities. Although the prevalence of age discrimination is hard to determine, both the public at large and employers themselves believe that it exists. Indeed, as Graebner (1980) argued, the institution of retirement itself may be best understood as a manifestation of age discrimination, being a mechanism where workers are forced from the labor market in the absence of any individual shortcoming and thus with no need to fire them.

Apart from pensions of various kinds, however, public law did not explicitly recognize the existence of age discrimination until passage of the Age Discrimination in Employment Act in 1967. In the most recent amendments to the act in 1986, the long-standing practice of mandatory retirement—forcing the retirement of workers attaining a given age—was outlawed for virtually all occupations. Nonetheless, age discrimination continues to be a problem of older workers, as demonstrated by the rising number of cases brought before the Equal Opportunity Employment Commission, which enforces the Age Discrimination in Employment Act as well as other civil rights laws.

Pull Factors
Despite the ongoing presence of this series of push factors, beginning in the middle decades of the 20th century, pull factors making retirement increasingly attractive began accounting for the preponderance of older workers leaving the workplace. Thus, as Costa's (1996) and others' studies have shown, the overall health status of older workers has steadily improved over the years, a trend that modulates the push–pull factors tied to health. Although improved health might allow workers to work longer (National Academy on an Aging Society, 2000), it also

introduces the possibility of an active and enjoyable retirement. In the 1950s few believed that American workers would, in fact, learn to prefer retirement to continued work, a view captured by Flint (cited in Schulz, 1988):

> There used to be a stigma to going out. He was over the hill. But now it's a looked-for status. Those retirement parties, they used to be sad affairs. They are darn happy affairs now. The peer pressure is for early retirement. (p. 81)

Indeed, by the 1980s, poor health was cited by only about 20 percent of respondents and layoffs by about 15 percent as the reason for retirement. At that time, nearly one-half of respondents cited a desire to leave work as the reason for retirement, suggesting that improved health made retirement even more attractive than it made work possible. The desire to retire was itself an important cultural shift in that it pulled at the long-held expectation that men at least should work as long as possible. However, by 1980, more than 80 percent of adults over the age of 50 had a positive attitude about prospects for their own retirement (Atchley, 2000).

Beyond improved health and elevated expectations, a third critical factor inducing individuals toward retirement was the availability of adequate retirement income and means for protecting that income. The advent and growth of public and private pensions have had the most profound effect here, although economists argue that the more fundamental factor behind pension growth was the enormous increase in national wealth that took place over much of the 20th century. Also of critical importance was the development over time of both employer- and government-sponsored health insurance. Employer-sponsored retiree health insurance, in covering retired workers before Medicare coverage commences at age 65, contributes directly and significantly to the ability of late-middle-aged employees to leave work (Fronstin, 1999; Gruber & Madrian, 1995).

Role of Public and Private Pensions in Retirement
Pensions, of course, lie at the heart of retirement (and are discussed in greater detail in the second section of this entry). Traditional private plans were developed for selected occupations in the early part of the century (Graebner, 1980), and they expanded greatly (though selectively) in the years after World War II, with coverage reaching roughly one-half of American workers by the 1970s (Schulz, 1988). Social

security began slowly, but has expanded considerably since 1960. One measure of social security's contribution to retirement is seen in the remarkable historical comparison that at the time of its passage in the 1930s, over one-half of the income of older people came from their adult children (Upp, 1982); by 1998 adult children were responsible for less than 2 percent of elders' income, social security for 38 percent, and private pensions for 19 percent (U.S. Social Security Administration, 2000).

Understood in social welfare policy terms, social security is primarily about maintaining income in old age, thereby protecting against one of the contingencies of modern industrial life (Rubinow, 1934). However, in labor market terms the importance of social security lies in its historically having put in place significant disincentives to work. By creating a normal retirement age of 65 and, later, an early retirement age of 62, social security directly pulled—or induced—individuals out of the labor force. There are big dips in labor force participation rates among older workers attaining these key ages. And before 2000 social security imposed a retirement test on older workers earning above about $13,000, reducing the benefit of workers ages 62 to 65 by one-half and workers ages 65 to 69 by one-third.

Traditional private pensions have also discouraged continued labor force participation by older workers. Although such plans mandate vesting periods designed to discourage younger workers departing the firm, they also contain provisions designed to encourage the retirement of older employees. The plans tend to penalize workers who stay at the job beyond a certain age by reducing subsequent retirement contributions to the worker and, in turn, the worker's ultimate pension benefit.

This set of factors accounts for much of the long-term increase in retirement rates that were found consistently through the early 1980s. Improving individual health, growing national wealth, heightened acceptance of retirement, and the overt intent of both public and private retirement policies each contributed to exiting the labor force.

More recently, however, significant modifications in social security and private pension provisions can be seen as contributing to the stabilization of older men's retirement levels and the modest increases in the proportion of older women remaining at work. Legislative changes in social security, beginning in 1983 and continuing to the present, have reversed the program's long-term bias toward encourag-

ing retirement among older workers. Specifically, the normal retirement age is now gradually increasing for workers born after 1938 and will ultimately rise to age 67 by 2027; the retirement test for workers ages 65 to 69 was completely eliminated in 2000 (and never existed for workers age 70 and over); and the credit for workers who delay taking social security benefits is being gradually increased so that a long-standing actuarial bias against delaying receipt of benefits is being eliminated. Regarding private pensions, participation in defined contribution plans has increased threefold since 1977, whereas the traditional defined benefit plan has fallen by nearly one-half; the importance of this shift being that, unlike the latter, defined contribution plans contain no bias encouraging retirement (VanDerhei, 2001).

Whether this flattening or partial reversal of the earlier retirement trend is temporary or not is a subject of much current debate. Improved health status can hypothetically be associated with either more work or more leisure; the recent strong economy encouraging worker retention may or may not endure; and the growing presence of partial or bridge employment makes the very definition of work and retirement harder to discern. Because of the growing number of Americans who will be in their late fifties to early seventies, these questions of work and retirement will be important for individuals, employers, the larger society, and public policy.

PRIVATE PENSIONS AND INDIVIDUAL RETIREMENT ACCOUNTS
Private pensions and Individual Retirement Accounts (IRAs) are important sources of income for many retired Americans. Indeed, in a long-standing metaphor used in the retirement literature, private pensions (including IRAs) are posited as one leg of a three-legged stool, the other two legs being social security benefits and personal savings. In fact, however, the private pension leg is considerably shorter than the social security one, and this is especially true for lower-income retirees. The personal savings leg tends to be shorter yet.

As with retirement, private pensions are designed with the sometimes conflicting concerns of employers, employees, and public policy in mind. For employers, certain pension plans may work to tie younger and middle-aged employees to the firm, but there may also be provisions that discourage older workers from staying on the job beyond certain ages or lengths of service. Employees may accumulate retirement assets through private pensions, but this option is available to only about one-half of American workers; employers do not always contribute to retirement plans even when they exist; and employees may have difficulty managing their plans when they, rather than the employer, are charged with that responsibility. Government regulations have provided added safeguards to workers in private pension plans, but there is no government requirement that private pensions be offered by employers, resulting in the retirement well-being of low-income and part-time workers—disproportionately women and people of color—being overwhelmingly reliant on social security, the nation's principal public retirement program.

Development of Private Pensions

The first company pension plan in the United States was instituted by the American Express Company in 1875 (Schulz, 1988), though a rudimentary plan existed for Plymouth Colony (Massachusetts) veterans as early as 1636 (Employee Benefit Research Institute, 2000). The first federal pensions were for northern veterans of the Civil War (Skocpol, 1992), and the first nonmilitary pensions for federal employees were begun in 1920 (Graebner, 1980). An important element in the development of both public and private pensions is that they were directed at employees who were either deemed critical to national welfare and/or who could exert considerable leverage on the incumbents of political office. In the case of public pensions, the armed forces and civil servants in virtually all countries were invariably covered before members of the citizenry at large, and in the United States today, over 90 percent of all government employees have employer pension coverage. And, in the case of private sector pensions, workers in critical arenas such as mining, steel, and railroads were invariably among the first covered. Although coverage has by today extended to roughly one-half of employees, it continues to be the case that workers in large industrial firms in core economic sectors have much greater coverage than do employees working in smaller firms in areas more marginal to the functioning of the overall economy.

Pension coverage in the United States was very spotty through the 1930s, with only an estimated 15 percent of workers being covered and then only under very stringent conditions (Schulz, 1988). The passage of social security—and in particular the popular acceptance of social insurance as something other than a "foreign" idea (Rimlinger, 1971)—generated interest and considerable imitation in the business community (Quadagno & Hardy, 1996). It was during World War II that private pension (and health) coverage was more broadly extended to compensate workers for wage freezes the government imposed during the conduct of the war. From about 10 million workers in 1950, private pension coverage was extended to 33 million workers by 1975 and to 40 million by the mid-1980s, a level that has held roughly constant in the years since. As of 1993, 67 million workers (57 percent of all workers) worked for an employer that sponsored a retirement plan; of these workers, 76 percent actually participated in such a plan (Yakoboski, 1994).

Types of Private Pensions

Today, there are two principal types of private pension plans: defined benefit plans (DBPs) and defined contribution plans (DCPs). DBPs are often referred to as "traditional" pension plans, and it is only these that are summarized above. DBPs are company (or multiemployer) sponsored, administered, and guaranteed. There are three types of DBPs: *flat benefit formulas*, where a flat amount is paid for years of service; *career-average formulas*, where either a percentage of pay for years of service or a career average over the period of participation is paid; and *final-pay formulas*, where benefits are based on an average of earnings during a number of years at the end of the participant's career (Employee Benefit Research Institute, 2000).

In the case of a DCP, an employer arranges for contributions to an account established for each participating employee. There are several types of DCPs, including money purchase, profit sharing, and 401(k) plans. Under such plans the retirement benefit is not guaranteed by the employer but results over time from the sum of employer contributions, employee contributions (if any), and the gains or losses from those investments. As a result of increased federal regulation and the risk burden they assume under DBPs, employers have shifted their coverage away from DBPs and toward DCPs in recent years. Thus, while the number of workers in DBPs has remained relatively flat over the past two decades, the number of active participants in DCPs has increased from 12 million in 1975 to 44 million in 1993, and in 1997 the accumulated assets in DCPs exceeded those in DBPs for the first time (Employee Benefit Research Institute, 1997b).

The critical distinction between the two types of plans centers on the nature of the guarantee. A worker under a DBP is assured a given retirement benefit, and this benefit is a legal responsibility of the sponsoring employer or plan. Thanks primarily to the Employee Retirement Income Security Act (ERISA) of 1974 and the Tax Reform Act of 1986, workers are vested in their plans after five years and, through the Pension Benefit Guarantee Corporation (created through ERISA), federal protections are in place against plan bankruptcy or forfeiture. Under a defined contribution plan the only guarantee lies in the periodic contribution into the plan by the participating employee, which in some cases may be matched by the employer. The employer is not responsible for the subsequent investment results, and the employee will not know the exact accumulation until the retirement date arrives. Concern about the growth in DCPs was sharpened by the revelation that in 2000 the average DCP account lost money for the first time in the program's 20-year history (Hakim, 2001).

It is worth noting here briefly that the debate over the relative merits of defined benefits or contributions has now been extended to public as well as private pensions. Schemes have recently been proposed that would partially transform social security, by far the nation's largest DBP, into a DCP by allowing workers to invest a portion of the contributions they currently make into the social security trust funds instead into private financial instruments such as stocks and bonds (Scheiber, 1996). Workers would enjoy the heightened returns proponents of privatization believe would result from such investments, but depending on the particular proposal they would forego the benefit guarantee covering all of their contributions. (There are also proposals pending that would transform Medicare, the health insurance program for the elderly, into a DCP from the current DBP; in one such proposal beneficiaries would be provided vouchers to use for purchasing health insurance in the private market, a step that would be a major departure from the current system in which beneficiaries pay insurance premiums in exchange for an assured range of benefits [Moon, 2001].)

Individual Retirement Accounts
IRAs were established under ERISA of 1974 and were expressly designed to allow workers who did not have employer-based plans to save for retirement on a tax-deferred basis. During a five-year period in the early 1980s, all individuals were permitted to contribute up to $2,000 annually to an IRA account on a tax-deferred basis during which time participation, especially among higher-income taxpayers, skyrock-

eted. However, in 1986 tax-deductible IRAs were once again restricted only to those individuals (and their spouses) who are not active participants in an employer-sponsored plan or who are in such plans but whose income does not exceed $32,000 for single individuals or $62,000 for a couple. Individuals may also participate in nondeductible IRAs if they so choose or in so-called Roth IRAs in which the contributions are not tax deductible but the withdrawals are. IRAs are a potentially important vehicle for individuals without employer-based plans to prepare for retirement. The relative importance of IRAs can be seen in the amount of assets held in IRA accounts compared with assets in DBPs and DCPs in 1999: $2.47 trillion (IRA), $2.45 trillion (DCPs), $2.21 trillion (DBPs; VanDerhei, 2001).

Private Pension and IRA Coverage
There are important issues around the degree and distribution of private pension and IRA coverage in the United States. These coverage issues are of particular importance because of the relatively heavier reliance the United States places on private pension protection than do many other industrial nations (Schulz & Myles, 1990) despite the fact that coverage is very uneven and that there are no governmental mandates that employers must provide pension coverage.

Private pension coverage in the United States is heavily skewed along important demographic, economic, and employer dimensions. Table 1 shows that participation in employee benefit retirement plans varies in important ways by employer type and by employees' full- or part-time status. Full-time workers employed by medium and large private firms are nearly twice as likely to be covered by a private pension plan than those employed in small firms, and virtually all full-time workers employed by state and local governments are covered. Among both types of private employers, the trend away from DBPs toward DCPs is seen, with a higher proportion of workers in both categories being in DCP plans in the 1994 to 1995 period. The private pension picture for part-time workers is noticeably worse than for full-time workers. Among large and medium-sized firms, participation falls by roughly half, and among small firms the rates of participation for part-time workers are roughly one-fourth of the already comparatively low rate for full-time workers in such firms. The situation of part-time workers regarding pensions and other fringe benefits

TABLE 1
Percentage of Employees Participating in Employer Benefit Programs

Benefit Program	Medium and Large Private Employer		Small Private Employer		State and Local Governments	
	1990–1991	1994–1995	1990–1991	1994–1995	1990–1991	1994–1995
	Full-Time Workers					
All retirement	78	80	42	42	96	96
DBP	59	52	20	15	90	91
DCP	48	55	31	34	9	9
	Part-Time Workers					
All retirement	40	37	10	10	48	58
DBP	28	22	4	5	45	55
DCP	20	24	7	6	3	5

NOTE: DBP = defined benefit plan; DCP = defined contribution plan. Individuals may participate in both DBPs and DCPs.
SOURCE: Reprinted with permission from Employee Benefit Research Institute. (2000). *Fundamentals of employee benefit programs* (5th ed.). Washington, DC: Author.

may erode further, given the increase in the growing number of secondary part-time jobs in the service sector and the precarious situation of such contingent workers in the face of a slowing economy (Gonyea, 2001).

Additional pension coverage concerns emerge when examining employee rather than employer characteristics. In part, this is because women and populations of color are more highly concentrated in lower-income jobs than are white men. Yet, adding to these disparities is that women and individuals of color also tend to be employed disproportionately in the types of firms where pension coverage is spotty. As seen in Table 2, Chen and Leavitt (1997) found both lower participation in pension plans and steeper declines in participation over time among black and Hispanic workers than for white workers. The advent of voluntary salary reduction plans (which did not exist in 1979) further exacerbated the problem as higher proportions of whites were able to and

chose to participate than did black or Hispanic workers. Regarding gender, older women rely more heavily than men on social security benefits in retirement and derive a lower proportion of their retirement income from private pensions than do men (Table 3).

Overall, as Smeeding (2001) noted, women are less likely than men to qualify for private pensions (48 percent versus 30 percent); when women do qualify, they receive benefits that are roughly one-half of what men receive; and about one-third of husbands do not elect joint and survivor options for their private pensions upon retirement, leaving wives unprotected when they die.

The picture of IRA participation is similar to that found for private pensions. As seen in Table 4, women, African Americans, and workers who do not have employer-based pension coverage and who work on a part-time basis are underrepresented among those holding IRA accounts. These clusterings suggest that

TABLE 2
Coverage Rates of Workers by Race

Year	White		Black		Hispanic	
	With Salary Reduction Plans (%)	Without Salary Reduction Plans (%)	With Salary Reduction Plans (%)	Without Salary Reduction Plans (%)	With Salary Reduction Plans (%)	Without Salary Reduction Plans (%)
1979	49.90	49.90	45.10	45.10	37.70	37.70
1988	44.10	43.30	35.00	33.60	26.10	25.00
1993	45.10	36.80	33.80	30.30	24.60	21.30

SOURCE: Reprinted with permission from Chen, Y., & Leavitt, T. (1997). The widening gap between white and minority pension coverage. *Public Policy and Aging Report, 8*(1), 10.

TABLE 3
Proportion of Income Provided by Various Sources by Gender (1997)

Worker	Social Security	Assets	Pensions	Earnings	Other
Men	36	17	24	21	3
Women	49	25	14	11	2

Source: Reprinted with permission from Employee Benefit Research Institute. (1999). *Facts from EBRI: Income of the elderly, 1997.* Washington, DC: Author.

IRAs are a very imperfect mechanism for aiding those who otherwise have little or no private pension coverage in preparing for retirement.

Finally, contrasting income sources in retirement of current elders show the overall inadequacy of pensions and IRAs in helping protect low-income workers in retirement. The top half of Table 5 shows what the sources of total income for older people are divided into income quintiles from the poorest 20 percent to the richest 20 percent, and the bottom half of the table shows what the income levels are for elderly people in each of those five groups. The shortcomings of pensions (including IRAs) are seen in both relative and absolute terms: those with low incomes are shown, in addition, to derive very little of that low income from private pensions. Conversely, private pensions constitute an increasing share of incomes as they dramatically rise from the first to the fourth quintile. In further contrast, one sees the critical safety-net role played by social security, constituting the overwhelming proportion of retirement income for the lower quintile groups. By adding the second public income source, Supplemental Security Income benefits, to the respective totals, public benefits make up 92 percent of the income of the poorest quintile and only one-fifth of the income of the richest quintile.

Tax Treatment of Private Pensions and IRAs
A major factor accounting for the overall expansion of private pension and IRA plans and their patterns of coverage is federal tax policy toward these vehicles. In recent years tax policy has been explicitly designed to encourage growth in these programs. Most notably, contributions to employer-based pension plans and one type of IRA account are made in pretax dollars, meaning the tax on those contributions and the investment return on those investments is deferred until the individual retires (or, in the case of the IRA, attains age 59 ½).

TABLE 4
Individual Retirement Account Participation (1992)

Workers	Workers Participating in Any Employment-Based Retirement Plan		Workers Not Participating in Any Employment-Based Retirement Plan	
	Total (thousands)	Contributing to an IRA (%)	Total (thousands)	Contributing to an IRA (%)
Total	52,179	9.20	53,636	6.30
Annual hours				
1–499	210	10.7	3,227	3.2
500–999	540	16.6	4,486	4.6
1000–1499	1,940	9.4	6,145	4.5
1500–1999	5,518	10.0	6,837	4.4
2000 or more	41,889	8.6	26,725	6.5
Gender				
Male	28,927	9.9	26,655	6.6
Female	23,252	8.2	26,981	5.9
Race				
White	45,232	9.6	45,422	6.9
Black	5,402	4.7	6,330	1.7
Other	1,545	11.3	1,994	6.8

Note: Certain categories do not equal totals due to missing data.
Source: Adapted with permission from Employee Benefit Research Institute. (1997a). *Data book on employee benefits* (4th ed., Table 15.4). Washington, DC: Author.

TABLE 5
Shares of Elderly Income by Quintiles of Total Income (1996)

Source	First	Second	Third	Fourth	Fifth
Social security	81	80	66	47	21
Pensions	3	7	15	24	21
Asset income	3	6	9	15	25
Earnings	1	3	7	12	31
Public assistance	11	2	1		
Other	1	2	3	2	2

	Distribution of Elderly Income by Quintile Share, 1995				
Income ($)	< 10,620	10,620–20,306	20,306–32,583	32,583–51,200	> 51,200

SOURCE: National Academy on an Aging Society. (1999). Is demography destiny? *Public Policy and Aging Report, 9*(4), 11.

Two issues are worth noting briefly. First, these deferrals are of enormous magnitude. The tax exclusion for employer-based plans totaled $83.8 billion in 1999, $13.4 billion for IRAs, and $5.2 billion for Keogh plans for self-employed workers (U.S. Office of Management and Budget, 2001). Second, these deferrals are of greater value to higher-income workers because they shelter proportionately (as well as absolutely) more of their current income because they are in higher marginal tax brackets. Thus, not only are middle- and upper-income workers more likely to participate in pension plans, an element of what Titmuss (1965) and Abramovitz (1983) termed "occupational welfare," but they also derive an added value because of their tax savings, what Titmuss and Abramovitz termed "fiscal welfare."

ISSUES FOR PUBLIC POLICY AND SOCIAL WORK
These policy provisions and coverage patterns raise multiple issues for public policymakers in general and for the social welfare–social work community in particular. Conservative commentators have favored the rise of DCPs and IRAs (and the decline in DBPs) because they place increasing responsibility on workers to plan for their own retirements, relieving business, and potentially government, of much of that role. On the other hand, liberal commentators have expressed concern with exposing workers to heightened risk from poor market performance or unwise investment decisions. They also see such efforts as part of a larger strategy to include partial privatization of social security by introducing individual accounts into the system that would take the form of a

DCP. These differences will continue to be heated both because they touch on fundamental ideological perspectives of both camps and because public and private pensions constitute by far the largest source of capital, wealth, and income in the United States.

Beyond these broader issues, the fundamental concern of the social work community around private pensions must focus on the distribution of benefits. A number of issues stand out. One-half of American workers have no private pension coverage. Those that do tend to be concentrated in larger firms, belong to unions, and work in core manufacturing industries. The groups for whom private pension coverage is nonexistent or inadequate virtually mirror the populations with which social work has been historically concerned: populations of color, women, part-time workers, low-income workers, and nontraditional families. And these inequities in the occupational sector are exacerbated by the tax treatment afforded most pension vehicles, resulting in disproportionate tax savings on top of highly unequal contributions made to plans by the employee and often the employer.

The social work community should engage in the larger debate about the role of government, business, and individuals in ensuring well-being in retirement. And, where appropriate, social workers should make part of their practice informing clients and communities about pension issues, options, and needs. The pressures on the future financing of social security mean, among other things, that enhancing economic well-being in old age will very much involve private sector alternatives of which pensions are the principal item.

REFERENCES

Abramovitz, M. (1983). Everyone is on welfare. *Social Work, 28,* 440–445.

Atchley, R. (2000). *Social forces and aging* (9th ed.). Belmont, CA: Wadsworth.

Burtless, G., & Quinn, J. (2001). Living longer, living better: The policy challenge of an aging workforce. *Public Policy and Aging Report, 11,* 5–11.

Chen, Y., & Leavitt, T. (1997). The widening gap between white and minority pension coverage. *Public Policy and Aging Report, 8*(1), 10–11.

Costa, D. (1996). Health and labor force participation of older men, 1900–1991. *Journal of Economic History, 56,* 62–89.

Employee Benefit Research Institute. (1997a). *Data book on employee benefits* (4th ed.). Washington, DC: Author.

Employee Benefit Research Institute. (1997b). *Defined contribution plan dominance grows across sectors* (Issue Brief No. 190). Washington, DC: Author.

Employee Benefit Research Institute. (1999). *Facts from EBRI: Income of the elderly, 1997.* Washington, DC: Author.

Employee Benefit Research Institute. (2000). *Fundamentals of employee benefit programs* (5th ed.). Washington, DC: Author.

Fronstin, P. (1999). Retirement patterns and employee benefits: Do benefits matter? *Gerontologist, 39,* 37–47.

Gendell, M., & Seigel, J. (1992). 1992 trends in retirement by age and sex, 1950–2005. *Monthly Labor Review, 115,* 22–29.

Gonyea, J. (2001). *Part-time and full-time low-wage workers' retirement security* (Final Report to AARP–Andrus Foundation). Boston: Boston University School of Social Work.

Graebner, W. (1980). *A history of retirement.* New Haven, CT: Yale University Press.

Gruber, J., & Madrian, B. C. (1995). Health-insurance availability and the retirement decision. *American Economic Review, 85*(4), 938–948.

Hakim, D. (2001, July 9). 401(k) accounts are losing money for the first time. *New York Times,* pp. A1, A12.

Henretta, J. (2001). Work and retirement. In R. Binstock & L. George (Eds.), *Handbook of aging and the social sciences* (5th ed., pp. 255–271). San Diego: Academic Press.

Kohli, M., Rein, M., Guillemard A.-M., & van Gunsteren, H. (1991). *Time for retirement.* New York: Cambridge University Press.

Moon, M. (2001). Health issues in living longer and living better. *Public Policy and Aging Report, 11,* 15–19.

Morgan, L., & Kunkel, S. (2000). *Aging: The social context.* Thousand Oaks, CA: Pine Forge Press.

Mutchler, J., Burr, J., Pienta, A., & Massagli, M. (1997). Pathways to labor force exit. *Journal of Gerontology: Social Sciences, 52B*(1), S4–S12.

National Academy on an Aging Society. (2000). *Who are young retirees and older workers?* Washington, DC: Gerontological Society of America.

O'Grady-LeShane, R. (1995). Retirement and pension programs. In R. L. Edwards (Ed.-in-Chief), *Encyclopedia of social work* (19th ed., Vol. 3, pp. 2054–2059). Washington, DC: NASW Press.

O'Rand, A. (1990). Stratification and the life-course. In R. Binstock & L. George (Eds.), *Handbook of aging and the social sciences* (3rd ed., pp. 130–150). San Diego: Academic Press.

Packard, M., & Reno, V. (1989). A look at very early retirees. *Social Security Bulletin, 52,* 16–29.

Quadagno, J., & Hardy, M. (1996). Work and retirement. In R. Binstock & L. George (Eds.), *Handbook of aging and the social sciences* (4th ed., pp. 326–345). San Diego: Academic Press.

Quinn, J. (1997). Retirement trends and patterns in the 1990s: The end of an era? *Public Policy and Aging Report, 8,* 10–14.

Quinn, J., & Burkhauser, R. (1990). Work and retirement. In R. Binstock & L. George (Eds.), *Handbook of aging and the social sciences* (3rd ed., pp. 308–327). San Diego: Academic Press.

Quinn, J., Burkhauser, R., & Meyers, D. (1990). *Passing the torch: The influence of economic incentives on work and retirement.* Kalamazoo, MI: Upjohn Institute for Employment Research.

Rimlinger, G. (1971). *Welfare policy and industrialization in Europe, America, and Russia.* New York: John Wiley & Sons.

Rubinow, I. (1934). *The quest for security.* New York: Henry Holt.

Ruhm, C. (1989). Why older Americans stop working. *Gerontologist, 29,* 294–299.

Ruhm, C. (1995). Secular changes in the work and retirement patterns of older men. *Journal of Human Resources, 30,* 362–395.

Scheiber, S. (1996). A new vision for social security. *Public Policy and Aging Report, 7*(3), 1ff.

Schulz, J. (1988). *The economics of aging* (4th ed.). Westport, CT: Auburn House.

Schulz, J., & Myles, J. (1990). Old age pensions: A comparative perspective. In R. Binstock and L. George (Eds.), *Handbook of aging and the social sciences* (3rd ed., pp. 398–414). San Diego: Academic Press.

Skocpol, T. (1992). *Protecting soldiers and mothers.* Cambridge, MA: Harvard University Press.

Smeeding, T. (2001). Living longer, living better: Economic status in old age. *Public Policy and Aging Report, 11,* 1, 20–23.

Szinovacz, M. (1982). Research on women's retirement. In M. Szinovacz (Ed.), *Women's retirement: Policy implications of recent research* (pp. 13–21). Beverly Hills, CA: Sage Publications.

Titmuss, R. (1965). The role of redistribution in social policy. *Social Security Bulletin, 39,* 20–26.

Uchitelle, L. (2001, June 26). Lacking pensions, older divorced women remain at work. *New York Times,* pp. A1, C2.

Upp, M. (1982). A look at the economic status of the elderly then and now. *Social Security Bulletin, 45,* 16–20.

U.S. Bureau of the Census. (1992). *Statistical abstracts of the United States.* Washington, DC: U.S. Government Printing Office.

U.S. Office of Management and Budget. (2001). *Budget of the United States government: Analytical perspectives, fiscal year 2001.* Available: http://w3.access.gpo.gov/usbudget/fy2001/fy2001_srch.html

U.S. Social Security Administration. (2000). *Annual statistical supplement to the Social Security Bulletin.* Washington, DC: U.S. Government Printing Office.

VanDerhei, J. (2001). *The changing face of retirement plans* (Issue Brief No. 232). Washington, DC: Employee Benefit Research Institute.

Villani, P. J., & Roberto, K. A.. (1997). Retirement decision-making: Gender issues and policy implications. *Journal of Women and Aging, 9,* 151–163.

Weaver, D. (1994). The work and retirement decisions of older women: A literature review. *Social Security Bulletin, 57,* 3–24.

Wilensky, H., & Lebeaux, C. (1965). *Industrial society and social welfare.* New York: Free Press.

Yakoboski, P. (1994). *Employment-based retirement benefits: Analysis of the 1993 Current Population Survey* (Issue Brief No. 153). Washington, DC: Employee Benefit Research Institute.

Robert B. Hudson, PhD, is professor and chair, Department of Social Welfare Policy, School of Social Work, Boston University, 121 Bay State Road, Boston, MA 02215.

For further information see
Retirement and Pension Programs; Social Security

Key Words

individual retirement accounts	private pensions
	retirement

S

Social Work Education and the Future

Terry Mizrahi
Frank Baskind

This entry describes the major internal and external factors of social work education that have shaped its development since 1995 (Frumkin & Lloyd, 1995). Some world events, major trends, and political and economic changes that have affected the status and content of professional social work education include globalization and internationalism; deprofessionalization, downsizing, devolution, and privatization; race, racism, and ethnicity; the nation's social and economic health; mental and physical disability; aging and end of life; and community-based problems and solutions. Each of these is briefly analyzed, followed by implications for social work education. Finally, the last sections, which focus on the workplace of the future, include descriptions of those activities undertaken by professional and educational organizations, specifically, the Council on Social Work Education (CSWE) and the National Association of Social Workers (NASW), to prepare professional social workers for practice in that future. Among them are the Millennium Project, the Action Network for Social Work Education and Research (ANSWER) Coalition, and the Education Policy and Accreditation Standards (EPAS) Program.

The period from 1996 to 2003 includes some of the most far-reaching changes the United States has seen for some time. The millennium dawned in the context of globalization and interconnectedness; worldwide poverty and AIDS; racial, ethnic, religious, and tribal conflicts abroad; a domestic economic boom followed by a recession in 2001 with continuing devolution from federal to state responsibility; and a shift from public to private sector influence on health, education, and human services. These years span the presidencies of William Jefferson Clinton and George Walker Bush when contradictions and uncertainties related to public policies were prominent. There was a right-wing, ultraconservative takeover in congressional leadership in 1999; and in 2001, for only the second time in U.S. history, Democratic presidential candidate Al Gore, who won the popular vote by a half million votes, lost the presidency in the electoral college to George Bush. It is still considered a controversial election outcome. It was the period when the federal entitlement program—Aid to Families with Dependent Children established in 1935 as part of the Social Security Act—was replaced in 1996 by a minimalist restrictive program known as Temporary Aid for Needy Families, which is likely to be renewed in 2003 with almost as many restrictions.

These past several years have witnessed a continuing technology and telecommunications explosion, with Internet use increasing worldwide; however, a digital divide, within and among countries and continents, remains. The United States went from unprecedented economic growth and surpluses in the 1990s to economic recession and deficits by 2003. This was the era when genetic codes were broken, genes were mapped, animals were cloned, and stem cells were researched with fanfare and fear. It has been a period when the prospects for peace in Northern Ireland, the Balkans, the Koreas, and the Middle East seemed imminent. But then quickly in South Asia (India and Pakistan), in the Middle East (between the Palestinians and Israel), and in the Koreas, coexistence disintegrated amid increasing clashes and threats of violence.

Without precedent, the events of September 11, 2001, burst the sense of national security. The terrorist attacks on the United States, including the World Trade Center in New York and the Pentagon in Washington, DC, resulted in the deaths of thousands of innocent people. This has precipitated an aggressive global "war on terrorism" conducted by the United States in Afghanistan and includes a war on Iraq and conflicts with North Korea. The prospects for global conflict seem more viable than those of international cooperation. This is the complex and rapidly changing scenario in which the future of social work education and the profession is embedded.

GLOBALIZATION AND INTERNATIONALISM— WITH IMPLICATIONS FOR THE FUTURE

Globalization is increasing communication among peoples of the world as well as interdependence among groups and communities of interest and identity. Technology allows for an instant transfer of resources, culture, knowledge, and ideas and the possibility of promoting commonalties, basic human rights, and opportunities for enhancing health and human potential. It puts greater stake in international and regional organizations including the United Nations, the World Bank, and the International Monetary Fund.

Globalization has also been viewed as a phenomenon responsible for increasing disparities and inequities between rich and poor countries, between the northern and southern hemispheres, between European Americans and societies of color, and between the East and the West (Van Soest, 1997). The nature, status, and security of work have been affected by a global marketplace as companies follow the profit trail, and governments have been unable or unwilling to influence economic organization, production, and distribution (NASW, 2003b; Reisch & Jarman-Rohde, 2000). Unemployment rates in the United States and in other places (for example, the Caribbean) are the highest since the early 1990s, and real wages have been stagnant throughout the 1990s (Prigoff, 2000).

The connection between social work education in the United States and abroad has varied over the years, with most attention paid when international issues affect the domestic social work agenda. Infusion of international issues into curricula of most social work programs has been minimal. International work usually occurs apart from the core curriculum. Although CSWE and NASW have increased their focus on international issues in social work in recent years, most schools of social work appear to perceive international social work as a "specialty" rather than as a context or a framework embracing all practice and policy issues. There are several exceptions, however. Many schools of social work consult or collaborate with social work programs or projects in other countries. As examples, the University of South Carolina has a campus program in Korea; the Mandel School of Applied Social Sciences at Case Western Reserve University works in

Romania; faculty at the University of Illinois at Chicago are helping Ethiopians create a social work program; the Virginia Commonwealth University School of Social Work faculty works in Ukraine, Belarus, and Germany; the Wurzweiler School of Social Work of Yeshiva University has field sites in Israel; and the Monmouth University Department of Social Work, which has designed its whole curriculum around international social work, is assisting the country of Latvia in building its social work program.

CSWE has a well-recognized international commission charged with the responsibility of developing the international dimension of the social work curriculum. It has established the Katherine A. Kendall Endowed Fund to support social work curriculum development and international interaction among social work educators. NASW has revitalized its international committee to increase the influence of social work on international policies regarding human rights, political prisoners, and international social work practice. The leadership of CSWE and NASW has called for a new paradigm of social work education that recognizes both internationalism and multiculturalism (Beless, 1998; Mizrahi, Davidson, & Marshack, 2000; Newsome, 1998; O'Neill, 2002a). CSWE's *Educational Policy and Accreditation Standards* (2001a) recognizes the global context for practice. Clearly, the 21st century is the time to internationalize the social work curricula (Asamoah, Healy, & Mayadas, 1997; Healy, 2002; Park, 1999), especially as international issues intersect domestically with the increasing number of immigrants and immigrant-dominated communities needing assistance.

Moreover, there are opportunities for social work education and practice to partner to contribute to universal knowledge about individual and collective change and to deepen understanding of various cultures and religions around the world. Prospects for exchanges that help to empower poor and marginalized communities, are increasing, while exemplar community development approaches in resource-poor countries could serve as models for U.S. social work education (Campfens, 1997).

DEPROFESSIONALIZATION, DOWNSIZING, DEVOLUTION, PRIVATIZATION— WITH IMPLICATIONS FOR THE FUTURE

Today, there are increasing challenges to professional control coming from the corporate and politically conservative sectors. The 21st century could become an era of deprofessionalization in American society. All professions in the latter part of the 1990s, including social work, experienced the usurping of clinical judgment and competence by outsiders. Managed care companies and other insurance corporations are increasingly making judgments about professional medical and mental health–behavioral health practice (Munson, 1996). Yet they are removed from the clinical setting and do not always possess the appropriate professional specialization or credentials to evaluate competency. In the name of "cross training" and "management prerogatives," decisions about access to care and who provides it appear to be guided primarily by the "bottom line" (Schames & Lightburn, 1998). With the consolidation, mergers, and integration of hospitals in this era of increased competition and funding cuts in reimbursement for hospital-based health care, almost all discipline-based professional departments, including nursing and social work, have been reconfigured (Berger et al., 1996; Edwards, Cooke, & Reid, 1996; Neuman, 2001).

This is also a time of continuing devolution, that is, the transfer of responsibility from the federal to state and local government (DiNitto, 2003; Rock & Perez-Koenig, 2001). It is a period in which government has abdicated much of its responsibility to meet the needs of people by limiting resources and entitlements and lowering expectations about what government can and should provide its citizens. This direction became evident in the Reagan–Bush era and continued with a more humane application during the Clinton–Gore administration. It was President Clinton who signed into law the Personal Responsibility and Work Opportunity Reconciliation Act (PRWORA) of 1996 (Edelman, 1997). And this trend continues in the policies of the George W. Bush administration. The Bush proposals to reauthorize PRWORA, known as Temporary Aid for Needy Families, in 2002 have even more restrictive provisions targeted at poor people who need government assistance. For example, his proposals do not increase support for child care, job training, or higher education. The 2002 federal budget reveals major cuts or limited growth in the Older Americans Act, Medicare, Medicaid, and other long-standing social programs as the economic recession lingers, defense and homeland security allocations increase, and massive tax cuts loom.

As government programs are cut, there is also the concomitant move toward privatization, charity, and voluntarism, touted by social and political conservatives as appropriate venues to meet human needs. Corporations are encroaching into and, in some cases, dominating health and human services industries and limiting a notion of public responsibility (Fisher & Karger, 1997). When government funding or oversight is in the picture, it more frequently takes the form of contracting with nonprofit agencies, with ever-stricter demands placed on them (Fabricant & Fisher, 2002). In some parts of the country, privatization has meant contracting with for-profit corporations that are assuming a greater role in education, health care, corrections, and child welfare (Vourlekis, Ell, & Padgett, 2001).

"Compassionate conservatism," the current term used by President Bush as an approach to government, interacts with privatization, downsizing, and deregulation. It places greater responsibility on individuals, families, civic efforts, and religious institutions to do more, often without appropriating sufficient resources and supports. It is reinforced with the call for charity and voluntarism as answers to social ills. Bush has expanded the Peace Corps as well as AmeriCorps and Teach for America, both initiated by President Clinton, and he also has created the "Freedom Corps" and the Office of Faith-Based Services. His call for volunteers and community service assumes in its philosophy that it only takes a caring community to solve the social ills of the country. When this is juxtaposed with a downsized federal budget for many domestic discretionary programs, there is an implication that "anyone with a good heart can do good." This places the onus on those clients and families already struggling and diminishes the role of professionally educated social workers and other qualified personnel. Other Bush policies are steeped in moral pronouncements targeted primarily at poor people. His proposals include counseling on the virtues of marriage, increasing hours of required work, and promoting "abstinence only," while restricting access to birth control and family planning domestically and in international aid programs. His proposals also continue to prohibit access to resources by immigrants, including those residing legally in the United States.

The impacts of deprofessionalization, downsizing, privatization, and voluntarism have immense repercussions for social work education. The challenges are multiple—to analyze these trends in social policy courses; to develop field placements in new and alternative settings; to conduct research and evaluation to demonstrate the strengths and limitations of existing and proposed programs; and to advocate for humane and effective policies, especially for socially and economically oppressed people. There is an immediate need for social work educators and practitioners to develop case studies and alternative models for the classroom and the field that address these complex scenarios that blur distinctions among the public, nonprofit, and proprietary responses to social problems.

The new faith-based initiatives challenge social work education. The social work community has raised concerns with regard to the funding of religious institutions and the almost exclusive emphasis on volunteers. Concerns focus on the lack of attention paid to competence, skill, and standards; the lack of safeguards against proselytizing and other practices that violate the separation of church and state; and the possible discrimination against staff and clients based on their backgrounds and beliefs (NASW, 2002).

Social work has celebrated its sectarian roots in past and contemporary U.S. social welfare systems (Cnaan, 1999). While incorporating those aspects of spirituality that assist in the healing and well-being of people and communities (Martin & Martin, 2002), social work also needs to continue to focus public attention on systemic environmental causation of problems, on respect for and competence in multicultural diversity, and on the value of political pluralism in the United States. For example, social work educators can seize upon the Surgeon General's first conference on mental health (U.S. Department of Health and Human Services [DHHS], 2000) that urged professionals to explore the role of culture, spirituality, and family and community support as protective factors against the threat of mental disorders.

With respect to charity and voluntarism, social work educators should focus on funding and supporting a competent professional social welfare workforce. Educators also need to articulate that quality and accountable volunteer programs and academia–community partnerships with clients and constituent groups require professional oversight, supervision, and resources. A challenge is to resist moves to deprofessionalize by demonstrating and documenting social work competencies and the effectiveness of social work interventions and by focusing on outcomes evaluation and evidence-based practice (Fraser, 2003; Rubin, 2000). At the same time that it evaluates the quality of social work research (Gomory, 2001; Thyer, 2001), the social work research community needs to articulate the complexities of conducting human subjects research, as well as help shape the definition of and criteria for

measuring program and policy effectiveness so these reflect social work values.

Social work leaders will also need to focus on strengthening licensing and other means of increasing professional recognition and protection. Social work licensing has been part of the move to elevate practitioners, protect the public, and reimburse agencies and practitioners for the provision of clinical and general social work services. However, varying licensing standards and regulations, title protection, and scopes of practice have resulted in divisions within the profession and differences among schools of social work about the methods and competencies taught and needed (Green, 2000). The profession will need to examine the impact and direction of licensing without damaging the hard fought gains to attain professional status and parity with comparable mental health and health professions.

This era also challenges social work to develop and test credentials and standards, to validate competencies, to articulate the unique aspects of social work, and to advocate for the funding of a range of psychosocial services. At the same time, there is a need to continue to promote interdisciplinary collaboration and teamwork models with other professional groups (Abramson & Rosenthal, 1995).

RACE, RACISM, AND ETHNICITY— WITH IMPLICATIONS FOR THE FUTURE

The number of immigrants coming to the United States continues to increase. The percentage of newly arrived populations, especially from Latin American and Caribbean countries and from Asia, grew significantly in the last decade of the 20th century. People of Latino–Hispanic origin are now the largest ethnic group in the United States. It is predicted that by 2050 people of color, including African Americans, will comprise approximately 50 percent of the population in the United States (Davis, 2000).

There has clearly been ambivalence in this country about the culture and social status of many immigrant groups and, in some quarters, overtly anti-immigrant sentiments go unabated (Buchanan, 2002). Racism continues as a controversial issue for American society. Since September 11, 2001, increased incidences of perceived and actual negative attitudes toward and assaults on those communities of color from Middle East and Southeast Asian backgrounds, particularly those who are Muslim and Arab, have increased (Human Rights Watch, 2002).

Although there are countervoices that applaud the virtues of diversity and pluralism and the contributions of immigrants individually and collectively, many public policies and practices point in the other direction. When the government cuts back or restricts resources to people in need because of ideology, economics, or distrust, new arrivals in need of assistance and support could be disproportionately hurt. Additionally, during this period of scarce resources for human services, there is a tendency toward increased ethnocentrism and escalation of interminority conflicts (Natapoff, 1995; Yamamoto, 1997). At the same time, tensions between African Americans and white Americans continue, with differing perceptions about the extent to which racism exists and the remedies for it (Coleman, 1997; Rowan & Friedman, 1996).

Social work education has addressed issues of race and ethnicity actively through affirmative action policies reflected in elected and appointed leadership positions, EPAS, major curriculum development initiatives, and the Carl Scott Memorial Lecture Series. The CSWE Task Force on Multicultural Social Work Education has been working on developing instructional models since its formation in 1998 at the first working conference held at the University of Michigan. With the input of many social work educators and practitioners, NASW has produced the first set of *Standards for Cultural Competence in Social Work Practice* and is developing the implementation and evaluation criteria for them (NASW, 2001). Schools of social work continue to work hard to improve the diversity of their student and faculty bodies with positive results. At the baccalaureate level, the percentage of ethnic minority students increased from 27.5 percent to 32.7 percent between 1995 and 1999. The master's degree level had gains from 19.3 percent to 24.2 percent for the same period (CSWE, 2001b). Many schools have instituted special programs that address financial and educational disadvantages among potential students of color (Mizrahi et al., 2000); curricula are filled with courses ranging from addressing issues of "oppression" to "multicultural" social work. The *Journal of Social Work Education* continues to feature articles on diversity and multicultural education written by a diverse group of scholars.

Field practica will increasingly be affected by the changing backgrounds and living conditions of immigrant groups. It is anticipated that a larger portion of clients seen in social agencies will be from different cultures. Social work programs are continuing to examine methods and opportunities to work with diverse populations, reinforced by the diversity perspective from the curriculum mandated by CSWE's EPAS

Program. The objectives are to prepare students to practice without discrimination and to develop understanding, affirmation, and respect for people from diverse backgrounds. At the same time, social workers will continue to work with low-income communities that still lack resources and a social services infrastructure. As social workers continue to develop the best ways to serve disadvantaged white and African American, Puerto Rican, and Native American populations, there will be a need to continue to develop multicultural curricula that produce culturally competent practitioners and educators from an even wider variety of populations (Gutiérrez & Alvarez, 2000; Gutiérrez, Yeakley, & Ortega, 2000; Rivera & Ehrlich, 1998).

Schools of social work need to recruit more students and faculty whose backgrounds are similar to those of the communities and clients they serve. The challenge for social work education is to acknowledge racism, and the other "isms," and to create the structures and culture within academic institutions and social agencies that promote policies and practices to ensure equality of opportunity and inclusion. Section 6, "Nondiscrimination and Human Diversity," of CSWE's *Educational Policy and Accreditation Standards* presents a specific structure for social work education programs to follow that outlines the learning context, the educational program, and the need to understand and respect diversity (CSWE, 2001a).

SOCIAL AND ECONOMIC HEALTH— WITH IMPLICATIONS FOR THE FUTURE

Examination of a social health index to assess the progress of America by monitoring the well-being of its people has revealed some disheartening discrepancies in U.S. society (Miringoff, Miringoff, & Opdycke, 1999, 2001). During the last 20 years of the 20th century, the gross domestic product grew by 140 percent, whereas social health indicators have diminished by 38 percent overall. It appears that the economic growth in the United States has not been accompanied by comparable social progress in many areas. Miringoff and colleagues (2001) documented national improvements in such social indicators as infant mortality, high school dropouts (although still disproportionately high among African Americans and Latinos), poverty among those over 65 years of age, homicides, and alcohol-related fatalities. However, other social health indicators have declined—child abuse, child poverty, teenage suicide, average weekly earnings for individuals, health insurance coverage and out-of-pocket costs for health care, access to affordable housing, and gaps between rich and poor people (Miringoff et al., 2001).

The aftermath of September 11 coupled with the economic recession continuing into 2003 do not augur well for government funding of programs to address these long-standing health, education, and welfare problems. Nevertheless, there has been recognition of the need for crisis, disaster, and trauma programs by the government under the auspices of "homeland security." This has the potential of refocusing a public health agenda that includes the mental and emotional as well as physical well-being of the U.S. population.

These long-standing and more recent indicators have implications for the types of social conditions likely to be faced by clients and other constituencies of social services agencies and social work practitioners. Social work educators are strengthening the knowledge and competencies needed to address these issues, clinically and systemically. A renewed focus on policy formulation and analysis, economics, and advocacy is evident in many social work programs (Prigoff, 2000; Schneider & Lester, 2001).

The entire social work community mobilized its resources and used its expertise after September 11, 2001. Social work programs and practitioners expanded and intensified their involvement in many pertinent areas. These included disaster teams with the Red Cross and other community organizations, mediating intergroup conflict, and addressing the needs of especially vulnerable clients such as the elderly, the mentally ill, and people who were already suffering from posttraumatic stress. Models of collecting and dispersing public and private resources during that crisis offer policy and research opportunities for an alternative paradigm to existing means-tested programs, such as the way Medicaid Disaster Relief was organized after September 11 (Bernstein, 2001). Many social work programs are and will be collaborating with NASW state chapters to support the training of all social workers to become first-line responders. Social work expertise with crisis intervention, grief and bereavement, and program coordination evident in the 1995 bombing of the Federal Building in Oklahoma should be incorporated into curricula (Wedel & Baker, 1998; Zakour, 2000).

AGING AND END OF LIFE— WITH IMPLICATIONS FOR THE FUTURE

Among the demographic trends, one of the most critical for society and social work is the "aging of America." By 2030 more than 20 percent of the U.S. population will be 65 years of age or older (Scharlach, Damron-Rodriguez, Robinson, & Feldman, 2000). This shift is primarily due to increased longevity—the average life span has almost doubled since 1900 (from approximately 47 years to 77 years)—and to the reduction of infant and childhood mortality and morbidity. Yet, gender and ethnicity differentially affect the aging experience. As a result of divorce and widowhood, women are more likely to live alone and to be poor. People of color are likely to have a poorer health status, be socially isolated, and have fewer resources as they age. The prolongation of life, particularly considering that the fastest-growing sector consists of people over 85 years old, also has an impact on health, long-term care, and family configurations with accompanying intergenerational responsibilities. Families still provide most of the long-term care in the United States, sometimes at great cost and burden to family members. Nevertheless, elderly people move into nursing homes as they age, with 25 percent of those over 85 years of age living in institutional settings (Scharlach et al., 2000).

Most people who are living longer are staying healthier longer. This has repercussions for the experience of retirement because millions of people will or could be productive in work and leisure activities for many years after age 65. Nevertheless, people over 65 years of age also use a disproportionate amount of health services. Age-related medical and psychological ailments afflict people more as they get older—from chronic renal, cardiovascular, and joint diseases to dementias including, but not limited to, Alzheimer's disease and depression. These demographic and health trends are reflected in the first goal of Healthy People 2010, which is to improve "health expectancy," defined as living life longer with the major proportion of life lived in good health (Wagener, Molla, Crimmins, Pamuk, & Madans, 2001).

Perhaps reflecting societal ambivalence about aging, social workers in this field are among the lowest paid; moreover, only a small percentage of faculty and students are interested in or have expertise in working with the aging populations (CSWE, 2001c). Not surprisingly, there are shortages of social workers selecting gerontology as a field of practice. Attempts are underway to redress obstacles for the pursuit of gerontological social work practice through initiatives funded by the John A. Hartford Foundation, the William Randolph Hearst Foundations, and the Soros Foundation.

These include funding for field practica, faculty development institutes, faculty and doctoral student scholars, curriculum enrichment initiatives, endowed student scholarships, and research on death in America (CSWE, 2002; Tompkins, 2002). In the future, more social work practitioners will need to be prepared to work with the elderly. They will need to advocate for maintaining and improving benefits and supports for older adults along the continuum of social and health care from naturally occurring retirement communities to assisted living and other long-term care arrangements.

Ironically, as longevity and life expectancy have been extended due to both better health and medical technology, dying and death have gained greater prominence in society and in social work. The "right to die" movement is gaining momentum and, at the same time, the right to health care is still not a political reality. Until recently, resources for hospice and palliative care have been considered inadequate compared with high-tech, in-hospital interventions. This momentum toward quality-of-life needs at the end of life will increase the demand for ethics education and practice guides (NASW, 2003a; Reamer, 1998a, 1998b).

MENTAL AND PHYSICAL DISABILITY— WITH IMPLICATIONS FOR THE FUTURE

The gains that were made in equality of opportunity for people with physical and mental disabilities since the Americans with Disabilities Act of 1990 are in danger of being dissipated by the courts and administrative agencies through narrowed interpretations and restrictive regulations (Fleischer & Zames, 2001). These bodies are questioning the very definition of disability and the accommodations that should be made to enable people who are disabled to be fully functioning members of society. There is still a lack of parity in the reimbursement between mental and physical conditions. Moreover, substance abuse as an illness still has not been embraced by policymakers. Advocacy for including substance abuse as part of mental health and medical funding is critical.

One of the stated goals of the mental health report issued by the Surgeon General (DHHS, 1999) is to reduce the incidence and encourage the treatment of mental disorders. The supplement to the Surgeon General's mental health report (DHHS, 2000) acknowledges the disparities in obtaining treatment for mental disorders. It also identifies the poorer quality of the services received by members of racial and ethnic groups and the underrepresentation of racial and ethnic minorities in research. It concluded that an environment of inequality increases greater exposure to racism, discrimination, violence, and poverty. It suggested there might be a relationship between depression and anxiety, on the one hand, and racism and discrimination, on the other, and called for further research.

Possible causes of mental and physical disabilities are critical areas of attention in the 21st century. These causes come center stage in the scientific, professional, and public arenas. The mapping of the genome has the potential for life and health enhancement; yet, the problems associated with the application of that knowledge to decisions about the prediction, prevention, and cure of myriad diseases and disabilities, are enormous (Stoesen, 2002). The controversies are primarily between those whose religious and moral convictions result in defining life in vitro and assert that scientists should not create or destroy that life and those who believe that these scientific breakthroughs could save lives in the future. It is not clear whether the Bush administration will fully support the priorities established by the Surgeon General in 2000.

Social work education and practice confront societal contradictions about the way disabilities are treated. The challenge for social work education is to educate practitioners to be individual (case) and group (class) advocates. The CSWE curriculum resource, *Integrating Disability Content in Social Work Education* (2002), provides model syllabi, assignments, and references to this end. The CSWE Commission on Disability and Persons with Disabilities established by the Board of Directors in 1997 has initiated the development of curriculum materials and activities that bring social, political, and economic issues of disability within the framework of social work education.

The Human Genome Project will clearly have an impact on social work education and practice with the expansion of the social work biopsychosocial assessment. There is a need for increased research, policy, and advocacy as technology creates more choices for people (Johnson & Taylor-Brown, 1997). The knowledge and skills of social workers during the AIDS epidemic over the past 20 years could be similarly applied to understand better the relationship between genetics and the environment.

The advancement of research related to health systems and life science programs is crucially important for furthering social work knowledge and practice in the 21st century. For instance, properly informed mental health counselors who know about the biochemical makeup of anthrax and its contamination risk could contribute to a new practice area. For another example, there was a three-year investigation (from 2000 to 2003) on best practices for clinical social workers in psychopharmacotherapy (funded by the Ittleson Foundation) and data about the experiences of clinical social workers with respect to psychiatric medication collected by a team of social work researchers (Bentley, 2002). It could contribute to more influential roles in medication management, ethical problem solving, and collaboration with doctors and other health and mental health professionals.

Social work principles, policy, and practice are embedded in the Surgeon General's reports, from examining culture to addressing racism. If President Bush provides resources to support Healthy People 2010, social workers will have an opportunity to demonstrate their knowledge and skills in the fields of public, community, and mental health.

COMMUNITY-BASED PROBLEMS AND SOLUTIONS—WITH IMPLICATIONS FOR THE FUTURE

The move away from large government initiatives to solve social problems has been accompanied by a trend to focus solutions at the community level (Mizrahi, 1999). In the past decade, the promotion of interorganizational collaborations and partnerships as solutions to social problems and as ways to strengthen communities has been expanded (Bailey & Koney, 1995; Edelman, 2001). The support by large private foundations, such as Kellogg, and by federal agencies, such as the U.S. Departments of Health and Human Services, Education, and Housing and Urban Development and their state and local counterparts, enables various constituencies within a community to come together to address social needs (Svihula & Austin, 2001). Presumably, because various sectors of society have an interest in or are affected by such issues as infant mortality, substance abuse, teen unemployment, child abuse, housing, and business deterioration, they support attempts to harness a range of expertise and resources to solve them. Moreover, the goals of many of these programs are to create local ownership and to build a unified community in the process.

As a result, social work education has undergone a revival of community and macropractice in traditional, new, and reconfigured ways

(Johnson, 1998). Some programs have strengthened their long-standing community organizing sequences, whereas others have developed new models that include social action, community social work, political social work, community partnerships, community empowerment and development, and community building (Avery et al., 1998; Mizrahi, 2001). The range of field placements and career tracks for community social workers and macropractitioners includes traditional and innovative settings and auspices (Delgado, 1998, 1999). Among these are private and public sector community organizations, social and economic development corporations, community investment projects, consensus organizing, urban leadership, church-based neighborhood organizing, school-based health and mental health collaboratives, political jobs with elected and appointed officials, among many others (Ewalt, Freeman, & Poole, 1998; Rubin & Rubin, 2001).

Given the complexity of the issues and organizational mechanisms, the time is ripe for schools to capitalize on the community context, community practice methodology, and capacity-building approaches at the institutional levels (Ryan, DeMasi, Jacobson, & Ohmer, 2000; U.S. Department of Housing and Urban Development, 2000). Dual-degree programs with urban studies, public health, law, and business administration are also areas for considered expansion because these allow social workers to move beyond traditional roles and sectors into a larger community change and development arena.

The expanding number of students concentrating on community organizing, planning, policy, and macropractice, along with the newer configurations noted above, augurs well for the growth of the macro end of social work. At the same time, there is a need for systematic, professionwide campaigns to position social work community practitioners in interorganizational and grassroots leadership careers. Greater promotion of the social work profession to the wider community development and advocacy sector is essential so that it identifies the bachelor's or master's social work degree as necessary qualifications for those positions. Promoting lateral and vertical career mobility with adequate compensation also is essential (Starr, Mizrahi, & Gurzinsky, 1996).

PREPARATION FOR THE FUTURE

Social work education has grown steadily. In fall 1995, there were 400 accredited baccalaureate programs and 117 accredited master's programs. Also, at that time, 38 baccalaureate programs and 12 master's programs were in candidacy status. By 2002, there were 66 doctoral programs, 430 accredited baccalaureate programs, and 146 accredited master's programs with an additional 22 baccalaureate and 25 master's programs in candidacy. The capacity to prepare practitioners for the future has increased. At the same time, there has been an overall decline in the total admissions applications to social work programs. Challenges related to the quality and distribution of social work programs at all levels, and the articulations among them, remain. The question, "Is there a continuum in social work education?" is one that remains to be answered (Schriver, Steimla, & Quinney, 2000). Other questions include, "Is there a sufficient number of doctoral graduates to fill the projected vacancies in social work education?" "What is the impact of declining admissions applications on the quality of students accepted into social work education programs?"

Several institutional and professional activities took place during the latter part of the 1990s that positioned social work educators to prepare future practitioners. These included the CSWE Millennium Project, the strategic plan of the CSWE's board of directors, the Institute for the Advancement of Social Work Research (IASWR), the ANSWER Coalition, Influencing State Policy (ISP), and EPAS.

Millennium Project. Anticipating major changes occurring in the symbolic passing from the 20th to the 21st century, several CSWE bodies created the Millennium Project (CSWE, 1995). This ambitious and forward-looking initiative had several components. These included commissioning education and practice-focused research; using annual program meetings as the venue for discussions about the future of social work education; and fostering new conceptualizations for social work education and practice.

IASWR. IASWR has continued initiatives to connect policy, practice, and education through the advancement of social work research. IASWR has played an important role in building the visibility of the profession in the national scientific community. Social workers are underrepresented as federally funded researchers. Therefore, the goal of IASWR is to create opportunities for social work research and researchers. It has been implementing strategies that promote evidence-based practice,

serving as a technical resource to social work educators, providing guidance on funding proposals, and increasing strategies to enhance the research infrastructure (Zlotnik, Biegel, & Solt, 2002). There is an increasing need for social workers to produce more usable practice-oriented research and to disseminate it rapidly for immediate use by practitioners and policymakers.

ANSWER. The ANSWER coalition was created in 1995 by CSWE and NASW, along with the National Association of Deans and Directors (NADD), the Baccalaureate Program Directors (BPD), the Group for the Advancement of Doctoral Education (GADE), and the IASWR. The mission of ANSWER is to increase legislative and executive branch advocacy on behalf of social work education, training, and research. In addition to its focus on creating a National Center for Social Work Research, it has worked with the executive branch, in particular, the Centers for Disease Control and Prevention and the Office of Behavioral and Social Science Research. There, the goal is to increase visibility for social workers as researchers and to influence the type of research protocols to include social work themes and perspectives. Additional significant ANSWER achievements include the advocacy on appropriations that resulted in significant increases in funding for the Title IV-B Section 426 child welfare training program; the opposition to the block grant of child welfare funding that would have severely affected Title IV-E training funds; ongoing inclusion of recommendations on social work research related to National Institutes of Health activities; and increased attention to social work research at the National Institute of Mental Health.

ISP. In 1997, with the advent of government devolution, NADD and CSWE provided seed funding for a national network of social work educators known as Influencing State Policy. ISP's mission is to assist faculty and students in learning to influence effectively the formation, implementation, and evaluation of state-level policy and legislation. As of 2002 there were 347 undergraduate programs and 135 graduate programs that have ISP liaisons. Accomplishments include the creation of a Web site, the production of two videos, sponsorship of the Annual Influencing State Policy Contest, the publication of the *Influence* newsletter, and 3,596 student visits to state legislatures (Schneider, 2002).

Accreditation. The major initiatives affecting the future of social work leading up to EPAS began with initiating the Millennium Project and ensuring Commission on Educational Policy review of the 1992 Curriculum Policy Statement. These set the tone for the development of revised accreditation standards for the new millennium. The CSWE 21st Century Strategic Planning Process, initiated in 1997, which called for streamlining and simplifying the accreditation process, supported this.

Two major activities directly contributed to revisions in the 1992 Curriculum Policy Statement and Accreditation Standards, resulting in EPAS. This was the assessment of the 1992 Curriculum Policy Statement (Sheridan, 1998) and the Commission on Accreditation Quality Assurance Research Project. The purposes of assessment of the 1992 Curriculum Policy Statement for the Commission on Educational Policy were to identify the strengths and limitations of the current curriculum policy statement and to use this information to inform revisions. The emphasis was on educational competencies and the ongoing assessment of program outcome measures. The overriding themes of the report were to eliminate the redundancy that existed between and within accreditation standards and the curriculum policy statement and to provide clarification of items. In 1998 the Commission on Accreditation established the Quality Assurance Research Project to ensure the quality of social work education by analyzing the accreditation process and its impact on programs (Metrey & Johnson, 1999). In 1999 faculty development training programs were initiated to assist faculty in understanding how to develop a mission statement, program goals and objectives, and a student outcomes assessment plan.

As we entered the 21st century, members of the Commission on Accreditation and the Commission on Educational Policy, for the first time in their history, revised standards for accreditation and created a new educational policy (White, 1999). These activities set the stage for social work education to enter the millennium with renewed direction for the future—a future focused on the assessment of student learning outcomes. Implementation of EPAS began in July 2002.

EPAS is a consensus document that had three drafts. It is the product of the review of hundreds of comments from individuals, program faculty, and constituent groups. The development of EPAS was very controversial and was reflective of the fragmentation in social work education, with differing expectations expressed by several constituencies: schools of social work who have a major research agenda, faith-based social work education programs, and baccalaureate and graduate educators. The credentials of a social work program's chief executive officer, the number of years of practice experience, the breadth and depth of research content, and the inclusion of content on sexual orientation in the curricula are lingering controversies that challenge the solidarity of social work education in the future.

Interprofessional education. A related accreditation activity that focuses on the future is the publication of accreditation strategies for effective interprofessional education (Zlotnik et al., 2002). Findings from a national forum suggested that accreditation is not the primary barrier to interprofessional education. The report recommended addressing the sustenance of interprofessional education in the university, increasing understanding of accreditation in the university, and strengthening the university community connection.

WORKPLACE OF THE FUTURE

The ability of schools of social work to recruit and retain the best students, and prepare committed, competent, and confident social workers at all levels of practice, is dependent on the image and influence of the profession, as well its status and salaries. New initiatives with the Department of Labor and CSWE, NASW, and IASWR focus on how federal agencies define and collect data on social work—as a start to standardize and professionalize the definition. These are steps in the direction toward improving social work's domain and professionalism (O'Neill, 2002b).

The future will see a partnership between CSWE and NASW to target large public and private employers in child welfare, public assistance, and school systems to recognize the need for more highly qualified, professionally educated social workers in line, supervisory, and management positions. There will be collaborative training and upgrading and incentive programs between schools of social work and agencies targeting current and potential employees with financial support from the government. CSWE and NASW will join to promote policies that would mandate minimum professional credentials with salaries commensurate to such highly skilled positions.

The CSWE Commission on Accreditation approved guidelines for social work programs using distance education technologies. The guidelines were developed to help social work education programs create and implement distance education components comparable in quality to on-campus offerings.

The issues that U.S. social work educators are grappling with are not unique to America. Many social work professional and educational organizations abroad are addressing similar issues (Lyons, 2000; Mamphiswana & Noyoo, 2000; National Institute of Social Work, 1999). They are all trying to forecast the future and to be proactive in shaping social work education for changing times. Social work education in the United States is ready for the future. By embracing in the curriculum its emerging interest in globalization and the value of practice partnerships and interprofessional collaboration, tomorrow's practitioners will be prepared to respond to the controversies and challenges of social work practice.

REFERENCES

Abramson, J. S., & Rosenthal, B. B. (1995). Interdisciplinary and interorganizational collaboration. In R. L. Edwards (Ed.-in-Chief), *Encyclopedia of social work* (19th ed., Vol. 2, pp. 1479–1489). Washington, DC: NASW Press.

Asamoah, Y., Healy, L. M., & Mayadas, N. (1997). Ending the international–domestic dichotomy: New approaches to a global curricula for the millennium. *Journal of Social Work Education, 33,* 389–401.

Avery, D., Charski, M., Floyd, D., Loftus, M., Marcus, M. B., Mulrine, A., et al. (1998, October 26). 20 hot track jobs: Social work. *U.S. News & World Report,* p. 90.

Bailey, E. D., & Koney, K. M. (1995). Community-based consortia: One model for creation and development. *Journal of Community Practice, 2,* 1–20.

Beless, D. (1998). Social work education needs a world view. *Social Work Education Reporter, 46,* 2, 12.

Bentley, K. J. (2002). *Best practices for clinical social workers in psychopharmacotherapy* (Annual Rep.). New York: Ittleson Foundation.

Berger, C., Cayner, J., Jensen, G., Mizrahi, T., Scesny, A., & Trachtenberg, J. (1996). The changing scene of social work in hospitals: A report of a national study by the Society for Social Work Administrators in Health Care and NASW. *Health and Social Work, 21,* 166–177.

Bernstein, N. (2001, September 26). On Pier 94, a welfare state that works, and a possible model for the future. *New York Times,* p. B9.

Buchanan, P. (2002). *The death of the West: How dying populations and immigrant invasions imperil our country and civilization.* New York: St. Martin's Press.

Campfens, H. (1997). *Community development around the world: Practice, theory, research and training.* Toronto: University of Toronto Press.

Cnaan, R. A. (with Wineburg, R. J., & Boddie, S. C.). (1999). *The newer deal: Social work and religion in partnership.* New York: Columbia University Press.

Coleman, J. (1997). *A long way to go: Black and white in America.* New York: Atlantic Monthly Press.

Council on Social Work Education. (1995). Commission on Educational Policy outlines millennium project work plan. *Social Work Education Reporter, 43,* 1, 3, 6.

Council on Social Work Education. (2001a). *Educational policy and accreditation standards.* Alexandria, VA: Author.

Council on Social Work Education. (2001b). *Statistics on social work education in the United States: 1999.* Alexandria, VA: Author.

Council on Social Work Education. (2001c). *Strengthening the impact of social work to improve the quality of life for older adults and their families: A blueprint for the new millennium.* Alexandria, VA: Author.

Council on Social Work Education. (2002). *Integrating disability content in social work education.* Alexandria, VA: Author.

Davis, L. E. (2000, October 26). *Color and class diversity: Implications for 21st century social work practice.* Paper presented at the thirteenth annual Robert J. O'Leary Memorial Lecture, College of Social Work, Ohio State University, Columbus.

Delgado, M. (1998). *Social services in Latino communities: Research and strategies.* Binghamton, NY: Haworth Press.

Delgado, M. (1999). *Social work practice in nontraditional urban settings.* New York: Oxford University Press.

DiNitto, D. (2003). *Social welfare and public policy* (5th ed.). Boston: Allyn & Bacon/Longman.

Edelman, I. (2001). Participation and service integration in community-based initiatives. *Journal of Community Practice, 9,* 57–76.

Edelman, P. (1997, March). The worst thing Bill Clinton has done. *Atlantic Monthly, 279,* 43–58.

Edwards, R. L., Cooke, P. W., & Reid, P. N. (1996). Social work management in an era of diminished federal responsibility. *Social Work, 41,* 468–480.

Ewalt, P., Freeman, E. M., & Poole, D. L. (Eds.). (1998). *Community building: Renewal, well-being, and shared responsibility.* Washington, DC: NASW Press.

Fabricant, M., & Fisher, R. (2002). *Settlement houses under siege: The struggle to sustain community organizations in New York City.* New York: Columbia University Press.

Fisher, R., & Karger, H. J. (1997). *Social work and community in a private world: Getting out in public.* White Plains, NY: Longman.

Fleischer, D. Z., & Zames, F. (2001). *The disability rights movement: From charity to confrontation.* Philadelphia: Temple University Press.

Fraser, M. (2003, January). *Intervention research in social work: Recent advances and continuing challenges.* Lecture presented at the seventh annual Conference of the Society for Social Work and Research, Washington, DC.

Frumkin, M., & Lloyd, G. A. (1995). Social work education. In R. L. Edwards (Ed.-in-Chief), *Encyclopedia of social work* (19th ed., Vol. 3, pp. 2238–2247). Washington, DC: NASW Press.

Gomory, T. (2001). Critical rationalization (Gomory's blurry theory) or positivism (Thyer's theoretical myopia): Which is the prescription for social work research? *Journal of Social Work Education, 37*(1), 67–78.

Green, J. (2000). *Current issues in social work licensing* (Summary Rep.). Alexandria, VA: Council on Social Work Education.

Gutiérrez, L., & Alvarez, A. R. (2000). Educating students for multi-cultural practice. *Journal of Community Practice, 7,* 39–56.

Gutiérrez, L., Yeakley, A., & Ortega, R. (2000). Educating students for social work with Latinos: Issues for the new millennium. *Journal of Social Work Education, 36,* 541–557.

Healy, L. M. (2002). Internationalizing social work curriculum in the 21st century. In N. T. Tan & I. Dodd (Eds.), *Social work around the world—II* (pp. 179–194). Berne, Switzerland: International Federation of Social Work.

Human Rights Watch. (2002, November). *"We are not the enemy": Hate crimes against Arabs, Muslims, and those perceived to be Arab or Muslim after September 11* (Rep., Vol. 14, No. 6). New York: Author.

Johnson, A. K. (1998). The revitalization of community practice: Characteristics, competencies, and curricula for community-based services. *Journal of Community Practice, 5*(3), 37–62.

Johnson, A. M., & Taylor-Brown, S. (1997). Genetics research and social work education. *Social Work Education Reporter, 45,* 10.

Lyons, K. (2000). The place of research in social work. *British Journal of Social Work, 30,* 433–447.

Mamphiswana, D., & Noyoo, N. (2000). Social work education in a changing socio-political and economic dispensation: Perspectives from South Africa. *International Social Work, 43,* 21–32.

Martin, E. P., & Martin, J. M. (2002). *Spirituality and the black helping tradition in social work.* Washington, DC: NASW Press.

Metrey, G., & Johnson, A. (1999). *Interim report project of the Commission on Accreditation Research Committee.* Alexandria, VA: Council on Social Work Education.

Miringoff, M. L., Miringoff, M., & Opdycke, S. (1999). *The social health of the nation: How America is really doing.* New York: Oxford University Press.

Miringoff, M. L., Miringoff, M., & Opdycke, S. (2001). *The social report: A deeper view of prosperity.* Tarrytown, NY: Fordham Institute for Innovation in Social Policy.

Mizrahi, T. (1999). Strategies for effective collaborations in the human services: Building stronger coalitions in the age of downsizing. *Social Policy, 29,* 5–20.

Mizrahi, T. (2001). The status of community organizing in social work at the end of the 20th century: Community practice context, complexities, contradictions and contributions. *Research on Social Work Practice, 11,* 176–189.

Mizrahi, T., Davidson, K., & Marshack, E. (2000). Career paths of health workers: The impact of a presocial work course on professional development. *Journal of Teaching in Social Work, 20,* 103–120.

Munson, C. E. (1996). Autonomy and managed care in clinical social work practice. *Smith College Studies in Social Work, 66,* 241–260.

Natapoff, A. (1995). Trouble in paradise: Equal protection and the dilemma of interminority group conflict. *Stanford Law Review, 47,* 1059.

National Association of Social Workers. (2001). *Standards for cultural competence in social work practice* [Brochure]. Washington, DC: NASW Press.

National Association of Social Workers. (2002, January). *NASW priorities on faith-based human services initiatives* [Issue statement]. Washington, DC: Author.

National Association of Social Workers. (2003a). Client self-determination in end-of-life decisions. In T. Mizrahi & E. J. Clark (Eds.), *Social work speaks* (6th ed., pp. 45–54). Washington, DC: NASW Press.

National Association of Social Workers. (2003b). Role of government, social policy, and social work. In T. Mizrahi & E. J. Clark (Eds.), *Social work speaks* (6th ed., pp. 293–297). Washington, DC: NASW Press.

National Institute of Social Work. (1999, December). *National debate on the future of social work: Creating a new agenda* (Briefing No. 28). London: Author.

Neuman, K. (2001, April). Life after reengineering in hospital and social work departments. In *Selected Proceedings of the 36th annual Educational Conference of the National Society for Social Work Leadership in Health Care* (pp. 16–21), San Antonio, TX.

Newsome, M., Jr. (1998). Positioning CSWE for the 21st century. *Social Work Education Reporter, 46,* 1, 14.

O'Neill, J. (2002a, March). Profession has a global role: Social work's international stature is explored. *NASW News,* pp. 1–2.

O'Neill, J. (2002b, May). Better labor data on social work sought. *NASW News,* pp. 1, 8.

Park, K. S. (1999). Internationalization: Direction of social welfare policy education in the future. *Arete, 23,* 33–45.

Prigoff, A. (2000). *Economics for social workers: Social outcomes of economic globalization with strategies for social action.* Belmont, CA: Wadsworth.

Reamer, F. (Chair). (1998a). *Current controversies in social work ethics: Case examples.* Washington, DC: NASW Press.

Reamer, F. (1998b). *Ethical standards in social work: A review of the NASW code of ethics.* Washington, DC: NASW Press.

Reisch, M., & Jarman-Rohde, L. (2000). The future of social work in the United States: Implications for field education. *Journal of Social Work Education, 36,* 201–214.

Rivera, F., & Ehrlich, J. (1998). *Organizing in diverse communities* (3rd ed.). Boston: Allyn & Bacon.

Rock, B., & Perez-Koenig, R. (2001). *Social work in an era of devolution: Toward a just practice.* New York: Fordham University Press.

Rowan, C. T., & Friedman, F. (Eds.). (1996). *The coming race war in America.* Boston: Little, Brown.

Rubin, A. (2000). Social work research at the turn of the millennium: Progress and changes. *Research on Social Work Practice, 10,* 9–14.

Rubin, J., & Rubin, I. (2001). *Community organizing and development.* Boston: Allyn & Bacon.

Ryan, W. P., DeMasi, K., Jacobson, W., & Ohmer, M. (2000, July). *Aligning education practice: Challenges and opportunities in social work education for community-centered practice.* Washington, DC: Alliance for Children and Families.

Schames, G., & Lightburn, A. (Eds.). (1998). *Humane managed care?* Washington, DC: NASW Press.

Scharlach, A., Damron-Rodriguez, J. A., Robinson, B., & Feldman, R. (2000). Educating social workers for an aging society: A vision for the 21st century. *Journal of Social Work Education, 36,* 521–537.

Schneider, R. (2002). *Influencing state policy* [Fact sheet]. Richmond, VA: Influencing State Policy.

Schneider, R., & Lester, L. (2001). *Social work advocacy: A new framework for action.* Pacific Grove, CA: Brooks/Cole.

Schriver, J., Steimla, B., & Quinney, H. (Eds.). (2000). [Entire issue]. *Journal of Baccalaureate Social Work, 6*(1).

Sheridan, M. J. (1998). *Assessment of the 1992 curriculum policy statement.* Alexandria, VA: Council on Social Work Education.

Starr, R., Mizrahi, T., & Gurzinsky, E. (1996). Where have all the organizers gone? The career paths of community organizing social work alumni. *Journal of Community Practice, 6,* 23–48.

Stoesen, L. (2002, May). Genetics: Science takes on a human face. *NASW News,* p. 3.

Svihula, J., & Austin, M. J. (2001). Fostering neighborhood involvement in workforce development: The Alameda County neighborhood jobs pilot initiative. *Journal of Community Practice, 9,* 55–72.

Thyer, B. (2001). What is the role of theory in research on social work practice? *Journal of Social Work Education, 37,* 9–25.

Tompkins, C. (2002). SAGE–SW faculty development institutes in full swing. *Social Work Education Reporter, 50,* 16–17.

U.S. Department of Health and Human Services. (1999). *Mental health: A report of the Surgeon General.* Rockville, MD: Author.

U.S. Department of Health and Human Services. (2000). *Mental health: Culture, race and ethnicity* (Suppl.). Rockville, MD: Author.

U.S. Department of Housing and Urban Development and Office of Policy Development and Research. (2000, Summer). *Colleges and communities: Gateway to an American dream* [Annual rep.]. Rockville, MD: University Partnerships Clearinghouse.

Van Soest, D. (1997). *The global crisis of violence: Common problems, universal causes, shared solutions.* Washington, DC: NASW Press.

Vourlekis, B. S., Ell, K., & Padgett, D. (2001). Educating social workers for health care's brave new world. *Journal of Social Work Education, 37,* 177–191.

Wagener, D. K., Molla, M. T., Crimmins, E. M., Pamuk, E., & Madans, J. H. (2001, September). Summary measures of population health: Addressing the first goal of Healthy People 2010, improving health expectancy. In *Healthy People 2010 Statistical Notes* (No. 22). Washington, DC: U.S. Departments of Health and Human Services, Centers for Disease Control and Prevention, National Center for Health Statistics.

Wedel, K. R., & Baker, D. R. (1998). After the Oklahoma City bombing: A case study of the resource coordination committee. *International Journal of Mass Emergencies and Disasters, 16,* 333–362.

White, B. (1999). Quality in social work education. *Social Work Education Reporter, 47,* 1, 9.

Yamamoto, E. (1997). Critical race praxis: Race theory and political lawyering practice in post-civil rights America. *Michigan Law Review, 95,* 821.

Zakour, M. J. (Ed.). (2000). Disaster and traumatic stress research and intervention. *Tulane Studies in Social Welfare,* Vol. 21–22.

Zlotnik, J. L., Biegel, D. E., & Solt, B. E. (2002). The Institute for the Advancement of Social Work Research: Strengthening social work research in practice and policy. *Research on Social Work Practice, 12,* 318–337.

Terry Mizrahi, PhD, is professor of social work, Hunter College, 129 East 79th Street, New York, NY 10021 and the 2001–2003 president of the National Association of Social Workers; **Frank Baskind, PhD,** is professor and dean, School of Social Work, Virginia Commonwealth University, 1001 W. Franklin Street, P.O. Box 842027, Richmond, VA 23284-2027 and the 2001–2004 president of the Council on Social Work Education.

For further information see

Baccalaureate Social Workers, *1997;* Child Welfare Overview; Continuing Education; Council on Social Work Education; Environmental Health: Race and Socioeconomic Factors; International Social Work Education; Licensing, Regulation, and Certification; Peace and Social Justice; Policy Practice; Sexual Distress; Social Work Education; Social Work Education: Electronic Technologies, *1997;* Social Work Practice: History and Evolution; Social Work Profession: History; Social Work Profession Overview

Key Words

future directions	social work practice
social work education	social work profession

Spouse Abuse

See Domestic Abuse, *Volume 1*

Strengths-Based Practice
Dennis Saleebey

The lines between the modern-day strengths perspective and certain fashions, philosophies, movements, and appreciations of the past in American culture are faint but nonetheless real. Elements of strengths thinking can be traced back to the ideals of democracy, American idealism, romance of the frontier, transcendentalism, social gospel, and the persistent beat of positive thinking in American society. In this culture, strains of optimism, hope, positive expectations, promise of tomorrow, and the possibility of remaking of the self have flourished in one form or another. They have been manifest in philosophies, religions, nostrums, and panaceas peddled by a variety of gurus, shamans, evangelists, physicians, philosophers, and politicians. A person such as Norman Vincent Peale, the Protestant minister who has written, preached, and proselytized on the power of positive thinking for five decades, would probably not have been possible in, say, France. Even today, the shelves of libraries, bookstores, and online booksellers fairly burst with manifestos of self-development, self-righting, and self-improvement. Some attribute such a breed of thought to a frontier mentality where El Dorado is just over the next rise and the self is always provisional.

AMERICAN PRECURSORS AND MOVEMENTS IN GENERAL

Transcendentalism was and is a peculiarly American phenomenon. In the 19th century, Ralph Waldo Emerson, Henry David Thoreau, Walt Whitman, and Margaret Fuller, among others, created this philosophy, stitched together with strands of pragmatism, naturalism, spirituality, Puritanism, Quaker philosophy, and old-fashioned American individualism. Among other tenets the idea is the self, the soul, is the spiritual center of the universe and that virtue depends, in part, on self-realization—the expression of that soul in the human and natural world. Knowing one's self is the beginning of understanding the cosmos. Self-realization requires the integration of two discordant forces: the self as transcendent (the desire to become one, to identify with the world) and the self-asserting, autonomous self. To know oneself is to know nature because nature is reflected in our deepest psyche. The reverse is true as well. The contemplation of the natural world is revelatory of the soul itself. The individual soul is a miracle of sorts; every element of the cosmos from the tiniest gnat to the grandest mountain range is miraculous as well. The soul is also an active seeker of truth, and the moment for seeking and expressing is now. Finally, true reform of the secular and spiritual worlds will come from the light and understanding within and will not be imposed from without (Boller, 1974; Reuben, 2000).

The Social Gospel movement developed in many Christian religions in the latter part of the 19th century as a reaction against the incursions of Social Darwinism, unrestrained industrial expansion, and the oppression of workers. Scientific thinking, evolutionary theory, and the principles of democratic socialism contributed to the Gospel's notion that humans were innately good and that the progress of society was much like evolution was thought to be—toward a better fit with the environment. It was believed, however, that the intervention and good will of Christian people and institutions would be necessary to ensure the "good society." In a word, the Social Gospel movement was the application of the teachings of the church, more particularly Jesus, to the real world. The working classes were the focus of much of the concern and interest of the adherents of the Social Gospel movement in two ways: first, it was thought to be the obligation of Christians to address the brutal conditions many laborers faced; and second, that confrontation would be accompanied by bearing the teachings of Christianity to the working classes. Washington Gladden, a Congregationalist minister from Ohio, and Walter Rauschenbusch, a German Baptist minister from Rochester, New York, were the foremost advocates of the Social Gospel, lecturing, writing, and engaging in advocacy for the abolition of child labor; better working conditions for workers, especially women; and the right of every worker to a living wage. Gladden's *Social Salvation* (1918) and Rauschenbusch's *A Theology for the Social Gospel* (1917) were enormously influential and widely read. Again, the basic tenets of the Social Gospel movement involved the affirmation of the basic goodness and innate wisdom of people (institutions were another matter), the application of Christian principles to social problems, and the perfectibility of humankind. Some of the programs and proposals of the Social Gospel movement found their way into the New Deal legislation of the 1930s (Phillips, 1996; Social Gospel, 2000).

The incessant beat of optimism, perfectibility, individual transformation, innate goodness, and the transmutation of the possible into the actual come from many corners of American culture and history. Remnants and hints of these are a part of the heritage of the strengths perspective.

SOCIAL WORK TRADITIONS

Forerunners of the strengths orientation in the early years of social work include the settlement house movement and the writings of Jane Addams and others, and also the views of Virginia Robinson, Bertha Capen Reynolds, the functional school of social work, and, somewhat later, Ruth Smalley and Herbert Bisno. The words of Jane Addams (1902) reflected the thinking of many in this new profession of social work in the early 1900s:

> We are gradually requiring of the educator that he shall free the powers of each man and connect him with the rest of life. We ask this not merely because it is the man's right to be thus connected but because we have become convinced that the social order cannot afford to get along without *his special contribution.* [italics added] (p. 178)

Later, Bertha Capen Reynolds (1951) spoke for many of her colleagues with these words:

> The real choice before us as social workers is whether we are to be passive or active. . . . Shall we be content to give with one hand and withhold with the other, to build up or tear down at the same time the strength of a person's life? Or shall we be conscious of our own part in making a profession which will stand forthrightly for human well-being, including the right to be an active citizen? (p. 175)

More recent contributions to and extensions of the strengths perspective flow from the expanding empowerment literature in social work. Through the work of Paulo Freire, Barbara Simon, Barbara Solomon, and Anthony Maluccio and, more currently, Lorraine Gutiérrez and Judith A. B. Lee, multicultural and feminist critiques and frameworks have provided instruction for the emergent strengths approach. From these fertile and varied points of view, we can draw out some of the core ideas: (1) formulating a critical consciousness, what Freire (1996) called "conscientization"— the developing awareness of the sources of oppression, and the intentions and methods of the oppressors; (2) developing a sense of individual and collective efficacy and agency, moving toward liberation; (3) encouraging dialogue between those who would be freer and those who would assist in their liberation—so that people can "think, see, talk, and act for themselves" (Lee, 1994, p. 4)—assuring equity, enhancing collective responsibility, and providing connections to social resources so that all can move toward individual development and greater contributions to the social order (Freire, 1996; Gutiérrez, 1990; Lee, 1994).

The purposeful amplification of the strengths perspective began at the University of Kansas School of Social Welfare in 1982. At that time, the school was awarded $10,000 by a local community health center to provide case management services to people with persistent and severe ("chronic" was the term used) mental illness. With Ronna Chamberlain, Charles Rapp evaluated the standard practice of case management with this group and became convinced that, with its emphasis on linking clients only with formal mental health services, this approach could not achieve the desired outcomes—living in the community, real work, use of leisure time, independent living, and so forth. So they discarded that approach and developed another based on the identification and support of individual and community strengths to achieve "normalization." A small field unit of four students, supervised by Chamberlain, "field" tested the model, and at the end of the year found that 19 of 22 indicators of positive outcomes were achieved. The model expanded conceptually and practically, and by the mid-1980s, the strengths approach was becoming the centerpiece of community support services in mental health. The state of Kansas adopted the approach and training expanded to other states that were interested in the model. The model began to spread to other populations—the elderly, youth in trouble with the law, community development, child welfare, Aid to Families with Dependent Children recipients, and others. But it was the original work of Rapp and his associates at the University of Kansas that provided the conceptual, ethical, and methodological tools for the investiture of the model (Rapp, 1998).

Philosophy and Principles
The guiding and formative values and philosophy of the strengths perspective clearly intersect with the values of the social work profession. Included are the following:

- All people, individually and collectively, have the right to develop not only their human nature to the optimum, but also their inherent capacity as well.
- Out of misfortune and tragedy may come transformation and redemption.
- In the ideal of social justice inheres the notion that social resources must be distributed in a way that ensures the development of those internal and external assets that maximize our humanity, personally and communally.

We cannot hope to become the people, individually and collectively, that we hope to become without the discovery and development of those internal and external resources that underwrite optimal human development.

The central philosophical axis of the strengths perspective counterposes two large themes that reflect timeless elements of the human condition: oppression and liberation. Liberation refers to the unimagined bounty of possibilities for choice, commitment, action, and belief, sought and pursued in relative liberty or wrenched out of dire circumstances. All humans, somewhere within, have the urge to be heroic: to transcend circumstances, to develop their powers, to overcome adversity, to be recognized and responsible. Too often this impulse is driven underground or thoroughly trampled by despotic leaders, economic conditions, difficult relationships, regrettable decisions, bad luck, or unfortunate circumstances. But even locked in the confines of such oppressive conditions, some find the courage and the connections to liberate themselves, in spirit if not in reality. Social workers have always claimed that they are a part of the work of liberation, although they may not have used that language (Freire, 1996; Weick, Rapp, Sullivan, & Kisthardt, 1989). Oppression, on the other hand, involves the all too common muting of human capacities and possibilities; the diminishing of the human spirit; and the crushing of human autonomy and collective will. Oppression, like liberation, can be modest, hardly noticeable, or epic and grand. It can occur within an abusive intimate relationship. It can be found in political marginalization and sequestering. It can be a part of the struggle for the basic necessities of life, stamped by the template of poverty and disease. Many of the people social workers help are, in one way or another, oppressed by circumstance, condition, relationship, and reality. Oppression often obscures to the observer, and to those who experience it, the reality of their strengths and resources, and the dream of a better life. The manifestations of these ideas may be hard to see, or wonderfully or painfully obvious (Lee, 1994; Simon, 1994).

These general philosophical primary principles can be further reduced to a subset of three principles, each with some refining secondary principles.

Empowerment. The work of empowerment is joining and connecting people to each other in the discovery and use of their inner powers and environmental resources, all in the service of liberation. It is predicated on the belief that (1) every individual, every family, every community, every culture—no exceptions—has strengths, assets, resources, capacities, and wisdom to be used in the practice of liberation; (2) in the process of facing oppression of the body, spirit, and environment, no matter how devastating, people inevitably learn things, acquire capacities, discover resources, and develop personal traits and interpersonal connections that can be tools and can provide motivation and energy for change; (3) every human being has an innate wisdom, a sense of what is right, a capacity for self-righting that, although it might be obscured by negative expectations, labels, regrettable decisions, and bad luck, nonetheless remains an important resource to be tapped; and (4) differences of ability, of culture, of class, of sexual orientation, of age, and of geography should be regarded as potential sources of strength, as distinctive resources in the process of meeting challenges and achieving aspirations (Mills, 1995; Rapp, 1998; Saleebey, 1996; Swadener & Lubeck, 1995). The idea of empowerment is that people, with a little help from their friends, contingencies, and people like social workers, empower themselves (Saleebey, 1996).

Resources. McKnight (1995) made the point that, in approaching communities under stress or economically and socially distressed (or thought to be), professionals, including social workers, often turn community members into clients. Social workers should be mindful of the distinction between service and care. In real care, there is a consenting commitment on the part of all parties involved that care is the manifestation of community and that community is the site of connectedness and the sharing of natural and informal resources. Service too often involves the imposition of alien ideas and programs and making community members dependent on them. So, whoever works in the community must be cognizant and respectful of the capacities there. This means being attentive to the fact that (1) every environment, even where the streets are mean and the money lean, has untapped, bountiful natural resources and assets—people, associations, families, symbols, history and heritage, tools—that can be part of the stuff of liberation; (2) the power of a community is summed up by the collective capacities of each individual and family in that

community, and that people working together in common pursuit have a power that is transformative; (3) in terms of individuals, the possible resources and assets an individual might possess are incalculable—at the least these include talents, skills, personal traits and virtues, lessons learned from experience, connections to others, cultural meaning systems and rituals, beliefs and values, and hopes and dreams; and (4) we cannot presume to know the limits and parameters of one's talents and capacities nor can we know the upper limits of a person's potential for development and transformation (Goldstein, 1997; Rapp, 1998; Saleebey, 1996).

Possibilities. Many people who come to social workers and other professionals seem stuck—unable to surmount the trauma and pain inflicted on them by others or by themselves. They live in the past and cannot imagine a future. Many of the labels affixed on them, and the approaches taken with them, exacerbate that. But human beings are nothing if not always immanent and full of possibilities, even though these may be obscured at the moment by pain, despair, and relationship ruts (Hoyt, 1996). It is important to help individuals, families, and communities rekindle and recapture their hopes and dreams for a better or different life. Existing aspirations and goals should be taken seriously and elaborated as colorfully and powerfully as possible, and steps toward them should be made explicit and conceived as a collaborative project between the social worker and the individual or family. Finally, hopes are generally wrapped in positive expectations, and those expectations become blueprints for the future (Benard, 1997; Snyder, 1994).

These principles and their correlates provide a way of thinking about those we help, their day-to-day lives, and the environments around them. Working from a strengths perspective does require something of a different language and an unconventional way of looking at the world of professional work. At the very least, using a strengths approach as a basis for practice encourages us, as Emily Dickinson once put it, to "dwell in possibility" and to be hopeful, to be respectful, and to believe in the individual, family, or community.

Core Elements of Humane and Effective Helping and the Strengths Perspective
In a survey of the research done on psychotherapy over the past couple of decades,

Lambert (1992) concluded that, when it works, psychotherapy is driven by four common factors that reach across schools of thought, theories of psychotherapy, and clinical practice of all kinds. Duncan, Hubble, and Miller (1997) have elaborated on these factors. It is possible to take them even further to provide some ballast for a strengths-based approach to helping.

The environment: Strengths, resources, and contingencies. The capacities, interests, beliefs, and skills of a client and the social, interpersonal, and economic resources in the environment are the most potent contributions to a change for the better. This is a reflection of the fabric of the lives of individuals and families—the web of resources in their surroundings, social support networks, their own assets and knowledge, personal or collective traits and virtues, and, importantly, the unforeseen contingencies (luck) in their lives. These are much more important than what professional helpers do, be they social workers, psychologists, or physicians. As a matter of fact, the people who get better while waiting for a first appointment (this includes some people with medical problems as well) are testament to the power of the person and the environment. Lambert (1992) claimed that in his research these factors accounted for 40 percent of the positive change. The strengths perspective encourages one to capitalize on these resources in a mindful, careful way.

The caring relationship. For years social workers have emphasized the importance of the helping relationship as the medium of change (Shulman, 1992). Half a century ago, Rogers (1951) stated that there were special qualities to relationships that were, in fact, therapeutic—caring, empathy, respect, and genuineness. These were the "core conditions" of positive change. Rogers spoke of the relationship as an alliance. Over the last 30 years, Strupp (1995) has done research on the effectiveness of psychotherapy and reiterated that the quality of the helping relationship is the root factor in positive change. Practitioners of the strengths perspective add to these conditions the importance of collaboration—developing a mutually crafted project to work on, to lay a concrete path to dreams and hopes. Likewise, practitioners of a strengths perspective also believe in the power of straightforward caring, empathic, and engaged relationships with clients. Rapp (1998) and his associates

defined the effective helping relationship as purposeful, reciprocal, friendly, trusting, and empowering and the core conditions, as we might suspect, as empathy, genuineness, and unconditional positive regard. Lambert (1992) reckoned in his review of research that relationships accounted for about 30 percent of the positive changes in clients' lives.

Positive expectations, hope, and the placebo effect. Often forgotten, but truly important to the process of change, is the power of positive expectations; belief in the possibilities inherent in the individual, family, or community; and the mysterious placebo effect. It would be hard to overstate the negative thinking that abounds with regard to many people who are experiencing difficulty in their lives, who have faced trauma, the excesses of their own appetites, the disasters of bad decisions, and the grinding effects of daily life: poverty, racism, illness, and so on. In the Western world, but especially in our society, medical, mental health, and other professionals have developed a language of "progressive infirmity" for an ever-increasing number of people. "How may I fault thee? Let me count the ways: impulsive personality, malingering, reactive depression, anorexia, mania, attention deficit disorders, psychopathia, external control orientation, low self-esteem, narcissism, bulimia, neurasthenia" (Gergen, 1994, pp. 147–148). Each of these carries heavy symbolic and linguistic freight, creating expectations and suffusing into identities of those so named. Most of all, unleavened by the acknowledgment of positive attributes, they constitute a kind of whammy, an amassing of negative, even dire, expectations.

But the reverse of such medical/psychiatric "hexing" is the creation of hope and positive expectancy, a buoyant and realistic orientation to a better future rather than an obsession with a dreary and painful past. To express belief in the possibilities inherent in the individual and the resources available in the environment is to fashion an evolving dream toward which steps can be taken. The placebo effect, although a testament to the power of the mind to shape reality, is an often-ignored phenomenon. The word "placebo" is from the Latin meaning "I shall please." These inert substances ("sugar pills"), on occasion, appear to relieve headaches, shrink some tumors, elevate mood, cure infections, and, yes, grow hair. In clinical studies of drug or treatment efficacy, two groups are formed randomly. One group receives the actual medication or procedure; the other, an inert one. Neither group, including those who administer the pills, knows who gets what. An advertisement for Rogaine when it was a prescription drug carried on the back of the presentation the specifications and contraindications for the use of this hair-growing drug. Also included was a description of the clinical trials. Over a period of six months, about 22 percent of the men who received Rogaine grew hair in all the right places. But 11 percent of the men who received the placebo also grew hair— an amazing testament to the power of expectation and to the healing properties within the human body. These three factors—hope, positive expectation, and the placebo effect—offer a powerful trio of appreciations for the helper. However, the positive expectations must be genuine.

Technical operations of theory or perspective. Technical operations contribute about as much to "therapeutic" gain as do positive expectations and hope—they do make a difference, of course, but not as much as we might think. It is clear, for example, that interpersonal therapy is an effective treatment for moderate depression. It is also clear that without the other three factors, interpersonal therapy is much less potent.

STRENGTHS MODEL OF PRACTICE: DIRECT PRACTICE AND CASE MANAGEMENT

A general but systematic account of the emerging models of strengths-based social work practice can be drawn from practice and research in a variety of fields: mental health, juvenile justice, aging, community development, child welfare, and clinical social work. Like any practice, the process of work from a strengths perspective is always subject to the vagaries and idiosyncrasies of the moment, the quality of the helping relationship, and the immediate context in which the work takes place. Nonetheless, a general understanding of the process is possible, as outlined below.

Direct Practice across Various Theoretical Approaches

The work of Wolin and Wolin (1996) on promoting the resilience of adults who have surmounted childhood trauma, the ideas that give shape to solution-focused therapy (DeJong & Miller, 1995), the approach of Benard (1997) in turning around the lives of "at-risk" adolescents and their families, the reports of Kaplan and Girard (1994) and Walsh (1998) in working with families where there are

serious problems, as well as the experiences of numerous practitioners have helped construct the general outlines of a strengths-based practice.

Acknowledging and metabolizing the pain and trauma—Stimulating critical consciousness. For many individuals and families, as well as communities, there is real use and purpose in addressing, acknowledging, reexperiencing, and putting into perspective the pains and traumas of one's life, especially those that seem insistent. Grief, rage, and anxiety, and the metabolization and catharsis of those feelings, are critical to developing an understanding of where individuals have been, what their current struggles are, and what emotional, cognitive, social, and spiritual burdens they shoulder. This process is also important in understanding what they have called upon in order to survive to this point. But it is also a step toward letting go of the past, and beginning to envision a present and future that are organically better. For some people, it may be beneficial to explore the roots of trauma in family, community, and culture. It certainly is important to assess current risks, for example, in a family in which vulnerable members have been traumatized. All of this is undertaken with the purpose of helping individuals, families, and communities develop a critical understanding of those elements in their lives that have oppressed, stunned, marginalized, and isolated them. But even within that, the purpose always is to encourage them to look for the seeds of resilience and rebound; the lessons taken away from adversity; the cultural, ethnic, and familial sources of adaptability; and the individual, communal, cultural, and spiritual resources they have or can use in lessening risk and confronting the trials of life.

Stimulating discourse and narratives of resilience and strength. There is often great reluctance to acknowledge and affirm one's competence, reserves, and resourcefulness. In addition, many traits and capacities that are signs of strength or at least potentially so are hidden by years of self-doubt, the blame and abuse of others, or the wearing of a diagnostic label. Sometimes the problem of discovering strengths lies in the relative poverty of words, sometimes it is the disbelief of others, and sometimes it is lack of trust in oneself. The social worker may have to be the one to help identify strengths; to provide the words and imagery; to give relevant feedback about the evidence of wisdom, virtues, and resources in the stories and narratives of life; to give name and life to those resiliencies the individual has developed and accumulated in the past and that extend into the present (Cowger, 1994; DeJong & Miller, 1995).

Social workers can do at least two things here by providing a vocabulary of strengths (in the language of the client) and a mirror that can give a glimmering and durable positive reflection of the client's abilities and accomplishments (Wolin & Wolin, 1996). The incremental but vivid creation of hope and realistic positive expectancies, as the impact of these strengths on future possibilities is discussed, is important as a central focus of the process; and as the process unfolds, a new narrative may begin to be written—a narrative of a better quality of life, and surcease from the pains and ordeals of the past.

Acting in context: Education, advocacy, and connection. This aspect continues the process of linking the individual's (or family's) capacities, virtues, and strengths and the resources of the community with the formation and pursuit of goals and hopes. The individual or family is encouraged to take the risk of acting on fresh expectancies using the newly articulated competencies as well as the already active ones. This is usually done with the development of a collaborative project between the client and social worker, a project designed to move toward specific goals by employing those resources within and around the individual. This often involves connecting and reconnecting people with others—as well as social, health, and educational services—as part of the mutual creation of multiple strategies for reaching one's goals. This is precarious business for many people who have been through hell. But as they decide and act, as they identify multiple strategies for redirecting their lives, they are encouraged and shown how to employ their assets and resiliencies to work, however tentatively and modestly, toward the realization of their dreams. They will also discover the limits of their resilience and the effect of still active sore spots and scars. They will encounter the intransigence of some institutions and agencies, people, and groups. It is here that advocacy, brokerage, and mediation on the part of the social worker play important roles. It is at this juncture, too, that the natural resources of the environment—people, associations, and tools—are summoned and employed. But, in the end, it is the individual or family's decision

making, risk taking, strengths, will, and persistence that lead to changes in feeling, thinking, and relationships that are more congruent with their goals and talents.

Normalizing and capitalizing upon one's strengths. Over a period of time, often a short period of time, the social worker and the individual or family will begin to consolidate the strengths that have emerged and grown, will reinforce and fill out the new vocabulary of strengths and competency, and will bolster the capacity to discover the resources within and without. The celebration and amalgamation of strengths and resources discovered and developed as well as an accounting of the steps and measures that have been taken toward a better quality of life are of the moment in this process. One important element of this part of the process is normalization and extension—teaching and sharing with others what one has learned in this journey, a kind of mentorship, a wedding of reminiscence and reinforcement. This is also the point of ritual and gradual disengagement between worker and client, and it occurs only with the assurance that personal strengths and communal resources are in place, and that the tempo of progress established by the client is sustained.

Strengths Model of Case Management

The development of the strengths model of case management, especially with people who have persistent and severe mental illness, has been the most robust expression of the strengths perspective. The theory behind, the principles of, and the character inherent in the helping relationship are a part of the roots of all strengths-based approaches. The work of Charles Rapp (1998) and his associates is the foundation of this model.

Theoretical assumptions. The propositions that make up the theory are that the individual strengths of a person are manifest, however meagerly or abundantly, in his or her aspirations, competencies, and degree of confidence (willingness, intentions, and beliefs). On the other hand, the environment provides, however meagerly or abundantly, tangible, natural or formal resources and services, social relationships, and access to opportunities relevant to the individual's goals and aspirations. The niches in which people lead their lives provide—or not—resources around living arrangements, work, education, and social relationships. The environmental niches of the oppressed, for instance, are characterized by entrapment, social stigmatization, isolation, poverty, and few routes out. More fortunate people live in enabling niches where there are rich job and educational opportunities; connections between people; avenues for growth, change, and development; and family involvement. The work of the strengths perspective is to do whatever it may take to increase and put into play the individual and environmental resources toward creating an "enabling niche"—a coming together of personal desires and capacities and the environmental opportunities and resources "needed to live, play, and work in a normally interdependent way in the community" (Rapp, 1998, p. 44; see also Sullivan, 1997; Taylor, 1997).

Principles. The following principles are derived from the theoretical assumptions about how and why people succeed in life and are meant to offer specific orientations and methods for assisting those struggling with mental illness to achieve that end (Rapp, 1998):

- Focus is on individual strengths rather than pathology.
- Environment is viewed as an oasis of resources.
- Interventions are based on client self-determination.
- Case manager–client relationship is primary and essential.
- Aggressive outreach is a preferred mode of intervention.
- People who suffer from major mental illness can continue to grow, learn, and change.

Three very important elements of case management include (1) development of a partnership between case manager and client; (2) thorough assessment of individual and environmental resources and strengths; and (3) on the basis of the assessment, development of a personal planning agenda, a mutual agenda for work between the client and case manager focused on achieving goals set by the client. The goals should be specific, doable, concrete, positive, and have a good chance of success. In addition, it should be possible to break them into discrete tasks. Finally, the goals should reflect the real context of the individual's life and a glimmer of that person's hopes. The community is the site for the acquisition of needed resources—people, tools, skills and expertise, groups, organizations—and the preference, where possible, is for natural resources, not

formal ones, to be used toward the normalization of life (Rapp, 1998; Sullivan, 1997).

In summary, the strengths model of case management is a set of orientations, appreciations, and methods that flow from the idea of empowerment. Although some factors in the lives of those who suffer and struggle with major mental illness, and in the work situation of those who help them, cannot be ameliorated, empowerment here means (1) becoming a genuine partner with the client; (2) encouraging the persistent and devoted search for strengths and resources and mutually devising ways that they may be employed; (3) trusting in the regenerative powers of individuals; (4) looking at the community as a fountain of resources and possibilities; and (5) believing in the client's dream as a possible outcome (Rapp, 1998; Saleebey, 2002).

COMMUNITY BUILDING: EMERGENCE OF STRENGTHS APPROACHES IN COMMUNITY WORK

There has been a sudden rise in and expansion of approaches to community development that rely upon a strengths and assets philosophy. Generally speaking, the philosophy of these approaches is based upon (1) working to develop resources and programs from within the community rather than imposing programs from outside agencies and organizations; (2) developing and articulating relationships and connections between residents, and between residents and helpers; (3) focusing on identifying and employing the available assets in the community—people, associations, institutions, and their talents, interests, knowledge, and physical, social, financial, and symbolic resources; (4) trusting in the self-righting capacities of a community once a critical mass of involved and motivated residents is achieved; and (5) developing community-built projects that move the community toward solidarity, celebration, ownership, and recognition, and in which residents' needs are met (Delgado, 2000; Kretzmann & McKnight, 1993; Mills, 1995).

The work of the community psychologist Roger Mills (1995), based on the "psychology of mind" of George Pransky, is a groundbreaking and strengths-based approach that applies to communities. The original work done by Mills in the Modello/Homestead Gardens public housing project in Miami beginning in 1987, and since replicated in many economically distressed communities, is truly amazing. The approach is based on the idea that many people have covered over their primal and indigenous healthy sense of self with socialized thinking (the language and views of others that have become embedded in identity) that is negative, destructive, and discouraging. People act on the latter and inadvertently produce consequences that reinforce this thinking. The work of Mills was to instruct people, in groups, on this phenomenon and show the impact it had on their daily lives and on their well-being and that of those around them. Collectively, this kind of self-expression can make life in a community difficult. Once people begin to see and understand this, their innate wisdom and urge to health come to the fore and begin to dominate their thinking, emotions, behavior, and self-image. Lest this sound too much like a "pop–psych nostrum," consider the results. In Miami over the years from 1987 to 1990, a pre-test and posttest analysis of 142 families and their 604 youth revealed the following: improved parent–child relationships in 87 percent of the families; 75 percent reduction in delinquency and school-related problem behaviors; 65 percent decrease in drug trafficking; and 66 percent increase in school attendance and achievement (Mills, 1995). In Coliseum Gardens in Oakland, California, a community wracked with violence, gang wars, and ethnic tensions over the previous 10 years, there has not been one homicide since this strengths-based approach was initiated in 1989 in a community that had had one of the highest murder rates in the Bay Area (personal communication with B. Benard, senior program associate with Human Development Program at WestEd's Oakland, California Office, May 1, 2000).

A lengthy quote from Mills (1995) reveals his philosophy and what he did as an effective community developer:

> We did everything we could to reduce stress when we began our public housing programs in 1987. We helped our clients with emergency rental needs, paid utility bills, and provided supplementary food, clothing, and physical security. We offered job training and day care assistance. We worked hard to make circumstances easier for our clients. . . . At the same time we never lost sight of the bottom line. . . . We wanted to see what could happen when people learned some practical ideas about how they could take charge of their own thinking. We hypothesized that they would begin to handle adversity with more hope and self-respect and find ways to improve their circumstances as a community and on their own. We trusted that our clients' innate intelligence would surface as soon as they would drop their

attachment to alienated or insecure patterns of thinking. We suspected and hoped that the buoyancy of the human spirit would deliver the resiliency they needed to frame their prospects and capabilities in a more hopeful light. (p. 128)

They certainly did.

So, in one sense, the approach of Mills (1995) is based on teaching residents to listen and hear their internal message of health, resilience, hope, and wisdom. But this teaching can be done only within a positive, caring, and real relationship with clients. "Perhaps the most vital ingredient," said Mills, "is the establishing of an empowering relationship . . . and being in a state of service" (pp. 29, 30). Finally, it is ultimately the residents who pass on the teaching to their peers, creating a forum for not only self-discovery but also community action and development. The model builds at the grass-roots level a critical mass of individuals capable of these practices who, together with newly involved residents, help create change and put pressure in the right places to move toward policy changes (educational, health, housing, child welfare) that support collective well-being, efficacy, and unity. When Mills and his staff leave, the community is already healing and most definitely empowered—to stay.

COMING TOGETHER: CONFLUENCE OF IDEAS FROM OTHER DISCIPLINES AND PRACTICES

Fortunately, for the strengths perspective, a number of initially unexpected developments have provided sources of philosophical guidance, conceptual innovation, and enhancement of practice methods. The following sections are some capsule descriptions of these developments.

Youth Development and Resiliency Research

A capacious volume of writing, clinical work, and research has demonstrated that many children—perhaps the majority—who suffer the most flagrant and egregious blows in their young lives (abuse, the addictions of parents, grinding poverty) turn out better than anyone might have predicted (Benard, 1997; Katz, 1997; Werner & Smith, 1992; Wolin & Wolin, 1993). This does not mean they do not suffer, nor does it mean that they do not bear the scars of their struggles. It does mean that because of "protective" and "generative" factors in their lives, they surmount, as adults, the adversities they faced as children. The good offices of caring adults in their lives, their own innate hardiness, schools that support and nurture, activities that instruct and strengthen skills and resolve, and traits and healthy defenses they develop in response to the stresses and demands all play a role in their rebound. Of course, any child can be overwhelmed by challenges. But because some children do seem, over time and with help, to overcome the critically damaging effects of a traumatic childhood does not mean that we, as a society, do not have an obligation to intervene and ensure respite and safety. Nonetheless, as Walsh (1998) said:

> We may . . . be drawn into villainizing men who have been abusive, or mothers who have failed to protect their children. While addressing problem behavior, we need to resist the pull to pathologize the person. We can gain empathy from seeing each person in the context of his or her relationships and life struggles: a single parent who is overwhelmed and undersupported; a wife whose trust has been shattered by past sexual abuse; a father who himself was abused and knows no other way to discipline children. (p. 265)

The idea, then, is to build upon the capacity for youths' resilience while acknowledging and working on those processes and dynamics that are destructive.

Health and Wellness

The wildly expanding literature on wellness seems, in part, a response to the narrowness and negativity of the medical model and medical research. For example, all the research done on the effects of risk factors on heart disease—stress, smoking, high blood pressure, high cholesterol—have led to campaigns to obliterate those factors. This is fine as such factors may compromise health and energy or are harmful; but most people who have three of these risk factors over a 10-year period, for example, do not die—some live quite a while (Moore, 1989). In other words, these particular factors may not predict completely, as well as we imagine, who stays healthy. There are other factors that we need to know more about, from genetically predisposed protections to peoples' daily practices (like exercise or meditation), their beliefs (meaning systems and spirituality and religious observances, for example), and their personal traits (such as patience, a sense of humor, or creativity; Ornstein & Sobel, 1989; Pelletier, 2000; Weil, 1995). Focusing on the factors that enhance health and bolster a sense of wellness is far different from focusing on the

signs and symptoms, and risk factors, of illness. Some assumptions of such holistic practices are essential and well-understood:

- People have an innate capacity for health and regeneration.
- Positive beliefs about oneself and one's condition seem indispensable for recovery and the maintenance of health.
- Certain emotions (like love, happiness, and optimism) and activities (such as meditation, massage, pleasurable love making, and regular exercise) seem to be health promoting, possibly because they elevate the functioning of the immune system; whatever else they are, they are significant hormonal events.
- Involvement in a network of meaningful relationships and membership in a community play important roles—connections between people and their stories, hopes, supports, resources, and common visions and activities create a community where body, mind, and environment truly come together (Mills, 1995; Ornstein & Sobel, 1989; Saleebey, 2001; Weil, 1995).

Recovery from Severe and Persistent Mental Illness

The literature increasingly documents that people do actually recover from severe mental disorders. Some aspects of their recovery seem related to an inherent physical, neurobiological process. Some recoveries, however, appear to be the result of the interplay between a variety of personal, sociocultural, and spiritual factors. In this sense, recovery does not necessarily mean being symptom free. It may mean the emergence of healing, a reintegration of body, mind, and environment through a variety of determined efforts, catalytic events, faith and hope, connections with others, and finding or renewing purpose and meaning. Certainly, finding a steadfast and caring relationship is a major force in healing. But learning to assume some degree of control over one's experience and fate, recasting the understanding of one's demons, is important, too. A person struggling with schizophrenia put it this way: "Sometimes you keep fighting and fighting. Like I have a fight in me all the time that I've got to keep going. I've got to keep going and I've got determination. I could just sit down, yeah, I'm not going to do nothing" (Tooth, Kalyanansundaram, & Glover, 1997, p. 43). This, in a sense, is a struggle for agency, autonomy, and control. For some, finding a new environment that is more hospitable and welcoming gives a boost to healing. These elements of healing clearly are promoted by the presence of someone who has a firm belief in positive expectations and hope for the person, showing him or her the way and providing a road map to a more satisfying life and to specific goals.

Kay Redfield Jamison (1995), a psychologist who has studied and suffered from manic–depressive illness (she prefers that stirring term to the barren "bipolar disorder" label) for most of her adult life, knows that she will always confront unsettling swings of mood, intensity, and energy. She knows, too, that lithium saved her life. Although lithium spoke to the molecular aspect, love spoke to the narrative aspect of her life:

> But love is, to me, the ultimately more extraordinary part of the breakwater wall: it helps to shut out the terror and awfulness, while, at the same time, allowing in life and beauty and vitality. . . . After each seeming death within my mind or heart, love has returned to re-create hope and to restore life. It has, at its best, made the inherent sadness of life bearable, and its beauty manifest. It has, inexplicable and savingly, provided not only cloak but lantern for the darker seasons and grimmer weather. (p. 215)

Enough said.

There are other intersecting contributions to a strengths perspective, including the work done in solution-focused therapy, narrative and constructionist approaches to helping, and the ecological perspective.

CONCLUSION

Studies of the strengths approach to this point have generally shown its efficacy—particularly in case management. Evaluations of related approaches (solution focused, resiliency based, health realization) have generally been positive (Duncan et al., 1997; Mills, 1995; Rapp, 1998; Wolin & Wolin, 1996). The importance of a strengths approach, however, is that it is concordant with social work values; it dramatically expands the scope and venues of helping; it gives the client a critical role in the process; it redresses some of the excesses of the expert role; it summons community resources; it fulfills the obligation of the person-in-environment perspective by drawing upon the energies of body, mind, spirit, and environment in helping; it has a vocabulary that is ordinary; it respects

the indigenous psychology of all peoples (their theories); and it can create positive atmospherics in agency and organization

Much work, however, needs to be done in terms of the theoretical and conceptual development of the perspective. And evaluation of this perspective must expand and become more rigorous. But

> at the very least, the strengths [perspective and the resilience literature] obligate us to understand that however downtrodden, beaten up, sick, or disheartened and demoralized, individuals [and families and communities] have survived and in come cases flourished. They have taken steps, summoned up resources, coped or maybe just raged at the darkness. We need to know what they have done, how they did it, and what resources provided ballast in their struggles. People are always engaged in their situations, working on them, even if they just decide to resign themselves to their fate. Circumstance can overwhelm and debilitate. We do know a lot about that. But dire circumstance can also bring a surge in resolve and resilience. We must know more about that. (Saleebey, 2001, p. 120)

REFERENCES

Addams, J. (1902). *Democracy and social ethics.* New York: Macmillan.

Benard, B. (1997). Fostering resiliency in children and youth: Promoting protective factors in the school. In D. Saleebey (Ed.), *The strengths perspective in social work practice* (2nd ed., pp. 167–182). New York: Longman.

Boller, P. F. (1974). *American transcendentalism, 1830–1860: An intellectual inquiry.* New York: Putnam.

Cowger, C. D. (1994). Assessing client strengths: Clinical assessment for client empowerment. *Social Work, 39,* 262–268.

DeJong, P., & Miller, S. D. (1995). How to interview for client strengths. *Social Work, 40,* 729–736.

Delgado, M. (2000). *Community social work practice in an urban context: The potential of a capacity-enhancement perspective.* New York: Oxford University Press.

Duncan, B. L., Hubble, M. A., & Miller, S. D. (1997). *Psychotherapy with "impossible" cases: The efficient treatment of therapy veterans.* New York: W. W. Norton.

Freire, P. (1996). *The pedagogy of hope: Reliving pedagogy of the oppressed.* New York: Continuum.

Gergen, K. J. (1994). *Realities and relationships: Soundings in social construction.* Cambridge, MA: Harvard University Press.

Gladden, W. (1918). *Social salvation.* Hicksville, NY: Regina Press.

Goldstein, H. (1997). Victors or victims. In D. Saleebey (Ed.), *The strengths perspective in social work practice* (2nd ed., pp. 21–36). New York: Longman.

Gutiérrez, L. M. (1990). Working with women of color: An empowerment perspective. *Social Work, 35,* 149–155.

Hoyt, M. F. (1996). Welcome to possibility-land: A conversation with Bill O'Hanlon. In M. F. Hoyt (Ed.), *Constructive therapies* (Vol. 2, pp. 87–123). New York: Guilford Press.

Jamison, K. R. (1995). *An unquiet mind: A memoir of moods and madness.* New York: Vintage Books.

Kaplan, L., & Girard, J. L. (1994). *Strengthening high-risk families: A handbook for practitioners.* New York: Lexington Books.

Katz, M. (1997). *On playing a poor hand well: Insights from those who have overcome childhood risks and adversities.* New York: W. W. Norton.

Kretzmann, J. P., & McKnight, J. (1993). *Building communities from the inside out: A path toward finding and mobilizing a community's resources.* Chicago: ACTA Publications.

Lambert, M. J. (1992). Implications of outcome research for psychotherapy integration. In J. C. Norcross & M. R. Goldfried (Eds.), *Handbook of psychotherapy integration* (pp. 94–129). New York: Basic Books.

Lee, J.A.B. (1994). *The empowerment approach to social work practice.* New York: Columbia University Press.

McKnight, J. (1995). *The careless society: Community and its counterfeits.* New York: Basic Books.

Mills, R. (1995*). Realizing mental health.* New York: Sulzberger & Graham.

Moore, T. J. (1989, September). The cholesterol myth. *The Atlantic, 264,* 37–70.

Ornstein, R., & Sobel, D. (1989). *Healthy pleasures.* Reading, MA: Addison-Wesley.

Pelletier, K. R. (2000). *The best alternative medicine: What works? What does not?* New York: Simon & Schuster.

Phillips, P. T. (1996). *A kingdom on earth: Anglo-American social Christianity, 1880–1940.* State College: Pennsylvania State University Press.

Rapp. C. A. (1998). *The strengths model: Case management with people suffering from severe and persistent mental illness.* New York: Oxford University Press.

Rauschenbusch, W. (1917). *A theology for the social gospel.* New York: Macmillan.

Reuben, P. P. (2000, January 24). Early 19th century American transcendentalism: A brief introduction [Online]. *Perspectives in American literature: A research and reference guide.* Available: http://www.csustan.edu/english/reuben/pal/chap4/4intro.html

Reynolds, B. C. (1951). *Social work and social living: Explorations in policy and practice.* New York: Citadel Press.

Rogers, C. (1951). *Client centered therapy: Its current practice, theory, and implications.* Boston: Houghton Mifflin.

Saleebey, D. (1996). The strengths perspective in social work practice: Extensions and cautions. *Social Work, 41,* 296–303.

Saleebey, D. (2001). *Human behavior and social environments: A biopsychosocial approach.* New York: Columbia University Press.

Saleebey, D. (Ed.). (2002). *The strengths perspective in social work practice* (3rd ed.). New York: Allyn& Bacon/Longman.

Shulman, L. (1992). *The skills of helping* (3rd ed.). Itasca, IL: F. E. Peacock.

Simon, B. L. (1994). *The empowerment tradition in American social work: A history.* New York: Columbia University Press.

Snyder, C. R. (1994). *The psychology of hope.* New York: Free Press.

Social Gospel. (2000). *Columbia encyclopedia* (6th ed.). New York: Columbia University Press.

Strupp, H. H. (1995). The psychotherapist's skills revisited. *Clinical Psychology, 2,* 70–74.

Sullivan, W. P. (1997). On strengths, niches, and recovery from serious mental illness. In D. Saleebey (Ed.), *The strengths perspective in social work practice* (2nd ed., pp. 183–198). New York: Longman.

Swadener, B. B., & Lubeck, S. (1995). *Children and families "at promise": Deconstructing the discourse of risk.* Albany: State University of New York Press.

Taylor, J. B. (1997). Niches and practice: Extending the ecological perspective. In D. Saleebey (Ed.), *The strengths perspective in social work practice* (2nd ed., pp. 217–228). New York: Longman.

Tooth, B. A., Kalyanansundaram, V., & Glover, H. (1997). *Recovery from schizophrenia: A consumer perspective.* Red Hill, Queensland, Australia: Centre for Mental Health Nursing Research.

Walsh, F. (1998). *Strengthening family resilience.* New York: Guilford Press.

Weick, A., Rapp, C. A., Sullivan, W. P., & Kisthardt, W. (1989). A strengths perspective for social work practice. *Social Work, 89,* 350–354.

Weil, A. (1995). *Spontaneous healing.* New York: Knopf.

Werner, E., & Smith, R. S. (1992). *Overcoming the odds.* Ithaca, NY: Cornell University Press.

Wolin, S., & Wolin, S. J. (1996). The challenge model: Working with strengths in children of substance-abusing parents. *Adolescent Substance Abuse & Dual Disorders, 5,* 243–256.

Wolin, S. J., & Wolin, S. (1993). *The resilient self: How survivors of troubled families rise above adversity.* New York: Villard.

Dennis Saleebey, DSW, is the 2002–2003 Lucy and Henry Moses Visiting Professor, Hunter College School of Social Work, 129 East 79th Street, New York, NY 10021 and professor of social welfare at the University of Kansas, Lawrence, KS 66045.

For further information see
Aging: Social Work Practice; Lesbians: Parenting

Key Words

empowerment	strengths-based
Social Gospel movement	practice

T

Temporary Assistance for Needy Families
Jan L. Hagen

Temporary Assistance for Needy Families (TANF), enacted as part of a major welfare "reform" package in 1996, represents a fundamental transformation in the nation's response to poor families and their children. As Title I of the Personal Responsibility and Work Opportunity Reconciliation Act of 1996 (commonly referred to as the welfare reform law), TANF did "end welfare as we know it" (President Bill Clinton, 1996, p. 2891) by terminating the federal entitlement to cash assistance previously authorized under Aid to Families with Dependent Children (AFDC). The welfare reform law abolishes AFDC and associated programs for emergency assistance and welfare employment programs. In their place, states have been authorized to receive two block grants, one for TANF and the other for child care services under Title VI of the Child Care and Development Block Grant. This block grant funding mechanism is the primary vehicle for achieving the overriding objective of TANF: to increase state flexibility in operating welfare programs for poor families and their children (42 U.S.C. § 601[a]). With the passage of TANF, states now have a level of autonomy and discretion in serving women and children who are poor that has not existed in the United States since states enacted mothers' aid or widows' pension laws during the early years of the 20th century. Following a brief review of efforts to reform welfare with work, this entry reviews the major provisions of TANF, state responses, initial effects, and emerging implementation issues.

Reforming Welfare with Work

During the 1960s, welfare caseloads and expenditures grew dramatically. Additionally, the demographic characteristics of the AFDC population changed. Increasingly, the AFDC population included mothers who had been deserted, divorced, or separated or who had never married, and included women of color and their children. Concurrent with these changes was the broader societal change of mothers with children entering the workforce, a trend that continued to escalate for two decades. These factors, as well as others, contributed to a public outcry against employable women receiving public assistance and for reform of the welfare system.

Strategies to reform AFDC focused on replacing welfare with work. Work requirements for AFDC mothers were imposed for the first time in 1967 under the Work Incentive Program (WIN). Initially, WIN provided employment services, job training, remedial education, and such supportive services as child care and transportation. By 1971, however, program priorities shifted to emphasize direct job placement. In general, WIN was regarded as a failure. Relatively few recipients participated in WIN, primarily because insufficient funds were authorized for meaningful implementation (Rein, 1982).

Enacted early in the Reagan administration, the Omnibus Budget Reconciliation Act (OBRA) of 1981 introduced significant changes in work requirements for AFDC recipients and, in keeping with the "New Federalism," gave states new options for operating welfare employment programs. With the latitude given them under OBRA and related legislation, states began to experiment with employment and training programs for AFDC recipients. Evaluations of the states' welfare-to-work programs (for example, Gueron, 1987; U.S. General Accounting Office [GAO], 1987, 1988) showed neither dramatic employment gains nor welfare savings, but the general conclusion was that welfare employment programs produced positive gains for adult AFDC recipients and led to welfare savings (Gueron, 1987). Against this backdrop of research on welfare employment programs as well as research identifying various patterns of welfare use (Bane & Ellwood, 1983), Congress moved to enact the next generation of welfare employment programs under the Family Support Act of 1988.

The Family Support Act was viewed as introducing a new social contract based on mutual obligation between welfare agencies and welfare recipients (Lurie & Sanger, 1991; Moynihan, 1990). Recipients were obligated to make an effort to achieve economic self-sufficiency. In return, the government was obligated to provide income support to eligible families; provide a range of education, training, and employment services through a new welfare employment program called Job Opportunity and Basic Skills Training (JOBS); and provide needed child care and other supportive services to foster work preparation or work itself. In a significant departure from previous legislation, all AFDC mothers, including those with preschool children (three years of age and older), were expected to work or prepare for work if child care was available. States were required to guarantee child care if it was necessary for participation in the JOBS program. Additionally, Congress required states to meet specific rates of participation in their JOBS programs and to target services on those at high risk for long-term welfare dependency. To help states finance their JOBS programs, federal funding was increased significantly over previous levels, with generous federal matching rates. The legislation also authorized the provision of transitional health and child care benefits for up to 12 months to serve as a bridge between receiving financial assistance and becoming economically self-sufficient (Hagen, 1995).

Evaluation studies of the JOBS program found that labor force attachment strategies increased employment rates and earnings, and decreased the number of participants remaining on AFDC. These impacts, however, were modest, with significant numbers of participants remaining on welfare. Human capital investment strategies—those involving education and training—produced modest savings for AFDC but did not demonstrate gains in earnings or employment at two-year follow-up studies (Freedman & Friedlander, 1995). The major impediment to implementation was inadequate funding for JOBS services as well as for child care and other supportive services to serve all eligible JOBS participants (Hagen & Lurie, 1994).

INCREASING MOMENTUM TO REFORM WELFARE

Almost concurrent with implementation of the JOBS program in October 1990, Bill Clinton began his first presidential campaign in which he promised, as president, he would "end welfare as we know it." He also promoted "two years and you're off," a proposal sounding like a time limit on benefits (Edelman, 1997). After becoming president, Clinton's major efforts were directed toward health care policy, and there was a two-

year delay before his administration presented its own welfare reform proposal.

During this period, at least two events unfolded that contributed further to reconceptualizing welfare. First, President Clinton was committed to allowing state experimentation in welfare and to supporting governors' welfare initiatives. Through the federal waiver process, the Clinton administration dramatically increased the number and types of state experiments with welfare, including limiting benefits even if family size increased (family cap) or reducing benefits if children failed to meet school attendance requirements (Learnfare). Second, in 1994 the Republican leadership of the 104th Congress put forward its Contract with America, an agenda that included welfare reform as a major feature and a commitment to end the federal guarantee of income support to poor mothers and their children. The Republican Congress, with strong support from several prominent Republican governors, seized the legislative initiative in welfare reform, and after two vetoed bills Congress and the President compromised on the welfare reform law in August 1996, just several months prior to the presidential election.

TEMPORARY ASSISTANCE FOR NEEDY FAMILIES

The primary purpose of TANF is to increase state flexibility in operating welfare programs (42 U.S.C. § 601[a]). The legislation continues the traditional focus of AFDC with a goal of assisting "needy families so that children may be cared for in their own homes or in the homes of relatives" (42 U.S.C. § 601[a][1]). Additional goals are to reduce welfare dependence through job preparation, work, and marriage; prevent and reduce the incidence of nonmarital pregnancies; and encourage the formation of two-parent families. To accomplish these purposes, the federal government altered the structural arrangement for providing funds to state welfare programs. AFDC was a categorical, grant-in-aid program that guaranteed cash assistance to all needy families and children meeting the eligibility requirements. Although states were required to invest their own funds, the federal government obligated itself to match those funds at a rate based on each state's per capita income. Under TANF, a block grant provides a fixed amount of funding to each state based on the state's prior spending levels under AFDC. To receive full block grant funding, states must meet several requirements including placing time limits on federal benefits for families, meeting federal participation rates in work programs, and spending their own funds to support poor and low-income families. Although this structural shift suggests a straightforward alteration in financing, TANF has fundamentally changed the nation's welfare programs.

Ending the Guarantee

For recipients. The most significant and far-reaching provision of TANF is the explicit ending of the federal entitlement to cash assistance for needy families and their children (42 U.S.C. § 601 [b]). Under AFDC, if mothers and their children met the income requirements set by the states and the eligibility requirements set by the federal government, they were guaranteed cash assistance. Under TANF, states have the authority to establish all eligibility requirements, and they are under no obligation to serve any particular type of family or any particular family. States have always had the authority to set income requirements and benefit levels for welfare; TANF expands this authority to cover all aspects of program eligibility, including the imposition of behavioral conditions on the receipt of welfare. For most purposes, the federal government now serves as a funding source for state programs—but a funding source with limited obligations (Hagen, 1998).

For states. Under TANF, there is no longer the guarantee that federal funding will automatically expand to help states meet the needs of poor families. Under AFDC, the federal government obligated itself to match state spending for all families meeting the eligibility requirements, and this funding was open-ended—if states were willing to invest their dollars to support poor families, the federal government guaranteed an investment of federal funding based on a matching rate, ranging from 50 percent to 79 percent. Under the block grant, the amount of federal money each state receives is a fixed amount based on prior federal expenditures to that state for AFDC. Federal funding for TANF is $16.4 billion annually through 2002. Over the short term, nearly all states have received more under TANF than they would have under AFDC because welfare caseloads have declined dramatically since TANF allocations were calculated. For fiscal years (FYs) 1997 through 1999, states spent or obligated 95 percent of the TANF block grant (U.S. Department of Health and Human Services [HHS], 2000).

Back-up funding for block grant. The welfare reform law recognized that states may need additional assistance in special circumstances, and several additional funds were established. A contingency fund of $2 billion over five years was established to assist states during economic downturns. An additional backup for states if they lacked sufficient resources for welfare programs is a revolving federal loan fund of $1.7 billion. Both of these funds are modest, potentially difficult for states to access, and generally regarded as insufficient for addressing an economic downturn. Finally, for FYs 1998 through 2001, $800 million was available to selected states that experienced high levels of population growth or had historic low levels of federal spending.

Maintenance of effort. Although there are no matching funds requirements under the block grant funding, TANF prevents states from withdrawing their funds completely from welfare programs through a "maintenance of effort" (MOE) provision that requires states to maintain spending for "eligible families" at 80 percent of their FY 1994 spending for AFDC. Failure to meet this provision carries a penalty of a reduced block grant the following year. State spending under the MOE provision is reduced to 75 percent if federally mandated work participation requirements are met. In FY 1999, all states met MOE spending requirements, and some states exceeded those requirements. Overall, $11.3 billion in state funds were spent in FY 1999 (HHS, 2000).

Time Limits: Creating a Welfare Cliff

TANF has three separate time triggers. The first, which requires adult recipients to participate in community service after two months, is a state option. The second occurs after adult recipients have received benefits for two years; at that point, they must meet specific work requirements, which are discussed below. The third time trigger creates, in effect, a welfare cliff: a five-year, lifetime limit for receiving assistance from federal TANF funds (Hagen, 1999). States are free to use their own funds to support families after five years—and they are free to establish shorter time limits.

State time limits for assisting families vary, and some are complex. A majority (37) of states use the five-year federal time limit as the lifetime limit, but in four of these states, the lifetime limit applies only to adults. Eight states have established lifetime limits that are shorter than the federal limit. These shorter limits range from 21 to 48 months. Thirteen states also have established "intermittent" time limits, which limit the number of consecutive months that assistance may be received, for example, 24 out of 60 months. Still other states have no time limits on welfare benefits, either because they have a preexisting waiver or have chosen to use state funds if the 60-month limit for federal benefits is exceeded (HHS, 2000).

Part of the intent of the five-year time limit for benefits is to give a different message to welfare recipients—that welfare is not a way of life. This message stems from the stereotype that those receiving welfare do so for extended periods of time. In fact, most recipients use welfare only temporarily for relatively short periods of time. In considering lifetime use of welfare for women beginning their first spell period on AFDC, Bane and Ellwood (1994) reported that 46.5 percent may be expected to rely on welfare for two years or less and that 71.4 percent will rely on welfare for five years or less. Pavetti (1995) reported similar findings. Although these estimates are based on patterns of use under AFDC and data limitations suggest caution in generalizing from these findings to TANF, these analyses suggest that a significant proportion of mothers who receive welfare at some point will reach the time limits—more than half will meet the two-year limit and about 30 percent will confront the five-year time limit. At this point, however, the actual percentage and characteristics of families who will reach the time limits are unknown because most families have not encountered the "welfare cliff" (GAO, 2002). Additionally, in states with shorter time limits such as Connecticut, extensions to the time limits as well as exclusions from the time limits have been granted for those who comply with program requirements but do not secure employment.

Although TANF sends a clear message that mothers, regardless of their children's ages, are expected to work and become economically self-sufficient, Congress recognized that for some adult welfare recipients, achieving economic self-sufficiency within five years might not be a realistic expectation. To accommodate this possibility, states are allowed to exempt up to 20 percent of their welfare caseloads from the five-year time limit for TANF because "of hardship or if the family includes an individual who has been battered or subjected to extreme cruelty" (42 U.S.C. § 608[a][7][C][I]).

The GAO (2002) reported that in the fall of 2001, 11 percent of the families with adults receiving cash assistance were excluded from

state or federal time limits. For 11 percent of those excluded from time limits, states have used the federal hardship exemption. A number of states continue to operate under preexisting waivers, making them exempt from the federal time limits. Waivers accounted for 43 percent of the exclusions. An additional 45 percent of the adults were excluded from the time limits by "stopping the clock"—that is, states used state-only funds to provide cash assistance to these families. Maryland and Illinois used this strategy to provide support for working families who did not earn enough to leave TANF (GAO, 2002). Some might view this stopping the clock as a strategy for welfare recipients as well, that is, the time limits might encourage welfare recipients to "bank" their months of TANF eligibility or to avoid "starting the clock" in the first place by avoiding welfare. The evidence to date suggests that

> the anticipatory impacts of time limits are modest [for recipients], and if impacts are modest for those most directly affected, it seems likely that impacts on welfare applications would be even smaller. (Pavetti & Bloom, 2001, p. 257)

In addition to excluding those who are working but still eligible for TANF, states are excluding families who are cooperating with program requirements or making an effort to find employment. Additionally, families regarded as "hard to employ" are excluded from the time limits. For example, most states exclude those with a disability, those caring for a disabled family member, and those experiencing domestic violence (GAO, 2002).

Although the percentage excluded from the time limits is currently relatively low, it is anticipated that it will increase as more families reach the time limits on cash assistance. What are the characteristics of those who are likely to reach the time limits? Research findings suggest that they will be mothers with preschool children who had less than a high school education, little or no recent work experience, and were relatively young (under age 25) when they began receiving welfare (Pavetti, 1995; Petersen, 1995). In addition to low educational levels and limited mastery of basic skills such as reading, barriers to employment include learning disabilities, physical disabilities (either the mother's own or her child's), substance abuse, depression, post-traumatic stress disorder, and domestic violence (Danziger et al., 1999a, 1999b; Grant &

Dawson, 1996; Olson & Pavetti, 1996; Raphael, 1996; Salomon, Bassuk, & Brooks, 1996; Sweeney, 2000).

Work Requirements

TANF continues the tradition begun under WIN to replace welfare with work, and a work-based welfare program is the major feature of the welfare reform law. Adult recipients are required to engage in work or work-related activities when the state indicates they are ready or after two years on assistance, whichever comes first. If a recipient fails to comply with the work requirements, states may sanction the recipient by reducing or terminating benefits to the family. Unlike prior programs, the law allows few exceptions to the work requirements. For all families, the average minimum number of hours of required work activity is 30 hours a week. For two-parent families, 35 hours of work are required each week. For single mothers with children under six years of age, 20 hours of work activity are expected each week.

In order to receive full block grant funding, states must meet two major work participation requirements. First, the state must meet overall participation rates, which are 50 percent of the entire caseload and 90 percent for two-parent families. These percentages are reduced, however, if the state's caseload declines in comparison to the FY 1995 caseload. Second, the state is required to have all adult recipients who have received assistance for two years participate in work or work-related activities. The work activities that may be counted toward the participation rate reflect a clear congressional preference for using a labor force attachment strategy rather than a human capital investment one under TANF. Acceptable activities include unsubsidized employment, subsidized private or public employment, work experience, community service, on-the-job training, job search, and job readiness. Vocational educational training is also allowed but restricted to no more than 12 months. Job skills training and education (for those without a high school education) must be directly related to work and is restricted to a limited percentage of the caseload. The reduction in educational services, particularly at the postsecondary level, is troubling given the reduction in low-skill jobs and research findings that suggest completion of high school and any postsecondary education reduce return to welfare, facilitate exit from welfare, and significantly reduce poverty (Gittell & Covington, 1993; Harris, 1996).

State Responses to Work Requirements

Although states have not modified benefit levels, which averaged $357 in 1999, or altered the categories of those eligible for benefits (HHS, 2000), they have made a significant shift by moving from a welfare system focused on the accurate provision of financial assistance to one emphasizing "finding employment as quickly as possible and becoming more self-sufficient" (GAO, 1998b, p. 3). As part of this "work first" strategy, 34 states have developed programs to divert applicants from ongoing welfare benefits by providing a one-time, lump-sum payment to assist with a temporary financial crisis; supportive services such as child care, food stamps, and Medicaid; and referrals to job search or placement services and to alternative programs for services or assistance (HHS, 2000). Whereas the use of "work first" strategies has been facilitated by a strong economy, "it is not yet known . . . how states' welfare reform programs will perform under weaker economic conditions" (GAO, 1998b, p. 7). Additionally, a recent review of experimental evaluations of welfare employment programs since 1985 suggests that the most effective programs are those "that used a mix of initial activities, where some people started with job search and others with short-term, work-focused education or training" (Gueron & Hamilton, 2002, pp. 3–4). This "work first" strategy also has been accompanied by an increased use of sanctions for noncompliance with work participation requirements. In applying these sanctions, 37 states have opted to terminate the benefit to the entire family rather than to reduce the amount of the benefit.

Additionally, an adult's Medicaid is terminated in one-fourth of the states, and food stamp benefits are terminated for the entire household in one-third of the states when an adult fails to comply with work requirements (GAO, 2000). The actual implementation of these policies varies across the states, particularly in terms of steps taken to address the reasons for noncompliance, but all states provide an appeals mechanism for sanctioning decisions (GAO, 2000). The GAO (2000) reported that in 1998 about 5 percent of the TANF caseload was under sanctions in an average month; the vast majority of these were partial rather than full family sanctions. Relatively little is known about families who are sanctioned, but studies suggest that those who are sanctioned tend to have lower educational levels and to face barriers to compliance such as transportation, child care, and physical and mental health problems (Bloom & Winstead, 2002; GAO, 2000). The effectiveness of a sanctioning strategy in fostering work activities, as well as accuracy in applying sanctions, has not been demonstrated and merits monitoring and evaluation, especially in light of previous research suggesting high rates of errors by welfare agencies in imposing sanctions (GAO, 1997b).

In operating their "work first" programs, 28 states require adult recipients to engage in work or work-related activities immediately upon receiving benefits. Thirteen states require work within 24 months, and eight states require work within six months or less of receiving benefits. Most states give exemptions from the work participation requirements based on the age of the youngest child. In 24 states, single mothers are exempt until the child is one year of age, and in 18 states until the child is six months old (HHS, 2000).

In FY 2000, the national average work participation rate for all families was 34 percent and for two-parent families, 49 percent. Because of the declines in caseloads compared to FY 1995, all states received reductions in their minimum participation rates for FY 2000, and no state was required to meet the minimum work participation rate of 40 percent for all families and 90 percent for two-parent families. Under the adjusted rates based on declines in caseloads in FY 2000, all states met or exceeded the work participation rate for all families. Of the 34 states with TANF for two-parent families, 27 states met or exceeded the work participation rate. About 631,000 adults participated in work activities in FY 2000, and the vast majority (61 percent) were engaged in unsubsidized employment. An additional 16 percent participated in work experience and community service, 12 percent in job search, and 14 percent in vocational education, employment-related education, and job skills training. (Percentages exceed 100 percent because people were involved in multiple activities.)

Other Federal Provisions for TANF Programs

Family Violence Option. Congress responded specifically to the potential vulnerability and needs of battered women by including the Family Violence Option (42 U.S.C. § 602[a][7]) as part of the TANF legislation, a step that for the first time recognized in federal policy the link between domestic violence and welfare for some welfare recipients (Brandwein, 1999). The link between welfare and domestic violence and

the extent to which domestic violence interferes with participation in welfare-to-work programs, as well as employment, have been investigated only recently, emerging in the mid-1990s concurrently with the political initiatives to reform welfare (for example, Browne, Salomon, & Bassuk, 1999; Danziger et al., 1999a, 1999b; Lloyd & Taluc, 1999; Raphael, 1996; Raphael & Tolman, 1997; Salomon et al., 1996).

If selected by the states, the Family Violence Option provides flexibility in applying TANF rules to victims of domestic violence. States may waive time limits, family caps, work requirements, and child support enforcement requirements for domestic violence victims if complying with them places clients at risk or unfairly penalizes them. Additionally, the Family Violence Option allows states to offer confidential screening and identification of battered women and to provide referrals for supportive and counseling services.

The Family Violence Option has been adopted by 37 states and the District of Columbia. States not adopting the Family Violence Option have developed state policies for serving victims of domestic violence (HHS, 2000). Early findings on the implementation of the Family Violence Option suggest that procedures for notifying clients of the option and screening for domestic violence vary widely across the states, with notification and screening classified as inadequate in 20 states (Raphael & Haennicke, 1999). If a waiver is granted, most states require the woman to cooperate with domestic violence services and to work toward eliminating domestic violence as a barrier to work (Raphael & Haennicke, 1999).

Immigrants. With the passage of Title IV of the Personal Responsibility and Work Opportunity Reconciliation Act of 1996 and subsequent legislation (for example, Illegal Immigration Reform and Immigrant Responsibility Act of 1996; Balanced Budget Act of 1997), provisions regarding the eligibility of legal immigrants for a range of public assistance programs, including TANF, have become increasingly complex, but in general states are prohibited from using TANF funds to assist new legal immigrants during their first five years in the United States. Additionally, states may elect whether to provide benefits to prewelfare reform immigrants and to new immigrants after five years of U.S. residency. At present, almost all states have opted to continue benefits to prewelfare reform immigrants and to new immigrants after five years of U.S. residency. Further, about one-third of the states provided benefits to immigrants during their first five years of residency using state funds (GAO, 1998a). Overall, however, participation in TANF has declined by 60 percent for families of noncitizens (Fix & Haskins, 2002).

Teen parents and nonmarital births. The legislation gives considerable attention to teenage parents and "out-of-wedlock" births. States are given explicit permission to end cash payments to unwed teenage parents and to deny payment increases for parents who have additional children while on welfare, referred to as a family cap. Family caps have been imposed by 16 states, two states provide a partial increase in benefits, two states have flat grants for all families, and three states provide payments to a third party or use vouchers (HHS, 2000). In an analysis of 20 of these 23 states with family cap provisions, the GAO (2001b) found that about 9 percent of TANF families were affected by family caps in an average month during 2000. The effectiveness of family caps in reducing out-of-wedlock births cannot be determined, however, given the limited research in this area, the lack of a national database, and the inability to separate the effects of family caps from other welfare changes and the overall societal change of declining birth rates among teens (GAO, 2001b). A provision affecting teens is the prohibition against using TANF funds to assist teen parents who are not in school and not living in an adult-supervised setting. Other provisions of the legislation that foster program development include funding for abstinence education programs and "bonus grants" to states that are most successful in reducing the number of out-of-wedlock births while decreasing abortion rates.

Child support enforcement. State leverage for child support enforcement has been enhanced by requiring families to assign support rights to the states as a condition of eligibility and imposing at least a 25 percent reduction in benefits for refusal to cooperate in paternity establishment and securing child support. Additionally, the legislation provided for a new hire reporting system, streamlined paternity establishment, created uniform interstate child support forms, and computerized statewide collections (HHS, 2000). In 1999 the child support enforcement program collected $16 billion, twice the amount collected in 1992, and paternity establishment rose to 1.5 million men acknowledging paternity in 1998, a three-fold increase since 1992 (HHS, 2000).

RELATED CHILD CARE PROVISIONS

Child Care and Development Fund

It is widely recognized that for any program requiring mothers to work or participate in work-related activities, access to child care services is essential. In conjunction with TANF, Congress enacted the Child Care and Development Block Grant in 1996, referred to as the Child Care and Development Fund (CCDF). The CCDF consolidated several previous funding streams and uses a block grant structure that limits federal obligations for child care funding to a total of $20 billion over six years. To receive full block grant funding, states must meet a "maintenance of effort" provision by using at least 70 percent of the funds on families who are at risk for needing welfare assistance, are receiving TANF, or are making the transition from welfare to work. At least 4 percent of state spending must be directed toward consumer education and improving the quality and availability of child care. States have the option of transferring up to 30 percent of their TANF allocation to the CCDF or to use it directly to support child care programs.

As with TANF, states have wide-ranging authority and flexibility in the use of these child care funds. Unlike prior legislation, child care is not guaranteed under TANF for the children of mothers who are required to work or participate in work-related activities. Additionally, transitional child care services are no longer guaranteed for those leaving welfare because of increased earnings but who continue to need child care subsidies to accept or maintain jobs. However, the consolidation of funding streams accompanied by a single set of eligibility criteria provides the opportunity for states to simplify the eligibility and administrative procedures and to create "seamless" child care services that avoid disruptions or gaps in services for children as their mothers move from one type of classification to another, for example, from recipient to low-income earner.

Child Care Issues

State spending for child care has been high, with states drawing on the CCDF, spending TANF funds, and accessing their own state funds. In FY 1999, total child care spending reached almost $7 billion (GAO, 2001a). This level of spending reflects the high demand for child care services needed by TANF families as well as for those transitioning to work. HHS (2000) estimated that about 1.5 million children were served under CCDF in 1998; however, an estimated 15 million children were potentially eligible for service. States currently are meeting the child care needs of TANF families and those families transitioning off welfare. All states provide transitional child care for 12 months, and 23 states offer these benefits for longer periods (HHS, 1999).

However, states are unable to meet the child care needs of other low-income families who meet the federal eligibility guidelines (GAO, 1998c, 2001a). Various mechanisms are being used to restrict access to state programs, including setting income limits and requiring copayments (GAO, 1998c, 2001a). The demand for child care subsidies can be expected to increase further as work participation rates increase and time limits take effect. Additionally, there is a shortage of child care for infants, sick children, and children with special needs as well as for care during nonstandard work hours and in rural areas (GAO, 1997a, 1998c). Finally, relatively little is known about the quality of child care services received by children covered under these programs. Adams and Rohacek (2002) identified several barriers to accessing quality care by low-income families, including limited supply of regulated providers in low-income communities, low reimbursement rates restricting access to lower cost providers, and problems in receiving reimbursements that may limit the number of providers willing to accept subsidies.

Monitoring TANF

Welfare Rolls

In recent years, welfare rolls have declined dramatically. The AFDC caseload peaked in March 1994 with 14.4 million recipients. By September 2001, there were 5.3 million recipients. Between January 1993 and June 2000, the number of families receiving welfare declined by 56 percent and the number of recipients by 59 percent. As these figures reflect, the welfare caseload began to decline prior to the enactment of TANF, but the trend increased with the law's passage. Explaining these caseload changes is complex because the implementation of TANF coincided with an extended period of economic expansion and a significant expansion of the earned income tax credit (EITC; Ziliak, 2002). Analyses by the U.S. Council of Economic Advisors (1997, 1999) suggested that for 1993 through 1996, less than one-third of the decline was due to state welfare waivers and more than 40 percent was due to declining unemployment. For the 1996 through 1998

period, however, changes stemming from welfare reform were the most important factors contributing to caseload declines, accounting for slightly more than one-third of the caseload decline. This suggests that a downturn in the economy will probably result in increasing welfare caseloads (Ziliak, 2002). How well TANF will function in a recessionary climate is unknown. The current legislative provisions aimed at assisting states during an economic downturn are generally regarded as inadequate (see, for example, Blank, 2001).

Poverty Rates

Like welfare caseloads, poverty rates have declined since 1993, from 15 percent in that year to 12 percent in 1999. Child poverty has declined significantly as well—reaching its lowest level since 1979—but child poverty still remains high, particularly for children 5 years of age and under. In 1999 the poverty rate for young children was 18 percent. Additionally, the percentages of single-mother working families living in poverty have changed only marginally, from 31 percent in 1993 to 30 percent in 1999 (Porter & Dupree, 2001). The percentage of the population in extreme poverty (those with incomes below 50 percent of the federal poverty line) has declined. However, of those who are poor, the proportion of those in extreme poverty has increased over the past two decades. Those people with incomes below 50 percent of the poverty level comprised 39 percent of the poverty population in 1999 (HHS, 2001). As with the declines in welfare caseloads, multiple factors contributed to declining poverty rates and, certainly, the strong economy contributed significantly.

Welfare Leavers

Despite the numerous tracking studies being conducted by states, quality information on those who have left welfare is limited because many state studies have serious limitations, including lack of representative samples, high nonresponse rates, lack of comprehensive data, and inability to compare data across states (GAO, 1999). Within these limitations, the findings from state "welfare leavers" studies indicate that between one-half and three-fourths of former welfare recipients are employed shortly after leaving welfare. Although they work a significant number of hours, former recipients tend to earn low wages from jobs in sales, clerical support, or other services jobs that do not provide employer-sponsored benefits, including health insurance (Brauner & Loprest, 1999;

Loprest, 2001; Parrott, 1998). A longitudinal study (Cancian & Meyer, 2000) of former AFDC recipients suggested that employment alone would not be a route to economic self-sufficiency for many women leaving welfare because wages tend to remain low and employment histories are characterized by part-time work, intermittent work, and unemployment.

Loprest's (1999) study, based on a nationally representative sample, suggested that about 30 percent of those who leave welfare for at least a month return to the welfare rolls and that 25 percent of welfare leavers are not working and have either no partner or a partner who is unemployed. Some studies suggest that one-third or more of former welfare recipients are experiencing economic hardships, including problems paying the rent or utilities and providing enough food for their families (Brauner & Loprest, 1999; Loprest, 2001). These families may be turning to local charities as well as to families and friends for assistance, but the extent of this trend is not documented. The demands placed on local not-for-profit agencies by some current and former welfare recipients who are encountering hardships may also have an effect on the capacity of these agencies to respond to their clients (Abramovitz, 2002).

Participation in Food Stamps and Medicaid
Research suggests that declines in TANF caseloads may be contributing to declines in food stamp participation, as well as to stable Medicaid enrollments despite eligibility expansions for this program (Families USA Foundation, 1999; Primus, Rawlings, Larin, & Porter, 1999; Zedlewski & Brauner, 1999). As people left welfare for employment or because of sanctions, some were losing their food stamps and Medicaid as well, even though they continued to be eligible. Administrative barriers, including not informing recipients of their continuing eligibility and complicated reporting requirements, appear to have contributed to these declines. Additionally, some people were diverted from applying for TANF and may not have learned of their eligibility for the other two programs. Legislative changes in October 2000 for the food stamp program may reduce some of these barriers (Zedlewski, 2001).

Work Pays
Although most of those leaving welfare are not earning enough to reach or exceed the poverty level (Brauner & Loprest, 1999), going to work "pays" for welfare recipients in most

states, even if they are working in low-wage part-time jobs. Work pays because some states set very low benefit levels whereas others allow employed recipients to keep more of their TANF benefits as they begin working. With few exceptions, states have liberalized policies regarding earned income, allowing recipients to retain a higher percentage of their earnings. Additionally, and perhaps most important, work pays when combined with two other programs—food stamps and the EITC. Full-time work at minimum wage along with these supplements will bring a family of three to an income level that is 20 percent above the poverty line. If a family relied solely on government benefits, the income level would be 32 percent below the poverty line (Coe, Acs, Lerman, & Watson, 1998).

Current TANF Recipients
In light of the dramatic declines in caseloads, concerns have been raised about people who remain on welfare rolls. Research suggests current welfare recipients are more likely than former recipients to report at least two obstacles to work, including low educational attainment, limited or no work experience, and physical and mental health problems (Loprest & Zedlewski, 1999). Zedlewski (1999), using a nationally representative sample, found that more than four out of 10 current welfare recipients report at least two obstacles to work and that up to 38 percent of the current TANF recipients are at risk for remaining on welfare. Danziger and colleagues (1999a), in a study of women receiving welfare in Michigan, found that 37 percent had two or three barriers to work and 27 percent had four or more barriers. The more barriers a woman had, the less likely she was to be working. One of the most challenging issues now facing states is finding ways to involve recipients with multiple barriers in work activities (GAO, 1998b). For this group, "work first" strategies will have limited effectiveness and other, more comprehensive services will be required (Danziger et al., 1999b), including education, training, and an array of personal social services.

Program Innovations
The state flexibility allowed under TANF has given states increased opportunities to modify and create programs that are responsive to their needs. The array of programs and services being developed is extensive. These programs include expansion of transportation assistance through provision of bus passes,

reverse commuter programs, and support of car purchases; enhanced services to children and youth through such programs as home visiting to new and expectant parents, school dropout prevention, teen pregnancy prevention, after-school programs, and family support centers; postemployment services, including child care, transportation, health coverage, case management, and peer counseling; services to noncustodial parents whose children receive assistance, including job search, employment training, parental skills, and family mediation services; and services to promote job advancement, including education, training, and tuition grants (HHS, 2000).

Additionally, programs to serve special populations have been developed. For example, in New York, welfare employees working with welfare recipients who are victims of domestic violence are required to complete an intensive training program developed by the state's welfare agency in conjunction with the state's office on prevention of domestic violence and the advocacy community. In California, a program serving "hard-to-serve" Southeast Asian American welfare recipients was developed that combined outreach, day socialization and job readiness, and family support services. Known as AsianWORKS, this program is an innovative practice model designed to engage a vulnerable population by providing services that are culturally and linguistically appropriate (Chow, Bester, & Shinn, 2001). For the entrepreneurial, the First Step Fund of Kansas City offers a program for former and current TANF recipients to prepare them to operate micro businesses (Straatmann & Sherraden, 2001). These are but a few of the programs that states and localities have developed to respond to the needs of TANF recipients and other low-income families.

IMPLICATIONS FOR SOCIAL WORK: PRACTICE, POLICY, AND RESEARCH

In responding to challenges and opportunities under TANF, social workers have new obligations for practice, advocacy, and research. For social workers in direct practice, to provide access services to poor and low-income families is central. Included in these access services is the provision of accurate and timely information to ensure that clients understand the time-limited nature of welfare benefits and the services to which they are entitled under each state's welfare program. With the "delinking" of welfare benefits from Medicaid and food stamps, particular attention must be given to ensure clients obtain these benefits as well as

transitional child care, child care subsidies for low-income families, and EITC. Given the economic hardships experienced by some families who have left welfare, social workers will be called upon also to effectively broker services for their clients from community-based agencies. Case advocacy is important to ensure that the use of sanctions is accurate and to secure exceptions from work requirements and time limits for those experiencing "hardships" or domestic violence. Advocacy efforts may also be required to ensure clients are not subject to inappropriate administrative discretion, including discrimination. Finally, social workers in direct practice are called upon to develop and evaluate new services models to assist current recipients who experience multiple barriers to employment and who interface with multiple services systems.

With the "devolution" of welfare programs, ongoing policy analysis and advocacy must maintain a dual focus on national and state policies. At the federal level, policy analysis must consider not only the federal law and regulations, but also the interaction and interrelatedness of federal policies, including Medicaid, food stamps, child health insurance, EITC, child credit, and child care tax credit. Because the welfare reform law severely restricts federal oversight, ongoing monitoring and analysis of each state's program by policy analysts becomes mandatory. State policy analysis should focus on the adequacy of benefits, effectiveness of welfare employment programs for diverse groups of welfare recipients, use of sanctioning, and adequacy of supportive services and program exemptions. The emphasis given to economic self-sufficiency under TANF calls for continual attention to the structural and societal barriers restricting the ability of many women with children to become economically self-sufficient. These factors include geographic restrictions on job availability; pay inequities based on gender and ethnicity; inability of full-time, low-wage jobs to support families; and lack of societal supports for dependent care. Although welfare debates in the past several decades have been framed around welfare dependency, the broader issue is poverty, which must remain as the benchmark for policy analyses.

Based on comprehensive and thoughtful policy analyses and research, advocacy agendas can be developed for both federal and state levels. At the federal level, an obvious policy direction is to recast the goal of TANF from one that emphasizes the reduction of welfare dependency to one that focuses on reducing poverty. Additional policy directions include expanding and refunding the child and child care tax credits, developing paid family leave policies, guaranteeing access to health care, providing universal child care subsidies, developing a child support assurance program, and expanding funding for education and training for less skilled workers. At the state level, advocacy efforts might be effectively focused on increasing benefit levels, providing state-funded welfare benefits for those people no longer eligible for federal TANF benefits, building welfare employment programs and associated supports that are responsive to client needs, and developing refundable state EITCs.

Social work researchers have a critical role to play as well. Longitudinal studies are needed to evaluate the impact of each state's program on mothers and their children and to give "voice" to the realities of clients' experiences under TANF. Research is also needed on those whose benefits are terminated by sanctioning and those who are diverted from welfare. Given the number of those at risk for confronting the five-year time limit, research on innovative programs that are designed for those people with severe or multiple barriers to employment is urgently needed.

REFERENCES

Abramovitz, M. (2002, February). *In jeopardy: The impact of welfare reform on nonprofit human service agencies in New York City.* Research conducted for the Task Force on Welfare Reform, New York City NASW Chapter, funded by United Way of New York City.

Adams, G., & Rohacek, M. (2002). *Child care and welfare reform* (Welfare Reform & Beyond Policy Brief Series No. 14). Washington, DC: Brookings Institution.

Bane, M. J., & Ellwood, D. T. (1983). *The dynamics of dependence: The routes to self-sufficiency.* Cambridge, MA: Harvard University, John F. Kennedy School of Government.

Bane, M. J., & Ellwood, D. T. (1994). *Welfare realities: From rhetoric to reform.* Cambridge, MA: Harvard University Press.

Blank, R. M. (2001). *Welfare and the economy* (Welfare Reform & Beyond Policy Brief Series No. 7). Washington, DC: Brookings Institution.

Bloom, D., & Winstead, D. (2002). *Sanctions and welfare reform* (Welfare Reform & Beyond Policy Brief Series No. 12). Washington, DC: Brookings Institution.

Brandwein, R. A. (1999). Family violence and social policy: Welfare "reform" and beyond. In R. A. Brandwein (Ed.), *Battered women, children and welfare reform: The ties that bind* (pp. 142–172). Thousand Oaks, CA: Sage Publications.

Brauner, S., & Loprest, P. (1999). *Where are they now? What states' studies of people who left welfare tell us* (Assessing the New Federalism: Issues and Options for States, Policy Brief, Series A, No. A-32). Washington, DC: Urban Institute. Available: http://www.urban.org/UploadedPDF/anf32.pdf

Browne, A., Salomon, A., & Bassuk, S. S. (1999). The impact of recent partner violence on poor women's capacity to maintain work. *Violence Against Women, 5,* 393–426.

Cancian, M., & Meyer, D. R. (2000). Work after welfare: Women's work effort, occupation, and economic well-being. *Social Work Research, 24,* 69–86.

Child Care and Development Block Grant of 1996, P.L. 104-193, Title VI.

Chow, J., Bester, N., & Shinn, A. (2001). AsianWORKS: A TANF program for Southeast Asian Americans in Oakland, California. *Journal of Community Practice, 9,* 111–124.

Clinton, W. J. Address upon signing H.R. 3734. (1996, August 26). *The weekly compilation of presidential documents* (pp. 2891–2893). Washington, DC: U.S. Government Printing Office.

Coe, N. B., Acs, G., Lerman, R. I., & Watson, K. (1998). *Does work pay? A summary of the work incentives under TANF* (Assessing the New Federalism: Issues and Options for States, Policy Brief, Series A, No. A-28). Washington, DC: Urban Institute. Available: http://www.urban.org/UploadedPDF/anf28.pdf

Danziger, S., Corcoran, M., Danziger, S., Heflin, C., Kalil, A., Levine, J., et al. (1999a). *Barriers to the employment of welfare recipients.* Unpublished research report, University of Michigan, Poverty Research and Training Center, Ann Arbor.

Danziger, S., Corcoran, M., Danziger, S., Heflin, C., Kalil, A., Levine, J., et al. (1999b). Barriers to work among welfare recipients. *Focus, 20,* 31–35.

Edelman, P. (1997, March). The worst thing Bill Clinton has done. *Atlantic Monthly,* pp. 43–58.

Families USA Foundation. (1999, May). *Losing health insurance: The unintended consequences of welfare reform* (Report 99-103). Washington, DC: Families USA Foundation. Available: http://www.familiesusa.org/media/reports/uninten.htm

Family Support Act of 1988, P.L. 100-485, 102 Stat. 2343.

Fix, M., & Haskins, R. (2002). *Welfare benefits for non-citizens* (Welfare Reform & Beyond Policy Brief Series No. 15). Washington, DC: Brookings Institution.

Freedman, S., & Friedlander, D. (1995). *The JOBS evaluation: Early findings on program impacts in three sites: Executive summary.* New York: Manpower Development Research Corp.

Gittell, M., & Covington, S. (1993). *Higher education in JOBS: An option or an opportunity? A comparison of nine states.* New York: City University of New York, Howard Samuel State Management and Policy Center.

Grant, B. F., & Dawson, D. A. (1996). Alcohol and drug use, abuse, and dependence among welfare recipients. *American Journal of Public Health, 86,* 1450–1454.

Gueron, J. (1987). *Reforming welfare with work* (Ford Foundation Project in Social Welfare and the American Future Occasional Paper 2). New York: Ford Foundation.

Gueron, J., & Hamilton, G. (2002). *The role of education and training in welfare reform* (Welfare Reform & Beyond Policy Brief Series No. 20). Washington, DC: Brookings Institution.

Hagen, J. L. (1995). The JOBS program. In R. L. Edwards (Ed.-in-Chief), *Encyclopedia of social work* (19th ed., Vol. 2, pp. 1546–1552). Washington, DC: NASW Press.

Hagen, J. L. (1998). The new welfare law: "Tough on work." *Families in Society, 79,* 596–605.

Hagen, J. L. (1999). Time limits under TANF: A look at the welfare cliff. *Affilia, 14,* 294–314.

Hagen, J. L., & Lurie, I. (1994). *Implementing JOBS: Progress and promise.* Albany, NY: Rockefeller Institute of Government.

Harris, K. M. (1996). Life after welfare: Women, work, and repeat dependency. *American Sociological Review, 61,* 407–426.

Lloyd, S., & Taluc, N. (1999). The effects of male violence on female employment. *Violence Against Women, 5,* 370–392.

Loprest, P. (1999). *How families that left welfare are doing: A national picture* (Assessing the New Federalism: National Survey of America's Families, B-1). Washington, DC: Urban Institute. Available: http://www.urban.org/UploadedPDF/anf_b1.pdf

Loprest, P. (2001). *How are families that left welfare doing? A comparison of early and recent welfare leavers* (Assessing the New Federalism: National Survey of America's Families, B-36). Washington, DC: Urban Institute. Available: http://www.urban.org/UploadedPDF/anf_b36.pdf

Loprest, P., & Zedlewski, S. R. (1999). *Current and former welfare recipients: How do they differ?* (Assessing the New Federalism: Discussion Papers, 99-17). Washington, DC: Urban Institute. Available: http://www.urban.org/UploadedPDF/discussion99-17.pdf

Lurie, I., & Sanger, B. (1991). The Family Support Act: Defining the social contract in New York. *Social Service Review, 65,* 43–67.

Moynihan, D. P. (1990, November 25). The children of the state. *Washington Post,* p. C1.

Olson, K., & Pavetti, L. (1996). *Personal and family challenges to the successful transition from welfare to work.* Washington, DC: Urban Institute. Available: http://www.urban.org/welfare/report1.htm

Omnibus Budget Reconciliation Act of 1981, P.L. 97-35, 95 Stat. 357.

Parrott, S. (1998). *Welfare recipients who find jobs: What do we know about their employment and earnings?* Washington, DC: Center on Budget and Policy Priorities.

Pavetti, L. (1995). *Who is affected by time limits?* (Welfare Reform Briefs No. 7). Washington, DC: Urban Institute.

Pavetti, L., & Bloom, D. (2001). State sanctions and time limits. In R. M. Blank & R. Haskins (Eds.), *The new world of welfare* (pp. 245–269). Washington, DC: Brookings Institution.

Personal Responsibility and Work Opportunity Reconciliation Act of 1996, P.L. 104-193; 42 U.S.C. § 1305 note.

Petersen, C. D. (1995). Female-headed families on AFDC: Who leaves welfare quickly and who doesn't. *Journal of Economic Issues, 29,* 619–628.

Porter, K. H., & Dupree, A. (2001). *Poverty trends for families headed by working single mothers, 1993–1999.* Washington, DC: Center on Budget and Policy Priorities.

Primus, W., Rawlings, L., Larin, K., & Porter, K. (1999). The initial impacts of welfare reform on the incomes of single-mother families [Executive summary]. Washington, DC: Center on Budget and Policy Priorities.

Raphael, J. (1996). *Prisoners of abuse: Domestic violence and welfare receipt.* Chicago: Taylor Institute.

Raphael, J., & Haennicke, S. (1999). *Keeping battered women safe through the welfare-to-work journey: How are we doing?* Chicago: Taylor Institute.

Raphael, J., & Tolman, R. M. (1997). *Trapped by poverty/trapped by abuse: New evidence documenting the relationship between domestic violence and welfare.* Chicago: Taylor Institute and University of Michigan Research Development Center on Poverty, Risk, and Mental Health.

Rein, M. (1982). Work in welfare: Past failures and future strategies. *Social Service Review, 56,* 211–229.

Salomon, A., Bassuk, S. S., & Brooks, M. G. (1996). Patterns of welfare use among poor and homeless women. *American Journal of Orthopsychiatry, 66,* 510–525.

Straatmann, S., & Sherraden, M. (2001). Welfare to self-employment: A case study of the First Step Fund. *Journal of Community Practice, 9,* 73–94.

Sweeney, E. P. (2000). *Recent studies indicate that many parents who are current or former welfare recipients have disabilities or other medical* conditions. Washington, DC: Center on Budget and Policy Priorities.

U.S. Council of Economic Advisors. (1997). *Explaining the decline in welfare receipt, 1993–1996* [Online]. Available: http://www.whitehouse.gov/WH/EOP/CEA/Welfare/Welfare/Report.html

U.S. Council of Economic Advisors. (1999). *The effects of welfare policy and the economic expansion on welfare caseloads: An update* [Online]. Available: http://www.whitehouse.gov/WH/EOP/CEA/html/welfare/nontech.pdf

U.S. Department of Health and Human Services. (1999). *Temporary Assistance to Needy Families (TANF) program: Second annual report to Congress* [Online]. Available: http://www.acf.dhhs.gov/programs/opre/tanifreports/tan19995.pdf

U.S. Department of Health and Human Services. (2000). *Temporary Assistance to Needy Families (TANF) program: Third annual report to Congress* [Online]. Available: http://www.acf.dhhs.gov/programs/opre/annual3.pdf

U.S. Department of Health and Human Services. (2001). *Indicators of welfare dependence: Annual report to Congress 2001.* Washington, DC: Author.

U.S. General Accounting Office. (1987). *Work and welfare: Current AFDC work programs and implications for federal policy* (GAO/HRD-87-34). Washington, DC: Author.

U.S. General Accounting Office. (1988). *Work and welfare: Analysis of AFDC employment programs in four states* (GAO/HRD-88-33). Washington, DC: Author.

U.S. General Accounting Office. (1997a). *Welfare reform: Implications of increased work participation for child care* (GAO/HEHS-97-95). Washington, DC: Author.

U.S. General Accounting Office. (1997b). *Welfare reform: States' early experiences with benefit termination* (GAO/HEHS-97-94). Washington, DC: Author.

U.S. General Accounting Office. (1998a). *Welfare reform: Many states continue some federal or state benefits for immigrants* (GAO/HEHS-98-132). Washington, DC: Author.

U.S. General Accounting Office. (1998b). *Welfare reform: States are restructuring programs to reduce welfare dependence* (GAO/HEHS-98-109). Washington, DC: Author.

U.S. General Accounting Office. (1998c). *Welfare reform: States' efforts to expand child care programs* (GAO/HEHS-98-27). Washington, DC: Author.

U.S. General Accounting Office. (1999). *Welfare reform: Information on former recipients' status* (GAO/HEHS-99-48). Washington, DC: Author.

U.S. General Accounting Office. (2000). *Welfare reform: State sanction policies and numbers of families affected* (GAO/HEHS-00-44). Washington, DC: Author.

U.S. General Accounting Office. (2001a). *Child care: States increased spending on low-income families* (GAO-01-293). Washington, DC: Author.

U.S. General Accounting Office. (2001b). *Welfare reform: More research needed on TANF family caps and other policies for reducing out-of-wedlock births* (GAO-01-924). Washington, DC: Author.

U.S. General Accounting Office. (2002). *Welfare reform: States are using TANF flexibility to adapt work requirements and time limits to meet state and local needs* (GAO-02-501T). Washington, DC: Author.

Work Incentive Program of 1967, P.L. 90-248, § 201; 81 Stat. 821.

Zedlewski, S. R. (1999). *Work-related activities and limitations of current welfare recipients* (Assessing the New Federalism, Discussion Papers, 99-06). Washington, DC: Urban Institute. Available: http://www.urban.org/UploadedPDF/discussion99-06.pdf

Zedlewski, S. R., & Brauner, S. (1999). *Declines in food stamp and welfare participation: Is there a connection?* (Assessing the New Federalism, Discussion Papers, 99-13). Washington, DC: Urban Institute. Available: http://www.urban.org/UploadedPDF/discussion99-13.pdf

Zedlewski, S. R. (with Gruber, A.). (2001). *Former welfare families and the food stamp program: The exodus continues* (Assessing the New Federalism: National Survey of America's Families, B-33). Washington, DC: Urban Institute. Available: http://www.urban.org/UploadedPDF/anf_b33.pdf

Ziliak, J. P. (2002). Social policy and the macroeconomy: What drives welfare caseloads? *Focus, 22,* 29–34.

FURTHER READING

Abramovitz, M. (1996). *Regulating the lives of women* (rev. ed.). Boston: South End Press.

Berrick, J. D. (1995). *Faces of poverty: Portraits of women and children on welfare.* New York: Oxford University Press.

Blank, R. M., & Haskins, R. (2001). *The new world of welfare.* Washington, DC: Brookings Institution.

Danziger, S. H. (Ed.). (1999). *Economic conditions and welfare reform.* Kalamazoo, MI: WE Upjohn Institute for Employment Research.

Hagen, J. L. (1999). Public welfare and human service: New directions under TANF? *Families in Society, 80,* 78–90.

Seccombe, K. (1999). *"So you think I drive a Cadillac?" Welfare recipients' perspectives on the system and its reform.* Boston: Allyn & Bacon.

Weil, A., & Finegold, K. (2002). *Welfare reform: The next act.* Washington, DC: Urban Institute.

Jan L. Hagen, PhD, ACSW, is Distinguished Teaching Professor, School of Social Welfare, University at Albany, State University of New York, 135 Western Avenue, Albany, NY 12222.

For further information see
Aid to Families with Dependent Children; Federal Social Legislation from 1994 to 1997, *1997;* General Assistance; Public Social Services; Temporary Assistance to Needy Families, *1997*

Key Words

Child Care and Development Fund	public assistance
Family Violence Option	TANF
	welfare reform

Temporary Work

See Contingent Work in the United States, *2003;* Working Poor, *1997*

Treatments for People with Severe and Persistent Mental Illness
Ellen P. Lukens

Mental illness affects a large percentage of the population in the United States, with estimates of lifetime prevalence among adults ranging from 32 to 48 percent (Kessler et al., 1994; Robins & Regier, 1991). Included in these numbers are some 5 percent of the adult population described as having severe mental illness (SMI), also referred to as severe and persistent mental illness, which typically includes major depression, bipolar disorder, schizophrenia, and obsessive–compulsive disorder in adults (U.S. Department of Health and Human Services [HHS], 1999). These particular illnesses are characterized as severe primarily because of the chronicity and intensity of symptoms and the impact on a person's ability to function adequately over time at home, at work, or in school. They are counted among the 10 leading causes of disability worldwide, with major depression ranked first among all illnesses whether medical or psychiatric (HHS, 1999). Although the causes of these illnesses are not fully understood, there is strong evidence that they are biological in nature and that stress and other environmental factors can trigger or increase symptoms. Because of the fact that SMI affects cognition and behavior, and at times limits the ability to recognize illness or monitor one's own care, creating a comprehensive treatment regimen that builds on both professional and nonprofessional support systems is critical to care planning (Pescosolido, Wright, & Sullivan, 1995).

DESCRIPTION OF ILLNESS
Any illness can be described in terms of both epidemiological characteristics and diagnosis. Epidemiology refers to the study of variations in the distribution of a specific illness or disorder and the variables that affect the disorder within a population or subset of a population. Diagnosis refers to the common set of symptoms that characterize a particular disorder.

All of the severe mental illnesses are subject to individual differences in presentation. This contributes significantly to difficulty in establishing reliable and valid methods of both epidemiological measurement and clinical diagnosis. Estimates of incidence (of new cases) and prevalence (of existing cases) for SMI are typically based on epidemiological studies of both community and clinical samples. In the United States, the best estimates for prevalence are based on the Environmental Catchment Area study and the National Comorbidity Survey, completed in the early 1980s and 1990s, respectively. The environmental study collected data on over 20,000 individuals in five communities (Robins & Regier, 1991). The comorbidity survey was a community-based survey conducted between 1990 and 1992 and included approximately 8,100 individuals (Kessler et al., 1994). Together, they provide the most accurate information to date for estimating the extent of mental illness within the United States, although they are far from comprehensive in describing the existence of mental illness and the use of mental health services in this country (HHS, 1999).

Among mental health professionals, the third, third revised, and fourth editions of the *Diagnostic and Statistical Manual of Mental Disorders* (American Psychiatric Association, 1980, 1987, 1994) have served as critical points of reference for establishing clinical diagnoses for SMI. The manuals, which are updated regularly, include descriptive and definitional data outlining the symptoms associated with mental disorders among adults and children. These definitions serve as critical starting points for the identification, assessment, and treatment of illness.

Major Depression

Both major depression and bipolar disorder are considered mood or affective disorders. Major depression is the most common of this group, with an estimated lifetime prevalence of 5 percent, and occurs most frequently among women, particularly those between 30 and 44 years of age (Robins & Regier, 1991). It is characterized by episodes of persistent depressed mood or loss of pleasure in combination with at least four additional symptoms. These may include significant weight loss or gain; insomnia or hypersomnia; psychomotor agitation or retardation; fatigue or loss of energy; feelings of worthlessness or guilt; diminished ability to think, concentrate, or make decisions; or thoughts of death, particularly suicidal threats, attempts, or plans.

Bipolar Disorder

Bipolar disorder is relatively rare compared with major depression. It is diagnosed when an episode of mania has occurred, regardless of whether depression has been present or not, with estimated prevalence ranging from 0.8 percent for Bipolar I (without episode of depression) to 0.5 percent for Bipolar II (with episode of some form of depression). Prevalence rates for bipolar disorder are comparable in men and women, with little ethnic variation (Robins & Regier, 1991). Mania includes symptoms of expansiveness or irritable mood; irrational, unpredictable, bizarre, or self-destructive behavior; hyperactivity; pressured speech, inflated self-esteem, or distractibility (American Psychiatric Association, 1994).

Schizophrenia

Schizophrenia is considered the most serious and devastating of the psychotic disorders and is associated with a tremendous burden and cost to the individual, the family, and society (American Psychiatric Association, 1994).

Although there is variation in prevalence across cultures, with a reported range of 0.2 to 2 percent, the estimated lifetime prevalence rate worldwide is about 1 percent. Reported prevalence for men and women is approximately equal, although there are some discrepancies based on whether samples are community or hospital based (Robins & Regier, 1991). The illness typically becomes manifest in early adulthood or late adolescence, with a median age of onset in the early or mid-twenties for men and late twenties for women, and is diagnosed by symptoms referred to as positive (or psychotic) and negative (American Psychiatric Association, 1994). The positive symptoms include hallucinations, delusions, bizarre behavior, disorganized speech, and disorganized or withdrawn behavior. The negative symptoms include affective flattening, alogia, or loss of volition, accompanied by a significant disturbance in ability to maintain work, interpersonal relations, or self-care.

Obsessive–Compulsive Disorder

Obsessive–compulsive disorder is an anxiety disorder characterized by obsessions, compulsions, or both, with a prevalence of 2.5 percent. Among those suffering from the illness, about 15 percent experience progressive deterioration in occupational and social functioning, whereas approximately 5 percent have a more episodic course with minimal or no symptoms between episodes. The initial presentation of the illness varies; in some individuals it is acute, in other cases, gradual. Women are somewhat more likely to develop obsessive–compulsive disorder although men tend to have an earlier age of onset (Pigott, 2000). Obsessions relate to cognitive processes and include intrusive, repeated, and persistent ideas or thoughts that are uncontrollable and cause marked distress. Compulsions include repetitive behaviors or mental acts, such as hand washing, checking and rechecking, or other dysfunctional and uncontrollable tasks intended to reduce or control anxiety (American Psychiatric Association, 1994).

Common Themes

For all the severe mental illnesses, there are some problematic or prodromal indicators that appear before a person seeks help, relapses, or both, but these may be elusive and difficult to characterize. Course and severity of illness is individual, which complicates diagnosis, assessment, and treatment. The unpredictable nature of the illnesses makes planning difficult and is disruptive to the life cycle of both people with symptoms and their families (Lefley, 1996). Most significantly, SMI affects the ability to perform adequately in everyday life.

Although new cases of SMI develop equally across class, ethnicity, and gender with little variation, poverty is associated with mental disorders (Polak & Warner, 1996). Lack of individual resources such as power, money, knowledge, and prestige is generally associated with the impaired functioning that is endemic to persons with SMI and may be further confounded by discrimination, differential access to services, and stigma (Link & Phelan, 1995; Neighbors et al., 1992). Once people of minority status enter the mental health system, they tend to be more readily diagnosed with more severe levels of illness (HHS, 1999). They may be more ill by the time they come in formal contact with the mental health system and thus require more intensive treatment, or they may receive less adequate care overall for reasons of discrimination or bias on the part of providers or less accessible or comprehensive services (HHS, 1999; Neighbors et al., 1992).

SMI occurs across cultures with little variation in prevalence (Fellin, 1996). However, symptoms may differ somewhat, depending on the cultural and religious belief systems in a given society. For example, certain behaviors or beliefs considered unusual or dysfunctional in one culture might be normal or acceptable in another, which adds to the complexity of accurate cross-cultural diagnosis (Fellin, 1996; Lefley, 1996). Understanding illness (that is, attribution) and help-seeking behaviors can vary radically as well and depend on a cultural frame of reference. For example, seeking the advice of traditional healers or spiritualists might be a valued aspect of help seeking in certain cultures and is important to consider and understand in developing a culturally sensitive and comprehensive plan for treatment intervention (Al-Krenawi, 1998; Sue & Sue, 1999).

ASSOCIATED FACTORS

SMIs are also associated with other factors, including suicide, homelessness, and incarceration, which make the symptoms particularly frightening and challenging to persons with illness and their families. Individual situations may be further complicated by coexistence or comorbidity of other mental illness, substance abuse, or medical illness. Overlying these factors is the societal stigma attached to mental illness that contributes to misunderstanding

and negative attitudes among the greater community and disenfranchisement among those with illness (Link & Phelan, 1995).

Among persons formerly hospitalized for major depression, some 10 to 15 percent commit suicide, and among all deaths by suicide, an estimated 20 to 35 percent are diagnosed with major depression (Angst, Angst, & Stassen, 1999). Among people with schizophrenia, approximately 10 to 15 percent complete and approximately 20 to 40 percent attempt suicide at some point in their lives (Harkavey-Friedman & Nelson, 1997). For those diagnosed with bipolar disorder, the suicide completion rate is 19 percent (HHS, 1999).

Among chronically homeless people in the United States, an estimated 25 to 50 percent are mentally ill. Within that group, approximately half have a comorbid substance abuse disorder (Fellin, 1996; HHS, 1999). Because the data are difficult to collect regarding numbers of persons without dwellings, estimates are generally considered inaccurate.

The number of people diagnosed with SMI who enter the criminal justice system is also difficult to calculate. However, recent clinical studies estimate that 6 to 15 percent of those in city or county jails and 10 to 15 percent of those in state prisons have some form of SMI. A large proportion are homeless before incarceration (Lamb & Weinberger, 1998). Once persons with SMI are imprisoned, focus tends to be placed on the safety of the greater community rather than on the alleviation of symptoms, and any active treatment for the mental illness is reduced (Lamb, Weinberger, & Gross, 1999). Violence has also become of increasing concern. Data on whether the incidence of significant acts of violence among those with SMI is higher than among the general public are inconclusive (HHS, 1999). However, widespread media coverage of particularly dramatic situations in which violence occurs among persons labeled with mental illness reinforces anxiety and stigma among the general public (Lefley, 1996; Mechanic, 1998).

The coexistence of other disorders worsens the course and outcome of the severe mental illnesses and complicates treatment. Up to half of those with SMI develop problems with alcohol or substance abuse at some point during their illness (Drake & Osher, 1997; Regier et al., 1993). Symptoms of SMI also interfere with the ability to monitor, attend to, or even care about established guidelines for self-care and personal health, putting individuals at risk for both acute and chronic medical and dental problems as well.

CHANGES IN TREATMENT OVER TIME

Both knowledge and attitudes regarding the cause and treatment of SMI changed over the course of the 20th century. Before the 1960s, psychoanalytic models predominated, with responsibility for illness assigned to the individual or family. Depending on the diagnosis, treatment followed an illness- or deficit-based model, which focused on a combination of long-term hospitalization, medication, and intensive individual or family therapy (Grob, 1994; Lefley, 1996). At midcentury antipsychotic medications became increasingly available, and mental health professionals began to move toward more community-based models of care as large numbers of people were deinstitutionalized and returned to the community. But the communities and the social services system were ill prepared for the needs of people with severe illness who had resided for long periods in hospital settings, and services were fragmented and inadequate (Grob, 1994). As a result, a new federal initiative, referred to as the community support program, was launched in 1977 to provide a more flexible and integrated approach to services and to integrate federally based resources with state-based community services. From 1955 to the present, the number of beds in public psychiatric hospitals decreased from 560,000 to about 77,000. Meanwhile, the average length of stay for psychiatric beds also decreased. Today, individuals are hospitalized only if they are considered a danger to themselves or others and then rapidly discharged to the community after a brief period of stabilization.

Current approaches to treatment, rehabilitation, and recovery have grown out of these community support efforts and go well beyond an emphasis on the individual or family as the focal point in treatment. Recent attention to "best practice" approaches, as outlined by the American Psychiatric Association and sanctioned by other mental health organizations and consumer groups, builds on a multisystem approach to care, focusing on coordinated care in collaboration with families and the client, attention to critical periods of transition from hospital to community, outreach, and prevention with increasing attention placed on strengths and resiliency (Frances, Kahn, Carpenter, Docherty, & Donovan, 1998; Lehman & Steinwachs, 1998; Schulberg, Katon, Simon, & Rush, 1999). However, best practice approaches are not always readily available and have been complicated by recent emphasis on managed care models for private and public insurance coverage that emphasize cost containment, demonstrated need, and measured outcome (HHS, 1999; Lehman & Steinwachs, 1998). Continued coverage under managed care plans is dependent on both initial and ongoing review to justify type, intensity, and duration of care (Center for Mental Health Services, 2001). As a result, insurers actively monitor both health and mental health services for effectiveness. Although insurance monitoring is useful to a point, this can also be associated with denial of adequate or needed treatment or poorly defined descriptions of what constitutes effective or good practice and care (Mechanic, 1998).

TREATMENT-RELATED CHALLENGES

Social workers and other mental health professionals face multiple challenges in working with individuals who suffer from SMI. Barriers to implementing a coordinated system of care include lack of resources, underfunded or non-existent programs, impediments to funding created by managed care, dated attitudes among mental health professionals, or confusion on the part of those in need of services as to what they need, where or when to go for help, or even what to ask for.

From a cross-systems perspective, these challenges include psychic and interpersonal manifestations of the illness as exemplified through the cognitions and behaviors associated with severe psychiatric symptoms, family variables, and a range of environmental variables, including social, community, and professional attitudes, biases, supports, and resources. For these reasons, diagnosis and ongoing assessment are fundamental to comprehensive treatment and care. Diagnosis serves as a critical first step in this ongoing process. Because medication is required for the treatment of the most disturbing symptoms and because knowledge of effects and side effects of these medications is essential for monitoring progress, a psychiatrist or primary physician is necessarily involved in this process.

SMI is always diagnosed through clinical dialogue or observation and information drawn from collaborative sources. This means there is room for error, disagreement among professionals, and change over time. Diagnosis is grounded in symptom presentation rather than the critical environmental and cultural factors that are essential to understand context.

Given the complexity of diagnosis, ongoing assessment is critical to treatment. As with any illness, multiple factors can interfere with the treatment process once a diagnosis is made. With SMI this may be further complicated when the person will not or cannot acknowledge the illness (Amador & David, 1998; Amador, Strauss, Yale, & Gorman, 1991) or when associated cognitive deficits interfere with the person's ability to evaluate situations accurately and respond appropriately (Silverstein, 1997).

Strengths-based models of assessment focus on effectiveness, empowerment, and function in the context of social, community, and professional support rather than pathology, disease, and dysfunctional relationships (Marsh, 1994). They assume that any form of illness is worsened by stress and that a reciprocal relationship exists among stress and other variables in the person's environment (Nicholson & Neufeld, 1992). Such transactional models address both individual resources and environmental demands in the context of symptom formation, resiliency, and protective factors, social supports, and overall level of functioning. Stress-related demands range from internal or external situations that create little or no support or stimulation to situations creating too much or excessive stimulation (Heinrichs & Carpenter, 1983; Penn, Mueser, Spaulding, Hope, & Reed, 1995). Internal stressors include cognitive deficits associated with illness; external stressors cover availability of resources across system levels, including society, community, and family (Link & Phelan, 1995). Resiliency refers to the internal strengths that a person is able to draw on under duress and stress; protective factors represent resources that facilitate resiliency and promote self-determination (Zubin, Steinhauer, & Condray, 1992).

SMI affects every aspect of a person's daily life. Because it attacks the brain, it interferes with the integrity of the self (Lefley, 1996; Marsh et al., 1996). Hence, constant vigilance is necessary to help the person keep on track and avoid the demoralization and stigma attached to repeated hospitalizations or insufficient or inappropriate outpatient care. With early identification of symptoms, use of carefully regulated medication, availability of ongoing professional services or consultation, and existence of a collaborative relationship among professionals, the person with illness and members of his or her support system can genuinely contribute to improved functioning and outcome (Lefley, 1996; McGlashan & Johannessen, 1996). Family members can help to fulfill this function as can other members of the community, such as friends, clergy, partners, or other consumers. Therefore, determining the nature and extent of social and familial relationships available to an individual, as characterized by social supports and network, is critical to assessment (Cohen & Wills, 1985; Mueller, 1980).

Availability of concrete resources must be carefully considered as well. These include any benefits to which the person is entitled, such as social security income, social security disability income, Medicaid, Medicare, access to housing, and information on how to use these benefits. If the person wishes to work, this must be evaluated in the context of stage of recovery and the availability of proper supports to ensure preparation, access, and adequate functioning on the job. Work settings bring their own set of environmental challenges and stresses—another arena for the individual to cope with and manage (Bond, 1992; Lehman & Steinwachs, 1998).

APPROACHES TO TREATMENT, REHABILITATION, AND RECOVERY

The preferred treatments for SMI vary somewhat, depending on the diagnosis, but combined or multimodal approaches are critical to effective intervention (HHS, 1999). It is commonly agreed that exemplary care includes (1) medication, education or psychoeducation, various forms of psychotherapeutic intervention ranging from case management to family and group therapy; (2) well-coordinated care among an interdisciplinary team of mental health providers who are readily available over time; and (3) collaboration among professionals and informal supports (Lundwall, 1996; Pescosolido et al., 1995). Self-help groups can serve a critical function in this process. In addition, treatment must be overlaid with attention to cross-cultural and ethical factors, particularly regarding disclosure of information and right to self-determination. Other considerations include timing and duration of intervention (HHS, 1999).

Medication

Medication, or pharmacotherapy, is critical to the treatment of SMI. In making decisions regarding the use of a particular medication or combination of medications, the treating physician must attend to diagnosis, symptoms, dose titration and monitoring, side effects, and the ability of the individual patient to monitor and adhere to treatment (Center for Mental Health Services, 2001).

Over the past decade, new medications have become available and have served to more effectively control symptoms and to increase levels of functioning for some people with SMI. At their most effective levels, these medications are associated with improved cognitive functioning and increased insight. However, they are also associated with unwanted or unexpected side effects of medication, such as excessive weight gain, or other physical symptoms, or emotionally loaded reactions (Duckworth, Nair, Patel, & Goldfinger, 1997). As an individual becomes both more well and more cognizant, associated depression, suicidal behavior, fear, mourning, and a sense of loss of "what might have been" may emerge. The disappearance of familiar symptoms may also be experienced as a kind of loss. In these situations, physicians monitoring the medication and other involved mental health professionals are challenged to help the individual effectively cope with and reach some level of acceptance of the illness while adjusting to a new level of functioning (Duckworth et al., 1997).

Psychotherapy and Counseling

Various models of psychotherapy are appropriate for SMI, including individual, family, and groups models, and are commonly used in combination with well-monitored medications. Variations of cognitive–behavioral intervention that focus on skills training, increased self-esteem, and treatment adherence have been particularly effective in the treatment of all of the severe mental illnesses.

Personal therapy is based on staged interventions and responses to the poorly regulated affects (that is, losing control, inability to regulate mood) that characterize schizophrenia. The three-stage treatment is strengths based and individualized; participants must attain clearly stated objectives regarding personal functioning before moving to the next stage in the process. Findings support the efficacy of this clearly defined model that is fine-tuned for the individual, particularly when presence of family serves as a stabilizing force (Hogarty et al., 1997).

Social skills training is a behavioral model designed for treating schizophrenia and other forms of SMI that focuses on those areas of behavior that allow individuals to interact and function in a socially acceptable manner. Training in problem solving, communication skills, and conflict resolution is central to the approach. The training can be conducted with individuals, in groups, or with families or couples (Bellack, Mueser, Gingerich, & Agresta, 1997; Mueser & Glynn, 1990).

Interpersonal therapy and variations of cognitive–behavioral therapy are particularly important as interventions for major depression, bipolar disorder, and obsessive–compulsive disorder. They are present focused and time limited and emphasize education and collaboration between therapist and the person with an illness. Interpersonal therapy focuses on role conflicts and life transitions, mourning and loss, and social functioning (Frank, Kupfer, Wagner, McEachran, & Cornes, 1991; Klerman, Weissman, Rounsaville, & Sherron, 1984). Cognitive–behavioral techniques provide specific and structured approaches to identifying problem areas, identifying response patterns, and challenging and restructuring assumptions and response. For persons with obsessive–compulsive disorder, specific cognitive–behavioral techniques using exposure and response to ritual prevention have been effective. In these treatments, individuals are guided to expose themselves to anxiety-provoking situations while learning how not to perform rituals in response (Ross, Simpson, & Fallon, 2000).

Electroconvulsive Therapy

Electroconvulsive therapy (ECT), first introduced in 1934 and commonly referred to as "electroshock therapy," has been increasingly used for the treatment of severe depression, bipolar disorder, and some forms of schizophrenia (American Psychiatric Association, 1990). In some situations, it is considered the treatment of choice, particularly when there is need for rapid response (for example, acute suicidality or psychosis; Sackheim, 1989, 1998). It is also used when medication, or medication in combination with some form of psychotherapeutic intervention, is unsuccessful or not tolerated (American Psychiatric Association, 1990). The treatment consists of inducing brief seizures by passing an electric current through the brain under carefully controlled circumstances. Typically, a full course of ECT involves six to 12 treatments, but there is individual variability in the number needed (Sackheim, 1998). Providing initial and ongoing education to individuals and involved family or friends about the benefits and risks involved in this treatment is critical, particularly given the misunderstanding and fear surrounding the intervention (Katz, 1992; Sackheim, 1998).

Education and Psychoeducation

One of the most critical components in providing comprehensive care and promoting resilience is education across system levels. For individuals and families, education serves as an important bridge for maintaining open and mutually respectful lines of communication, both within the family and with professionals. It creates a common language that facilitates dialogue between consumer and provider and serves to enhance the levels of trust and alliance that are so fundamental to effective treatment (McFarlane et al., 1995).

From an educational perspective, helping families and individuals to recognize both internal and external stressors is paramount because the ability to recognize and use personal strengths and build on external supports is easily impaired by symptoms and exacerbated during an acute episode of illness (Saleebey, 1996). Professional expertise is critical to provide information, support, and distance. Because SMI tends to be episodic, helping people understand what is generally known about the illness as well as learning how to monitor these episodes as they play out for any one individual are critical. If the person and his or her caregivers can learn how to identify and monitor early warning signs of decompensation, significant progress can be made toward keeping the illness in check through anticipatory planning during periods when the person is doing relatively well. This sets the stage for proactive medical and environmental intervention during more difficult or crisis periods (McGlashan & Johannessen, 1996; Mueser, Bellack, Wade, Sayers, & Resenthal, 1992).

Various educational and psychoeducational models have been developed and tested, particularly for schizophrenia, bipolar disorder, and major depression. The more strictly educational models concentrate on the dissemination of information (Solomon, 1996). The psychoeducation models tend to include an added emphasis on solving problems, managing crisis and stress, developing coping skills, and overcoming barriers to understanding and treatment adherence (Lukens, Thorning, & Herman, 1999; McFarlane et al., 1995). Interventions have been designed for individual families, for multiple family groups, and for individual or group sessions with patients (Lukens & Thorning, 1998). Psychoeducational multiple family groups have been used effectively with families and persons with various forms of SMI to contain symptoms, to improve compliance, and to reduce relapse. The models build on social learning, cognitive–behavioral and group theory, and maximize collaboration among professionals and family members (Lukens et al., 1999; McFarlane et al., 1995).

Case Coordination

Case coordination or case management is particularly important for persons with SMI who are not in a position to manage their own care or have limited informal or family support. Such collaboration among social workers and other mental health professionals (including psychiatrists, nurses, rehabilitation specialists, occupational and recreational therapists, and teachers) and between professional and client enhances the potential for extending and reinforcing both the formal (professional) and informal (family and community) systems of care that are so important for health care monitoring (Borkman, 1976; Lundwall, 1996; Pescosolido et al., 1995).

Although many valuable models of case coordination exist, the most widely replicated of these approaches is assertive community treatment (ACT), initially developed in Wisconsin in the late 1970s to help people with schizophrenia who were not able to live successfully outside of a hospital (Stein & Test, 1980). In this model, an interdisciplinary team of mental health professionals provides round-the-clock outreach in the community to groups of clients at high risk. The goals are to lessen a person's tendency to be defined as a patient; increase personal strength, control, and self-esteem; meet basic needs and enhance social skills; expand employment opportunities; and enhance quality of life. Services are usually provided in the community or neighborhood and range from assistance with shopping to comprehensive mental health, substance abuse, and physical health treatment, as well as vocational, educational, and recreational services. More recently, consumer or peer specialists have been included on the teams. Extensive research has documented the effectiveness of these programs in reducing relapse and days in the hospital and in increasing stability in the community and in residences (Lehman & Steinwachs, 1998; Mueser, Drake, & Bond, 1997).

Rehabilitation and Recovery

Persons with SMI need a range of well-coordinated services and resources that are readily available over time and that may be intensified during periods of increased symptoms or relapse. In addition to inpatient and community programs, such services include attention to work, housing, and quality of life.

SMI interferes with the ability to function adequately in the workplace. Currently, only an estimated 5 to 10 percent of those diagnosed with SMI are able to maintain any form of competitive employment (HHS, 1999). Others attend sheltered workshops or vocational training programs where they are responsible for relatively unskilled or semiskilled tasks, or participate in day hospitals with little attention to vocational training. As medications and other interventions become increasingly sophisticated and effective and employers become sensitized to their needs, people with SMI will be more emotionally available to meet the demands required to maintain regular employment. The structure and potentially rewarding nature of the work environment may also serve to focus and ground the individual if appropriate supports are available. This demands that social workers and other mental health professionals involved with this group of clients become well versed in the policies and services related to the rights of persons with disabilities in the workplace (Kurzman & Akabas, 1993).

Housing is particularly important. Among the homeless population in the United States, approximately 10 percent have SMI (Brekke, Ansel, Long, Slade, & Weinstean, 1999). Among all persons with SMI, an estimated 60 to 75 percent reside with relatives (Lefley, 1996). Although this may be functional for some, in other instances it undermines attempts to move toward more independent living. Matching individuals with appropriate housing, in a setting where needed supports are in place, provides an ongoing challenge and a critical priority, particularly given limited availability and funding support (Lefley, 1996). Recently, programs such as Pathways to Housing in New York City, which provides housing to persons with comorbid symptoms of SMI and substance abuse, have been particularly effective in maintaining people in the community (Tsemberis & Eisenberg, 2000). Founded on the belief that housing is a basic right, the program blends two community mental health models—supported housing and proactive community outreach. As with psychoeducation, the consumers are considered partners in treatment. When tenants relapse due to substance abuse or an increase of psychiatric symptoms, their housing status remains constant; they do not have to leave their apartments. The team and tenant manage relapse crises collaboratively, and services are intensified during these periods.

Self-Help Groups
Encouraging involvement in the family and consumer organizations promotes education of clients and families. The family advocacy groups, particularly the National Alliance for the Mentally Ill (NAMI), have become a major resource for both the lay and professional community and a force for change among national and local policymakers through advocacy, policy analysis and information dissemination, support, and antistigma campaigns (Lefley, 1996).

Local and national advocacy or consumer groups organized by persons with illness have enabled individuals to work together, educate each other, raise self-esteem, and create opportunities for themselves through advocacy, client-run businesses, and support groups (Deegan, 1992). These groups serve a unique and critical function, either alone or in concert with professionally based intervention, because of their emphasis on peer support, self-determination, and hope. They serve a particularly critical function for those who are unwilling to participate in professional treatments (March, Frances, Carpenter, & Kahn, 1997).

As the movement has expanded, professionals have become increasingly sensitized to the need for consumer and family input into program development and planning, and consumers are beginning to serve as consultants and collaborators not only for each other, but also for professional program initiatives as well (for example, assertive community treatment teams). This provides meaningful work for consumers, peer role models for work and recovery, and increased levels of empathy and sensitivity among professionals to the needs of people with illness (Mowbray et al., 1996).

CURRENT CHALLENGES AND CONCLUSIONS
Several themes emerge in reviewing the needs of those with SMI. These include combined forms of treatment, including medication and psychotherapeutic interventions; family, and community-based education and prevention; continuity of care; increased availability of self-help models and consideration as to how these can best work in tandem with professional treatment models; unique and sometimes unexpected issues that evolve as people move toward recovery; and the continuing need to increase opportunities for rehabilitation, housing, employment, and workplace supports for those facing the particular challenges of these illnesses.

It is important to consider what directions social workers might take to actively confront the needs of those with SMI. These illnesses are profoundly debilitating, stigmatized, and widely misunderstood. Interventions are clearly complicated by the fact that the client may be unaware of or unwilling to admit the presence of illness. Strengths-based models can be used to place illness in context and help individuals move toward rehabilitation and recovery. However, this requires ongoing education not only for the consumers of services (that is, individuals with illness and families), but also for the professional providers themselves and for the larger community.

At the community level, educational campaigns can be used to sensitize people to the fact that SMI can be described and treated, that associated behaviors are not merely willful but have a biological base, and that early intervention is important to improved outcome and prognosis. Such campaigns include programs designed to promote understanding and early identification of symptomatic behaviors because there is increasing evidence that early intervention and carefully monitored treatment can slow and curb the potentially debilitating course of mental illness (McGlashan & Johannessen, 1996). Community-based educational strategies also increase awareness that for many people, the most disturbing and overt symptoms of SMI can be adequately controlled (Duckworth et al., 1997).

As issues regarding mental health become increasingly visible and complex in all strata of society, developing innovative and effective strategies for education, prevention, and treatment is paramount. Historically, social workers have played major roles in mental health care in this country. As SMI continues to be better understood in terms of etiology and epidemiology, social workers and other mental health professionals must stay abreast of such knowledge as an important step toward developing and evaluating educational and psychosocial interventions, models, and resources that are readily available both nationally and locally. The challenges of SMI demand that social workers intervene across systems to provide and coordinate everyday and crisis care for consumers and families; develop and evaluate programs that define effective practice-based interventions; and, in turn, influence policies that provide guidelines for both services and preventive measures for persons and communities as they face such complex illness. Creating active links among primary health care providers, social services, community-based rehabilitation and recovery programs, housing, criminal justice, and advocacy groups is critical to this process. Such links will set the stage for

the development and potential for combined or complementary professional and consumer-based models that draw on both professional and practical expertise, build on the recent availability of more effective psychotropic medications, provide support and opportunity for rehabilitation and recovery over time, and improve quality of life and hope for those facing the complex symptoms of SMI.

REFERENCES

Al-Krenawi, A. (1998). Reconciling Western tradition and traditional healing: A social worker walks with the wind. *Reflections, 4*(3), 6–21.

Amador, X. F., & David, A. S. (Eds.). (1998). *Insight and psychosis.* New York: Oxford University Press.

Amador, X. F., Strauss, D. H., Yale, S. A., & Gorman, J. M. (1991). Awareness of illness in schizophrenia. *Schizophrenia Bulletin, 17,* 113–132.

American Psychiatric Association. (1980). *Diagnostic and statistical manual of mental disorders* (3rd ed.). Washington, DC: Author.

American Psychiatric Association. (1987). *Diagnostic and statistical manual of mental disorders* (3rd ed., rev.). Washington, DC: Author.

American Psychiatric Association. (1990). *The practice of electroconvulsive therapy: Recommendations for treatment, training, and privileging—A task force report of the American Psychiatric Association.* Washington, DC: Author.

American Psychiatric Association. (1994). *Diagnostic and statistical manual of mental disorders* (4th ed.). Washington, DC: Author.

Angst, J., Angst, F., & Stassen, H. H. (1999). Suicide risk in patients with major depressive disorder. *Journal of Clinical Psychiatry, 60*(Suppl. 2), 57–62.

Bellack, A. S., Mueser, K., Gingerich, S., & Agresta, J. (1997). *Social skills training for schizophrenia: A step-by-step guide.* New York: Guilford Press.

Bond, G. R. (1992). Vocational rehabilitation. In L. P. Liberman (Ed.), *Handbook of psychiatric rehabilitation* (pp. 244–275). New York: Macmillan.

Borkman, T. (1976). Experiential knowledge: A new concept for the analysis of self-help groups. *Social Service Review, 50,* 445–456.

Brekke, J. S., Ansel, M., Long, J., Slade, E., & Weinstein, M. (1999). Intensity and continuity of services and functional outcomes in the rehabilitation of persons with schizophrenia. *Psychiatric Services, 50*(2), 248–256.

Center for Mental Health Services. (2001). *Mental Health, United States, 2000* (DHHS Publication No. SMA 01-3537). Washington, DC: U.S. Government Printing Office.

Cohen, S., & Wills, T. A. (1985). Stress, social support, and the buffering hypothesis. *Psychological Bulletin, 98,* 310–357.

Deegan, P. E. (1992). The independent living movement and people with psychiatric disabilities: Taking back control over our own lives. *Psychosocial Rehabilitation Journal, 15*(3), 3–19.

Drake, R. E., & Osher, F. C. (1997). Treating substance abuse in patients with severe mental illness. In S. W. Henggler & A. B. Santos (Eds.), *Innovative approaches for difficult-to-treat populations* (pp. 131–163). Washington, DC: American Psychiatric Press.

Duckworth, K., Nair, V., Patel, J. K., & Goldfinger, S. M. (1997). Lost time, found hope and sorrow: The search for self, connection and purpose during "awakenings" on the new antipsychotics. *Harvard Review of Psychiatry, 5*(4), 227–233.

Fellin, P. (1996). *Mental health and mental illness: Policies, programs, and services.* Itasca, IL: F. E. Peacock.

Frances, A. J., Kahn, D. A., Carpenter, D., Docherty, J. P., & Donovan, S. L. (1998). The expert consensus guidelines for treating depression in bipolar depression. *Journal of Clinical Psychiatry, 59*(Suppl. 4), 73–79.

Frank, E., Kupfer, D. J., Wagner, E. F., McEachran, A. B., & Cornes, C. (1991). Efficacy of interpersonal therapy as a maintenance treatment of recurrent depression: Contributing factors. *Archives of General Psychiatry, 48,* 1053–1059.

Grob, G. N. (1994). *The mad among us: A history of the care of America's mentally ill.* New York: Free Press.

Harkavey-Friedman, J. M., & Nelson, E. A. (1997). Assessment and intervention for the suicidal patient. *Psychiatric Quarterly, 68*(4), 361–375.

Heinrichs, D., & Carpenter, W. (1983). The coordination of family therapy with other treatment modalities. In W. R. McFarlane (Ed.), *Family therapy in schizophrenia* (pp. 267–288). New York: Guilford Press.

Hogarty, G. E., Greenwald, D., Ulrich, R. F., Kornblith, S. J., DiBarry, A. L., Cooley, S., et al. (1997). Three-year trials of personal therapy among schizophrenic patients living with or independent of family: II. Effects on adjustment of patients. *American Journal of Psychiatry, 154*(11), 1514–1524.

Katz, G. (1992). Electroconvulsive therapy from a social work perspective. *Social Work in Health Care, 16*(4), 55–68.

Kessler, R. C., McGonagle, K. A., Zhao, S., Nelson, C. B., Hughes, M., Eshleman, S., et al. (1994). Lifetime and 12-month prevalence of DSM III-R psychiatric disorders in the United States: Results from the national comorbidity study. *Archives of General Psychiatry, 51,* 8–19.

Klerman, G. L., Weissman, M. M., Rounsaville, B. J., & Sherron, E. S. (1984). *Interpersonal therapy of depression.* New York: Basic Books.

Kurzman, P. A., & Akabas, S. H. (Eds.). (1993). *Work and well-being: The occupational social work advantage.* Washington, DC: NASW Press.

Lamb, H. R., & Weinberger, L. E. (1998). Persons with severe mental illness in jails and prisons: A review. *Psychiatric Services, 1998*(49), 483–492.

Lamb, H. R., Weinberger, L. E., & Gross, B. H. (1999). Community treatment of severely mentally ill offenders under the jurisdiction of the criminal justice system: A review. *Psychiatric Services, 50*(7), 907–913.

Lefley, H. P. (1996). Family caregiving in mental illness. Thousand Oaks, CA: Sage Publications.

Lehman, A. F., & Steinwachs, D. M. (1998). Translating research into practice: The schizophrenia patient outcomes research team (PORT) treatment recommendations. *Schizophrenia Bulletin, 24*(1), 1–10.

Link, B., & Phelan, J. (1995). Social conditions as fundamental causes of disease [Extra issue]. *Journal of Health and Social Behavior, 36,* 80–94.

Lukens, E. P., & Thorning, H. (1998). Psychoeducation and severe mental illness: Implications for social work practice and research. In J.B.W. Williams & K. Ell (Eds.), *Advances in mental health research: Implications for practice* (pp. 343–364). Washington, DC: NASW Press.

Lukens, E. P., Thorning, H., & Herman, D. B. (1999). Family psychoeducation in schizophrenia: Emerging themes and challenges. *Journal of Practical Psychiatry and Behavioral Health, 5,* 314–325.

Lundwall, R. A. (1996). How psychoeducational support groups can provide multidiscipline services to families of people with mental illness. *Psychiatric Rehabilitation Journal, 20*(2), 64–71.

March, J. S., Frances, A., Carpenter, D., & Kahn, D. A. (1997). Treatment of obsessive–compulsive disorder: The Expert Consensus Panel for Obsessive–Compulsive Disorder. *Journal of Clinical Psychiatry, 58,* 2–72.

Marsh, D. T. (1994). *The psychodynamic model and services for families: Issues and strategies.* Chur, Switzerland: Harwood Academic Publishers.

Marsh, D. T., Lefley, H. P., Evans-Rhodes, D., Ansell, V. I., Doerzbacher, B. M., LaBarbera, L., et al. (1996). The family experience of mental illness: Evidence for resilience. *Psychiatric Rehabilitation Journal, 20*(2), 3–12.

McFarlane, W., Lukens, E., Link, B., Dushay, R., Deakins, S., Newmark, M., et al. (1995). Multiple family groups and psychoeducation in the treatment of schizophrenia. *Archives of General Psychiatry, 52,* 679–687.

McGlashan, T. H., & Johannessen, J. O. (1996). Early detection and intervention with schizophrenia: Rationale. *Schizophrenia Bulletin, 22,* 201–222.

Mechanic, D. (1998). Emerging trends in mental health policy and practice. *Health Affairs, 17*(6), 82–98.

Mowbray, C. T., Moxley, D. P., Thrasher, S., Bybee, D., McCrohan, N., Harris, S., et al. (1996). Consumers as community support providers: Issues created by role innovation. *Community Mental Health Journal, 32,* 47–67.

Mueller, D. P. (1980). Social networks: A promising direction for research on the relationship of the social environment to psychiatric disorder. *American Journal of Psychiatry, 14,* 147–161.

Mueser, K. T., Bellack, A. S., Wade, J. H., Sayers, S. L., & Resenthal, C. K. (1992). An assessment of the educational needs of chronic psychiatric patients and their relatives. *British Journal of Psychiatry, 160,* 674–680.

Mueser, K. T., Drake, R. E., & Bond, G. R. (1997). Recent advances in psychiatric rehabilitation for patients with severe mental illness. *Harvard Review of Psychiatry, 5,* 123–137.

Mueser, K. T., & Glynn, S. M. (1990). Behavioral family therapy for schizophrenia. *Progressive Behavior Modification, 26,* 122–149.

Neighbors, H. W., Bashshur, R., Price, R., Selig, S., Donabedian, A., & Shannon, G. (1992). Ethnic minority mental health service delivery: A review of the literature. *Research in Community and Mental Health, 7*(1), 39–47.

Nicholson, I., & Neufeld, R. (1992). A dynamic vulnerability perspective on stress and schizophrenia. *American Journal of Orthopsychiatry, 62,* 117–130.

Penn, D. L., Mueser, K. T., Spaulding, W., Hope, D. A., & Reed, D. (1995). Information processing and social competence in chronic schizophrenia. *Schizophrenia Bulletin, 21*(2), 269–281.

Pescosolido, B., Wright, E., & Sullivan, W. (1995). Communities of care: A theoretical perspective on case management models in mental health. *Advances in Medical Sociology, 6,* 37–79.

Pigott, T. A. (2000). Obsessive–compulsive disorder: Symptom overview and epidemiology. *Bulletin of the Menninger Clinic, 62*(Suppl. 4), A4–A32.

Polak, P., & Warner, R. (1996). The economic life of seriously mentally ill people in the community. *Psychiatric Services, 47,* 270–274.

Regier, D. A., Narrow, W. E., Rae, D. S., Manderscheid, R. W., Locke, B. Z., & Goodwin, F. K. (1993). The de facto U.S. mental and addictive service system: Epidemiological catchment area prospective 1-year prevalence rates of disorders and services. *Archives of General Psychiatry, 50,* 85–94.

Robins, L. N., & Regier, D. A. (Eds.). (1991). *Psychiatric disorders in America: The Epidemiologic Catchment Area Study.* New York: Free Press.

Ross, R. W., Simpson, H. B., & Fallon, B. A. (2000). Treatment of obsessive-compulsive disorder. *Journal of Psychiatric Practice, 6,* 173–174.

Sackheim, H. A. (1989). The efficacy of electroconvulsive therapy in the treatment of major depression. In S. Fisher & R. P. Greenberg (Eds.), *The limits of biological treatments for psychological distress: Comparisons with psychotherapy and placebo* (pp. 234–272). Hillsdale, NJ: Lawrence Erlbaum.

Sackheim, H. A. (1998). *ECT: Electroconvulsive therapy: What you need to know, a patient information booklet.* New York: New York State Psychiatric Institute.

Saleebey, D. (1996). The strengths perspective in social work practice: Extensions and cautions. *Social Work, 41,* 296–305.

Schulberg, H. C., Katon, W. J., Simon, G. E., & Rush, A. J. (1999). Best clinical practice: Guidelines for managing major depression in primary medical care. *Journal of Clinical Psychiatry, 60*(Suppl. 7), 19–26.

Silverstein, S. M. (1997). Information processing, social cognition, and psychiatric rehabilitation in schizophrenia. *Psychiatry, 60,* 327–340.

Solomon, P. (1996). Moving from psychoeducation to family education for families of adults with serious mental illness. *Psychiatric Services, 47*(12), 1364–1370.

Stein, L. I., & Test, M. A. (1980). Alternative to mental hospital treatment: I. Conceptual model, treatment program, and clinical evaluation. *Archives of General Psychiatry, 37,* 392–397.

Sue, D. W., & Sue, D. (1999). *Counseling the culturally different: Theory and practice* (3rd ed.). New York: John Wiley & Sons.

Tsemberis, S., & Eisenberg, R. F. (2000). Pathways to housing: Supported housing for street-dwelling homeless individuals with psychiatric disabilities. *Psychiatric Services, 51*(4), 487–493.

U.S. Department of Health and Human Services. (1999). *Mental health: A report of the Surgeon General.* Rockville, MD: National Institutes of Health, National Institute of Mental Health, Substance Abuse and Mental Health Services Administration, Center for Mental Health Services.

Zubin, J., Steinhauer, S. R., & Condray, R. (1992). Vulnerability to relapse in schizophrenia. *British Journal of Psychiatry, 161*(Suppl. 18), 13, 18.

Ellen P. Lukens, PhD, is associate professor, Columbia University School of Social Work, McVickar Hall, 622 West 113th Street, New York, NY 10025.

For further information see

Adult Day Care; Aging: Alzheimer's Disease and Other Disabilities, *1997;* Deinstitutionalization; Mental Health Overview; Psychosocial Rehabilitation; Serious Mental Illness: A Biopsychosocial Perspective, *1997*

Key Words	
best practices	rehabilitation, recovery
integrated practice models	severe mental illness

Appendix 1. NASW Code of Ethics

The primary mission of the social work profession is to enhance human well-being and help meet the basic human needs of all people, with particular attention to the needs and empowerment of people who are vulnerable, oppressed, and living in poverty. A historic and defining feature of social work is the profession's focus on individual well-being in a social context and the well-being of society. Fundamental to social work is attention to the environmental forces that create, contribute to, and address problems in living.

Social workers promote social justice and social change with and on behalf of clients. "Clients" is used inclusively to refer to individuals, families, groups, organizations, and communities. Social workers are sensitive to cultural and ethnic diversity and strive to end discrimination, oppression, poverty, and other forms of social injustice. These activities may be in the form of direct practice, community organizing, supervision, consultation, administration, advocacy, social and political action, policy development and implementation, education, and research and evaluation. Social workers seek to enhance the capacity of people to address their own needs. Social workers also seek to promote the responsiveness of organizations, communities, and other social institutions to individuals' needs and social problems.

The mission of the social work profession is rooted in a set of core values. These core values, embraced by social workers throughout the profession's history, are the foundation of social work's unique purpose and perspective:

- service
- social justice
- dignity and worth of the person
- importance of human relationships
- integrity
- competence.

This constellation of core values reflects what is unique to the social work profession. Core values, and the principles that flow from them, must be balanced within the context and complexity of the human experience.

Purpose of the NASW Code of Ethics

Professional ethics are at the core of social work. The profession has an obligation to articulate its basic values, ethical principles, and ethical standards. The *NASW Code of Ethics* sets forth these values, principles, and standards to guide social workers' conduct.

The *Code* is relevant to all social workers and social work students, regardless of their professional functions, the settings in which they work, or the populations they serve.

The *NASW Code of Ethics* serves six purposes:

1. The *Code* identifies core values on which social work's mission is based.
2. The *Code* summarizes broad ethical principles that reflect the profession's core values and establishes a set of specific ethical standards that should be used to guide social work practice.

3. The *Code* is designed to help social workers identify relevant considerations when professional obligations conflict or ethical uncertainties arise.
4. The *Code* provides ethical standards to which the general public can hold the social work profession accountable.
5. The *Code* socializes practitioners new to the field to social work's mission, values, ethical principles, and ethical standards.
6. The *Code* articulates standards that the social work profession itself can use to assess whether social workers have engaged in unethical conduct. NASW has formal procedures to adjudicate ethics complaints filed against its members.[1] In subscribing to this *Code,* social workers are required to cooperate in its implementation, participate in NASW adjudication proceedings, and abide by any NASW disciplinary rulings or sanctions based on it.

The *Code* offers a set of values, principles, and standards to guide decision making and conduct when ethical issues arise. It does not provide a set of rules that prescribe how social workers should act in all situations. Specific applications of the *Code* must take into account the context in which it is being considered and the possibility of conflicts among the *Code*'s values, principles, and standards. Ethical responsibilities flow from all human relationships, from the personal and familial to the social and professional.

Further, the *NASW Code of Ethics* does not specify which values, principles, and standards are most important and ought to outweigh others in instances when they conflict. Reasonable differences of opinion can and do exist among social workers with respect to the ways in which values, ethical principles, and ethical standards should be rank ordered when they conflict. Ethical decision making in a given situation must apply the informed judgment of the individual social worker and should also consider how the issues would be judged in a peer review process where the ethical standards of the profession would be applied.

Ethical decision making is a process. There are many instances in social work where simple answers are not available to resolve complex ethical issues. Social workers should take into consideration all the values, principles, and standards in this *Code* that are relevant to any situation in which ethical judgment is warranted. Social workers' decisions and actions should be consistent with the spirit as well as the letter of this *Code.*

In addition to this *Code,* there are many other sources of information about ethical thinking that may be useful. Social workers should consider ethical theory and principles generally, social work theory and research, laws, regulations, agency policies, and other relevant codes of ethics, recognizing that among codes of ethics social workers should consider the *NASW Code of Ethics* as their primary source. Social workers also should be aware of the impact on ethical decision making of their clients' and their own personal values and cultural and religious beliefs and practices. They should be aware of any conflicts between personal and professional values and deal with them responsibly. For additional guidance social workers should consult the relevant literature on professional ethics and ethical decision making and seek appropriate consultation when faced with ethical dilemmas. This may involve consultation with an agency-based or social work organization's ethics committee, a regulatory body, knowledgeable colleagues, supervisors, or legal counsel.

Instances may arise when social workers' ethical obligations conflict with agency policies or relevant laws or regulations. When such conflicts occur, social workers must make a responsible effort to resolve the conflict in a manner that is consistent with the values, principles, and standards expressed in this *Code.* If a reasonable resolution of the conflict does not appear possible, social workers should seek proper consultation before making a decision.

The *NASW Code of Ethics* is to be used by NASW and by individuals, agencies, organizations, and bodies (such as licensing and regulatory boards, professional liability insurance providers,

---

[1]For information on NASW adjudication procedures, see *NASW Procedures for the Adjudication of Grievances.*

courts of law, agency boards of directors, government agencies, and other professional groups) that choose to adopt it or use it as a frame of reference. Violation of standards in this *Code* does not automatically imply legal liability or violation of the law. Such determination can only be made in the context of legal and judicial proceedings. Alleged violations of the *Code* would be subject to a peer review process. Such processes are generally separate from legal or administrative procedures and insulated from legal review or proceedings to allow the profession to counsel and discipline its own members.

A code of ethics cannot guarantee ethical behavior. Moreover, a code of ethics cannot resolve all ethical issues or disputes or capture the richness and complexity involved in striving to make responsible choices within a moral community. Rather, a code of ethics sets forth values, ethical principles, and ethical standards to which professionals aspire and by which their actions can be judged. Social workers' ethical behavior should result from their personal commitment to engage in ethical practice. The *NASW Code of Ethics* reflects the commitment of all social workers to uphold the profession's values and to act ethically. Principles and standards must be applied by individuals of good character who discern moral questions and, in good faith, seek to make reliable ethical judgments.

ETHICAL PRINCIPLES

The following broad ethical principles are based on social work's core values of service, social justice, dignity and worth of the person, importance of human relationships, integrity, and competence. These principles set forth ideals to which all social workers should aspire.

Value: *Service*

Ethical Principle: *Social workers' primary goal is to help people in need and to address social problems.*

Social workers elevate service to others above self-interest. Social workers draw on their knowledge, values, and skills to help people in need and to address social problems. Social workers are encouraged to volunteer some portion of their professional skills with no expectation of significant financial return (pro bono service).

Value: *Social Justice*

Ethical Principle: *Social workers challenge social injustice.*

Social workers pursue social change, particularly with and on behalf of vulnerable and oppressed individuals and groups of people. Social workers' social change efforts are focused primarily on issues of poverty, unemployment, discrimination, and other forms of social injustice. These activities seek to promote sensitivity to and knowledge about oppression and cultural and ethnic diversity. Social workers strive to ensure access to needed information, services, and resources; equality of opportunity; and meaningful participation in decision making for all people.

Value: *Dignity and Worth of the Person*

Ethical Principle: *Social workers respect the inherent dignity and worth of the person.*

Social workers treat each person in a caring and respectful fashion, mindful of individual differences and cultural and ethnic diversity. Social workers promote clients' socially responsible self-determination. Social workers seek to enhance clients' capacity and opportunity to change and to address their own needs. Social workers are cognizant of their dual responsibility to clients and to the broader society. They seek to resolve conflicts between clients' interests and the broader society's interests in a socially responsible manner consistent with the values, ethical principles, and ethical standards of the profession.

Value: *Importance of Human Relationships*

Ethical Principle: *Social workers recognize the central importance of human relationships.*

Social workers understand that relationships between and among people are an important vehicle for change. Social workers engage people as partners in the helping process. Social workers seek to strengthen relationships among people in a purposeful effort to promote, restore, maintain, and enhance the well-being of individuals, families, social groups, organizations, and communities.

Value: *Integrity*

Ethical Principle: *Social workers behave in a trustworthy manner.*

Social workers are continually aware of the profession's mission, values, ethical principles, and ethical standards and practice in a manner consistent with them. Social workers act honestly and responsibly and promote ethical practices on the part of the organizations with which they are affiliated.

Value: *Competence*

Ethical Principle: *Social workers practice within their areas of competence and develop and enhance their professional expertise.*

Social workers continually strive to increase their professional knowledge and skills and to apply them in practice. Social workers should aspire to contribute to the knowledge base of the profession.

ETHICAL STANDARDS

The following ethical standards are relevant to the professional activities of all social workers. These standards concern (1) social workers' ethical responsibilities to clients, (2) social workers' ethical responsibilities to colleagues, (3) social workers' ethical responsibilities in practice settings, (4) social workers' ethical responsibilities as professionals, (5) social workers' ethical responsibilities to the social work profession, and (6) social workers' ethical responsibilities to the broader society.

Some of the standards that follow are enforceable guidelines for professional conduct, and some are aspirational. The extent to which each standard is enforceable is a matter of professional judgment to be exercised by those responsible for reviewing alleged violations of ethical standards.

1. Social Workers' Ethical Responsibilities to Clients

1.01 Commitment to Clients
Social workers' primary responsibility is to promote the well-being of clients. In general, clients' interests are primary. However, social workers' responsibility to the larger society or specific legal obligations may on limited occasions supersede the loyalty owed clients, and clients should be so advised. (Examples include when a social worker is required by law to report that a client has abused a child or has threatened to harm self or others.)

1.02 Self-Determination
Social workers respect and promote the right of clients to self-determination and assist clients in their efforts to identify and clarify their goals. Social workers may limit clients' right to self-determination when, in the social workers' professional judgment, clients' actions or potential actions pose a serious, foreseeable, and imminent risk to themselves or others.

1.03 Informed Consent

(a) Social workers should provide services to clients only in the context of a professional relationship based, when appropriate, on valid informed consent. Social workers should use clear and understandable language to inform clients of the purpose of the services, risks related to the services, limits to services because of the requirements of a third-party payer, relevant costs, reasonable alternatives, clients' right to refuse or withdraw consent, and the time frame covered by the consent. Social workers should provide clients with an opportunity to ask questions.

(b) In instances when clients are not literate or have difficulty understanding the primary language used in the practice setting, social workers should take steps to ensure clients' comprehension. This may include providing clients with a detailed verbal explanation or arranging for a qualified interpreter or translator whenever possible.

(c) In instances when clients lack the capacity to provide informed consent, social workers should protect clients' interests by seeking permission from an appropriate third party, informing clients consistent with the clients' level of understanding. In such instances social workers should seek to ensure that the third party acts in a manner consistent with clients' wishes and interests. Social workers should take reasonable steps to enhance such clients' ability to give informed consent.

(d) In instances when clients are receiving services involuntarily, social workers should provide information about the nature and extent of services and about the extent of clients' right to refuse service.

(e) Social workers who provide services via electronic media (such as computer, telephone, radio, and television) should inform recipients of the limitations and risks associated with such services.

(f) Social workers should obtain clients' informed consent before audiotaping or videotaping clients or permitting observation of services to clients by a third party.

1.04 Competence

(a) Social workers should provide services and represent themselves as competent only within the boundaries of their education, training, license, certification, consultation received, supervised experience, or other relevant professional experience.

(b) Social workers should provide services in substantive areas or use intervention techniques or approaches that are new to them only after engaging in appropriate study, training, consultation, and supervision from people who are competent in those interventions or techniques.

(c) When generally recognized standards do not exist with respect to an emerging area of practice, social workers should exercise careful judgment and take responsible steps (including appropriate education, research, training, consultation, and supervision) to ensure the competence of their work and to protect clients from harm.

1.05 Cultural Competence and Social Diversity

(a) Social workers should understand culture and its function in human behavior and society, recognizing the strengths that exist in all cultures.

(b) Social workers should have a knowledge base of their clients' cultures and be able to demonstrate competence in the provision of services that are sensitive to clients' cultures and to differences among people and cultural groups.

(c) Social workers should obtain education about and seek to understand the nature of social diversity and oppression with respect to race, ethnicity, national origin, color, sex, sexual orientation, age, marital status, political belief, religion, and mental or physical disability.

1.06 Conflicts of Interest

(a) Social workers should be alert to and avoid conflicts of interest that interfere with the exercise of professional discretion and impartial judgment. Social workers should inform clients when a real or potential conflict of interest arises and take reasonable steps to resolve the issue in a manner that makes the clients' interests primary and protects clients' interests to the greatest extent possible. In some cases, protecting clients' interests may require termination of the professional relationship with proper referral of the client.

(b) Social workers should not take unfair advantage of any professional relationship or exploit others to further their personal, religious, political, or business interests.

(c) Social workers should not engage in dual or multiple relationships with clients or former clients in which there is a risk of exploitation or potential harm to the client. In instances when dual or multiple relationships are unavoidable, social workers should take steps to protect clients and are responsible for setting clear, appropriate, and culturally sensitive boundaries. (Dual or multiple relationships occur when social workers relate to clients in more than one relationship, whether professional, social, or business. Dual or multiple relationships can occur simultaneously or consecutively.)

(d) When social workers provide services to two or more people who have a relationship with each other (for example, couples, family members), social workers should clarify with all parties which individuals will be considered clients and the nature of social workers' professional obligations to the various individuals who are receiving services. Social workers who anticipate a conflict of interest among the individuals receiving services or who anticipate having to perform in potentially conflicting roles (for example, when a social worker is asked to testify in a child custody dispute or divorce proceedings involving clients) should clarify their role with the parties involved and take appropriate action to minimize any conflict of interest.

1.07 Privacy and Confidentiality

(a) Social workers should respect clients' right to privacy. Social workers should not solicit private information from clients unless it is essential to providing services or conducting social work evaluation or research. Once private information is shared, standards of confidentiality apply.

(b) Social workers may disclose confidential information when appropriate with valid consent from a client or a person legally authorized to consent on behalf of a client.

(c) Social workers should protect the confidentiality of all information obtained in the course of professional service, except for compelling professional reasons. The general expectation that social workers will keep information confidential does not apply when disclosure is necessary to prevent serious, foreseeable, and imminent harm to a client or other identifiable person. In all instances, social workers should disclose the least amount of confidential information necessary to achieve the desired purpose; only information that is directly relevant to the purpose for which the disclosure is made should be revealed.

(d) Social workers should inform clients, to the extent possible, about the disclosure of confidential information and the potential consequences, when feasible before the disclosure is made. This applies whether social workers disclose confidential information on the basis of a legal requirement or client consent.

(e) Social workers should discuss with clients and other interested parties the nature of confidentiality and limitations of clients' right to confidentiality. Social workers should review with clients circumstances where confidential information may be requested and where disclosure of confidential information may be legally required. This discussion should occur as soon as possible in the social worker–client relationship and as needed throughout the course of the relationship.

(f) When social workers provide counseling services to families, couples, or groups, social workers should seek agreement among the parties involved concerning each individual's right to confidentiality and obligation to preserve the confidentiality of information shared by others. Social workers should inform participants in family, couples, or group counseling that social workers cannot guarantee that all participants will honor such agreements.

(g)   Social workers should inform clients involved in family, couples, marital, or group counseling of the social worker's, employer's, and agency's policy concerning the social worker's disclosure of confidential information among the parties involved in the counseling.

(h)   Social workers should not disclose confidential information to third-party payers unless clients have authorized such disclosure.

(i)   Social workers should not discuss confidential information in any setting unless privacy can be ensured. Social workers should not discuss confidential information in public or semipublic areas such as hallways, waiting rooms, elevators, and restaurants.

(j)   Social workers should protect the confidentiality of clients during legal proceedings to the extent permitted by law. When a court of law or other legally authorized body orders social workers to disclose confidential or privileged information without a client's consent and such disclosure could cause harm to the client, social workers should request that the court withdraw the order or limit the order as narrowly as possible or maintain the records under seal, unavailable for public inspection.

(k)   Social workers should protect the confidentiality of clients when responding to requests from members of the media.

(l)   Social workers should protect the confidentiality of clients' written and electronic records and other sensitive information. Social workers should take reasonable steps to ensure that clients' records are stored in a secure location and that clients' records are not available to others who are not authorized to have access.

(m)   Social workers should take precautions to ensure and maintain the confidentiality of information transmitted to other parties through the use of computers, electronic mail, facsimile machines, telephones and telephone answering machines, and other electronic or computer technology. Disclosure of identifying information should be avoided whenever possible.

(n)   Social workers should transfer or dispose of clients' records in a manner that protects clients' confidentiality and is consistent with state statutes governing records and social work licensure.

(o)   Social workers should take reasonable precautions to protect client confidentiality in the event of the social worker's termination of practice, incapacitation, or death.

(p)   Social workers should not disclose identifying information when discussing clients for teaching or training purposes unless the client has consented to disclosure of confidential information.

(q)   Social workers should not disclose identifying information when discussing clients with consultants unless the client has consented to disclosure of confidential information or there is a compelling need for such disclosure.

(r)   Social workers should protect the confidentiality of deceased clients consistent with the preceding standards.

1.08 Access to Records

(a)   Social workers should provide clients with reasonable access to records concerning the clients. Social workers who are concerned that clients' access to their records could cause serious misunderstanding or harm to the client should provide assistance in interpreting the records and consultation with the client regarding the records. Social workers should limit clients' access to their records, or portions of their records, only in exceptional circumstances when there is compelling evidence that such access would cause serious harm to the client. Both clients' requests and the rationale for withholding some or all of the record should be documented in clients' files.

(b)   When providing clients with access to their records, social workers should take steps to protect the confidentiality of other individuals identified or discussed in such records.

1.09 Sexual Relationships

(a)   Social workers should under no circumstances engage in sexual activities or sexual contact with current clients, whether such contact is consensual or forced.

(b) Social workers should not engage in sexual activities or sexual contact with clients' relatives or other individuals with whom clients maintain a close personal relationship when there is a risk of exploitation or potential harm to the client. Sexual activity or sexual contact with clients' relatives or other individuals with whom clients maintain a personal relationship has the potential to be harmful to the client and may make it difficult for the social worker and client to maintain appropriate professional boundaries. Social workers—not their clients, their clients' relatives, or other individuals with whom the client maintains a personal relationship—assume the full burden for setting clear, appropriate, and culturally sensitive boundaries.

(c) Social workers should not engage in sexual activities or sexual contact with former clients because of the potential for harm to the client. If social workers engage in conduct contrary to this prohibition or claim that an exception to this prohibition is warranted because of extraordinary circumstances, it is social workers—not their clients—who assume the full burden of demonstrating that the former client has not been exploited, coerced, or manipulated, intentionally or unintentionally.

(d) Social workers should not provide clinical services to individuals with whom they have had a prior sexual relationship. Providing clinical services to a former sexual partner has the potential to be harmful to the individual and is likely to make it difficult for the social worker and individual to maintain appropriate professional boundaries.

1.10 Physical Contact
Social workers should not engage in physical contact with clients when there is a possibility of psychological harm to the client as a result of the contact (such as cradling or caressing clients). Social workers who engage in appropriate physical contact with clients are responsible for setting clear, appropriate, and culturally sensitive boundaries that govern such physical contact.

1.11 Sexual Harassment
Social workers should not sexually harass clients. Sexual harassment includes sexual advances, sexual solicitation, requests for sexual favors, and other verbal or physical conduct of a sexual nature.

1.12 Derogatory Language
Social workers should not use derogatory language in their written or verbal communications to or about clients. Social workers should use accurate and respectful language in all communications to and about clients.

1.13 Payment for Services
(a) When setting fees, social workers should ensure that the fees are fair, reasonable, and commensurate with the services performed. Consideration should be given to clients' ability to pay.

(b) Social workers should avoid accepting goods or services from clients as payment for professional services. Bartering arrangements, particularly involving services, create the potential for conflicts of interest, exploitation, and inappropriate boundaries in social workers' relationships with clients. Social workers should explore and may participate in bartering only in very limited circumstances when it can be demonstrated that such arrangements are an accepted practice among professionals in the local community, considered to be essential for the provision of services, negotiated without coercion, and entered into at the client's initiative and with the client's informed consent. Social workers who accept goods or services from clients as payment for professional services assume the full burden of demonstrating that this arrangement will not be detrimental to the client or the professional relationship.

(c) Social workers should not solicit a private fee or other remuneration for providing services to clients who are entitled to such available services through the social workers' employer or agency.

1.14 Clients Who Lack Decision-Making Capacity

When social workers act on behalf of clients who lack the capacity to make informed decisions, social workers should take reasonable steps to safeguard the interests and rights of those clients.

1.15 Interruption of Services

Social workers should make reasonable efforts to ensure continuity of services in the event that services are interrupted by factors such as unavailability, relocation, illness, disability, or death.

1.16 Termination of Services

(a) Social workers should terminate services to clients and professional relationships with them when such services and relationships are no longer required or no longer serve the clients' needs or interests.

(b) Social workers should take reasonable steps to avoid abandoning clients who are still in need of services. Social workers should withdraw services precipitously only under unusual circumstances, giving careful consideration to all factors in the situation and taking care to minimize possible adverse effects. Social workers should assist in making appropriate arrangements for continuation of services when necessary.

(c) Social workers in fee-for-service settings may terminate services to clients who are not paying an overdue balance if the financial contractual arrangements have been made clear to the client, if the client does not pose an imminent danger to self or others, and if the clinical and other consequences of the current nonpayment have been addressed and discussed with the client.

(d) Social workers should not terminate services to pursue a social, financial, or sexual relationship with a client.

(e) Social workers who anticipate the termination or interruption of services to clients should notify clients promptly and seek the transfer, referral, or continuation of services in relation to the clients' needs and preferences.

(f) Social workers who are leaving an employment setting should inform clients of appropriate options for the continuation of services and of the benefits and risks of the options.

2. Social Workers' Ethical Responsibilities to Colleagues

2.01 Respect

(a) Social workers should treat colleagues with respect and should represent accurately and fairly the qualifications, views, and obligations of colleagues.

(b) Social workers should avoid unwarranted negative criticism of colleagues in communications with clients or with other professionals. Unwarranted negative criticism may include demeaning comments that refer to colleagues' level of competence or to individuals' attributes such as race, ethnicity, national origin, color, sex, sexual orientation, age, marital status, political belief, religion, and mental or physical disability.

(c) Social workers should cooperate with social work colleagues and with colleagues of other professions when such cooperation serves the well-being of clients.

2.02 Confidentiality

Social workers should respect confidential information shared by colleagues in the course of their professional relationships and transactions. Social workers should ensure that such colleagues understand social workers' obligation to respect confidentiality and any exceptions related to it.

2.03 Interdisciplinary Collaboration

(a) Social workers who are members of an interdisciplinary team should participate in and contribute to decisions that affect the well-being of clients by drawing on the perspectives, values, and experiences of the social work profession. Professional and ethical obligations of the interdisciplinary team as a whole and of its individual members should be clearly established.

(b)   Social workers for whom a team decision raises ethical concerns should attempt to resolve the disagreement through appropriate channels. If the disagreement cannot be resolved, social workers should pursue other avenues to address their concerns consistent with client well-being.

2.04 Disputes Involving Colleagues
(a)   Social workers should not take advantage of a dispute between a colleague and an employer to obtain a position or otherwise advance the social workers' own interests.
(b)   Social workers should not exploit clients in disputes with colleagues or engage clients in any inappropriate discussion of conflicts between social workers and their colleagues.

2.05 Consultation
(a)   Social workers should seek the advice and counsel of colleagues whenever such consultation is in the best interests of clients.
(b)   Social workers should keep themselves informed about colleagues' areas of expertise and competencies. Social workers should seek consultation only from colleagues who have demonstrated knowledge, expertise, and competence related to the subject of the consultation.
(c)   When consulting with colleagues about clients, social workers should disclose the least amount of information necessary to achieve the purposes of the consultation.

2.06 Referral for Services
(a)   Social workers should refer clients to other professionals when the other professionals' specialized knowledge or expertise is needed to serve clients fully or when social workers believe that they are not being effective or making reasonable progress with clients and that additional service is required.
(b)   Social workers who refer clients to other professionals should take appropriate steps to facilitate an orderly transfer of responsibility. Social workers who refer clients to other professionals should disclose, with clients' consent, all pertinent information to the new service providers.
(c)   Social workers are prohibited from giving or receiving payment for a referral when no professional service is provided by the referring social worker.

2.07 Sexual Relationships
(a)   Social workers who function as supervisors or educators should not engage in sexual activities or contact with supervisees, students, trainees, or other colleagues over whom they exercise professional authority.
(b)   Social workers should avoid engaging in sexual relationships with colleagues when there is potential for a conflict of interest. Social workers who become involved in, or anticipate becoming involved in, a sexual relationship with a colleague have a duty to transfer professional responsibilities, when necessary, to avoid a conflict of interest.

2.08 Sexual Harassment
Social workers should not sexually harass supervisees, students, trainees, or colleagues. Sexual harassment includes sexual advances, sexual solicitation, requests for sexual favors, and other verbal or physical conduct of a sexual nature.

2.09 Impairment of Colleagues
(a)   Social workers who have direct knowledge of a social work colleague's impairment that is due to personal problems, psychosocial distress, substance abuse, or mental health difficulties and that interferes with practice effectiveness should consult with that colleague when feasible and assist the colleague in taking remedial action.
(b)   Social workers who believe that a social work colleague's impairment interferes with practice effectiveness and that the colleague has not taken adequate steps to address the impairment

should take action through appropriate channels established by employers, agencies, NASW, licensing and regulatory bodies, and other professional organizations.

2.10 Incompetence of Colleagues

(a) Social workers who have direct knowledge of a social work colleague's incompetence should consult with that colleague when feasible and assist the colleague in taking remedial action.

(b) Social workers who believe that a social work colleague is incompetent and has not taken adequate steps to address the incompetence should take action through appropriate channels established by employers, agencies, NASW, licensing and regulatory bodies, and other professional organizations.

2.11 Unethical Conduct of Colleagues

(a) Social workers should take adequate measures to discourage, prevent, expose, and correct the unethical conduct of colleagues.

(b) Social workers should be knowledgeable about established policies and procedures for handling concerns about colleagues' unethical behavior. Social workers should be familiar with national, state, and local procedures for handling ethics complaints. These include policies and procedures created by NASW, licensing and regulatory bodies, employers, agencies, and other professional organizations.

(c) Social workers who believe that a colleague has acted unethically should seek resolution by discussing their concerns with the colleague when feasible and when such discussion is likely to be productive.

(d) When necessary, social workers who believe that a colleague has acted unethically should take action through appropriate formal channels (such as contacting a state licensing board or regulatory body, an NASW committee on inquiry, or other professional ethics committees).

(e) Social workers should defend and assist colleagues who are unjustly charged with unethical conduct.

3.   Social Workers' Ethical Responsibilities in Practice Settings

3.01 Supervision and Consultation

(a) Social workers who provide supervision or consultation should have the necessary knowledge and skill to supervise or consult appropriately and should do so only within their areas of knowledge and competence.

(b) Social workers who provide supervision or consultation are responsible for setting clear, appropriate, and culturally sensitive boundaries.

(c) Social workers should not engage in any dual or multiple relationships with supervisees in which there is a risk of exploitation of or potential harm to the supervisee.

(d) Social workers who provide supervision should evaluate supervisees' performance in a manner that is fair and respectful.

3.02 Education and Training

(a) Social workers who function as educators, field instructors for students, or trainers should provide instruction only within their areas of knowledge and competence and should provide instruction based on the most current information and knowledge available in the profession.

(b) Social workers who function as educators or field instructors for students should evaluate students' performance in a manner that is fair and respectful.

(c) Social workers who function as educators or field instructors for students should take reasonable steps to ensure that clients are routinely informed when services are being provided by students.

(d) Social workers who function as educators or field instructors for students should not engage in any dual or multiple relationships with students in which there is a risk of exploitation or potential harm to the student. Social work educators and field instructors are responsible for setting clear, appropriate, and culturally sensitive boundaries.

3.03 Performance Evaluation
Social workers who have responsibility for evaluating the performance of others should fulfill such responsibility in a fair and considerate manner and on the basis of clearly stated criteria.

3.04 Client Records
(a) Social workers should take reasonable steps to ensure that documentation in records is accurate and reflects the services provided.
(b) Social workers should include sufficient and timely documentation in records to facilitate the delivery of services and to ensure continuity of services provided to clients in the future.
(c) Social workers' documentation should protect clients' privacy to the extent that is possible and appropriate and should include only information that is directly relevant to the delivery of services.
(d) Social workers should store records following the termination of services to ensure reasonable future access. Records should be maintained for the number of years required by state statutes or relevant contracts.

3.05 Billing
Social workers should establish and maintain billing practices that accurately reflect the nature and extent of services provided and that identify who provided the service in the practice setting.

3.06 Client Transfer
(a) When an individual who is receiving services from another agency or colleague contacts a social worker for services, the social worker should carefully consider the client's needs before agreeing to provide services. To minimize possible confusion and conflict, social workers should discuss with potential clients the nature of the clients' current relationship with other service providers and the implications, including possible benefits or risks, of entering into a relationship with a new service provider.
(b) If a new client has been served by another agency or colleague, social workers should discuss with the client whether consultation with the previous service provider is in the client's best interest.

3.07 Administration
(a) Social work administrators should advocate within and outside their agencies for adequate resources to meet clients' needs.
(b) Social workers should advocate for resource allocation procedures that are open and fair. When not all clients' needs can be met, an allocation procedure should be developed that is nondiscriminatory and based on appropriate and consistently applied principles.
(c) Social workers who are administrators should take reasonable steps to ensure that adequate agency or organizational resources are available to provide appropriate staff supervision.
(d) Social work administrators should take reasonable steps to ensure that the working environment for which they are responsible is consistent with and encourages compliance with the *NASW Code of Ethics*. Social work administrators should take reasonable steps to eliminate any conditions in their organizations that violate, interfere with, or discourage compliance with the *Code*.

3.08 Continuing Education and Staff Development
Social work administrators and supervisors should take reasonable steps to provide or arrange for continuing education and staff development for all staff for whom they are responsible. Continuing education and staff development should address current knowledge and emerging developments related to social work practice and ethics.

3.09 Commitments to Employers

(a) Social workers generally should adhere to commitments made to employers and employing organizations.

(b) Social workers should work to improve employing agencies' policies and procedures and the efficiency and effectiveness of their services.

(c) Social workers should take reasonable steps to ensure that employers are aware of social workers' ethical obligations as set forth in the *NASW Code of Ethics* and of the implications of those obligations for social work practice.

(d) Social workers should not allow an employing organization's policies, procedures, regulations, or administrative orders to interfere with their ethical practice of social work. Social workers should take reasonable steps to ensure that their employing organizations' practices are consistent with the *NASW Code of Ethics*.

(e) Social workers should act to prevent and eliminate discrimination in the employing organization's work assignments and in its employment policies and practices.

(f) Social workers should accept employment or arrange student field placements only in organizations that exercise fair personnel practices.

(g) Social workers should be diligent stewards of the resources of their employing organizations, wisely conserving funds where appropriate and never misappropriating funds or using them for unintended purposes.

3.10 Labor–Management Disputes

(a) Social workers may engage in organized action, including the formation of and participation in labor unions, to improve services to clients and working conditions.

(b) The actions of social workers who are involved in labor–management disputes, job actions, or labor strikes should be guided by the profession's values, ethical principles, and ethical standards. Reasonable differences of opinion exist among social workers concerning their primary obligation as professionals during an actual or threatened labor strike or job action. Social workers should carefully examine relevant issues and their possible impact on clients before deciding on a course of action.

4. Social Workers' Ethical Responsibilities as Professionals

4.01 Competence

(a) Social workers should accept responsibility or employment only on the basis of existing competence or the intention to acquire the necessary competence.

(b) Social workers should strive to become and remain proficient in professional practice and the performance of professional functions. Social workers should critically examine and keep current with emerging knowledge relevant to social work. Social workers should routinely review the professional literature and participate in continuing education relevant to social work practice and social work ethics.

(c) Social workers should base practice on recognized knowledge, including empirically based knowledge, relevant to social work and social work ethics.

4.02 Discrimination

Social workers should not practice, condone, facilitate, or collaborate with any form of discrimination on the basis of race, ethnicity, national origin, color, sex, sexual orientation, age, marital status, political belief, religion, or mental or physical disability.

4.03 Private Conduct

Social workers should not permit their private conduct to interfere with their ability to fulfill their professional responsibilities.

4.04 Dishonesty, Fraud, and Deception
Social workers should not participate in, condone, or be associated with dishonesty, fraud, or deception.

4.05 Impairment
(a) Social workers should not allow their own personal problems, psychosocial distress, legal problems, substance abuse, or mental health difficulties to interfere with their professional judgment and performance or to jeopardize the best interests of people for whom they have a professional responsibility.

(b) Social workers whose personal problems, psychosocial distress, legal problems, substance abuse, or mental health difficulties interfere with their professional judgment and performance should immediately seek consultation and take appropriate remedial action by seeking professional help, making adjustments in workload, terminating practice, or taking any other steps necessary to protect clients and others.

4.06 Misrepresentation
(a) Social workers should make clear distinctions between statements made and actions engaged in as a private individual and as a representative of the social work profession, a professional social work organization, or the social worker's employing agency.

(b) Social workers who speak on behalf of professional social work organizations should accurately represent the official and authorized positions of the organizations.

(c) Social workers should ensure that their representations to clients, agencies, and the public of professional qualifications, credentials, education, competence, affiliations, services provided, or results to be achieved are accurate. Social workers should claim only those relevant professional credentials they actually possess and take steps to correct any inaccuracies or misrepresentations of their credentials by others.

4.07 Solicitations
(a) Social workers should not engage in uninvited solicitation of potential clients who, because of their circumstances, are vulnerable to undue influence, manipulation, or coercion.

(b) Social workers should not engage in solicitation of testimonial endorsements (including solicitation of consent to use a client's prior statement as a testimonial endorsement) from current clients or from other people who, because of their particular circumstances, are vulnerable to undue influence.

4.08 Acknowledging Credit
(a) Social workers should take responsibility and credit, including authorship credit, only for work they have actually performed and to which they have contributed.

(b) Social workers should honestly acknowledge the work of and the contributions made by others.

5.   Social Workers' Ethical Responsibilities to the Social Work Profession

5.01 Integrity of the Profession
(a) Social workers should work toward the maintenance and promotion of high standards of practice.

(b) Social workers should uphold and advance the values, ethics, knowledge, and mission of the profession. Social workers should protect, enhance, and improve the integrity of the profession through appropriate study and research, active discussion, and responsible criticism of the profession.

(c) Social workers should contribute time and professional expertise to activities that promote respect for the value, integrity, and competence of the social work profession. These activities may include teaching, research, consultation, service, legislative testimony, presentations in the community, and participation in their professional organizations.

(d) Social workers should contribute to the knowledge base of social work and share with colleagues their knowledge related to practice, research, and ethics. Social workers should seek to con-tribute to the profession's literature and to share their knowledge at professional meetings and conferences.

(e) Social workers should act to prevent the unauthorized and unqualified practice of social work.

5.02 Evaluation and Research

(a) Social workers should monitor and evaluate policies, the implementation of programs, and practice interventions.

(b) Social workers should promote and facilitate evaluation and research to contribute to the development of knowledge.

(c) Social workers should critically examine and keep current with emerging knowledge relevant to social work and fully use evaluation and research evidence in their professional practice.

(d) Social workers engaged in evaluation or research should carefully consider possible consequences and should follow guidelines developed for the protection of evaluation and research participants. Appropriate institutional review boards should be consulted.

(e) Social workers engaged in evaluation or research should obtain voluntary and written informed consent from participants, when appropriate, without any implied or actual deprivation or penalty for refusal to participate; without undue inducement to participate; and with due regard for participants' well-being, privacy, and dignity. Informed consent should include information about the nature, extent, and duration of the participation requested and disclosure of the risks and benefits of participation in the research.

(f) When evaluation or research participants are incapable of giving informed consent, social workers should provide an appropriate explanation to the participants, obtain the participants' assent to the extent they are able, and obtain written consent from an appropriate proxy.

(g) Social workers should never design or conduct evaluation or research that does not use consent procedures, such as certain forms of naturalistic observation and archival research, unless rigorous and responsible review of the research has found it to be justified because of its prospective scientific, educational, or applied value and unless equally effective alternative procedures that do not involve waiver of consent are not feasible.

(h) Social workers should inform participants of their right to withdraw from evaluation and research at any time without penalty.

(i) Social workers should take appropriate steps to ensure that participants in evaluation and research have access to appropriate supportive services.

(j) Social workers engaged in evaluation or research should protect participants from unwarranted physical or mental distress, harm, danger, or deprivation.

(k) Social workers engaged in the evaluation of services should discuss collected information only for professional purposes and only with people professionally concerned with this information.

(l) Social workers engaged in evaluation or research should ensure the anonymity or confidentiality of participants and of the data obtained from them. Social workers should inform participants of any limits of confidentiality, the measures that will be taken to ensure confidentiality, and when any records containing research data will be destroyed.

(m) Social workers who report evaluation and research results should protect participants' confidentiality by omitting identifying information unless proper consent has been obtained authorizing disclosure.

(n) Social workers should report evaluation and research findings accurately. They should not fabricate or falsify results and should take steps to correct any errors later found in published data using standard publication methods.

(o)   Social workers engaged in evaluation or research should be alert to and avoid conflicts of interest and dual relationships with participants, should inform participants when a real or potential conflict of interest arises, and should take steps to resolve the issue in a manner that makes participants' interests primary.

(p)   Social workers should educate themselves, their students, and their colleagues about responsible research practices.

6.   Social Workers' Ethical Responsibilities to the Broader Society

6.01 Social Welfare
Social workers should promote the general welfare of society, from local to global levels, and the development of people, their communities, and their environments. Social workers should advocate for living conditions conducive to the fulfillment of basic human needs and should promote social, economic, political, and cultural values and institutions that are compatible with the realization of social justice.

6.02 Public Participation
Social workers should facilitate informed participation by the public in shaping social policies and institutions.

6.03 Public Emergencies
Social workers should provide appropriate professional services in public emergencies to the greatest extent possible.

6.04 Social and Political Action
(a)   Social workers should engage in social and political action that seeks to ensure that all people have equal access to the resources, employment, services, and opportunities they require to meet their basic human needs and to develop fully. Social workers should be aware of the impact of the political arena on practice and should advocate for changes in policy and legislation to improve social conditions in order to meet basic human needs and promote social justice.

(b)   Social workers should act to expand choice and opportunity for all people, with special regard for vulnerable, disadvantaged, oppressed, and exploited people and groups.

(c)   Social workers should promote conditions that encourage respect for cultural and social diversity within the United States and globally. Social workers should promote policies and practices that demonstrate respect for difference, support the expansion of cultural knowledge and resources, advocate for programs and institutions that demonstrate cultural competence, and promote policies that safeguard the rights of and confirm equity and social justice for all people.

(d)   Social workers should act to prevent and eliminate domination of, exploitation of, and discrimination against any person, group, or class on the basis of race, ethnicity, national origin, color, sex, sexual orientation, age, marital status, political belief, religion, or mental or physical disability.

Appendix 2. Reader's Guides

The Reader's Guides from the 19th edition of the *Encyclopedia of Social Work* have been updated wherever appropriate. Entries found in this *Supplement* are followed by the year "*2003.*" Entries found in the *1997 Supplement* are followed by the year "*1997.*" All other entries can be found in alphabetic order in the three-volume *Encyclopedia*.

Abuse and Neglect
  Child Abuse and Neglect Overview
  Child Abuse and Neglect: Direct Practice
  Domestic Violence
  Domestic Violence: Gay Men and Lesbians, *1997*
  Domestic Violence: Legal Issues
  Elder Abuse

Adolescents
  Adolescence Overview
  Adolescent Pregnancy
  Adolescents: Direct Practice
  Gay and Lesbian Adolescents
  Runaways and Homeless Youths

Adults
  Adult Corrections
  Adult Courts
  Adult Day Care
  Adult Foster Care
  Adult Protective Services
  Aging Overview
  Aging: Alzheimer's Disease and Other Disabilities, *1997*
  Aging: Direct Service
  Aging: Public Policy Issues and Trends
  Aging: Racial and Ethnic Groups, *1997*
  Aging: Services
  Aging: Social Work Practice
  Baby Boomers
  Elder Abuse
  Men Overview
  Men: Direct Practice
  Women Overview
  Women: Direct Practice

African Americans
  African Americans Overview
  African American Pioneers in Social Work

African Americans: Caribbean
African Americans: Immigrants
Haitian Americans

Aging
  Adult Day Services
  Adult Foster Care
  Adult Protective Services
  Aging Overview
  Aging: Alzheimer's Disease and Other Disabilities, *1997*
  Aging: Direct Practice
  Aging: Public Policy Issues and Trends
  Aging: Racial and Ethnic Groups, *1997*
  Aging: Services
  Aging: Social Work Practice
  Elder Abuse
  End-of-Life Decisions
  Family Caregiving
  Hospice
  Long-Term Care
  Medicare and Medicaid: Health Policy, *2003*
  Retirement and Pension Programs
  Retirement, Private Pensions, and Individual Retirement Accounts, *2003*

AIDS/HIV
  HIV/AIDS Overview
  HIV/AIDS: Direct Practice
  HIV/AIDS: Men
  HIV/AIDS: Pediatric
  HIV/AIDS: Women

Asian Americans
  Asian Americans Overview
  Asian Americans: Chinese
  Asian Americans: Japanese
  Asian Americans: Southeast Asians
  Asian Indians
  Pacific Islanders

Health Care: Homeless People
Homelessness
Hunger, Nutrition, and Food Programs
Income Distribution
Income Security Overview
JOBS Program
Oppression, *1997*
Poverty
Rural Poverty
Social Development
Social Security
Supplemental Security Income
Temporary Assistance for Needy Families, *2003*
Temporary Assistance to Needy Families, *1997*
Welfare Employment Programs: Evaluation
Working Poor, *1997*

Professional Associations
Council on Social Work Education
International Social Welfare: Organizations and Activities
National Association of Social Workers
Special-Interest Professional Associations

Public Assistance
Aid to Families with Dependent Children
General Assistance
Income Security Overview
JOBS Program
Supplemental Security Income
Temporary Assistance for Needy Families, *2003*
Temporary Assistance to Needy Families, *1997*
Welfare Employment Programs: Evaluation

Public Policy
Advocacy
Aging: Public Policy and Trends
Conservatism and Social Welfare, *2003*
Deinstitutionalization
Developmental Disabilities: Definitions and Policies
Federal Legislation and Administrative Rule Making
Federal Social Legislation from 1961 to 1994
Federal Social Legislation from 1994 to 1997, *1997*
Health Care: Policy Development, *1997*
Health Services Systems Policy

Income Security Overview
Mass Media
Medicare and Medicaid: Health Policy, *2003*
Policy Analysis
Public Social Services, *See* Reader's Guide
Social Welfare Policy
Social Workers in Politics
Substance Abuse: Federal, State, and Local Policies

Public Social Services
Child Welfare Overview
Family Preservation and Home-Based Services
General Assistance
Health Services Systems Policy
Hunger, Nutrition, and Food Programs
Income Security Overview
JOBS Program
Medicare and Medicaid: Health Policy, *2003*
Public Health Services
Public Policy, *See* Reader's Guide
Public Social Services
Social Security
Social Service Delivery, *See* Reader's Guide
Social Welfare Expenditures: Public
Social Welfare Policy
Supplemental Security Income
Temporary Assistance for Needy Families, *2003*
Temporary Assistance to Needy Families, *1997*
Veterans and Veterans Services
Welfare Employment Programs: Evaluation

Racial and Ethnic Groups
African American Pioneers in Social Work
African Americans Overview
African Americans: Caribbean
African Americans: Immigrants
Aging: Racial and Ethnic Groups, *1997*
Alaska Natives
American Indians
Asian Americans Overview
Asian Americans: Chinese
Asian Americans: Japanese
Asian Americans: Southeast Asians
Asian Indians
Ethnic-Sensitive Practice
Haitian Americans
Hispanics Overview
Hispanics: Cubans

Appendix 3. Acronyms

AA	Alcoholics Anonymous
AAFP	American Academy of Family Practice
AAFRC	American Association of Fund-Raising Counsel
AAGW	American Association of Group Workers
AALL	American Association for Labor Legislation
AAMD	American Association on Mental Deficiency
AAMFT	American Association of Marriage and Family Therapists
AAMR	American Association on Mental Retardation
AAMSW	American Association of Medical Social Workers
AAP	affirmative action program
AAPSW	American Association of Psychiatric Social Workers
AARP	American Association of Retired Persons
AASSW	American Association of Schools of Social Work
AASSWB	American Association of State Social Work Boards
AASW	American Association of Social Workers
AB	Aid to the Blind
ABE	American Board of Examiners in Clinical Social Work
ABW	average body weight
ACEHSA	Accrediting Commission on Education for Health Services Administration
ACLU	American Civil Liberties Union
ACM	anticult movement
ACOAs	adult children of alcoholics
ACOSA	Association of Community Organization and Social Administration
ACSUS	AIDS Cost and Service Utilization Survey
ACSW	Academy of Certified Social Workers
ACT	assertive community treatment
ACT-UP	AIDS Coalition to Unleash Power
ADA	Americans with Disabilities Act of 1990
ADAMHA	Alcohol, Drug Abuse, and Mental Health Administration
ADC	adult day care
ADC	Aid to Dependent Children
ADHD	attention-deficit hyperactivity disorder
ADL	activities of daily living
AFAR	American Foundation for AIDS Research
AFDC	Aid to Families with Dependent Children
AFDC-UP	Aid to Families with Dependent Children-Unemployed Parent program
AFL-CIO	American Federation of Labor–Congress of Industrial Organizations
AFRAIDS	fear of AIDS
AFSCME	American Federation of State, County, and Municipal Employees
AFSW	Association of Federation Social Workers
AFT	American Federation of Teachers
AGI	adjusted gross income
AHA	American Hospital Association
AID	Agency for International Development
AIDS	acquired immune deficiency syndrome

AIM	Aid to Imprisoned Mothers
AIME	average indexed monthly earnings
AIRS	Alliance of Information and Referral Systems
ALMACA	Association of Labor-Management Administrators and Consultants on Alcoholism
AMA	American Medical Association
AMFAR	American Foundation for AIDS Research
ANCSA	Alaska Native Claims Settlement Act
ANSWER	Action Network for Social Work Education and Research
AoA	Administration on Aging
APA	American Psychiatric Association
APMs	annual program meetings
APS	adult protective services
APTD	Aid to the Permanently and Totally Disabled
APWA	American Public Welfare Association
ARC	AIDS-related complex
ARIES	Assistance to Resource Institutions for Enterprise Support Project
ARROW	Americans for Restitution and Righting of Old Wrongs
ASAP	Automated Screening and Assessment Package
ASAT	Association for Science in Autism Treatment
ASCO	Association for the Study of Community Organizations
ASH	Action on Smoking and Health
ASL	American Sign Language
ASO	AIDS services organizations
ASPA	American Society for Personnel Administrators
ASSA	American Social Science Association
ASSIST	American Stop Smoking Intervention Study
ASWB	Association of Social Work Boards
AUPHA	Association of University Programs in Health Administration
AZT	azidothymidine
BCRS	Bertha Capen Reynolds Society
BLS	Bureau of Labor Statistics
BPD	Baccalaureate Program Directors
BSW	bachelor of social work
CAB	Citizens Advice Bureau (British)
CAP	Community Action Program
CAPTA	Child Abuse Prevention and Treatment Act
CARE	Community and Resource Exchange
CARE	Comprehensive AIDS Resources Emergency
CARE	Cooperative for American Relief Everywhere, Inc.
CASA	court-appointed special advocate
CASP	Comprehensive Annual Services Plan
CASS	computer-assisted social services
CASSP	Child and Adolescent Service System Program
CBR	community-based research
CCC	Competence Certification Commission
CCDBG	Child Care and Development Block Grant
CCDF	Child Care and Development Fund
CCETSW	Central Council for Education and Training in Social Work
CCIP	Center for Children of Incarcerated Parents
CCMC	Committee on the Costs of Medical Care

CCMS	Child Care Management Service
CCS	Crippled Children's Services
CCSSO	Council of Chief State School Officers
CDC	Centers for Disease Control and Prevention
CDC	community development corporation
CDF	Chapter Development Fund
CD-I	compact disk-interactive
CD-ROM	compact disk-read-only memory
CEOs	chief executive officers
CES	Current Employment Statistics
CETA	Comprehensive Employment and Training Act
CEUs/CECs	continuing education units/credits
CFC	Combined Federal Campaign
CFS	Community Financial Service
CHAMPUS	Civilian Health and Medical Program of the Uniformed Services
CHAP	Children Have a Potential
CHAP	Comprehensive Homeless Assistance Plan
CHAS	Comprehensive Housing Affordability Strategy
CHIP	Comprehensive Health Insurance Plan
CHP	Comprehensive Health Planning and Public Health Services Amendments
CIA	Central Intelligence Agency
CIAS	Committee on Inter-Association Structure
CIP	Council of International Programs
CLAIM	Chicago Legal Aid for Imprisoned Mothers
CMHC	community mental health centers
CMHCA	Community Mental Health Centers Act
CMHS	Center for Mental Health Services
CMHSA	Community Mental Health Services Act
CMV	cytomegalovirus
CNHI	Committee of One Hundred for National Health Insurance
COA	Commission on Accreditation
COAs	children of alcoholics
COBRA	Comprehensive Omnibus Budget Reconciliation Act
CODAs	children of deaf adults
COI	Committee on Inquiry
COMPSYCH	computerized software service for psychologists
CON	certificate of need
COPA	community-oriented primary care
CORE	Congress of Racial Equality
CORPA	Commission on Recognition of Postsecondary Accreditation
COS	Charity Organization Societies
COSAs	children of substance abusers
COSSMHO	Coalition of Spanish-Speaking Mental Health Organizations
CPAI	Correctional Program Assessment Inventory
CPC	child protective services
CPI	consumer price index
CPS	Child Protective Services
CPS	Current Population Survey
CPS	curriculum policy statement
CRA	Community Reinvestment Act
CREP	Cuban Refugee Emergency Program
CSA	Child Support Assurance

C-SAP	Centers for Substance Abuse Prevention
C-SAT	Centers for Substance Abuse Treatment
CSCE	Commission on Security and Cooperation in Europe
CSFII	Continuing Survey of Food Intakes by Individuals
CSHCN	children with special health care needs
CSOs	Community Service Organizations
CSWE	Council on Social Work Education
CVS	chorionic villus sampling
CWA	Communications Workers of America
CWEP	Community Work Experience Program
CWLA	Child Welfare League of America
CWS	Child Welfare Services
CWV	Community Wealth Ventures
DAWN	Drug Abuse Warning Network
DB	decibel
DBMS	database management system
DBP	defined benefit plan
DCC	dependent care credit
DCP	defined contribution plan
D&D	design and development
DdC	dideoxycytidine
Ddl	dideoxyinosine
DEA	Drug Enforcement Administration
DHEW	U.S. Department of Health, Education, and Welfare
DHHS	U.S. Department of Health and Human Services
DII	Disability Insurance
DipSW	Diploma in Social Work
DMA	Department of Memorial Affairs
DNA	deoxyribonucleic acid
DNR	Do Not Resuscitate
DoD	U.S. Department of Defense
DRG	diagnosis-related group
DSM	*Diagnostic and Statistical Manual of Mental Disorders*
DSS	decision support system
DSW	doctor of social work
DUI	driving under the influence
DVB	Department of Veterans Benefits
DVI	digital video interactive
DWI	driving while intoxicated
EAP	employee assistance program
EAPA	Employee Assistance Professionals Association
EBP	evidence-based practice
EBRI	Employee Benefit Research Institute
EBT	electronic benefits transfer
ECA	Epidemiologic Catchment Area
ECOSOC	Economic and Social Council
EDI	economic development initiative
EEO	equal employment opportunity
EEOC	Equal Employment Opportunity Commission
EIC	earned income credit

EITC	earned income tax credit
ELAN	Education Legislative Action Network
ELISA	enzyme-linked immunosorbent assay
E-mail	electronic mail
EMSC	emergency medical services for children
ENIAC	Electronic Numerical Integrator and Computer
EOA	Economic Opportunity Act
EPA	Environmental Protection Agency
EPO	exclusive provider organization
EPSS	electronic performance support system
ERISA	Employee Retirement Income Security Act of 1974
ES	effective size
ESL	English as a second language
EZ	empowerment zone
EZ-EC	empowerment zone and enterprise community
FAO	Food and Agriculture Organization
FAP	Family Assistance Program
FAS	fetal alcohol syndrome
FBI	Federal Bureau of Investigation
FDA	Food and Drug Administration
FEHBA	Federal Employees Health Benefits Act
FEMA	Federal Emergency Management Agency
FERA	Federal Emergency Relief Administration
FHA	Federal Housing Administration
FICA	Federal Insurance Contributions Act
FIDCR	Federal Interagency Day Care Requirements
FLE	Family Life Education
FLSA	Fair Labor Standards Act
FmHA	Farmers Home Administration
FMLA	Family and Medical Leave Act
FNS	Food and Nutrition Service
FOSR	Function, Organization, and Structure Review
FPAs	Family Program Administrators
FSA	Federal Security Administration
FSAA	Family Service Association of America
FTC	Federal Trade Commission
FWAA	Family Welfare Association of America
FY	fiscal year
FYSB	Family and Youth Services Bureau
GA	General Assistance
GADE	Group for the Advancement of Doctoral Education
GAI	guaranteed annual income
GAIN	Greater Avenues to Independence
GAO	U.S. General Accounting Office
GARF	Global Assessment of Relational Functioning
GDP	gross domestic product
GED	general equivalency diploma
GEM	Geriatric Evaluation and Management
GEMINI	Growth and Equity through Microenterprise Investments and Institutions
GNP	gross national product

GRECC	Geriatric Research Education and Clinical Centers
GRID	gay-related immune disorder
4-H	Head, Heart, Hands, and Health
HCFA	Health Care Financing Administration
HCSA	Hate Crime Statistics Act
HHS	U.S. Department of Health and Human Services
HI	Hospital Insurance
HIP	Helping Incarcerated Parents
HIV	human immunodeficiency virus
HIV/AIDS	HIV disease
HMO	health maintenance organization
HRD	(National) Health, Planning, and Resources Development Act
HRR	Human Rights Report
HRSA	Health Resources and Services Administration
HSAs	health system agencies
HTML	hypertext markup language
HUD	U.S. Department of Housing and Urban Development
Human SERVE	Human Service Employees Registration and Voter Education
Hz	hertz
IASSW	International Association of Schools of Social Work
IASWR	Institute for the Advancement of Social Work Research
ICD	International Classification of Diseases
ICSSW	International Committee of Schools of Social Work
ICSW	International Congress of Social Welfare
ICWA	Indian Child Welfare Act
IDA	individual development account
IDA	injection drug abusers
IDEA	Individuals with Disabilities Education Act
IDU	injecting drug use
IEP	individualized educational program
IFSW	International Federation of Social Workers
IHHS	In-Home Health Services
IHS	Indian Health Service
ILO	International Labour Organization
INS	Immigration and Naturalization Service
IOM	Institute of Medicine
IPEC	International Programme on the Elimination of Child Labour
IPO	independent practice organization
IQ	intelligence quotient
I&R	information and referral
IRCA	Immigration Reform and Control Act of 1986
IRS	Internal Revenue Service
IS	information system
ISP	Influencing State Policy
ITV	interactive television
IUCISD	Interuniversity Consortium on International Social Development
IUDs	intrauterine devices
IUPAE	Independent Union of Public Aid Employees
IV	intravenous
IVD	interactive video disk

JAMA	*Journal of the American Medical Association*
JCAHO	Joint Commission on Accreditation of Healthcare Organizations
JJDPA	Juvenile Justice and Delinquency Prevention Act
JOBS	Job Opportunities and Basic Skills Training
JTPA	Job Training and Partnership Act
LAN	local area network
LEAA	Law Enforcement Assistance Administration
LRU	La Raza Unida
LULAC	League of United Latin American Citizens
LULU	locally unwanted land uses
MADD	Mothers Against Drunk Driving
MAG	Mothers Against Gangs
MAGIC	Merced Automated Global Information Control
MALDEF	Mexican American Legal Defense and Education Fund
MAP	membership assistance program
MAPA	Mexican American Political Association
MASH	Make Something Happen
MCC	Metropolitan Community Church
MCH	maternal and child health
MCHS	Maternal and Child Health Services
MDRC	Manpower Development Research Corporation
MIS	management information system
MOE	maintenance of effort
MORE	Member-Organized Resource Exchange
MPSW	military psychiatric social worker
MRI	magnetic resonance imaging
MSA	metropolitan statistical area
MSSP	Multipurpose Senior Services Project
MSW	master of social work
NA	Narcotics Anonymous
NAACP	National Association for the Advancement of Colored People
NABSW	National Association of Black Social Workers
NACW	National Association of Colored Women
NADD	National Association of Deans and Directors
NAEYC	National Association for the Education of Young Children
NAMI	National Alliance for the Mentally Ill
NAOSW	National Association of Oncology Social Workers
NAPWA	National Association of People with AIDS
NARCEA	National Aging Resource Center on Elder Abuse
NASHP	National Academy for State Health Policy
NASPAA	National Association of Schools of Public Affairs and Administration
NASSA	National Association of Schools of Social Administration
NASSW	National Association of School Social Workers
NASUA	National Association of State Units on Aging
NASW	National Association of Social Workers
NCATE	National Council for Accreditation of Teacher Education
NCCC	National Conference of Charities and Correction
NCCS	National Center on Charitable Statistics
NCF	National Civic Federation

NCHS	National Center for Health Statistics
NCLC	National Child Labor Committee
NCN	NASW Communications Network
NCOI	National Committee on Inquiry
NCOLGI	National Committee on Lesbian and Gay Issues
NCOMA	National Committee on Minority Affairs
NCORED	National Committee on Racial and Ethnic Diversity
NCOWI	National Committee on Women's Issues
NCPCR	National Center for the Prevention and Control of Rape
NCRP	National Committee for Responsive Philanthropy
NCSPP	National Center for Social Policy and Practice
NCSW	National Conference of Social Work
NCSWE	National Council on Social Work Education
NCVS	National Crime Victimization Survey
NFB	National Federation of the Blind
NFSCSW	National Federation of Societies for Clinical Social Work
NGO	nongovernmental organization
NGT	nominal group technique
NHIP	National Health Insurance Program
NHIS	National Health Interview Survey
NHO	National Hospice Organization
NIAAA	National Institute on Alcoholism and Alcohol Abuse
NIADC	National Institute on Adult Day Care
NIDA	National Institute on Drug Abuse
NIDS	National Inventory of Documentary Sources
NIH	National Institutes of Health
NIMH	National Institute of Mental Health
NIT	negative income tax
NLRA	National Labor Relations Act
NLRB	National Labor Relations Board
NLS	National Library Service
NLS	national longitudinal survey
NMES	National Medical Expenditure Survey
NMHA	National Mental Health Association
NPR	national public radio
NRA	normal retirement age
NRM	new religious movement
NSFG	national surveys of family growth
NSWA	nonstandard work arrangement
NTEE	National Taxonomy of Exempt Entities
NVRA	National Voter Registration Act of 1993
NYCOS	New York Charity Organization Society
OAA	Old-Age Assistance
OAA	Older Americans Act of 1965
OASDI	Old-Age and Survivors and Disability Insurance
OASI	Old-Age and Survivors Insurance
OBRA	Omnibus Budget Reconciliation Act
ODP	Orderly Departure Program
OJJDP	Office of Juvenile Justice and Delinquency Prevention
OJT	on-the-job training
O&M	orientation and mobility

OMB	Office of Management and Budget
OSAP	Office of Substance Abuse Prevention
OSIQ	Offer Self-image Questionnaire for Adolescents
OXFAM	Oxford Committee on Famine
PACE	Political Action for Candidate Election
PAR	participatory action research
PAR	population-attributed risk
PASSO	Political Association of Spanish-Speaking Organizations
PATCH	Planned Approach to Community Health
PCP	*Pneumocystis carinii* pneumonia
PET	positron emission tomography
PG	practice guideline
PIA	primary insurance amount
PIE	person-in-environment
PIN	personal identification number
PIRC	Prevention Intervention Research Center
PISCES	Program for Investment in the Small Capital Enterprise Sector
PKU	phenylketonuria
POS	purchase of service
PPO	preferred provider organization
PRWOA	Personal Responsibility and Work Opportunity Act
PSE	public service employment program
PSID	Panel Study of Income Dynamics
PSIR	presentence investigation report
PSR	psychosocial rehabilitation
PTSD	posttraumatic stress disorder
PVO	private voluntary organization
PVS	persistent vegetative state
PWA	people with AIDS
QMB	qualified medical beneficiary
RCT	randomized clinical trial
RDA	recommended dietary allowance
REA	Retirement Equity Act of 1984
RFP	request for proposal
RICO	Racketeer Influenced and Corrupt Organization (1970 statute)
RLIN	research libraries information network
RMP	Regional Medical Programs Act
RMP	regional medical program
RR	risk ratio
RTR	Reintegration Through Recreation
SAMHSA	Substance Abuse and Mental Health Services Administration
SCHIP	State Children's Health Insurance Program
SCLC	Southern Christian Leadership Conference
SCMWA	State, County, and Municipal Workers of America
SDI	strategic defense initiative
SE	supported employment
SEED	Self-Employment and Enterprise Development Demonstration
SEID	Self-Employment Investment Demonstration

SEIU	Service Employees International Union
SEM	standard error of measurement
SERVE	Service Employees Registration and Voter Education
SES	socioeconomic status
SGA	substantial gainful activity
SHARE	Source of Help in Airing and Resolving Experiences
SHPDA	state health planning and development agency
SIC	Standard Industrial Classification
SIECUS	Sex Information and Education Council of the United States
SIPP	Survey of Income and Program Participation
SMHAs	State Mental Health Authorities
SMI	severe mental illness
SMI	Supplementary Medical Insurance
SNCC	Student Non-Violent Coordinating Committee
SNF	skilled nursing facility
SOFAS	Social & Occupational Functioning Assessment Scale
SOS	Secular Organization for Sobriety
SOS	Share Our Strength
SOSAD	Save Our Sons and Daughters
SPL	sound pressure level
SPLC	Southern Poverty Law Center
SPRANS	Special Programs of Regional and National Significance
SRO	single-room occupancy
SSA	Social Security Administration
SSBG	social services block grant
SSD	single-subject (or -system) design
SSDI	Social Security Disability Insurance
SSEU	Social Service Employees Union
SSI	Supplemental Security Income
SSRD	single-system research design
SSWR	Society for Social Work and Research
STD	sexually transmitted disease
STEPA	Street Terrorism Enforcement Prevention Act
SVREP	Southwest Voter Registration Education Project
SWIM	Saturated Work Initiative Model
SWOT	Strengths, Weaknesses, Opportunities, and Threats
SWRG	Social Work Research Group
TANF	Temporary Assistance to Needy Families
TB	tuberculosis
TDHS	Texas Department of Human Services
TFP	Thrifty Food Plan
TIAC	Temporary Inter-Association Council of Social Work Membership
TVA	Tennessee Valley Authority
UAW	United Automobile Workers
UCR	Uniform Crime Reports
UFWA	United Federal Workers of America
UN	United Nations
UNDP	United Nations Development Program
UNESCO	United Nations Education, Scientific, and Cultural Organization
UNHCR	United Nations High Commission for Refugees

UNICEF	United Nations Children's Fund (formerly United Nations International Children's Emergency Fund)
UNRRA	United Nations Relief and Rehabilitation Agency
UOPWA	United Office and Professional Workers of America
UPWA	United Public Workers of America
USAID	U.S. Agency for International Development
USCC	U.S. Catholic Conference
USCRA	U.S. Coordinator for Refugee Affairs
USDA	U.S. Department of Agriculture
USDHHS	U.S. Department of Health and Human Services
USINS	US. Immigration and Naturalization Service
USNCHS	U.S. National Center for Health Statistics
UWASIS	United Way of America Services Identification System
UWI	University of the West Indies
VA	Veterans Administration
VCIS	Voluntary Cooperative Information System
VCR	videocassette recorder
VET Centers	Vietnam-era Veterans Outreach and Counseling Centers
VHA	Veterans Health Administration
VISTA	Volunteers in Service to America
VOCA	Victims of Crime Act
VS	vital signs
VSC	voluntary surgical contraception
WAN	wide area network
WASP	white Anglo-Saxon Protestant
WHO	World Health Organization
WHO/GPA	World Health Organization/Global Programme on AIDS
WHO/SPA	World Health Organization/Special Programme on AIDS
WIC	Special Supplemental Nutrition Program for Women, Infants, and Children
WIN	Work Incentive Program
WPA	Works Progress Administration
YMCA	Young Men's Christian Association
YWCA	Young Women's Christian Association

Index

2003 Supplement to the Encyclopedia of Social Work, 19th Edition
Designed by Cohen Design
Composed by Electronic Quill Publishing Services in Cheltenham
Printed by Port City Press on 60# Chesapeake

MORE RESOURCES FROM NASW PRESS!

Encyclopedia of Social Work, *19th Edition, 2003 Supplement,* Richard L. English, Editor-in-Chief. The *2003 Supplement* is an essential addition to the three-volume *Encyclopedia of Social Work, 19th Edition* and the *1997 Supplement,* widely accepted as the profession's most comprehensive reference work. The *2003 Supplement* features new articles on timely topics, including conservatism and social welfare, issues of multiculturalism and cultural diversity, strengths-based practice, hate crimes, and a variety of economic issues.

ISBN: 0-87101-353-3. June 2003. Item #3533. $42.99.

Encyclopedia of Social Work, *19th Edition, 1997 Supplement,* Richard L. Edwards, Editor-in-Chief. The *Supplement* updates the *Encyclopedia* with current concerns in social work and over 400 pages of information, including 30 new entries and 15 new biographies.

ISBN: 0-87101-277-4. 1997. Item #2774. $37.95.

Encyclopedia of Social Work, *19th Edition,* Richard L. Edwards, Editor-in-Chief. Three volumes provide nearly 3,000 pages of information on virtually every aspect of social work. Expanded content areas include new technologies, research, global changes, U.S. policy developments, and evolving roles for social workers.

Casebound version—ISBN: 0-87101-255-3. 1995. Item #2553s. $159.00.
Softcover version—ISBN: 0-87101-256-1. 1995. Item #2561s. $129.00.

The Social Work Dictionary, *5th Edition,* Robert L. Barker. The dynamic vocabulary of social work, like the profession itself, continues to grow and become more complex. Since the first edition of *The Social Work Dictionary* in 1987, this essential reference work has been recognized as the definitive lexicon of social work. Now in its fifth edition, the *Dictionary* captures more than 9,000 terms, cataloging and cross-referencing the nomenclature, concepts, organizations, historical figures, and values that define the profession. It is used extensively in schools of social work, social service agency libraries, licensing exam preparation centers, and social work offices worldwide. Every social worker—from professor to student, from novice to experienced professional—should own this unparalleled resource for understanding the language of social work and related disciplines!

ISBN: 0-87101-355-X. July 2003. Item #355X. $49.99.

Social Work Speaks, 6th Edition, *NASW Policy Statements 2003–2006.* A comprehensive and unabridged collection of policy statements adopted by the NASW Delegate Assembly in August 2002. More than 60 policy statements, ranging from foster care and adoption to disasters, capital punishment, cultural competence, women's issues, HIV and AIDS, technology, substance abuse, and others are arranged alphabetically and topically for easy reference. For professional value, *Social Work Speaks, 6th Edition* is an unrivaled reference tool that can assist in developing organizational responses to policy issues, conducting policy analysis and study, and working in political action coalitions.

ISBN: 0-87101-354-1. February 2003. Item #3541. $42.99.

(Order form and information on reverse side)

ORDER FORM

Qty.	Title	Item #	Price	Total
__	Encyclopedia of Social Work, 2003 Supplement	3533	$42.99	_____
__	Encyclopedia of Social Work, 1997 Supplement	2774	$37.95	_____
	Encyclopedia of Social Work			
___	Casebound version	2553s	$159.00	_____
___	Softcover version	2561s	$129.00	_____
__	The Social Work Dictionary	355X	$49.99	_____
__	Social Work Speaks	3541	$42.99	_____

POSTAGE AND HANDLING
Minimum postage and handling fee is $4.95. Orders that do not include appropriate postage and handling will be returned.

DOMESTIC: Please add 12% to orders under $100 for postage and handling. For orders over $100 add 7% of order.

CANADA: Please add 17% postage and handling.

OTHER INTERNATIONAL: Please add 22% postage and handling.

	Total
Subtotal	_____
Postage and Handling	_____
DC residents add 6% sales tax	_____
MD residents add 5% sales tax	_____
Total	_____

❑ **Check** or **money order** (payable to NASW Press) for $ _____.

❑ **Credit card**
    ❑ NASW Visa* | ❑ Visa | ❑ NASW MasterCard* | ❑ MasterCard | ❑ Amex

_____   _____
Credit Card Number   Expiration Date

Signature _____

Use of these cards generates funds in support of the social work profession.

Name _____

Address _____

City _____ State/Province _____

Country _____ Zip _____

Phone _____ E-mail _____

NASW Member # (if applicable) _____

(Please make checks payable to NASW Press. Prices are subject to change.)

NASW PRESS
P. O. Box 431
Annapolis JCT, MD 20701
USA

Credit card orders call
1-800-227-3590
(In the Metro Wash., DC, area, call 301-317-8688)
Or fax your order to 301-206-7989
Or order online at http://www.naswpress.org

Visit our Web site at http://www.naswpress.org.   CPSU03